THE
BIOFEEDBACK
SYLLABUS

THE
BIOFEEDBACK
SYLLABUS

A HANDBOOK FOR THE PSYCHOPHYSIOLOGIC STUDY OF BIOFEEDBACK

Edited by

BARBARA B. BROWN, Ph.D.

Chief, Experiential Physiology
Veterans Administration Hospital
Sepulveda, California
Lecturer, Department of Psychiatry
UCLA Medical Center
Los Angeles, California

CHARLES   C   THOMAS   ·   PUBLISHER
Springfield   ·   Illinois   ·   U.S.A.

Published and Distributed Throughout the World by
CHARLES C THOMAS • PUBLISHER
BANNERSTONE HOUSE
301-327 East Lawrence Avenue, Springfield, Illinois, U.S.A.

© *1975 by* CHARLES C THOMAS • PUBLISHER
ISBN 0-398-03268-8 (cloth)
ISBN 0-398-03269-9 (paper)
Library of Congress Catalog Card Number: 74-19865

With THOMAS BOOKS *careful attention is given to all details of
manufacturing and design. It is the Publisher's desire to present
books that are satisfactory as to their physical qualities and artistic
possibilities and appropriate for their particular use.* THOMAS
BOOKS *will be true to those laws of quality that assure a good name
and good will.*

Printed in the United States of America
N-1

Library of Congress Card Number: 74:19865

Brown, Barbara
        Biofeedback syllabus.
Illinois   Charles C Thomas
Nov. 1974

9-12-74

INTRODUCTION

THE BIOFEEDBACK SYLLABUS is a handbook of abstracted summaries of research relevant to biofeedback, including all physiologic background, techniques, methodologies and related psychobiology.

Psychophysiology is a young discipline concerned with the intricate, complex and interfused relationships between mind and body. From it can derive information for the understanding of psychosomatic medicine and assistance for the development of new therapeutic directions. The evolvement of its most recent development, biofeedback, has not only provided new insights into the mechanisms and scope of mind-body interactions, but has also laid the groundwork for numerous practical applications.

Because of the remarkably rapid growth of interest and research in biofeedback and because of the unusual diversity of scientific disciplines involved, there has been considerable difficulty in obtaining adequate source material which bears upon the subject. There appear to be no comprehensive reviews of the psychophysiology of the cardiovascular, muscle, skin electrical or brain electrical systems.

The Biofeedback Syllabus represents an effort to provide a single reference which encompasses most of the factors necessary for a comprehensive understanding of the underlying factors and framework of the biofeedback phenomenon. Although the biofeedback phenomenon appears common to all physiologic systems, the Syllabus obviously cannot deal with information on all systems within a single volume, and is therefore confined to research reports concerned with the major body systems.

The productive exploration and use of biofeedback depends upon an unusually large number of factors such as instrumentation; recording techniques; measurement techniques; physiologic and neurophysiologic mechanisms; psychologic factors as emotion, learning, cognition, and system changes during abnormal activity. Fortunately, however, both the general characteristics of the phenomenon and the procedures employed for it effective operation appear to involve similar basic mechanisms and procedural needs for nearly all physiologic systems.

The major emphasis of the Syllabus, therefore, has been placed upon those systems where the greatest amount of information is available and which are most commonly used in research and applications. All references and abstracts covering the many diverse relevant factors have been included

*The compilation was supported in part by Silva Mind Control International, Inc.

only for the three major systems of skin, muscle and cardiovascular. The section on brain electrical activity, in contrast, has been focused chiefly on the biofeedback phenomenon itself, since the literature dealing with brain wave alpha activity is fully covered in *The Alpha Syllabus*.[1] Those reports specifically dealing with alpha biofeedback have also been included here for the convenience of the general reader.

The biofeedback phenomenon has been defined as a process in which information about an organism's biologic activity is supplied for perception by that same organism.

Because of the limitations and control inadequacies of the scientific method as applied to organisms capable of discriminating the significance of elements in their environment, there can be no sharp dividing line between biofeedback and other learning processes, particularly conditioned learning. That is, the majority of learning procedures supply the organism with information about their biologic activity either explicitly, implicitly or both. Ideally, a reference syllabus on biofeedback should contain all relevant material; however, the scientific literature on learning, especially experimental conditioned learning, is far too vast to be included in its entirety. Therefore, an arbitrary limit was set with respect to including references to conditioned learning. Essentially the criteria for inclusion were those references (with an occasional exception) which were concerned with studies in human beings. The exceptions included are for subjects where relatively few human studies are available and where animal studies are essential as background material. Certain less relevant or less studied areas of biofeedback were omitted because of the prohibitions of length of text. There may be omissions of scientific reports in the subjects covered; these are either the fault of the editor whose searches did not uncover the reports or the difficulty of inadequate descriptoring and indexing. No omissions were intentional.

Finally, the lack of standardized descriptors in psychophysiology and related fields, and consequently in biofeedback, may be slightly troublesome in certain areas. For this reason the following guidelines were used: use of reference author's terms wherever possible, and use of separate descriptor indices for each part.

---

[1]Barbara Brown and Jay Klug, *The Alpha Syllabus: A Handbook of Human EEG Alpha Activity* (Springfield, Charles C Thomas, 1974).

ACKNOWLEDGMENTS

THE FOLLOWING PUBLISHERS are thanked for permission to reprint abstracts of publications.

Academic Press, Inc.
Akadémiai Kiadó
American Academy of Pediatrics
American Association for the Advancement of Science
American Congress of Rehabilitation Medicine
American Psychological Association
American Society for Psychical Research
British Journal of Psychiatry
British Medical Association House
Brooklyn Medical Press, Inc.
Canadian Journal of Behavioral Science
Canadian Psychological Association
Duke University Press
Elsevier Publishing Company
Gerontological Society
Japanese Psychological Association
J. B. Lippincott Company
Journal of Clinical Psychology
The Journal Press
Macmillian (Journals), Ltd.
Munksgaard International Publishers
National Association for Mental Health, Inc.
Neurosciences Research Program Bulletin
North Holland Publishing Co.
Pergamon Press, Inc.
Physicians Post-Graduate Press
Psychological Association of Scandanavia
Psychology
Psychonomic Society Journals
S. Karger AG Basel
Society for Psychophysiological Research
Society for Research in Child Development
Society for the Experimental Analysis of Behavior
Southern Universities Press

Transpersonal Association
University Microfilms, A Xerox Co.
University of Alabama Medical Center
University of Illinois Press
University of Kansas, Dept. of Human Development
University of Michigan, Ann Arbor
Williams & Wilkins Company

ACKNOWLEDGMENTS

The editor wishes to thank the Silva Mind Control International and Company for their support of this project.

INSTRUCTIONS

The Biofeedback Syllabus is comprised of six major parts. Five of these are devoted to the physiologic systems which have received the greatest amount of research attention: electrodermal, cardiovascular (heart rate and blood pressure), skeletal muscle, and central nervous system. The sixth part contains abstracts directed toward the psychophysiology and biofeedback mechanisms of other physiologic systems: respiratory, salivary, renal, temperature and vasomotor.

Each part is self-contained, each being organized by classifying the abstracts according to general topics such as instrumentation, measurements, physiologic and psychologic correlates, and other major topic headings appropriate for the system reviewed, or occasionally where specialized areas have been studied, e.g. lie detection using electrodermal activity, relaxation using muscle system indices, etc.

The Table of Contents for each part provides a key to the major topics covered. The Descriptor Index provides the index for all subtopics and specific aspects treated by the individual studies abstracted.

To locate abstracts for special topics, refer either to the Table of Contents or to the Descriptor Index. Those abstracts which deal primarily with one principal variable or aspect are grouped under the appropriate heading for each of the major sections of the syllabus indicated by the name of the physiologic system reviewed. In each section, abstracts are organized by alphabetizing by author's name. The Miscellaneous Part is not indexed.

The Descriptor Index for each part lists all descriptors used and gives the location of all abstracts that are concerned with the subject matter indicated by the descriptor. Abstract location is indicated by letter and number; the letter refers to the section of each system part and the number refers to the number of the abstract in the section indicated. Abstract numbers which appear in boldface type denote the major sections whose headings are the same as the descriptor. To find related material in different sections, note the same or similar descriptors in the several Descriptor Indices.

Following the abstracts of all parts a listing of pre- 1965 references is given as an aid to collecting additional background. These are listed alphabetically by author and by part.

LIST OF ABBREVIATIONS

BC — basal conductance
BCL — basal conductance level
BP — blood pressure
BPSP — basal palmar skin potential
BSC — basal skin conductance
BSP — basal skin potential
BSPL — basal skin potential level
BSR — basal skin resistance
CNV — contingent negative variation
ECT — electroconvulsive shock therapy
EDA — electrodermal activity
EDR — electrodermal resistance
EEG — electroencephalogram
EKG — electrocardiogram
EMG — electromyogram
ESP — extrasensory perception
GSR — galvanic skin response
HR — heart rate
LIV — law of initial value
PC — palmar conductance
PGR — palmar galvanic resistance
PSC — palmar skin conductance
PVCS — premature ventricular contractions
REM — rapid eye movement (sleep)
SC — skin conductance
SP — skin potential
SPR — skin potential response
SR — skin resistance
SRR — skin resistance response

CONTENTS

PART I
ELECTRODERMAL ACTIVITY

Instruments
Recording Techniques
Measurement Indices
Response Analysis

Peripheral Factors
Cholinergic Factors
Central Factors

Skin Sites
Response Components
Response Stability and Distribution
Habituation, Adaptation, Stimulus Generalization

Response Characteristics
Habituation and Adaptation
Conditionability
Influence of other Variables

Vigilance
Arousal
Sleep
Hypnosis

PART II
HEART RATE

PART III
BLOOD PRESSURE

PART IV
MUSCLE SYSTEM

THE
BIOFEEDBACK
SYLLABUS

PART I

ELECTRODERMAL ACTIVITY

MEASUREMENTS

INSTRUMENTS

A 1   Borrey, R., Grings, W.W., and Longstreet, B.J.: A system for registering both true and false feedback of the galvanic skin response. *Psychophysiology, 6:366,* 1969.

A system has been presented which allows the presentation of either true galvanic skin responses (GSRs) or false GSRs to a recorder viewed by a subject (S). Transistor circuitry is used to produce a double RC circuit using a common capacitor with two variable resistors which control the time constants of the rise and decay of a pulse such that it reflects changes in time of a true GSR. An attenuator controls the proportion of true resistance change of the S which is passed through or added to the response of the false feedback generator. This provides a means of projecting to the S either completely false GSR responding, completely true GSR activity, or a mixture of both. A record of the true responses of the S is obtained by a second recorder viewed only by the experimenter.

instruments
feedback
false feed-back

A 2   Hicks, Ronald G., Giesige, Richard, and Fick, Arthur: An absolute ohmic readout of the galvanic skin response. *Psychophysiology, 4:349,* 1968.

A relatively linear Wheatstone bridge that quantifies skin resistance is described. Current through the skin is kept low and relatively constant in all ranges. Circuitry is simple, easy to calibrate, and reliable.

instruments
GSR meas-urement

A 3   Kuechenmeister, C.A.: Instrument for direct readout of log conductance (log 1/R) measures of the galvanic skin response. *Psychophysiology, 7:128,* 1970.

An automatic computing instrument is described which con- *instruments*
tinuously measures skin conductance in units of the log of *measure-*
skin conductance (log 1/R) without ranging or adjustment. *ment tech-*
Circuit assembly and alignment is described in detail. The *niques*
instrument is ideally suited to automation in conjunction *computer*
with computers or pen recorders. *analysis*

A 4   McGraw, C.R., Kleinman, K.M., Brown, M.L., Korel, B.:
       An accurate one-channel basal level/response signal separator
       for skin resistance, incorporating pulse coding of the basal
       level. *Psychophysiology, 6:*209, 1969.

We have developed a method for measuring SR which com- *instruments*
bines the accuracy of DC measurement of basal SR level *measure-*
with the convenience gained from the AC coupling of SR *ment tech-*
responses for purposes of separating the total signal into *niques*
basal SR level and SR responses. Our circuitry accomplishes *signal*
(1) amplification of total DC signal, (2) postamplification *separation*
signal separation and display of SR responses and, on the *BSR*
same display channel, (3) pulse coding of basal SR.

A 5   Macpherson, Leonard, Hutchings, Michael L., and Kopell,
       Bert S.: An electrically operated skin resistance switch. *Psy-*
       *chophysiology, 8:*673, 1971.

A touch operated switch is described that uses a simple skin *instruments*
resistance detection circuit. This "isometric push-button" *switch*
type switch has no moving parts, is noiseless, and absorbs the *operant con-*
minimum of energy from the subject. It was primarily de- *ditioning*
signed for psychophysiological experiments where an operant
response is required.

A 6   Miller, Ralph D.: Silver-silver chloride electrodermal elec-
       trodes. *Psychophysiology, 5:*92, 1968.

An electrolytic method is presented for the preparation of a *instrumenta-*
disc type Ag-AgCl electrode which has low bias potential and *tion*
drift, moderate resistance and low polarization, is relatively *electrodes*
durable, and can be easily replated if damaged or contami-
nated. The electrode has been used for measuring both skin
potential and conductance and is compatible with a pre-

viously published device which compensates for nonisothermal electrodes in skin potential recording. Although other applications have not been explored, the general design might be useful for the recording of other peripherally assessed bioelectric activity as well. A convenient electrode paste is described which does not dry out quickly and can be stored indefinitely.

7   Simons, David G., Lt Col, USAF, MC, and Perez, Robert E., B.S.: The B/GSR module: A technic for the combined recording of base skin resistance and galvanic skin reflex activity. Brooks Air Force Base, Texas, USAF School of Aerospace Medical Division (AFSC), May, 1965.

A B/GSR (base skin resistance/galvanic skin reflex) module combined BSR (base skin resistance) and GSR (galvanic skin reflex) activity into a one-channel recording. Three identical modules recorded three sites simultaneously on a series of normal subjects. Electrode sites included bilateral palmar locations and a location just beneath the medial malleolus. The GSR amplification factor was a fixed value of 3.0. The units provided a generally satisfactory combined record of base skin resistance and reflex activity. The BSR and GSR patterns observed simultaneously from three sites consistently showed very similar changes.

instruments
recording
* techniques*
measure-
* ment in-*
* dices*

8   Strahan, Robert: A simple device for the polygraphic recording of judgments. *Psychophysiology*, 7:135, 1970.

A device for recording judgmental data on the Grass Model 7 polygraph is described. Various modifications of the simple apparatus are discussed.

instruments
recording
* techniques*
subjective
* judgments*

9   Welford, N.T.: A constant current skin resistance coupler. *Psychophysiology*, 5:724, 1969.

A constant current skin resistance measuring device with separate outputs, linear in ohms, for skin resistance responses (SRR) and skin resistance level (SRL) is described. The unit is made as a coupler for an Offner Type R Dynograph® and has built-in calibration facilities.

instruments
measure-
* ment tech-*
* niques*
GSR

RECORDING TECHNIQUES

A 10   Kaplan, Stephen, and Hobart, James L.: New technique for recording skin resistance. *Am J Med Electron, 4:*117, 1965.

Since there is growing evidence that GSR and BRL are indices of a central state of arousal or nonspecific neural activity, a simple reliable inexpensive recording technique is of some interest. A recording system is described which utilizes any ten-millivolt, high impedance servo recorder and a control unit designed for the purpose. A particularly important feature of this system is the wideband rectilinear writeout of the servo recorder. This results in a record from which both BRL and GSR can be scored and eliminates the need for an operator and/or automatic scale-shifting necessary for certain widely used skin-resistance recording systems. A number of technical advantages of the system are also discussed. The use of the system is described not only for human and rat experiments in which skin resistance is a central variable, but also for many other experiments where arousal variations may be produced unintentionally. It is concluded that such auxiliary recording could lead to new insights and discoveries.

recording technique. servo mechanism scoring

A 11   McNair, Douglas M., Droppleman, Leo F., and Kussman, Michael: Finger sweat print tape bands. *Psychophysiology, 4:*75, 1967.

A simple inexpensive technique for obtaining finger sweat prints (FSPs) is described. Evidence for its validity is presented. The method proved approximately equal to a more elaborate procedure in sensitivity to an anticholinergic drug effect. FSP techniques, perhaps, have been technically refined without the compensating gains of increased reliability or validity.

recording technique. sweat prints

A 12   Niimi, Yosizumi: The studies on electrical skin conductance and galvanic skin reflex by exosomatic method. *J Child Development, 4:*1, 1968.

Presents an overview of progressive technological innovations in GSR recording techniques from exosomatic in 1946 to

recording techniques

endosomatic in 1963. Findings of various studies of GSR re- *review*
cording are collected and integrated on the utility of this *applications*
method with conditioned GSR to olfactory stimuli and auditory stimuli. GSR accompanying the Rorschach, and group
measurement.

13   Wilcott, R.C., and Hammond, L.J.: On the constant-current
error in skin resistance measurement. *Psychophysiology, 2:*
39, 1965.

A substantial reduction in skin resistance (SR) is produced *recording*
by a rise in induced voltage. This indicates that with a con- *techniques*
stant-current circuit, variations in voltage can have a signif- *review*
icant effect on the SR level. Therefore, SR levels obtained *GSR*
with a constant-current and constant-voltage circuits were
compared for a group of Ss. The higher the SR level, the
greater the discrepancy between the constant-current and
constant-voltage measurements. The use of a constant-voltage circuit when measuring high SR levels is recommended.

MEASUREMENT INDICES

14   Bonier, R.J., and Hanley, C.: Relationship among PGR indices. *J Psychosom Res, 9:*285, 1965.

Psychogalvanic reflex (PGR) has been widely employed in *measure-*
psychological research as an index of emotionality, autonomic *ment in-*
responsivity, subclinical response, etc., and has been an *dices*
integral part of research design investigating phenomena as *response*
disparate as perceptual vigilance and psychosomatic illness. *compon-*
Little attention is paid, however, to the identity of PGR as a *ents*
tool; studies tend to regard, and therefore employ, PGR as a *stress*
unitary measure devoid of facets which in themselves relate *resting*
to planning of a research design. The present study em- *levels*
ployed seven separate measures on sixty-four normal subjects with a mean age of 20.5 yrs., four measures relating to
different types of stress stimulation, and three different measures of the resting phase. While some measures correlated
highly with each other, others failed to correlate or showed
high negative correlations. Three separate PGR factors were
obtained.

A 15   Burstein, Kenneth R., Fenz, Walter D., Bergeron, James, and Epstein, Seymour: A comparison of skin potential and skin resistance responses as measures of emotional responsivity. *Psychophysiology*, 2:14, 1965.

Compared gradients of skin resistance (SR) and skin potential (SP) responses generated by differing degrees of psychologically disturbing stimuli and determined the significance of the different wave forms of skin potential. SR and SP were simultaneously recorded during a word-association test that included three levels of psychologically disturbing verbal stimuli. In addition to the a and b waves of the SP response, a second negative wave form, a₂, was recorded. SR and all SP wave forms yielded positive gradients as a function of increasing stimulus intensity. Gradients based upon SR and total SP were close to identical. Magnitude measures, which include zero responses, of the SP wave forms yielded steeper gradients than measures of amplitude or frequency. The relative contribution of different SP wave forms to total SP varied with stimulus level.

measurement indices
emotional responsivity
verbal stimuli
response components

A 16   Christie, Margaret J., and Venables, Peter H.: Basal palmar skin potential and the electrocardiogram T-wave. *Psychophysiology*, 8:779, 1971.

Palmar skin potential levels (SPLs) and the amplitude of the T-wave of the electrocardiogram (EEG) were measured in groups of habituated male subjects in conditions of bed rest and while resting in a sitting position. Significant correlations of −.70 and −.61 between the negativity of SPL and T-wave amplitude were obtained when there was minimal palmar sudorific activity and skin potential could be designated as "basal" (BSPL). Previous work had suggested that BSPL might be related to extracellular potassium (K+) levels, and evidence is presented which relates EKG T-wave amplitude to palmar K+ levels. The results thus provide support for the hypothesis that measured values of SPL reflect levels of body K+.

measurement indices
BPSP
EKG

A 17   Gaviria, Bernardo, Coyne, Lolafaye, and Thetford, Paul E.: Correlation of skin potential and skin resistance measures. *Psychophysiology*, 5:465, 1969.

Simultaneous measurements of skin potential (SP) and skin resistance (SR) obtained from twenty male and twenty female adult subjects during two sessions held two to nine days apart were used in studying (1) the correlation of change measurements and prestimulus level in the two measures, and (2) the amount of correlation between SP and SR using both simple difference and residual change scores in which the regression of poststimulus values on initial level (prestimulus) has been controlled. Correlations within Ss and correlations among Ss showed large individual variability, correlation differences between males and females, and high correlation between SP and SR change scores. Although the law of initial value (LIV) seemed to have little applicability to the measurement of electrodermal responses, the results underscored the need to control for contamination of change measures by initial level, regardless of direction.

*measure-
ment in-
dices*
SP
SR
LIV
*individual
differences*

A 18   Lockhart, Russell A.: Interrelations between amplitude, latency, rise time, and the Edelberg recovery measure of the galvanic skin response. *Psychophysiology, 9:437*, 1972.

This report describes relationships between the Edelberg recovery measure, latency, rise time, and amplitude measures of GSR response to cued, uncued and disparity USs. Under cued and uncued conditions all temporal measures were independent of amplitude. Rise time and recovery measures were highly correlated under all conditions, while correlations between latency and rise time or amplitude were quite weak, suggesting that latency and rise time-recovery are partly under the control of different mechanisms. When US was unexpected (disparity), latency remained independent of amplitude, but significant correlations developed between amplitude and the temporal measures of rise time and recovery. Latency and recovery, but not rise time or amplitude, distinguished between disparity and nondisparity conditions. The results demonstrate the need and utility for more complete response specification.

*measure-
ment in-
dices*
*response
compon-
ents*
*disparity
phenomena*

A 19   Lykken, David T.: Direct measurement of skin conductance: A proposal for standardization. *Psychophysiology, 8:656*, 1971.

A provisional standard method of measuring tonic skin conductance (SCL) and GSR (SCR) is advocated, using a constant-voltage method for which circuits are provided usable
with Beckman, Grass, and other common polygraphs. A
standard electrode methodology is also presented. The problem of units of measurement is considered in detail with an
analysis of the so-called Law of Initial Values. Methods are
given for correcting both tonic SC and SCRs for individual
differences in their respective ranges of variation and the
purpose and relative advantages of these range-correction
methods are discussed.

*measure-
ment in-
dices
review*

RESPONSE ANALYSIS

A 20 Kimmel, H.D.: GSR amplitude instead of GSR magnitude:
Caveat emptor! *Behav Res Methods Instrumentation, 1:*54,
1968.

Size of GSR made by 300 undergraduate Ss to twenty repetitions of a visual stimulus is presented as mean magnitude
and mean amplitude, illustrating that the amplitude method
(averaging only those responses which are greater than zero)
is susceptible to distortion resulting from a systematic elimination of Ss who initially make small responses. From trial
to trial, the amplitude function comes more to be due to the
behavior of Ss who initially make large responses. Even
though the latter Ss' responses actually reduce across trials,
the amplitude function rises. Magnitude (including zeroes)
does not suffer from this distortion. It is suggested that the
definition of a zero response is the source of the problem.

*response
analysis
data analysis
GSR ampli-
tude*

A 21 Lykken, David T.: Square-wave analysis of skin impedance.
Psychophysiology, 7:262, 1970.

A method is described for studying skin impedance phenomena based on analysis of waveforms of current through the
skin produced by square voltage pulses. In several experiments, the method is used to provide data relevant to the
choice of an appropriate equivalent circuit for skin. Removal
of the stratum corneum eliminates the parallel resistive and
capacitive elements, and slightly reduces the series or

*response
analysis
skin imped-
ance
polarization*

"ohmic" resistance. During healing the source of skin potential recovers before the other electrodermal parameters have returned to normal. The relationship of these parameters to electrode area, current density, and site temperature is studied. It is argued that the capacitance of skin may not vary with the frequency of the measuring current, in contrast to traditional views. The main purpose of the paper is to illustrate and advocate the square-wave method of analysis.

22   Prokasy, William F.: Toward a complete analysis of GSR data. *Behav Res Methods Instrumentation, 1*:99, 1969.

Discussed a critique of amplitude analyses in GSR conditioning. It was pointed out that when amplitudes are properly analyzed with all 300 Ss contributing equally to each repeated measures point, the concern of latency interval, definition of response probability, and distribution of GSR amplitudes apply to analyses of magnitude, probability and latency, as well as of amplitude. It was concluded that nothing is lost in separating magnitude into its amplitude and probability components, particularly when magnitude is included in the statistical analyses. Such a partitioning is considered significant.

response analysis

response components

SECTION B

MECHANISMS:
REGULATION AND CONTROL

PERIPHERAL FACTORS

B 1   Adams, Thomas, and Vaughan, John A.: Human eccrine sweat gland activity and palmar electrical skin resistance. *J Appl Physiol, 20:*980, 1965.

Sweat gland activity, monitored as a function of the rate at which water vapor was removed from the skin surface (EWL), was measured simultaneously with electrical skin resistance (ESR) from adjacent I-cm² areas on the human palm. Both ESR and EWL, and ESR and $\triangle$EWL, were correlated throughout twenty to thirty minutes of testing during which the subject rested or participated in conversation. The ratio $\triangle$ESR/$\triangle$EWL was greater and lower the EWL level. As EWL approached diffusion levels (0.06 mg/min cm²), ESR assumed the highest and most stable value (ca 170 kilohms). Subject differences in ESR at high EWL rates and the pattern of ESR-EWL relationships through the range of sudomotor activity (0.06/—0.18 mg/min cm²) are attributed to individual variation in the density and activity of sweat glands on the palmar surface. The character of ESR-EWL correspondence was also seen to vary with the phase of sweating activity for any one subject.

peripheral factors
epidermal hydration
rest
arousal

B 2   Christie, Margaret J., and Venables, Peter H.: Characteristics of palmar skin potential and conductance in relaxed human subjects. *Psychophysiology, 8:*525, 1971.

An investigation of mechanisms generating palmar skin potential level (SPL) was undertaken from relaxed subjects in a nonarousing environment. In these circumstances it was possible to obtain recordings where there were no skin potential responses (SPRs). At such times of quiescence,

peripheral factors
relaxation
arousal
cognitive tasks

14

SPLs, recorded with 0.5% KC[1] as the external electrolyte medium, had characteristics which differed from SPLs recorded when there were SPRs. The potentials recorded at the beginning of these periods of quiescence were designated "basal" skin potential levels (BSPLs). BSPLs were demonstrated in other than optimal conditions for achieving basal state, i.e. with nonhabituated subjects, and with subjects carrying out an undemanding cognitive task; the relevance of these findings to the use of SPL as an index of arousal in unstimulating conditions is discussed. An interpretation of BSPL phenomena is possible in terms of a relationship between electrode electrolyte and individual values of body fluid potassium.

BSPL

B 3   Christie, Margaret J., and Venables, Peter H.: Sodium and potassium electrolytes and "basal" skin potential levels in male and female subjects. *Jap J Physiol, 21:*659, 1971.

When palmar skin potential level (SPL) is recorded during periods of minimal arousal sweating, and a concentration of potassium chloride within physiological limits is used for the external electrolyte, the value of the "basal" SPL (BSPL) recorded can be expressed as a function of the external/epidermal potassium concentration gradient. The present study reports comparison of BSPL values obtained with the use of physiologically comparable concentrations of sodium and potassium chlorides. The results suggest the possibility that the BSPL methodology may provide a means of monitoring electrolyte shifts in the human subject. In addition, sex differences in BSPL values were demonstrated.

peripheral factors
BSPL
electrolytes
sex differ-ence

B 4   Christie, Margaret J., and Venables, P.H.: Effects on "basal" skin potential level of varying the concentration of an external electrolyte. *J Psychosom Res, 15:*343, 1971.

Palmar skin potential level, which has in the past been used to assess psychophysiological state, increases in its negativity is being associated with increases in arousal when sudorific activity is the determinant of such change. Evidence has been presented showing that when palmar skin potential level is recorded with quiescent sweat glands, then the concentration

peripheral factors
sweating
arousal
electrolytes

of both tissue and external electrolytes can become significant parameters. This can present problems if SPL is required as a direct index of arousal for use in low arousal states, but may prove to be of value for monitoring of electrolyte changes in the organism.

B 5   Darrow, Chester W., and Gullickson, Gary R.: The peripheral mechanism of the galvanic skin response. *Psychophysiology, 6*:597, 1970.

Darrow held that the galvanic skin response (GSR) appears to be a complicated phenomenon because a number of events are sequentially involved. The mechanism resulting in the peripheral components of electrodermal phenomena is not complicated. Following excitation, sympathetic impulses to cutaneous tissues and subsequent release of aceteylcholine account for initial negative polarity and resistance changes. When these incoming impulses are sufficiently persistent and strong, and when the cholinergic response of the sweat glands is sufficient, then if temperature and circulatory conditions are favorable, secretion by the sweat glands is initiated. Sweating is the major factor contributing to the positive potential and large drops in skin resistance during excitation, but at low levels of excitation, when skin resistance is high and before sweating has reached a critical level, epidermal activities other than those of the sweat glands may contribute appreciably to negative potential and resistance changes.

peripheral factors cholinergic mechanisms arousal sweating

B 6   Fowles, Don C., and Venables, P.H.: The effects of epidermal hydration and sodium reabsorption on palmar skin potential. *Psychol Bull, 73*:363, 1970.

Two factors important in measurements of palmar skin potentials are described: (1) Epidermal hydration, which occurs when aqueous solutions with low salt content are applied to the skin, promotes swelling of the epidermis and closure of the sweat gland pores. Poral closure, in turn, reduces the measured potential by increasing the resistance between the electrode and the negative potential in the duct, and probably also by altering ductal reabsorption. (2) The reabsorption of sodium from the sweat passing through the

peripheral factors sodium transport sweat glands SP

duct generates a transductal potential in which the duct lumen is negative relative to the interstitial fluid. This active transport of sodium under the control of the pituitary-adrenal axis may account for the large negative potentials recorded from the human palm. It may also account for the large positive waves recorded in humans.

7   Fowles, Don C., and Venables, P.H.: The reduction of palmar skin potential by epidermal hydration. *Psychophysiology, 7*:254, 1971.

Simultaneous measurements of palmar skin potential (SP) at four levels of epidermal hydration yielded a difference of 35 mv between the mean values for the least hydrated site (pretreated with polyethylene glycol) and the most hydrated site (pretreated with distilled water) during sweat gland activity. It was also demonstrated that there was a decline in SP during the first fifteen minutes of recording with aqueous electrolyte which can be attributed to the application of an electrolyte to the skin. Thus the hydration effect appears to be a large, uncontrolled source of variance which must be brought under control if physiologically meaningful results are to be obtained with SP measurements. The hydration effect may offer an alternative interpretation of data previously cited as supporting the hypothesis that an epidermal membrane contributes to SP.

peripheral factors
epidermal hydration
sweat glands
SP

8   Gibinski, Kornel, Giec, Leszek, Zmudzinski, Jerzy, Waclaw-czyk, Jerzy, and Dosiak, Jerzy: Body side related assymmetry in sweat gland function. *J Invest Dermatol, 57*:190, 1971.

Sweat sodium and potassium concentrations were determined in thirty-eight healthy young subjects exposed to a hot, humid environment. Sweat samples were taken from two symmetric areas on the back and/or the arms at ten-minute intervals during one hour. Sodium concentration was a little higher on the left than on the right side. The difference became more distinct and significant with an increasing rate of sweating. There was, however, no significant difference either in the sweating rate between the left and the right sides of the body or in the potassium concentration. The

peripheral factors
bilateral responses
electrolytes
sweating

sweat glands on the left side are less efficient in elaborating a
sodium concentration gradient.

B 9   Katkin, E.S., Weintraub, G.S., and Yasser, A.M.: Stimulus
specificity of epidermal and sweat gland contributions to
GSR. *J Comp Physiol Psychol, 64:*186, 1967.

To investigate the independence of sweat gland and epidermal contributions to the GSR, and to try to elucidate
their stimulus specificity, responses were simultaneously recorded from the palmar and dorsal surfaces of the hand to
two classes of stimuli: those which elicited motor responses
and those which did not. The sweat gland component was
facilitated by stimuli which elicit motor activity, but not by
stimuli eliciting nonmotor activity.

*peripheral
factors
epidermal
compon-
ents
sweat gland*

B 10   Lykken, D.T., Miller, R.D., and Strahan, R.F.: GSR and
polarization capacity of skin. *Psychonde Sci, 4:*355, 1966.

By applying a square voltage pulse to skin through GSR electrodes and observing the voltage waveform across a small
series resistance, the conductivity of skin may be seen to decrease sharply (e.g. by 80% or more) during the first 50 to
500 microsec. to a steady-state or DC value. At the end of the
pulse, a back e.m.f. may be observed across the skin, equal to,
e.g. 80 percent of the pulse voltage, and opposite in polarity.
During the GSR this polarization voltage decreases, producing an increase in apparent DC conductance, while the initial
peak conductance does not change. This indicates that the
GSR involves a change in polarization capacity of some membrane (s) in the epidermis.

*peripheral
factors
polarizatio
SC
GSR*

B 11   Martin, Irene, and Venables, P.H.: Mechanisms of palmar
skin resistance and skin potential. *Psychol Bull, 65:*347, 1966.

An attempt is made to analyze peripheral and central factors
responsible for four electrical properties of palmar skin: (1)
skin-resistance level (SRL), (2) skin-resistance responses
(SRRs), (3) skin-potential level (SPL), and (4) skin-potential responses (SPRs), these latter being often diphasic—an
initial negative change in potential followed by a positive

*peripheral
factors
central
mecha-
nisms
review*

wave. There seems little doubt that SRL and SRRs are closely linked with sweat gland activity, but, in addition, there is probably some contribution from epidermal factors. Available data suggest that SPL is largely independent of sweat gland activity and may relate to certain membrane characteristics of the epidermis. In the case of SPR, the latency of the negative wave seems to correlate closely with the latency of the SRR, and both are probably functions of the presecretory activity of sweat glands. The mechanism of the positive wave is in doubt; it is regarded by some as a secondary aspect of sweat gland activity and by others as being of independent epidermal origin.

12 Maxwell, R.D.H., and Barton, J.L.: The apparent skin resistance. *Acta Psychiatr Scand, 47:*92, 1971.

It is confirmed that the greater part of the skin resistance measured, the apparent skin resistance, is due to the appearance of a polarization potential which is actively generated by the skin at the electrode contact areas, at each of which a potential of up to ten volts may be produced to oppose the voltage applied. This polarization potential is subject to fatigue in proportion to the voltage and time of application. These findings explain many of the anomalies described in the behavior of organic as compared with electrical resistors. A practical method of measurement has been evolved by which consistent results can be obtained by using repeated measurements, each of short duration.

peripheral factors
polarization
measurement techniques

13 Prout, B.J.: Independence of the galvanic skin reflex from the vasoconstrictor reflex in man. *J Neurol Neurosurg Psychiatry, 30:*319, 1967.

The galvanic skin reflex and the vasoconstrictor reflex have been recorded on the same digit of healthy subjects at rest. The reflexes may fluctuate independently in size, and one reflex may occur in the absence of the other. A distended bladder may result in depression of one reflex without influencing the other. The experimental results have been discussed in the light of previous observations in the cat. It is concluded that in man vascular and sweat gland responses in the

peripheral factors
vasomotor influence
sweat glands

same area of skin can function independently of each other and have separate nervous pathways.

CHOLINERGIC FACTORS

B 14 Gullickson, Gary R., and Darrow, Chester W.: Is the skin resistance-skin potential relation complicated? *Psychophysiology, 4:*505, 1968.

Epidermal activities other than those of the sweat glands may contribute to negative resistance and potential changes at low level excitation when resistance is high and sweating is not at a critical level. Sweating is a significant factor in the larger responses associated with diphasic and positive potential when skin resistance is low. The peripheral neurophysiologic mechanism of the GSR is likewise basically simple. Sympathetic impulses over unmyelineated fibers from the ventral sympathetic rami activate the sweat glands and other cutaneous tissues, accounting for initial negative polarity and high resistance changes. Following these effects, secretion by the sweat glands is initiated if the cholinergic response mechanism of the sweat glands is active, if temperature and circulatory conditions are favorable, and if incoming impulses are persistent and strong. The low resistance saline contact of the positively active interior of the sweat glands with the surface electrode via the saline-filled sweat ducts accounts for the shift to positive surface potential and for greatly lowered resistance.

cholinergic factors
response characteristics
sweating
innervation
polarity

B 15 Juniper, Kerrison Jr., Blanton, David E., and Dykman, Roscoe A.: Palmer skin resistance and sweat gland counts in drug and non-drug states. *Psychophysiology, 4:*231, 1967.

Propantheline bromide, an anticholinergic blocking agent, was found to nullify all sizable changes in skin resistance. Betazole hydrochloride, a histamine isomer causing flushing of the skin, had no detectable effect on changes in skin resistance. Betazole hydrochloride did decrease the level of skin resistance, and it is possible that increased vasodilatation "pumps" more conductive (saline-like) substances into the skin. These results suggest that relatively rapid changes in

cholinergic factors
histamine
sweat gland
LIV

skin resistance depend more upon sweat gland activity than upon changes in the fluid content of the skin, without denying the importance of the latter. It may be that the level of skin resistance at any one time depends upon a combination of sweat gland and vasomotor activities. Hence, as basal levels of skin resistance decrease, the relative magnitude of changes in skin resistance to stimuli also decreases (law of initial values) .

B 16   Lader, M.H.: The unit of quantification of the GSR. *J Psychosom Res, 14*:109, 1970.

Atropine shows increasing systemic effects over forty to fifty minutes even when injected intra-arterially. The delay when the drug is administered by iontophoresis is not inconsistent. The rise in skin resistance and abolition of the GSR suggest a cholinergic mechanism mediating the response and present knowledge of the anatomy of the fingertip would strongly suggest that sweat glands, being cholinergic in man, subserve the GSR. If the sweat glands are regarded as small electrical shunts through the high resistance stratum corneum of the skin, as the sweat glands are essentially parallel, a conductance model would be appropriate. Be that as it may, it was an empirical finding in the present study that resistance units led to most improbable results whereas the conductance transformation yielded biologically meaningful results. It is concluded that conversion of skin resistance units to the reciprocal conductance units is most advisable. Further refinements such as log or square root transformations may then be performed on conductance data if statistical considerations warrant them.

cholinergic factors sweat glands measurement indices

B 17   Venables, P.H., and Martin, Irene: The relation of palmar sweat gland activity to level of skin potential and conductance. *Psychophysiology, 3*:302, 1967.

The role of sweat gland activity in the mediation of skin potential and skin conductance levels was investigated. 1-Hyoscyamine was introduced into the fingertips by iontophoresis to eliminate sweat gland activity, and d-hyoscyamine, an inert analog of the l-isomer, was used as a control for ion

cholinergic factors sweat glands innervation SP

size. Neostigmine was used to potentiate sweating. 1-Hyoscyamine significantly decreased skin conductance level and the number of active sweat glands and reduced the negativity of skin potential level, but neostigmine, which promoted sweating and skin conductance, did not increase the negativity of skin potential. The lowering of skin potential on the denervated hand of a hemisympathectomized patient was found to be similar in magnitude to the decrease in skin potential due to pharmacological elimination of sweat gland activity. The results are discussed in relation to hypotheses concerning the mechanism of skin potential.

B 18   Verghese, A.: Some observations on the psychogalvanic reflex. *Br J Psychiatry, 114:*639, 1968.

Some PGR studies in a female subject who had bilateral cervical sympathectomy were described. It was found that sympathectomy abolished PGR and that intra-arterial infusion of acetylcholine evoked marked PGR changes in the sympathectomized limb. These findings support the theory that the PGR is mediated through the cholinergic fibers of the sympathetic nervous system.

cholinergic factors
sympathectomy
PGR

B 19   Wilcott, R.C.: Adaptive value of arousal sweating and the epidermal mechanism related to skin potential and skin resistance. *Psychophysiology, 2:*249, 1966.

The following five experiments are reported. (1) After palmar sweating is abolished by atropine, the skin is easier to drill with a dental burr. This suggests that arousal sweating protects the skin against mechanical injury. (2) Intracutaneous injection of acetylcholine or mecholyl at the forearm will produce skin potential (SP) effects of both negative and positive polarity and also a reduction in skin resistance (SR). This suggests that a cholinergic substance is involved in the production of SP and SR. (3) Intracutaneous injection of mecholyl at the forearm will either lower or raise the pain threshold to a needle prick. A lowering of the pain threshold was associated with the presence of an SP negative effect and a rise was associated with an SP positive effect. It is concluded

cholinergic factors
arousal sweating
skin injury
pain threshold
sensory stimuli
electric shock

that the adaptive value of the cholinergic substance related to SP and SR is to modulate cutaneous sensitivity. (4) The pain threshold to an electric shock can be lowered or raised by mecholyl injection. This may show that the pain threshold can be varied by mecholyl injection independently of its effects on sweating. (5) Lowering of the electric shock pain threshold at the palm is associated with the appearance of both SP negative and positive responses. This further demonstrates a relation between SP activity and pain sensitivity but indicates that the direction of the change in the pain threshold is not dependent on SP response polarity.

CENTRAL FACTORS

B 20   Darrow, C.W.: Problems in the use of the galvanic skin response (GSR) as an index of cerebral function: implications of the latent period. *Psychophysiology, 3:*389, 1967.

The author reviewed the findings on relationships between EEG activity and the occurrence of the GSR. Not all GSRs were found to be centrally mediated. Alpha blocking, which occurs to any attention-centering stimulus, precedes the GSR during the latent period and acts as an indicator of central nervous system involvement. The author noted that EEG phase relationships, particularly diphasic activity in the latent period, may prove to be more important as an indicator of central involvement in the GSR.

central factors
cerebral function
arousal
response character-istics
EEG activity
applications
GSR

B 21   Fowles, D., and Venables, P.H.: Endocrine factors in palmar skin potentials. *Psychon Sci, 10:*387, 1968.

Sodium and potassium measurements in mixed and parotid saliva were used to compute an index of mineralocoid activity which was significantly related to maximum readings of palmar skin potential (r = + .459 to + .608) in two experiments. These results were interpreted as indicating an important influence of the adrenal cortex in palmar skin potential, possibly reflecting stress produced endocrine arousal.

central factors
stress
endocrine factors
SP

B 22   Surwillo, Walter W.: Relationship between electrical poten-
        tial of the skin and skin temperature. *Percept Mot Skills, 25:*
        465, 1967.

        The relationship between electrical potential of skin (SP)   *central*
        and temperature of the skin (ST) in the region of the re-   *factors*
        cording electrodes was investigated in 112 healthy Ss. SP be- *skin temper-*
        tween palm and ventral surface of the forearm was recorded   *ature*
        during a one-hr. test session in which S was asked to watch   *skin sites*
        for a rarely occurring stimulus. Forearm ST and SP proved   *SP*
        to be unrelated. The regression of SP on palm ST was
        statistically significant, but the low correlation suggested
        that, under the conditions investigated, SP and ST were
        largely independent.

B 23   Wilcott, R.C.: Arousal sweating and electrodermal phenom-
        ena. *Psychol Bull, 67:*58, 1967.

        Recent research supports the following conclusions: Various   *central*
        body parts display both arousal sweating and thermoregula-   *factors*
        tory sweating, but there are differences in the magnitude of   *review*
        the two types of sweating. The main adaptive function of   *sweating*
        arousal sweating may be to toughen the skin and protect it   *response*
        from mechanical injury. The negative wave of the skin po-   *compon-*
        tential response seems to be due to a sympathetic mediator,   *ents*
        and the positive wave may be primarily due to sweating.
        These two factors appear to summate in the production of
        skin resistance and skin impedance responses. However, skin
        resistance and skin impedance activity of the cat seem to be
        controlled entirely by sweating. The function of the sympa-
        thetic mediator may be to modify cutaneous sensitivity.

B 24   Wineman, E.W.: Autonomic balance changes during the
        human menstrual cycle. *Psychophysiology, 8:*1, 1971.

        Five female students were each tested five days a week   *central*
        throughout one menstrual cycle with a three-day overlap   *factors*
        into the next cycle. The autonomic variables reported are   *autonomic*
        sublingual temperature, heart period, diastolic blood pres-   *balance*
        sure, palmar and volar conductance, salivary output, and log   *menstrual*
        conductance change. These measures were taken in order to   *cycle*
                                                                       SC

estimate autonomic factor scores (Ā). Significant menstrual phase differences in Ā scores and sublingual temperature were demonstrated. The Ā score estimates an autonomic factor for an individual at a particular time; low scores represent relative sympathetic nervous system (SNS) dominance. During menses, the follicular and the ovulatory phases, Ā scores were higher; during the luteal phase the Ā scores were lowest. It was concluded that high estrogen levels are accompanied by decreased SNS function.

temperature
HR
BP

RESPONSE CHARACTERISTICS

SKIN SITES

C 1   Christie, Margaret J., and Venables, Peter H.: Site, state, and subject characteristics of palmar skin potential levels. *Psychophysiology, 9:*645, 1972.

Palmar skin potential levels (SPLs) were recorded with Ag/ AgCl electrodes and 0.5% KCl, in two degrees of relaxation, simultaneously from eight finger sites of twenty habituated and twenty nonhabituated male subjects. The SPLs were examined by analyses of variance computed with right/left, and dominant/nondominant distributions of hand data. There were significant finger site differences in all conditions; significant hand differences were observable only with greater relaxation, i.e. to "basal" levels of SP, and only with the dominant/nondominant distribution of data. There was evidence of significant interactions implicating the habituation factor. The results are interpreted in terms of the balance of sweat gland and nonsudorific contributions to the generation of palmar SPL.

*skin sites
habituation
relaxation
sweat glands
mechanisms
hand domi-
nance
SP*

C 2   Culp, William C., and Edelberg, Robert: Regional response specificity in the electrodermal reflex. *Percept Mot Skills, 23:* 623, 1966.

By comparing electrodermal response amplitudes from the right and left hands when either the right foot or left foot was flexed, it was possible to demonstrate relative augmentation of the response amplitude on the side ipsilateral to the active member. Comparison of responses from the left hand and left foot showed relative augmentation of the hand response with motor activity in the opposite hand and of the foot response

*skin sites
bilateral
 responses
motor activ-
 ity
orienting
 response*

with motor activity of the opposite foot. These regional influences also appeared when the response to motor activity was compared with centrally elicited orienting responses.

C 3 Fuhrer, Marcus J.: Effects of unilateral stimuli on the magnitude and latency of bilaterally recorded skin conductance responses. *Psychophysiology, 8:*740, 1971.

This experiment examined the effects of unilateral stimulation on the relative magnitude and latency of skin conductance responses recorded bilaterally from the palms. The unilaterally applied stimuli were shocks to either the left or right forefinger and voluntary flexion of either the left or right foot. Additional stimuli consisted of binaurally presented tones and deep breaths. In a within-Ss design, the 22 Ss were submitted to eighteen repetitions of each stimulus. The unilateral shocks, as well as the foot movements, had the effect of augmenting the relative magnitude of skin conductance responses from the palm ipsilateral to the site of stimulation. The shocks were found to be somewhat more effective than foot flexion in producing this effect. The relative latencies of responses were also influenced by the shocks, with shorter latency responses occurring from the palm ipsilateral to the stimulus site. Consideration is given to the role of both suprasegmental and spinal cord mechanisms in mediating these effects of unilateral stimuli.

bilateral responses
sensory stimuli
electric shock
motor stimuli
GSR

C 4 Rickles, W.H., Jr., and Day, J.L.: Electrodermal activity in nonpalmar skin sites. *Psychophysiology, 4:*421, 1968.

Explored the human body for GSR sites which would parallel palmar GSR activity, but would not impede the S or be prone to artifact. Specific resistance values ranged from 10,000 to 800,000 ohm X cm^2. Ss were sixteen 17 to 20-year-old airmen. Specific resistance of the scalp was consistently lower than other areas. Spontaneous activity was observed at all nonpalmar, nonplantar sites except the scalp. At times, this activity was present when the palm was quiescent. Evoked nonpalmar, nonplantar activity was present irregularly, but was always accompanied by evoked responses. Nonpalmar, nonplantar sites responded to exertional stimuli

skin sites
spontaneous GSR
rhythmicity
arousal

with rhythmic, 16 to 21/min GSR activity. Some Ss demonstrated this rhythmic activity spontaneously, and one revealed abrupt suppression of this phenomenon in response to psychosensory stimulation. Medial and lateral hypomalleolar areas of the ankle paralleled plantar-specific GSR responses and are recommended as useful GSR skin sites under conditions of moderate arousal.

C 5   Varni, John G., Doerr, Hans O., and Franklin, Jill R.: Bilateral differences in skin resistance and vasomotor activity. *Psychophysiology, 8:*390, 1971.

Obtained bilateral basal skin resistance (BSR) and bilateral photoplethysmographic vasomotor measures for sixteen female undergraduates. Ten Ss were found to have bilateral differences in BSR. The direction of these differences was not related to handedness. Bilateral differences in vasomotor resting levels, variability, and reactivity were also observed in the majority of Ss. Some relationships among bilateral patterns of vasomotor responsivity and BSR emerged. Thus, the side of the body having lower BSR was identical to the side with the lesser vasomotor constriction during experimental stress (breath-holding). Also, the side of the body having the lower vasomotor amplitude had less vasomotor variability. Findings suggest that asymmetry of autonomic activity is typical rather than atypical for the normal individual, and that various autonomic variables form patterns of asymmetry.

bilateral differences vasomotor activity BSR

C 6   Wyatt, R., and Tursky, B.: Skin potential levels in right- and left-handed males. *Psychophysiology, 6:*133, 1969.

From twelve left-handed and twelve right-handed males, skin potential levels were recorded simultaneously from both sides of the body. In both groups, significantly higher skin potential levels were found on the right side. Unilateral stimuli and handedness did not unilaterally affect maximum response level.

handedness SP

RESPONSE COMPONENTS

C 7   Edelberg, Robert: The information content of the recovery limb of the exosomatic electrodermal response. *Psychophysiology, 4:*505, 1968 (abstr).

Recent studies support the hypothesis that the skin conduct- *response compon-ents*
ance response manifests (in the shape of its recovery limb) a
slow component associated with the negative skin potential
response and sweating and a faster one associated with the *recovery time*
positive skin potential response and with the sweat reabsorption reflex. Part of the recovery limb has an exponential *arousal*
form, and its time constant (recovery rate) is interpreted as *reaction time*
a measure of the relative participation of these two compon-
ents. A simple manual method, utilizing an overlay, allows *goal-directed behavior*
rapid determination of the time constant. The measure is
independent of amplitude and capable of differentiating be- *SC*
tween spontaneous responses during rest and during a simple
task, between orienting responses to a meaningless light
flash and to the same flash used as a task-alerting signal, and
between responses to tones and those to an RT effort. The
time constant taken during a standard stimulus was also
correlated across individuals with the rate of adaptation to a
series of RT trials. The results indicate that the fast component of the electrodermal response is preferentially activated
during goal-directed behavior.

C 8   Edelberg, Robert: Electrodermal recovery rate, goal-orientation, and aversion. *Psychophysiology, 9*:512, 1972.

To distinguish between goal-orientation and the attending *recovery time*
activation as causes of acceleration of electrodermal recovery,
sixteen subjects were examined during task performance and *E D fre-quency*
during an activating, nontask condition, cold pressor. Re-
covery limb time constants (tc) were significantly related to *defensive responses*
two activation measures, electrodermal frequency (EF) and *apprehen-sion*
skin conductance level (SCL). EF, SCL, and change in log
conductance were similar for cold pressor and mirror tracing
despite significant differences in tc values. Since, in addition,
tc decreased with better performance and with increasing
task complexity, goal-orientation is considered the primary
determinant of acceleration of recovery. There are characteristic individual differences in recovery rate which are relatively stable over five consecutive weeks. Rate constant, the reciprocal of tc, has more uniform variance and is preferred
for parametric statistical analysis. A warning of shock introduced during a reaction time series caused slowing of re-

covery. This, coupled with slow recovery during cold pressor, suggests that enhanced electrodermal activity with retarded recovery may signal a defensive reaction.

C 9   Furedy, John J.: Novelty and the measurement of the GSR. *J Exp Psychol, 76:*501, 1968.

Electrodermal effects of presenting a familiar stimulus (last of fifteen tones or lights) and a novel stimulus (light or tone, respectively, after the fifteenth tone or light) to forty college Ss were examined with the levels and changes-in-levels techniques. Only the latter technique produced greater responding to novelty, suggesting that the GSR, defined as a transient electrodermal variation following stimulation, is not necessarily insensitive to stimulus change.

recovery time anticipatory responses stimulus intensity

C 10   Furedy, John J.: Electrodermal recovery time as a suprasensitive autonomic index of anticipated intensity of threatened shock. *Psychophysiology, 9:*281, 1972.

The electrodermal recovery time was examined in a classical conditioning paradigm demonstrating that this parameter reliably and differentially reflected anticipated intensities of threatened shocks.

response components recovery time anticipatory responses

C 11   Neumann, Eva: Thermal changes in palmar skin resistance patterns. *Psychophysiology, 5:*103, 1968.

In contrast to the usual description of a uniformly low basal skin resistance at the human palmar surface as compared with other parts of the body (Richter, Woodruff, and Eaton, 1943; Wilcott, 1963), the present studies reveal skin resistance patterns (SRPs) with different resistance values at different subregions of palm and forearm. The shape of these patterns is related to the season in which the experiment was performed. Three basic SRPs are described for winter, summer, and prolonged summer heat spell, respectively: (1) an alternating pattern, (2) an oblique pattern, (3) a so-called

temperature response patterns skin sites

summer reversal pattern. The distinguishing factor for this categorization is the reciprocal electrodermal behavior of the mid-palm and arm regions. The resistance of the palm is relatively low in the winter, intermediate in the early summer, and high in a summer heat spell, while the resistance of the arm is high in winter and summer and low in the heat spell. Experimental heating and cooling leads to independent variation of the skin resistance values at different subregions and differs as a function of the basic seasonal SRP. A follow-up study shows that children have a less differentiated pattern, which, at all seasons tested, is similar to the oblique summer pattern of adults. The studies are considered exploratory.

RESPONSE STABILITY AND DISTRIBUTION

12 Doctor, Richard F., and Friedman, Louis F.: Thirty-day stability of spontaneous galvanic skin responses in man. *Psychophysiology,* 2:311, 1966.

response stability GSR frequency arousal

Measures of long-range stability of spontaneous GSRs (Galvanic Skin Response) were obtained from twenty-three male university students. Records were taken throughout a weekly recording period and compared with measures obtained under identical conditions thirty days later. In addition to the investigation of long-term spontaneous GSR stability, this design permitted analysis of the twenty-four-hour stability of measured responses within each of the recording periods. Results yielded significant correlations between measures obtained twenty-four hours apart, as well as a significant correlation between the median weekly rates of spontaneous GSR emission taken thirty days apart. Comparison of emission rates on comparable recording days thirty days apart failed to manifest a significant relationship. Present data support earlier studies of twenty-four-hour spontaneous GSR stability. In spite of the failure to find significant relationships between emission rates on comparable days of the two recording periods, the authors conclude that the significant relationship between median weekly rates of emission, taken thirty days apart, indicates that spontaneous GSR is an intra-individual characteristic which remains relatively stable, even over extended periods of time.

C 13   Germana, Joseph, and Chernault, George: Patterns of gal-
        vanic skin responses to signal and non-signal stimuli. *Psycho-
        physiology, 5:*284, 1968.

Two studies investigating the specific features of galvanic   *signal sig-*
skin responses (GSRs) to signal and non-signal stimuli are   *nificance*
reported. The results of experiment I indicate that stimuli   *novelty*
which have instructed behavioral associates (signal signific-   *GSR*
ance) produce GSRs which are both multiphasic and relatively persistent in nature. Multiple GSRs are produced by
the initial presentation of a signal stimulus and the persistence of the overall response appears to have at least a short-
term effect on baseline. Experiment II was designed to investigate the possible independence of these two characteristics through the manipulation of response certainty. The results suggest that multiplicity and persistence may be separ-
able features of the response to signal stimuli in which the
latter may be a correlate of response novelty.

C 14   Jones, B.E., and Ayres, J.J.B.: Significance and reliability of
        shock-induced changes in basal skin conductance. *Psycho-
        physiology, 2:*322, 1966.

Once weekly for five weeks, fifteen adult male postaddicts   *response*
were given twelve to fifteen shocks of 5.0 to 8.0 ma. Basal   *stability*
skin conductance (BSC) was recorded during the twenty-five-   *methodol-*
minute weekly sessions. Increases in BSC during each session   *ogy*
and the week-to-week reliabilities of the increases were de-   *electric*
termined. After the first week, subsequent increases showed   *shock*
reliability coefficients which ranged from 0.69 to 0.95 (P <   *BSC*
0.01). The reliabilities of the increases in BSC produced by
shock were considered favorable for the use of change in
BSC as a dependent variable in designs requiring repeated
measurements on the same Ss at weekly intervals.

C 15   O'Connell, Donald N., Tursky, Bernard, and Evans, Fred-
        erick J.: Normality of distribution of resting palmar skin
        potential. *Psychophysiology, 4:*151, 1967.

Resting skin potential level scores from three samples, two   *normal dis-*
of undergraduates and one of housewives, were analyzed for   *tribution*

normality of distribution. The first two samples showed no significant departure from normality. The third showed some significant positive skewness. In general, it was concluded that resting level scores were sufficiently normal not to require transformation for statistical analyses.

resting levels
SP

C 16 Surwillo, Walter W.: Statistical distribution of volar skin potential level in attention and the effects of age. *Psychophysiology, 6:*13, 1969.

Skin potential (SP) level was investigated in fifty-eight young (aged twenty-two to fifty-three years) and sixty-four old (aged fifty-four to eighty-five years) Ss. SP recordings were made during a fifteen-minute interval while Ss were taking part in a watch-keeping task. The Kolmogorov-Smirnov test revealed that while the distribution of SP level in young Ss deviated significantly from normality, the distribution in old Ss was normal. Evidence suggested that age of Ss needs to be taken into account when dealing with distributions of SP level recorded under attentive conditions.

normal distribution
age
SP

C 17 Tursky, Bernard, Greenblatt, David, and O'Connell, Donald: Electrocutaneous threshold changes produced by electric shock. *Psychophysiology, 7:*490, 1970.

Describes three experiments to investigate the effect of strong shock on absolute electrocutaneous thresholds. Experiment I with thirty-eight paid volunteer male undergraduates confirms the existence of a reliable elevation of absolute threshold after strong shock. Experiment II with 10 Ss shows the effect to be highly localized to the site of the strongly shocked electrode. It also shows that threshold elevation does not follow the same time course as do local vascular and impedance changes. Experiment III with 10 Ss used skin treatment to alter the local vascular and impedance levels and demonstrates that threshold elevation occurs after strong shock even after these measures have been stabilized. Data indicate that the threshold increase due to electric shock is probably analogous to auditory fatigue but does not rule out the possible involvement of more central control factors.

threshold changes
electric shock
vasomotor changes
impedance

C 18 Watanabe, T., Yamazaki, K., and Niimi, Y.: Skin potential level and its relation to the waveform of skin potential reflex. *Clin Electroencephalogr (Osaka), 9:269*, 1967.

Abstract not available.

HABITUATION, ADAPTATION, STIMULUS GENERALIZATION

C 19 Burstein, K.R., Epstein, S., and Smith, B.: Primary stimulus generalization of the GSR as a function of objective and subjective definition of the stimulus dimension. *J Exp Psychol, 74:124*, 1967.

Two experiments were conducted to determine whether the divergent results obtained on previous replications of Hovland's classic study of generalization to auditory frequency could be accounted for on the basis of Ss responding to a subjectively defined dimension rather than to the objective one defined by E. In two experiments Ss were asked to identify the test stimuli (tones of 153, 468, 1000 and 1967 cps). No support was obtained in either of the experiments for decremental gradients of stimulus generalization when response strength was plotted as a function of the perceived characteristics of the stimuli. Accuracy of labeling the generalization stimuli as the CS produced highly reliable negatively accelerated gradients.

stimulus generalization
stimulus characteristics
subjective judgments

C 20 Germana, Joseph: Rate of habituation and the law of initial values. *Psychophysiology, 5:31*, 1968.

The galvanic skin response (GSR) data of two experiments were analyzed in an attempt to determine the effects of tonic shifts in baseline conductance on apparent rate of habituation. The results of the first experiment indicated that rate of habituation is exaggerated when response measures which are not base-independent are employed. The positive correlation found between habituation slope and an index of base-level change in conductance was significantly reduced when autonomic lability scores (ALSs) were used. Thus, base-corrected responses produced less steep habituation functions.

habituation
response components
LIV
GSR

The second experiment demonstrated that a tonic increase in conductance occurs to an intense auditory stimulus and that rate of habituation is consequently overestimated in comparison to that associated with repeated presentation of a mild stimulus.

C 21 Kimmel, H.D., and Kimmel E.: Sex differences in adaptation of the GSR under repeated applications of a visual stimulus. *J Exp Psychol, 70:*536, 1965.

Eight men and eight women came to the laboratory on three occasions, one week apart to receive ten presentations of a visual stimulus on each occasion. The average galvanic skin response (GSR) to the light showed an intrasession (but no intersession) adaptation effect for both sexes, but this effect was almost gone for the males on the last session. In addition, the males made significantly larger GSRs than the women on all three occasions, especially on the last session. It was conjectured that the men became familiar with the procedure and anticipated the end of the third session by making larger GSRs, but that the women did not.

adaptation
visual
* stimuli*
sex differ-
* ences*
GSR

C 22 O'Gorman, J.G.: Latency and habituation of the electrodermal response. *Psychophysiology, 8:*280, 1971.

Reports two studies, with forty male and thirty-six female undergraduates, respectively, in which a variance common to habituation and latency was found. It is suggested that this may reflect "inhibitory influences within the electrodermal system, a strong inhibitory process giving rise to both long latency, and rapid suppression of response with repeated stimulus presentations."

habituation
latency

C 23 Orr, William C., and Stern, John A.: The relationship between stimulus information, reaction time, and cortical habituation. *Psychophysiology, 7:*475, 1970.

Studied the effects of uncertainty, or stimulus information, on habituation rate with thirty-nine 18 to 26-year-old females associated with nursing as Ss. Ss were randomly assigned to one of three conditions varying in uncertainty. EEG alpha

habituation
uncertainty
stimulus in-
* formation*

desynchrony duration, electrodermal conductance change, and RT were the dependent measures. Results show uncertainty to have no significant effect on any of the neurophysiological measures. There was a significant effect on the RT measure. There was no significant correlation between the EEG and electrodermal response measures, nor was there any correlation between either of these measures and RT. Results indicate that habituation could occur in the presence of cortical and behavioral arousal. It is concluded that information may be most meaningfully measured behaviorally and that habituation parameters are dependent upon the physiological system being measured.

SC
EEG alpha
reaction
*   time*

ORIENTING RESPONSE

RESPONSE CHARACTERISTICS

D 1   Gale, Elliot N., and Stern, John A.: Conditioning of the electrodermal orienting response. *Psychophysiology, 3:*291, 1967.

The present study demonstrates that the orienting response (OR) to the conditional stimulus can be conditioned with a delayed differential conditioning paradigm. Controls utilized were two "sensitization" and one backward-trace differential conditioning group. Conditioned ORs, conditioned anticipatory responses, and conditioned responses at latency of unconditioned response in the absence of the unconditioned stimulus were all demonstrated. In the backward conditioning group the amplitude of the OR to the tone preceded by shock was lower than that found for any other group. Refractoriness of the peripheral components of the electrodermal response (EDR) are invoked to account for this finding.

*orienting response
delayed differential conditioning
anticipatory responses*

D 2   Loveless, E., and Thetford, P.: Interpretation and conditioning of the positive and negative components of the skin potential response. *Psychol Rec, 16:*357, 1966.

Skin potential responses to tone and tone plus light were separated for analysis into positive and negative components. The positive component showed typical orienting response characteristics (in the Sokolov sense), whereas the negative seemed to reflect stimulus registration. Conditioning of the positive component did not occur.

*response components
conditioning
SP*

D 3   Raskin, David C.: Semantic conditioning and generalization of autonomic responses. *J Exp Psychol, 79:*69, 1968.

Semantic conditioning (SC) and semantic generalization (SG) of GSR and finger vasomotor responses were studied using auditory presentation of stimuli, white noise as the UCS, and a ten-second trace-conditioning procedure. The relationship of the orienting reflex (OR) and anxiety to the development of SC and SG was investigated. Prompting of SG was attempted by manipulating the instructions to Ss and the number of different conditioned stimulus (CS) words used. The results showed clear evidence of SC in both responses, strong SG of the GSR, and some evidence of vasomotor SG. The partially-informative instructions enhanced the SC and SG effects produced with the noncommittal instructions, and the number of different CS words had weak effects on SG. The OR and anxiety had different effects on SC and SG, and there was no evidence of any relationship between OR and anxiety.

classical conditioning
verbal stimuli
orienting response
anxiety
instructions
response generalization

D 4   Spence, Donald P., Fiss, Harry, and Varga, Michael: Sensitivity to latent cues as a function of two changes in skin resistance: Orienting response and basal drop. *Psychosom Med, 30:*311, 1968.

A test of sensitivity to low-level cues is described. The test consists of thirty-two pairs of items; one of each pair is similar, in some specific way, to a standard stimulus. Basal skin resistance was monitored continuously during each subject's performance. Sensitivity to a particular item was significantly related to subjective confidence on that item and to increase in relaxation during the judgment period for that item (change in basal skin resistance), and negatively related to an orienting response to that item. Implications for therapeutic sensitivity are discussed.

signal detection
response thresholds
arousal
BSR

D 5   Uno, Tadao, and Grings, William W.: Autonomic components of orienting behavior. *Psychophysiology, 1:*311, 1965.

Changes in skin conductance (GSR), skin potential (SP), heart rate (HR), finger blood volume (BV), and pulse volume (PV) were recorded in response to two-second bursts of white noise. Five intensity levels of sound (60, 70, 80, 90, and 100 db) were presented over five repetitions. Results

orienting response
stimulus intensity
HR

showed that (1) response magnitudes and latencies were *vasomotor*
directly related to stimulus intensity and inversely related to *activity*
number of repetitions; (2) for BV, SP and GSR the effect *finger pulse*
of repetition varied with stimulus intensity; (3) HR changes *volume*
were primarily monophasic; and (4) BV and PV were more
sensitive to stimulus intensity differences than were the electrodermal responses.

HABITUATION AND ADAPTATION

6 Beideman, Larry R., and Stern, John A.: Onset and terminal
orienting responses as a function of task demands. *Psychophysiology, 8:*376, 1971.

The frequency of response and trials to habituation of the *orienting*
electrodermal onset and terminal orienting response were *task demand*
manipulated as a function of discrimination tasks involving *response*
either stimulus content (pitch) or duration. There were no *components*
significant differences between the groups on either measure *ents*
for onset ORs; however, the duration task group demon- *habituation*
strated more TORs and required a greater number of trials
to habituate than the content task group. The results, interpreted in terms of the development of cortical models, supported Stern's suggestion that OR and TOR habituation are
related to the content and duration of the stimulus respectively.

7 Corman, C.D.: Stimulus generalization of habituation of the
galvanic skin response. *J Exp Psychol, 74:*236, 1967.

A generalization gradient of habituation of the orienting re- *orienting*
sponse occurred across groups when Ss were exposed to a new *response*
tone after hearing a similar one over a number of trials. The *habituation*
between-Ss design indicated that it is not necessary for S to *stimulus*
be exposed to the full range of test stimuli in order that a *generalization*
gradient may be demonstrated. *stimulus
character-
istics*

8 Firth, Hugh: Habituation during sleep. *Psychophysiology,
10:*43, 1973.

In some recent reports, authors have found no evidence for habituation during sleep, and have concluded that habituation and sleep are incompatible. This finding was tested using skin potential, heart rate, and EEG responses to a 70 dB, 1 sec, 1000 Hz tone, in sleep stages 2, 4, and REM, with daytime controls. Interstimulus intervals used ranged from ten to thirty seconds. Autonomic responses analyzed separately for each series of stimuli showed significant habituation, except for heart rate responses in REM and in the daytime (drowsy) controls. EEG responses also demonstrated habituation. An interstimulus interval effect was found with EEG K-complexes, habituation occurring more slowly or not at all with the longer, irregular interstimulus intervals. It is suggested that previous failure to detect habituation has been due to a technique of averaging responses over hourly periods and/or the use of long, irregular interstimulus intervals. It is concluded that habituation is indeed possible in human sleep if stimulus intervals are not long.

orienting response habituation sleep SP HR EEG

D 9   Fried, R., Korn, S.J., and Welch, L.: Effects of change in sequential visual stimuli on GSR adaptation. *J Exp Psychol,* 72:325, 1966.

GSR records were obtained for twenty Ss while they were presented with a series of eighty stimuli (four lights alternating in apparently random sequence). Records were obtained for twenty additional Ss using the same procedure, except that a novel stimulus (a light not previously presented) was substituted in place of one of the original four lights. Typical adaptation phenomena were observed for both groups. While the novel stimulus was perceived by all Ss in the second group, it had no effect on the adaptation curve for that group. It is concluded that novelty is a dimension which needs considerable reexamination.

novel stimuli GSR

D 10   Fried, Robert, Welch, Livingston, and Friedman, Miriam: Stimulus novelty and intraseries primacy in GSR adaptation. *Percept Psychophys, 1:*345, 1966.

GSR records were obtained for four groups of 20 Ss. Group 1 was presented with a series of four different lights (amber,

novel stimuli

blue, green and white) appearing twenty times each, in apparent random order. The procedure was similar for the other three groups except that in group 2, a novel stimulus (a red light) appeared instead of the sixth amber light; in group 3, it appeared instead of the eleventh amber light; and, in group 4, it appeared instead of the sixteenth amber light. Typical GSR adaptation phenomena were observed in all groups. The introduction of the novel stimulus appeared to have no effect on the course of GSR adaptation.

orienting response adaptation

11 Galbrecht, Charles R., Dykman, Roscoe A., Reese, William G., and Suzuki, Tetsuko: Intrasession adaptation and intersession extinction of the components of the orienting response. *J Exp Psychol, 70:*585, 1965.

Intrasession (adaptation) and intersession (extinction) changes in the skin resistance (SR), heart rate (HR), respiratory rate (RR), and muscle action potentials (MP) components of the orienting response (OR) to auditory stimuli of moderate intensity were compared. Adaptation and extinction curves were very similar in SR and similar in MP. There was essentially no evidence of adaptation or extinction in HR and RR or indeed systematic responsiveness. These findings support the logical inference that adaptation and extinction are equivalent processes mediated by the same neural mechanisms. Significant bilateral differences in prestimulus levels of SR did not affect responses; in each system Ss maintained their rank-order position in the group across sessions; the responses studied provided little evidence of startle components; and the generally larger reactions in SR and MP on the first tone each day were not related to arousal levels as measured by prestimulus levels of functioning.

orienting response procedures adaptation extinction

12 Johnson, L.C., and Lubin, A.: The orienting reflex during waking and sleeping. *Electroencephalogr Clin Neurophysiol,* 22:11, 1967.

A three-second tone was presented at thirty- to forty-five-second intervals to seventeen subjects before sleep and during all night sleep sessions. For twelve of these subjects twenty

habituation sleep wakefulness

tones were presented during a day awake session. The following components of the orienting reflex to the tone were
measured: EEG, heart rate, respiration, electrodermal, and
finger plethysmogram. All measures habituated during the
awake sessions. With sleep onset there was a return of the OR
for all variables, but the magnitude of the restored OR differed for each variable. There was little if any habituation of
the OR during sleep. While the smallest OR response was
generally during 1-REM, heart rate was a striking exception.
The presence of a stimulus-evoked K complex was associated
with increased responsiveness in all autonomic variables, but
presence of eye movement bursts was associated with decreased cardiovascular response to the tone.

*EEG activ-
ity
HR
finger pulse
volume
respiration
EDA
eye move-
ment*

D 13   Katkin, Edward S., and McCubbin, Robert J.: Habituation
of the orienting response as a function of individual differences in anxiety and autonomic lability. *J Abnorm Psychol,
74:54,* 1969.

This study evaluated the role of individual differences in
anxiety and autonomic lability on the habituation of GSR
responses to auditory stimuli of moderate and very low intensity. Sixty Ss were used. They were divided into high-
and low-anxious groups on the basis of Taylor MA scale
scores and high and low autonomic lability groups on the
basis of spontaneous GSR activity during a rest period. No
relationship between Taylor score and GSR habituation was
obtained for either stimulus intensity. Autonomically labile
Ss showed no habituation to the moderate tone, but did
habituate to the low intensity tone. Autonomically stabile
Ss habituated to both tones. It was concluded that individual
differences in autonomic lability may predict whether an S
will respond to moderate intensities with orienting or defensive reactions.

*habituation
anxiety
autonomic
responsiv-
ity
individual
differences*

D 14   Kimmel, H.D., Pendergrass, V.E., and Kimmel E.B.: Modi-
fying children's orienting reactions instrumentally. *Cond Reflex, 2:227,* 1967.

Normal Ss' GSRs to visual stimuli habituated more slowly
than retarded Ss' GSRs and were larger. During condition-

*operant con
ditioning
children*

ing, normal Ss' GSRs increased in magnitude under nonresponse-contingent reinforcement but not under response-
contingent reinforcement. Retarded children's GSRs increased in magnitude slightly under response-contingent
reinforcement but not under nonresponse-contingent reinforcement. More Ss who received response-contingent reinforcement improved in their performance on the Seguin
form board than got poorer; Ss who received reinforcement
contingent on nonresponding did not show this differential
tendency. The retarded Ss showed this effect substantially
more than normals. Children who were merely tested twice
but received no conditioning showed no differential tendency
toward improved form board performance. It was concluded
that normal and retarded children differ in their initial
orienting reaction (OR) tendencies, particularly in the persistence of OR under repeated stimulation, and that instrumental conditioning of ORs mediates improved performance on complex tasks requiring attention to relevant stimulus dimensions.

*mental re-
tardation
orienting
response
habituation*

D 15 Koepke, J.E., and Pribram, K.H.: Habituation of GSR as a
function of stimulus duration and spontaneous activity. *J
Comp Physiol Psychol, 61:442,* 1966.

Habituation of GSR to repeated stimulation with tones of
either two- or twenty-second duration was investigated with
college students. Subsequent to habituation stimulus durations were reversed immediately for one half of the Ss and
after a number of additional trials for the remaining Ss.
Speed of habituation did not vary with stimulus duration
but was significantly related to "spontaneous activity" as defined by spontaneous fluctuation scores. Orienting to the
reversal in stimulus duration was indicated by an overall
increase in latency and an increase in response duration for
Ss changed from a two- to a twenty-second stimulus.

*habituation
stimulus
character-
istics
spontaneous
GSRs*

D 16 Lovibond, S.H.: Habituation of the orienting response to
multiple stimulus sequences. *Psychophysiology, 5:435,* 1969.

The purpose of the study was to test the hypothesis that rate
of habituation of the orienting response (OR) to multiple

*habituation
uncertainty
SC*

stimulus sequences is a negative function of the uncertainty (H) in the stimulus series. Seven groups of 30 Ss received ten presentations of a ten second light stimulus (S_1) followed immediately by a one second 70 db auditory stimulus (S_2) on 0, 10, 20, 50, 80, 90 or 100 percent of trials. The response measure was change of skin conductance to S_1. Mean conductance change scores of the various groups were closely related to the degree of uncertainty (H) in the stimulus series. The results were interpreted as offering support for Sokolov's OR theory, and the view that, in human information processing, information concerning stimulus probabilities is integrated continuously to form the basis of predictive extrapolation.

D 17 O'Gorman, J.G., Mangan, G.L., and Gowen, Joan A.: Selective habituation of galvanic skin response component of the orientation reaction to an auditory stimulus. *Psychophysiology, 6:*716, 1970.

habituation
individual
differences
GSR

The prediction from Sokolov's (1960) theory that following OR habituation, size of OR return is proportional to the amount of difference between the new stimulus and the habituating stimulus was tested using an auditory stimulus varying in frequency and intensity. Five Ss were allocated to each of sixteen conditions, three conditions involving changes in frequency, three involving changes in intensity, nine involving changes in both frequency and intensity, with one control condition involving a repetition of the habituating stimulus. Following habituation of the GSR component of the OR to a criterion of response failure for three successive trials, magnitude of GSR under the sixteen conditions was measured. Contrary to Sokolov's theory, only increase in intensity had a significantly different effect on OR return. More importantly, it was found that Ss habituating rapidly to the initial stimulus were less likely to show OR return to stimulus change. It was concluded that individual differences in habituation rate may be more important than stimulus difference effects in selective habituation.

D 18 Stern, J.A., Surphlis, W., and Koff, E.: Electrodermal responsiveness as related to psychiatric diagnosis and prognosis. *Psychophysiology, 2:*51, 1965.

Electrodermal responsiveness as measured by orienting re- *ED respon-*
sponses to tone stimulation and to a word-association *siveness*
task was evaluated in a group of schizophrenic patients upon *word associ-*
admission to the hospital and after five weeks of hospitaliza- *ation task*
tion. Two evaluations were conducted, the first based on *habituation*
clinical recovery, the second based on electro-dermal respon- *applications*
siveness at time of first testing. Results indicate that patients
who demonstrate more rapid habituation at second time of
testing have a better hospital discharge record than those
who show no change in rate of habituation. Electrodermal
responsiveness to the word-association task at first time of
testing was related to such factors as clinical diagnosis, severity of illness, and adequacy of word associations. In general,
patients who were most responsive demonstrated less pathology than those who were less responsive at first time of testing.

19 Stern, Robert M., Gaupp, Larry, and Leonard, William C.:
A comparison of GSR and subjective adaptation to stressful
stimuli. *Psychophysiology, 7:3, 1970.*

Compared subjective and physiological adaptation, as mea- *adaptation*
sured by magnitude of GSRs, to electric shock and auditory *instructions*
noise. In Experiment I, forty-eight undergraduates received *stimulus*
fifteen shocks of constant intensity, one subgroup always re- *character-*
ceiving low shocks and the other high. Ss were told that shock *istics*
intensity would vary and rated the intensity of each shock *anticipation*
immediately following its presentation. In Experiment II,
the same procedure was followed with fifty different Ss, using
noises instead of shocks. Shock Ss showed subjective adaptation but no GSR adaptation. Noise Ss showed GSR adaptation with an increase in subjective intensity reports. The
importance of anticipation, in terms of level of arousal at the
onset of the session, is discussed.

20 Zimny, George H., and Schwabe, Leonard W.: Stimulus
change and habituation of the orienting response. *Psycho-*
physiology, 2:103, 1966.

Eight hypotheses derived from Sokolov's theory of habitu- *habituation*
ation of the orienting response were tested. Subjects were *condition-*
ing

given a series of thirty-six standard stimuli (SSs), each 500 cps. Four interpolations of a 1000-cps test stimulus (TS) for one group (N = 10) and of a 4000-cps TS for another group (N = 10) were made. Results for amplitude of galvanic skin response (GSR) for combined groups showed that habituation occurred over the first eight SSs and over the four TSs, a TS produced return of GSR and disrupted habituation to the SS, and response was greater to the TS than to the following SS. The 4000 TS disrupted habituation to the SS more than the 1000 TS and produced less drop from the TS to the next SS. Seven hypotheses were confirmed. Habituation of resistance level was found but spontaneous fluctuations were not. Sokolov's theory and the results obtained were related to the classical conditioning of autonomic processes.

spontaneo
GSRs

CONDITIONABILITY

D 21   Gale, Elliot N.: Long-term conditioning of orienting responses. *Psychophysiology, 5:*307, 1968.

The Russian literature suggests that as stable conditional responses develop, orienting responses (ORs) adapt. Prior research by Gale and Stern (1967 and 1968) indicated that in a differential conditioning situation the OR becomes conditioned (COR) and conditioned responses in the form of anticipatory responses (CAR) develop. The Russian literature suggests an inverse relationship between these two responses. As the CAR evolves the COR extinguishes. In the present study conditioning in the electrodermal and peripheral vasomotor systems was assessed utilizing 300 trials of conditioning. The results indicate that the COR does not extinguish in a series this long, nor does the CAR increase in amplitude as predicted. Rather the two CRs evolve in a similar manner. Possible explanations for the obtained results are discussed.

condition-
ing
adaptation
anticipator
responses
EDR
vasomotor
activity

D 22   Maltzman, Irving, and Mandell, Mary P.: The orienting reflex as a predictor of learning and performance. *J Exp Res Pers, 3:*99, 1968.

Noted the complex nature of the concept of the orienting reflex (OR), and summarized recent unpublished results of

condition-
ability

experiments which demonstrated individual differences in physiological measures of the orienting reflex predicted between response systems. For example, individual differences in the GSR measure of the OR predicted individual differences in semantic conditioning of alpha blocking, and differentiated between "aware" and "unaware" Ss in the experiment. It was also found that a GSR measure of the OR induced by verbal reinforcement differentiated "aware" from "unaware" Ss in an operant verbal conditioning task. The theoretical implications of these and related studies were discussed as well as the problems inherent in research on the orienting reflex in human Ss.

predictor
performance
verbal
  stimuli
individual
  differences
awareness
review

23   Morgenson, D.F., and Martin, Irene: The orienting response as a predictor of autonomic conditioning. *J Exp Res Pers, 3:* 89, 1968.

Orienting response (OR) amplitudes in three response modalities of skin resistance, pulse volume, and pulse rate were split at the group mean to distinguish subgroups of high and low orienters. These groups differed significantly on mean conditioning response (CR) amplitude within each specific response system, but relatively little on the degree of linear trend of CR over acquisition trials, both groups showing a substantial incremental trend. Highly significant correlations were obtained between OR and CR amplitudes within but not across response systems, suggesting that CR amplitude might be regarded as an augmentation of initial response amplitude differences. The correlation between OR amplitude and linear trend of the CR over trails was also significant, but dropped to zero when CR amplitude effects were partialled out. No evidence of a predictive effect of the OR on subsequent autonomic conditioning was obtained. This is discussed in relation to the problems of assessing a learning as distinct from a sensitivity factor.

condition-
  ability
predictor
GSR
HR
pulse
  volume

24   Ohman, Arne: Differentiation of conditioned and orienting response components in electrodermal conditioning. *Psychophysiology, 8:*7, 1971.

Discusses different criteria for CRs and orienting responses (ORs) and proposes that neither latency nor differences be-

conditioned
  responses

tween conditioning and sensitization treatments provide ade-   *criteria*
quate solutions to the problem. An additional criterion is
proposed based on differences in the slopes of the generalization gradients, i.e. ORs should show rising and CRs falling
generalization gradients with increased stimulus change.
This criterion was tested with a total of 132 undergraduates
for conditioning and sensitization groups in paradigms involving generalization along pitch and temporal continua.
It was found that the response to the onset of the CS (the
CS response) fulfilled the proposed criteria for an OR,
while responses in the interval of the UCR on trials where
the UCS was omitted (post-UCS responses) satisfied the
criteria for an OR early in training and the criteria for a CR
later in training. For the response preceding UCS (the pre-
UCS response) no definite conclusion was reached, but the
evidence could be interpreted to mean that both OR and CR
components participated in that response too. The relationships between these response components and stages of sensory integration and response acquisition of conditioning
are discussed.

D 25   Stern, John A.: Stability-lability of physiological response
        systems. *Ann NY Acad Sci, 134*:1018, 1966.

Speed of adaptation of electrodermal orienting responses   *orienting*
and conditionability of electrodermal responses were in most   *response*
studies found to be significantly related to the level of spon-   *habituation*
taneous fluctuations. The greater the number of spontaneous   *condition-*
fluctuations the more difficult it is to habituate orienting   *ability*
responses and the easier it is to develop conditioned electrodermal responses. We suspect that these findings are not
unique to the electrodermal system but are characteristic of
other physiological measures as well. We have preliminary
data which confirm these findings as far as peripheral vasomotor activity is concerned. We would thus like to hypo-
thesize that there are specific periods (critical periods) in an
organism's life when environmental influences can either ac-
celerate or inhibit the normal course of retardation of spontaneous fluctuations. That there are critical periods during
which specific types of behavior can be most successfully
elaborated is well demonstrated in the studies by Hess (1959)

on imprinting, as well as the studies by Fuller and Thompson (1960) and others on critical periods for socialization and other aspects of behavior.

26 van Olst, E.H., and Orlebeke, J.F.: The usefulness of GSR-conditioning in psychology. *Ned Tijdschr Psychol, 21:232,* 1966.

Investigated the following assumptions underlying GSR conditioning: (1) GSR is a reflex comparable to eyelid reflex, salivary reflex, etc., and (2) GSR can be considered a conditioned reflex. Because of their generality, these assumptions do not appear tenable because the GSR is part of both orienting and defensive reflexes. The influence that these assumptions might have had upon the results of four previous experiments was subjected to critical consideration. It was concluded that, in GSR conditioning, it is necessary to use a method by means of which orienting, defensive and conditioned reflexes (or anticipatory responses) can be distinguished. The use of a classical conditioning procedure is not necessary for the establishment of a conditioned GSR.

GSR conditioning defensive responses anticipatory responses review

27 Zeiner, Arthur R.: Individual differences in orienting, conditionability, and skin resistance responsivity. *Psychophysiology, 8:612,* 1971.

Forty-eight college students, after serving as Ss in a SRR discrimination conditioning experiment, were divided into quartiles on magnitude of SRR to both noxious (UCS) and innocuous (CS) stimuli. With both orienting response (OR) measures, i.e. to the CS and to the UCS, it was shown that subjects giving large ORs gave significantly larger responses to both CS+ and CS− (during conditioning) than did Ss giving small ORs. On the basis of the innocuous stimulus split, Ss giving large ORs demonstrated both significantly faster and greater discrimination conditioning than did Ss giving small ORs. Such differences in rate and amount of discrimination conditioning were not demonstrated with the noxious stimulus split. In other words, with the noxious stimulus measure there is only a significant response level effect, but with the innocuous stimulus definition of OR,

conditionability differential conditioning individual differences

there is a significant response level effect and a significant effect on rate and amount of discrimination conditioning. Thus noxious and innocuous stimulus definitions of OR do not appear to be measuring the same process.

D 28 Zimny, George H., and Kienstra, Randy A.: Orienting and defensive responses to electric shock. *Psychophysiology, 3:* 351, 1967.

The major purpose of this study was to test ten hypotheses *condition-* dealing with orienting responses and defensive responses that *ing* were derived from Sokolov's theory. Four presentations of a *defensive* 0.5-sec. tone were occasionally interpolated among a series *response.* of forty presentations of a 0.5-sec. electric shock administered *GSR* to one group of fourteen human subjects and among forty presentations of simultaneous 0.5-sec. shock and 0.5-sec. tone administered to another group of fourteen subjects. Skin resistance was recorded and analyses were carried out on amplitude and base level. With amplitude, seven hypotheses were completely and two were partially confirmed, thereby providing strong support for Sokolov's theory. The findings were discussed in relation to various problems involved in the classical conditioning of physiological processes.

INFLUENCE OF OTHER VARIABLES

D 29 Berlyne, D.E., and Borsa, Donna M.: Uncertainty and the orientation reaction. *Percept Psychophysics, 3:*77, 1968.

In Experiment I, blurred pictures evoked longer desyn- *uncertain* chronization than clear pictures but not more intense GSRs. *arousal* Experiment II confirmed that the EEG effect depended on *pictorial* subjective uncertainty by showing that it did not occur when *stimuli* a blurred picture was immediately preceded by a clear version of the same picture.

D 30 Fletcher, James E.: The orienting response as an index of mass communication effect. *Psychophysiology, 8:*699, 1971.

A study is described of the contribution of the electrodermal *mass com* response to the measurement of broadcast communication *municat* *effect*

effect. A 2 × 2 mixed between-within groups design was employed. The within groups variable was radio commercial content, while the between groups variable was production style. Electrodermal measurements included average log conductance change, number of responses, and recovery half time. Comparison measures included retention test, interest scales, and semantic differentials. Only average log conductance change significantly discriminated stimuli on both between and within groups variables. An explanatory model incorporating Sokolov's notion of the neuronal model and the Deutsch and Deutsch model for attention is offered.

attention
recovery
rate
GSR
EDR

31 Houck, Robert L., and Mefferd, Roy B. Jr.: Generalization of GSR habituation to mild intramodal stimuli. *Psychophysiology, 6:*202, 1969.

Subjects habituated to a mild stimulus failed to have GSRs upon the intrusion of a "novel" mild intramodal stimulus. However, an intruding intermodal stimulus of approximately the same intensity caused large GSRs. These results support an explanation based on expectancy or the "neuronal model" of Sokolov, provided suitable allowance is made for changes in specificity of the model as a result of variations in the experimental situation.

stimulus
generaliza-
tion
habituation
novel
stimuli

32 Korn, James H., and Moyer, K.E.: Effects of set and sex on the electrodermal orienting response. *Psychophysiology, 4:* 453, 1968.

Determined the extent to which brief instructions to "pay attention" would affect the magnitude and rate of habituation of the electrodermal orienting response (OR) and whether sex differences would be obtained. Ss were fifteen male and fifteen female college students. Compared to neutral (relaxation) instructions, it was found that Ss who were told to pay attention (1) had larger ORs to the first tone in each of two sets of twenty tones, (2) showed more irregular habituation over the second set of tones, and (3) exhibited decreases in base conductance during a rest period between sets of tones. Females habituated faster than males over the first set of tones. The results are discussed in terms of preparatory set variables.

instruction-
al set
sex differ-
ences
attention
habituation
GSR magni-
tude

CORRELATES OF
BEHAVIORAL STATES

VIGILANCE

E 1   Andreassi, J.L.: Skin conductance and reaction time in a con-
       tinuous auditory monitoring task. *Am J Psychol, 79:*470,
       1966.

Continuous measures of palmar skin-conductance (PSC)   *vigilance*
were taken as S responded to aperiodic auditory signs pre-   *vigilance*
sented against a white noise background. Thirty-two reac-   *task*
tion-time (RT) trials were taken for each of sixteen Ss over a   *reaction*
forty-minute session. The results indicated that Ss had sig-   *time*
nificantly faster RTs on the ten trials in which PSC was high-   *arousal*
est as compared to the RTs for the twelve middle and ten
lowest PSC trials. There were decreases in PSC as the experiment progressed. The sharp decrease in PSC between the
first and second ten-minute segments of the experiment was
accompanied by a significant increase in RT. There was no
upturn in RT at the highest levels of PSC, and it was suggested that in certain situations S's level of arousal must be
actively manipulated to achieve an inverted "U" relation
between bodily activity level and performance.

E 2   Coles, Michael G.H., and Gale, Anthony: Physiological re-
       activity as a predictor of performance in a vigilance task.
       *Psychophysiology, 8:*594, 1971.

The experiment was designed to determine the value of   *vigilance*
measures of physiological activity as predictors of perform-   *vigilance*
ance in a vigilance task. Subjects for whom resting (EEG,   *task*
heart rate, and skin conductance) and response (electro-   *autonomic*
dermal) measures were available were given an auditory   *reactivity*
vigilance task. Overall vigilance performance was significant-   *prediction*

ly correlated with one measure of electrodermal habituation, latency of response to the first of a series of stimuli, and total number of responses to stimuli. None of the measures of resting physiological activity were significantly related to vigilance performance. The results are discussed in terms of Mackworth's (1969) theory of vigilance.

response character-istics
habituation

3   Davies, D.R., and Krkovic, Andjelko: Skin-conductance, alpha-activity, and vigilance. *Am J Psychol, 78*:304, 1965.

An experiment is reported in which the relationship between skin-conductance, alpha-activity, and auditory vigilance was studied. A trend analysis shows that these three measures appear to be associated over a ninety-minute vigil. The results seem to indicate that during the course of a vigil, S becomes drowsy, as shown by the decrease in EEG alpha-activity, skin-conductance, and the level of performance. It is also confirmed by S's replies to a questionnaire. It is suggested that this drowsiness is produced by the lack of varied stimulation from the task and from the environment.

vigilance
auditory vigilance
drowsiness
task per-formance
EEG alpha
SC

4   Eason, Robert G., Beardshall, Ann, and Jaffee, Stanley: Performance and physiological indicants of activation in a vigilance situation. *Percept Mot Skills, 20*:13, 1965.

Changes in performance and in four physiological measures during the course of a one-hour vigil and as a function of signal presentation rate were studied. Based on data obtained from six Ss during a total of twenty-four vigils, performance (% correct detections) and skin conductance decreased during the course of a vigil, heart rate remained constant, and neck tension level increased. There was no consistent tendency for Ss to perform at a higher level when signals were presented at a relatively fast rate than when presented at a slower rate. However, their performance was differentially affected by presentation rate, some performing better during the fast rate, some during the slow rate, and others showing no change. A positive relationship was found between the relative performance level manifested during the two rates (fast rate expressed relative to slow) and the relative magnitudes of skin conductance, heart rate, and neck tension level.

vigilance
stimulus character-istics
activation
SC
HR
EMG

The results were interpreted as supporting the hypothesis that variations in vigilance performance are in part determined by changes in activation level. The feasibility of recording physiological information in order to ascertain more accurately which factors are contributing to variations in performance in a given vigilance situation seems to have been demonstrated.

E 5   Gale, Anthony, Bull, Ray, and Haslum, Mary: Cumulative expectancy, subjective report of alertness, and electrodermal activity. *Psychophysiology, 9*:383, 1972.

Skin conductance was monitored during a vigilance task in which the S responded to wanted signals. The wanted signal was a sequence of three consecutive odd digits (e.g. 1, 3, 7, +). Nonwanted signals also contained three consecutive digits; of these, two, one, or none were odd (e.g. 1, 1, 2, +, or 1, 4, 6, +, or 2, 4, 6, +). (The plus signs following each signal served to separate the individual signals from each other and may therefore be treated as rest periods.) Since the S must respond to a series of odd digits the different signal types vary in their power to induce a state of cumulative expectancy in the S. Ss were informed that a monetary reward was dependent upon fast and accurate response. Electrodermal activity was quantified in terms of change in conductance (SCR), either increase (SCR+) or decrease (SCR-) associated with particular sequences of digits. Results indicate (1) SCR+ for wanted signals progressively increases as the sequence accumulates, with maximum SCR+ on the final digit and a large SCR— on the plus sign. (2) Odd numbers are generally associated with SCR+, whereas even numbers and plus signs are associated with SCR—. (3) Ss report post-test that they were more alerted by odd digits. (4) Reaction time to wanted signals does not correlate with SCL at time of response, with latency of the associated SCR, nor with pre- and post-signal SCRs. (5) Intra-individual analysis yields no evidence for operation of the Law of Initial Value.

vigilance
expectancy
arousal
reaction time
subjective reports
SC

E 6   Krupski, Antoinette, Raskin, David C., and Bakan, Paul: Physiological and personality correlates of commission errors in an auditory vigilance task. *Psychophysiology, 8*:304, 1971.

To determine correlates of the tendency to make errors of commission in a vigilance task, 31 Ss worked at a task of listening to recorded digits for forty-eight minutes and reported odd-even-odd digit sequences. Reports of "signals" where signals did not actually occur constituted commission errors. While S was engaged in the vigilance task, skin conductance was continuously recorded. A measure of extraversion and neuroticism was available for each S. The tendency to make commission errors was associated with decrement in the detection of real signals over time, low GSR amplitude at detection points, and low initial orienting response. Commission errors were positively related to extraversion and unrelated to neuroticism. It was concluded that commission errors are made by Ss who are low in arousal level, subject to vigilance decrement, and likely to score higher on extraversion.

vigilance task
signal detection
arousal
extraversion
neuroticism
SC

7 Surwillo, Walter W., and Quilter, Reginald E.: The relation of frequency of spontaneous skin potential responses to vigilance and to age. *Psychophysiology, 1*:272, 1965.

Skin potential (Tarchanoff effect) was recorded in 132 healthy males, aged twenty-two to eighty-five years, while they performed an hour-long watchkeeping task. Vigilance level, as measured by S's detection or failure to detect certain critical stimuli, proved to be related to frequency of spontaneous skin potential responses (SPRs) in an interval immediately preceding the stimulus. Low vigilance was associated with fewer spontaneous SPRs per unit of time than high vigilance. This relationship did not appear to be the result of a correlation of the physiological and behavioral variables with time or with age. Old persons evinced a smaller number of spontaneous SPRs in a standard time interval than young persons. Lacey and Lacey's hypothesis that autonomic "labiles," or Ss who show a large number of spontaneous autonomic responses, have shorter reaction times than autonomic "stabiles" was confirmed. A related hypothesis, in which number of erroneous motor responses was the dependent variable, was not substantiated.

vigilance
vigilance task
signal detection
spontaneous SP
age
autonomic reactivity
motor responses

8 Surwillo, Walter W.: Level of skin potential in healthy males and the influence of age. *J Gerontol, 20:*519, 1965.

Skin potential (Tarchanoff effect of the GSR) was recorded *vigilance*
by Ag-AgCl electrodes, which were attached to the palm and *vigilance*
ventral surface of the forearm, in 122 healthy males aged   *tasks*
twenty-two to eighty-five years. Ss performed a watchkeeping *age*
task while the recordings were made. In all cases, the palm
proved to be electrically negative with respect to the forearm.
Average level of skin potential for the group was −31.5 mV,
and individual values ranged from −12.3 to −56.8 mV. A low
but statistically significant negative correlation was found
between age and skin potential level.

E 9   Verschoor, A.M., and van Wieringen, P.C.: Vigilance per-
       formance and skin conductance. *Acta Psychol (Amst), 33:*
       394, 1970.

Explored the relation between vigilance performance and *vigilance*
skin conductance level in twenty-two male undergraduates. *task per-*
A distinction is made between good and bad detectors. Dur- *formance*
ing the watch, performance and skin conductance of the   *signal*
good detectors remain constant; the bad detectors show a   *detection*
decrement on both variables. A second experiment with 40
Ss is reported with a more complicated signal presentation
(two types of signals). In comparison with the simple detection task (one type of signal) there is no difference in skin
conductance, while detection and RT show less decrement
in the more complicated task.

AROUSAL

E 10   Hupka, Ralph B., and Levinger, George: Within-subject
       correspondence between skin conductance and skin potential
       under conditions of activity and passivity. *Psychophysiology,*
       *4:*161, 1967.

This study investigated (1) the covariation between *arousal*
skin conductance and skin potential levels and (2) the *relaxation*
correspondence between the negative component of the *measure-*
skin potential response (SPR) and concurrent skin con- *ment*
ductance response deflections (SCR) during periods of rest *indices*
and activity. The study was restricted to the protocols of ten *mechanism*
female Ss who manifested predominantly the negative com-

ponent of the SPR during both periods. During rest periods, the results showed a positive correspondence between conductance and potential levels, and between the negative component of the SPR waves and concurrent SCR deflections. However, under conditions of active motor performance, the correspondence of levels was near zero and much lower between the negative and concurrent SCR deflections. It is suggested that an epidermal factor may be exerting its effects differentially during periods of passivity and activity.

11 Solley, C.M., and Thetford, P.E.: Skin potential responses and the span of attention. *Psychophysiology, 3/4:*397, 1967.

Experiment I tested whether an alerting signal would increase the span of visual attention. Female subjects (sixteen) were presented an array of letters exposed for two seconds by a tachistoscope. Half of the subjects had a series of trials with a loud tone contiguous with the tachistoscope, followed by a series of trials with tachistoscope only. The remaining subjects received a reverse procedure—half the trials with no tone initially, followed by tone. The group receiving only tachistoscope followed by a series of tachistoscope plus tone trials showed a significant improvement in the number of letters correctly reported. Experiment II repeated the above with skin potential (SP) recording throughout the session to test that the tone would generate a momentary state of arousal (an orienting response) and an increase in the span of attention. Tone significantly produced larger positive SP amplitudes and more diphasic SP responses and increased the number of letters correctly reported. All differences disappeared during the second trial series.

arousal
attention
visual
 signals

12 Taylor, Stuart P., and Epstein, Seymour: The measurement of autonomic arousal. *Psychosom Med, 29:*514, 1967.

Empirical evidence is presented to demonstrate that there is no true relationship between such physiological measures as heart rate and skin conductance, but that (depending on circumstances) heart rate and skin conductance covary directly, inversely, or not at all. It is contended that a solution to the general measurement of arousal will not be found

arousal
stress
aggression
HR
SC

by transforming single measures, by innovations in data reduction, or by combining measures. Instead, the solution lies in learning more about the unique properties of different physiological systems by establishing how they vary as a function of the parameters of stimulus input—such as intensity, rate of stimulation, and time since stimulus onset.

E 13   Thayer, Robert E.: Activation states as assessed by verbal report and four psychophysiological variables. *Psychophysiology, 7*:86, 1970.

Examines the validity of controlled verbal reports of various activation states. A different score design was used in which four psychophysiological measures and verbal ratings of various activation states were obtained in a baseline and an activation period from forty-one female undergraduates. Verbal reports were then correlated with individual physiological measures and composites or indices of physiological measures. Specifically, two kinds of physiological index were employed: one in which the S's physiological change score was represented by the single system showing the greatest change, and a second index weighted equally by all four physiological measures. The physiological index using the single system showing the greatest activation yielded slightly greater correlations with verbal report than the other index. Skin conductance and heart rate, the best combination of the four physiological systems measured, correlated as high as .62 with verbal report. Results demonstrate the usefulness and validity of controlled self-report and the relative superiority of skin conductance and heart rate among other physiological systems in correlations with verbal report.

arousal
activation
verbal
reports
individual
difference

SLEEP

E 14   Broughton, R.J., Poire, R., and Tassinari, C.A.: 1he electrodermogram (Tarchanoff effect) during sleep. *Electroencephalogr Clin Neurophysiol, 18*:691, 1965.

The electrodermal response (Tarchanoff effect) was studied during sleep. (1) Spontaneous EDRs were usually rare during wakefulness but, even if frequent, did not undergo striking changes during falling asleep. They increased in number

sleep
spontaneo
activity
REM slee

with passage to stage IV. During stage II they were isolated *skin sites*
or related to K complexes and, occasionally to the presence of *sensory*
generalized myoclonic jerks. During stage III and IV they *stimuli*
frequently become virtually continuous. In stage I^{rem}, how- *theory*
ever, they were infrequent and were either isolated or associated with bursts of rapid eye movements (REMs) and any of
the following: partial myoclonic jerks, tachycardia or respiratory changes. (2) EDRs could be elicited by various stimuli
in all stages, always with a one to four second latency. In
stages II, III and IV the threshold was lowered, whereas in
stage I^{rem} it was quite high. In stage II, successful stimuli
provoked a K complex before the EDR and, rarely, a startle
response. In stages III and IV the EEG changes were usually
less marked whereas other antonomic reactivity persisted.
EDRs provoked in stage I^{rem} were sometimes associated with
EEG changes (e.g. blocking of "saw-toothed" waves or a
burst of posterior alpha activity) but not with partial jerks
or REMs. (3) Topographically, the EDR in all phases was
seen to diffuse from the head caudally down the body axis
and peripherally along the limbs, where conduction occurred
at approximately 1 m/sec. In stage I^{rem} apparently randomly
distributed EDRs were occasionally recorded. (4) In further
studies EDRs were noted with various episodic sleep phenomena (enuresis nocturna, somnambulism, etc.), certain
abnormal movements, focal epileptic temporal lobe discharges, generalized or hemigeneralized epileptic discharges,
and tonic epileptic seizures, even when reduced to their
minimal expression. (5) Prefrontal bilateral lobotomy,
hemispherectomy, or congenital agenesis of the corpus callos-
um did not influence the evolution of the EDG. Congenital
analgesia was associated with difficulty in provoking EDRs by
painful stimuli. (6) The apparent neurophysiological basis
and certain psychological correlations are discussed.

15   Johnson, Laverne C., and Lubin, Ardie: Spontaneous electrodermal activity during waking and sleeping. *Psychophysiology, 3:8, 1966.*

Spontaneous electrodermal activity (EDA) (galvanic skin *sleep*
response [GSR] and skin potential response [SPR]) was re- *waking*
corded during daytime sleep and nighttime sleep. During all *spontaneous*
GSRs

sleep, spontaneous EDA occurred most frequently during   *SPR*
stages 3 and 4 (slow wave sleep) and least frequently during
stage 1 (rapid eye movement [REM] and non-REM). This
pattern was consistent over three nights of sleep. There was
no relation between waking and sleeping spontaneous EDA.
The spontaneous EDA during slow wave sleep significantly
exceeded that during waking. During sleep, spontaneous
SPRs often occurred without spontaneous GSRs.

E 16   Koumans, Alfred J.R., Tursky, Bernard, and Solomon,
Philip: Electrodermal levels and fluctuations during normal
sleep. *Psychophysiology, 5*:300, 1968.

All-night recordings of skin potential (SP) and skin resist-   *sleep*
ance (SR) levels and rapid electrodermal fluctuations (REFs)   *REM sleep*
were taken from a group of college students during two   *spontaneou*
nights of normal sleep. An attempt was made to associate   *GSR*
changes in these measures with stages of sleep as identified by   *SP*
EEG patterns. Electrodermal levels could differentiate between wake and sleep but could not clearly identify individual sleep stages or REM periods. REFs were found to
increase in number during slow wave sleep and decrease during Stage I REM periods. This diminution of REFs occurred
consistently about six minutes before the onset of each REM
period and then returned at a lower rate a few minutes after
the termination of the REM period.

E 17   Lester, B.K., Burch, N.R., and Dossett, R.C.: Nocturnal
EEG-GSR profiles: The influence of presleep states. *Psychophysiology, 3*:238, 1967.

The number of nocturnal galvanic skin responses (GSRs)   *sleep*
varied widely between the electroencephalograph (EEG)
stages of sleep as well as from night-to-night and from person-
to-person. As others have found, nonspecific GSRs occurred
much more frequently during stage IV than other EEG stages
and were rare in stage REM. However, night-to-night variation and individual differences were related to the presleep
state of the person. In general, electrodermal activity increased in all EEG stages as daytime stress increased, being
especially great on nights preceding important school exam-

inations. The nocturnal EEG profile was also related to the presleep state, the percentage of stage IV decreasing as daytime stress increased. The percentage of stage REM showed no systematic relation to stress. The occurrence of GSR "storms" during slow-wave sleep is consistent with the notion of release of cortical or other inhibitory influences during this state, but another mechanism is needed to explain the fact that presleep stress increases the frequency of GSRs in all stages of sleep, while simultaneously decreasing the percentage of slow-wave sleep.

18 Niimi, Y., Hori, T., and Watanabe, T.: Positive shifts of basal skin potentials during human sleep. *J Physiol Soc Japan, 29:*710, 1967.

Abstract Not Available.

19 Tart, Charles T.: Patterns of basal skin resistance during sleep. *Psychophysiology, 4:*35, 1967.

There are qualitative differences between Ss in the pattern of basal skin resistance (BSR) through a night's sleep. The most common is a rapid rise to maximum value of BSR in the first hour, with a steady fall the rest of the night. A steady rise through the night is also common. No relationship between BSR and the occurrence of stage 1 dreaming was found.

sleep
REM sleep
individual
  differences
BSR

20 Tizard, B.: Evoked changes in EEG and skin potential. *Electroencephalogr Clin Neurophysiol, 20:*122, 1966.

EEG and skin potential responses to repeated auditory stimuli of two different intensities were studied. Two sets of instructions, to attend to and to ignore the sounds, were given. Ratings of EEG stages of sleep and also a quantitative measure of 4 to 7 c/sec activity were used to measure drowsiness. It was found that significantly more evoked skin potential changes occurred in the "attend to sound" periods than in the "ignore sound" periods, but this variable did not affect the rate of habituation. Transient EEG responses, viz V waves and K complexes, did not habituate and their number

stimulus
  intensity
sleep
drowsiness
instructions
habituation
orienting
  response

was not affected by instructions to the subject, although significantly more occurred when the stimulus was loud. Changes in ongoing EEG activity during a stimulus also did not habituate, rather there was a tendency for these to increase in number during the experimental period. The nature of the instructions to the subject was a significant variable here, but the intensity of sound was not. In the case of all three types of response there was a significant correlation, positive or negative, between the number of responses recorded and the degree of drowsiness at that time, as assessed by the amount of 4 to 7 c/sec activity. There was also a significant association between the frequency with which responses were evoked and the stage of sleep obtaining at the time. The findings are discussed in relation to Sokolov's concept of the orienting reflex.

E 21   Weller, G.M., and Bell, R.Q.: Basal skin conductance and neonatal state. *Child Develop, 36*:647, 1965.

Basal skin conductance was correlated with activity and respiration measures in a sample of forty white bottle-fed human newborns divided into four equal groups by sex and parity. The age range was 60 use to 110 hours. A significant positive correlation average was obtained between activity level and conductance. The average correlation between respiration rate and conductance was not significant until internal recording was extended over several minutes. In general, conductance was not as strongly related to the sleep levels of the arousal continuum as it was to higher levels. Females were significantly higher in conductance than males, and infants born to multiparae were significantly higher than those born to primiparae.

infants
sleep
arousal
response
  rate
sex differ-
  ences
BSC

HYPNOSIS

E 22   O'Connell, D.N. and Orne, M.T.: Endosomatic electrodermal correlates of hypnotic depth and susceptibility. *J Psychiatr Res, 6*:1, 1968.

Correlations between endosomatic measures of electrodermal activity and hypnotic depth and susceptibility were made for fifty-one subjects. Significant correlations appeared between

hypnosis
hypnotic
  suscepti-
  bility

waking level of GSP and hypnotic performance; high sub-   *spontaneous*
jects tended to maintain a high level of GSP, low ones to   *SP*
show gradual drift during the experiment in a positive (lower) alertness direction. Apparent correlations between waking level and shift in level was taken into account. No correlations between spontaneous activity and either depths or
susceptibility were found. An interpretation in terms of more
sustained rapport is suggested.

RESPONSES TO EMOTION PRODUCING STIMULI

F 1   Abrams, S.: The polygraph and the psychiatrist. *Am J Psychiatry,* Jan., 1972.

The polygraph, or lie detector, monitors heartbeat rate and amplitude, breathing pattern and rate, and galvanic skin response. Changes in these areas indicate an emotional reaction and are considered to be at least 70 percent accurate in detecting lies. During psychotherapy an analyst determines areas of patient stress by noting physiological reactions such as blushing, perspiring or trembling. Stanley Abrams of the Permanente Clinic in Portland, Ore., says that the polygraph can be useful to analysts as a stress detector. Twenty of his patients were examined with the polygraph. Each was given a total of forty stimulus words alternating between assumed neutral words (window, book) and words thought to be relevant to each individual (sex, hate). The amount of stress indicated by reaction to the relevant words helps set up a hierarchy of stress useful later in the treatment process. But, says Abrams, patients also respond to some of the supposedly neutral words. When this happens, he says, it opens up the door to new material (some of it repressed) that can be dealt with in therapy.

psychiatric use polygraph stress detector emotional reactions

F 2   Beloff, J., Cowles, M., and Bate, D.: Autonomic reactions to emotive stimuli under sensory and extrasensory conditions of presentation. *J Am Soc Psychical Res, 64:*313, 1970.

Twenty schoolboys were tested for their GSR reactions on being presented unexpectedly with their self-image or own name. Presentation was sensory (by means of slides), and extrasensory, using a set of photoprints with one author acting as agent. Scoring was done blindly by another author who had to pick out the most salient deflections of the poly-

emotional stimuli self-image GSR responses extrasensory perception

64

graph record. On this basis 2 × 2 stimulus response contingency matrices were set up and analyzed. The sensory runs gave an overall phi contingency coefficient of .453, which is overwhelmingly significant, but the extrasensory runs gave a phi of only .008, which is almost exactly at chance expectation.

F 3   Brendsted, A.N., and Denisova, Z.V.: Changes of the galvanic skin response in children at play (Russian). *Zh Vyssh Nerv Deat, 21:*164, 1971.

GSR changes in children in the course of play behavior were analyzed by mathematical estimation of the parameters of reaction energy. It has been found that GSR energy in three to seven-year-old children in the process of playing exceeds that observed during a simple perception of a toy stimulus. A dependence has been shown of GSR prolongation on positive emotions originating in the course of playing. The data reveal that the GSR responds primarily to the elements of taking a decision in the play process of the child.

play
children
GSR
*   responses*
reaction
*   energy*
judgments

F 4   Craig, Kenneth D., and Wood, Keith: Physiological differentiation of direct and vicarious affective arousal. *Can J Behav Sci, 1:*98, 1970.

Examined the extent to which skin conductance and heart rate indices differentiated between responses to direct adverse stimulation and observing another experiencing the adverse stimulation (tolerating immersion of the hand in a −4°C brine solution). Forty-eight male and female undergraduates served as Ss. Differential patterns of autonomic response appeared. Both experiences produced increases in skin conductance. The direct experience produced acceleration of heart rate, whereas the vicarious experience tended to produce deceleration. Sequence of experiences and degree of stress were related to the heart rate.

aversive
*   stimuli*
affective
*   arousal*
vicarious
*   experience*
response
*   differenti-*
*   ation*
HR
SC

F 5   Dykman, R.A., Reese, W.G., Galbrecht, C.R., and Thomasson, P.J.: Psychophysiological reactions to novel stimuli: Measurement adaptation and relationship of psychological and physiological variables in the normal human. *Ann NY Acad Sci, 79:*45, 1959.

Forty male junior medical students, twenty-two to thirty-three years of age, served as subjects. The experiment ("test") consisted of three phases: (1) a rest period of fifteen minutes; (2) a tone period of eighteen minutes; and (3) a question period of eleven minutes. The subjects received eighteen tones (each lasting five seconds, 800 cps, about 60 db, and given at one-minute intervals) and were asked eleven alternating emotional and nonemotional questions (requiring two to four seconds to read and given at one-minute intervals). The subjects were instructed to think about the questions, but not to answer them aloud. Continuous recordings were made of skin resistance, heart rate, and respiration, with excellent instrumentation, except possibly for respiration. The autonomic responses were scaled by a modification of the regression method proposed by Lacey. Evidence was presented to indicate that: (1) Of the systems studied, skin resistance was the easiest to evaluate and the most consistent. (2) Autonomic responses to serially presented stimuli rapidly diminish to a relatively constant level in normal humans. (3) Subjects are more reactive in skin resistance than in heart rate or respiratory rate, both in terms of the magnitude and the frequency of response. (4) The magnitude of an autonomic response is dependent upon the initial level of functioning; in general, the higher the initial level the smaller the response (Wilder's rule).

sensory stimuli
emotional stimuli
autonomic response patterns
adaptation
response characteristics

F 6   Gaviria, Bernardo: Autonomic reaction magnitude and habituation to different voices. *Psychosom Med, 29:*598, 1967.

This experiment studied habituation to and magnitude of electrodermal, plethysmographic, and heart rate changes in response to four auditory stimuli: (1) noise, (2) the subject's own voice, (3) the subject's spouse's voice, and (4) unknown persons' voices. Although consistent interstimulus differences are small, habituation seems to be slowest to noise, next slowest to one's own voice and the spouse's voice, and fastest for unfamiliar voices. Interpersonal factors independent of the verbal message may be reflected in the pattern of autonomic reaction. However, an orienting reaction element seems to have been intense enough to obscure specific interstimulus response differences.

habituation
voices
familiarity
orienting response

7   Hare, Robert, Wood, Keith, Britain, Sue, and Shadman, Janice: Autonomic responses to affective visual stimulation. *Psychophysiology, 7:*408, 1970.

Recorded physiological responses while forty-eight male undergraduates viewed a series of thirty slides of homicide scenes, nude females, or ordinary objects. Half the Ss saw the same slide thirty times while the others saw a different slide on each trial. The physiological responses given by all six groups involved are those generally associated with an orienting response, i.e. increase in skin conductance, cardiac deceleration, and digital vasoconstriction. In addition, a biphasic cephalic vasomotor response, consisting of constriction followed by dilation, was observed. Stimulus presentation was also accompanied by a sharp reduction in eyeblink rate. The physiological and eyeblink responses given by Ss who saw a different homicide scene on each trial were generally greater and more resistant to habituation than were those given by other Ss. Ss repeatedly shown the same homicide scene gave relatively small cardiac and cephalic vasomotor responses, and showed rapid habituation of the electrodermal response.

affective stimuli
pictorial stimuli
orienting responses
habituation
HR
vasomotor responses

8   Hare, Robert D.: Response requirements and directional fractionation of autonomic responses. *Psychophysiology, 9:* 419, 1972.

Physiological responses were monitored while twenty-seven male Ss were shown a series of forty-five colored slides of homicide victims. Nine of the Ss were required to simply look at each slide (Nonraters), nine were required to push one of seven buttons after each trial to indicate how disturbing they found the slide to be (Raters). Evidence for directional fractionation of autonomic responses to the slides was obtained for only the Nonraters. Their responses included cardiac deceleration, an increase in skin conductance, digital vasoconstriction, and cephalic vasodilation. The Raters responded with cardiac acceleration, an increase in skin conductance, and both digital and cephalic vasoconstriction. The Raters also showed a larger increase in tonic skin conductance over trials than did the Nonraters. To determine whether the physiological responses of the Raters were in-

emotional stimuli
pictorial stimuli
directional fractionation
cognitive elaboration
subjective rating
judgment
vasomotor activity
HR
SC

fluenced by the requirement to make a motor response, nine other Ss pressed a button after each slide. The physiological responses of these latter Ss were almost identical with those of the Nonraters. The results are consistent with the hypothesis that the requirement to rate the stimuli was associated with appraisal and cognitive elaboration. They also indicate that response requirements can have a profound effect upon autonomic responsivity.

F 9   Hirschman, Richard, and Katkin, Edward S.: Relationships among attention, GSR activity, and perceived similarity of self and others. *J Pers, 39*:277, 1971.

Simulated taped interviews were prepared, varying the dimensions of amount of work and success in college. Emotional expression by the interviewees was kept to a minimum. College Ss responded with a significantly larger number of nonspecific GSRs to a tape identified by them as being more like themselves than to a tape identified as being less like themselves. The nonsignificant comparisons of tapes are discussed in terms of the importance of cognitive activity on autonomic responsivity.

affective stimuli
GSR frequency
cognitive influences
autonomic responsivity
identity

F 10   Nourse, James C., and Welch, Robert B.: Emotional attributes of color: A comparison of violet and green. *Percept Mot Skills, 32*:403, 1971.

In order to investigate the common belief that colors induce emotional states specific to hue (e.g. Norman and Scott, 1952; Nakshian, 1964), a study examining the relationship between exposure to color and electrical skin conductance was carried out recently by Wilson (1966). The experiment showed that the galvanic skin response (GSR) was greater when S was exposed to a red stimulus than to green. The author proposed that hues at the ends of the visible spectrum are more arousing than those located toward the middle. This U-shaped function, he speculated, might be due to natural selection and/or learning based on the association of "extreme" hues with dangerous wave lengths such as infrared or ultraviolet. Thus, according to this theory, violet, like red, should prove more arousing than green. The present study tested this prediction.

colored visual stimuli
arousal

11 Rimm, David C., Kennedy, Thomas D., Miller, Harold L., and Tchida, Gene R.: Experimentally manipulated drive level and avoidance behavior. *J Abnorm Psychol, 78:43*, 1971.

Examined forty-eight female undergraduates in five experimental conditions designed to effect a momentary change in arousal level and a control condition. The experimental conditions included threat of shock, frustration, information that they would be required to handle a snake, deep muscle relaxation, and exposure to soft background music. Self-ratings and changes in the number of GSR peaks provided strong evidence that drive or arousal level was modified by the experimental conditions. In a subsequent behavioral snake avoidance task, Ss who had undergone drive reduction showed considerably more approach behavior than Ss in the drive-induction conditions. Results suggest that behavioral avoidance is highly sensitive to momentary arousal level. Implications for therapy analogue studies which employ behavioral avoidance measures are discussed.

emotional arousal
spontaneous GSRs
motivation

12 Satterfield, James H., and Dawson, Michael E.: Electrodermal correlates of hyperactivity in children. *Psychophysiology, 8:*191, 1971.

Basal skin conductance, nonspecific GSRs, and specific GSRs were studied during two experimental sessions with two groups of twelve hyperkinetic children each and a group of twelve matched normal controls. Hyperkinetic children were found to have lower basal skin conductance, fewer and smaller nonspecific GSRs, and smaller specific GSRs than those of normal children. Stimulant drugs which were administered to one group of hyperkinetic children tended to raise basal level conductance and nonspecific GSR activity toward the levels of normal children. A tentative neurophysiological hypothesis is offered to account for these data as well as the clinical observations that stimulant drugs are effective in the treatment of hyperkinetic children.

children
hyperkinesis
minimal brain dysfunction
spontaneous GSRs
elicited GSRs
stimulants
BSC

13 Tursky, Bernard, and O'Connell, Donald: Reliability and interjudgment predictability of subjective judgments of electrocutaneous stimulation. *Psychophysiology, 9:*290, 1972.

The within and between day reliability and interjudgment predictability of subjective judgments (threshold, discomfort, pain and tolerance) produced in the laboratory by a highly controllable electrocutaneous stimulation technique were investigated. Results indicated low to moderate reliability and predictability at the threshold level, excellent reliability at all suprathreshold levels, as well as excellent predictability at the discomfort and pain levels. The implications of these findings for the use of electrocutaneous stimulation in the study, measurement of pain in the laboratory, and the possibility of using different psychophysical methods to measure the sensory and reactive components of the pain experience are discussed.

electric shock
pain
subjective judgment
reliability

F 14   Wenger, Marion A., Averill, James R., and Smith, David D.B.: Autonomic activity during sexual arousal. *Psychophysiology, 4:*468, 1968.

Autonomic activity was recorded from sixteen male subjects as they read sexually stimulating material. The resulting physiological response patterns included increases in systolic and diastolic blood pressures, palmar conductance, and number of galvanic skin responses. Heart and respiration rates remained relatively constant, and there was some indication of peripheral vasodilatation subsequent to initial constriction. The results suggest a differential change in the activity of both branches of the autonomic nervous system, in which neither the parasympathetic nor the sympathetic nervous system may be considered dominant.

sexual arousal
autonomic responsivity
GSR frequency
vasomotor responses
BP
PC

F 15   Wilson, Glenn D.: Arousal properties of red versus green. *Percept Mot Skills, 23:*947, 1966.

Twenty Ss were each exposed for sixty seconds to five red and five green slides in alternating order. Two electrodermal measures, conductance level and GSR, were taken. Results support the hypothesis that red is a more "arousing" color than green, the effect being particularly apparent in the GSR data (p. < .002).

colored visual stimuli
arousal

CORRELATES OF
TASK PERFORMANCE

G 1   Andreassi, John L.: Effects of regular and irregular signal patterns upon skin conductance and reaction time. *Percept Mot Skills, 23*:975, 1966.

An experiment was conducted to study the effects of stimulus patterning upon reaction time (RT) performance and palmar skin conductance (PSC) of one S over a period of ten consecutive days. The main findings were that PSC was significantly more variable with an irregular signal pattern than with a regular one, RTs were significantly faster with the regular pattern, there was a nonsignificant trend in which high PSC values were associated with fast RTs and low PSC values with slow RTs. The results were discussed in terms of wider variations in arousal produced by irregularly occurring signals and greater learning with regular signals.

reaction time performance
response characteristics
arousal
PSC

G 2   Corteen, R.S.: Basal conductance level and motor performance. *Br J Psychol, 58*:93, 1967.

The relations between log. basal conductance and performance on three tasks were investigated. Significant relations were found with end spurt and reminiscence on the pursuit rotor, with overall performance on a dotting task, and with abnormally slow responses and optimum response speed in reaction time. These results are consistent with a view of basal conductance as a measure of "tonic" activation or the ergotropic-trophotropic dimension of Hess.

reaction time
motor performance
activation
BCL

G 3   Coules, John, and Avery, Donald L.: Human performance and basal skin conductance in a vigilance-type task with and without knowledge of results. *Percept Mot Skills, 23*:1295, 1966.

This study showed no trends between reaction time and interstimulus intervals and reaction time and time blocks under knowledge of results or no knowledge of results. An ABC × S variance design of reaction time scores showed only knowledge of results by Ss was statistically reliable. The source of this variance was attributed to sex differences. Results showed that under knowledge of results, fast mean reaction time (males) was associated with high skin conductance. For females slow mean reaction time was associated with low conductance. Under the no knowledge of results condition, females showed slower mean reaction time than males. Their conductance scores showed significantly greater variability without knowledge of results than under the knowledge condition. Males under no knowledge show mean conductance scores as high as those under knowledge of results. However, their mean reaction time scores under the no knowledge condition was significantly lower than under knowledge of results. It was concluded that males, contrasted with females, respond differentially to knowledge and no knowledge of results in simple reaction time studies. As males show high conductance and females high variability in conductance under no knowledge of results, an inhibition-reinforcement theory for vigilance tasks appears inadequate.

vigilance reaction time knowledge of results sex differences BSC

G 4   Cowles, Michael P.: The latency of the skin resistance response and reaction time. *Psychophysiology, 10:*177, 1973.

Skin conductance level (SCL) and skin resistance response (SRR) latency to a foreperiod warning light were shown to be related to a measure of simple reaction time performance. Other physiological measures monitored immediately prior to the task were not related to performance nor were they interrelated. Speculation is offered on the possible mechanism whereby a central facilitation system is related to SRR latency and to performance.

reaction time performance SRR latenc arousal SC

G 5   Dureman, Ingmar, and Palshammar, Ake: Differences in tracking skill and psychophysiological activation dynamics in children high or low in persistence in schoolwork. *Psychophysiology, 7:*95, 1970.

Seven children (nine to ten years) rated by their school teachers as high in persistence (HP) and seven rated as low in persistence (LP) were compared in a simulated car-driving situation with a risk-taking game component. Increased reward was paid for every consecutive two minutes that they managed to drive without making more than five "off the road" errors within each of four ten-minute periods. More than five errors meant loss of accumulated reward, and the situation thus was meant to evoke a kind of temporal approach-avoidance conflict. Heart rate, skin conductance, and respiratory rate were recorded throughout the session. The LP children made significantly more "off the road" errors than the HP children during the four driving periods. They also had significantly lower skin conductance levels and lower respiratory rates during the work periods, as well as a suggested difference in the pattern of change in skin conductance.

tracking tasks persistence children individual differences SC respiration HR

6   Grim, P.F., and White, S.H.: Effects of stimulus change on GSR and reaction time. *J Exp Psychol, 69:*276, 1965.

Sixty subjects were given sixty RT trials using a colored light as a stimulus and then, without warning, lights differing in color but not in intensity were presented. Augmented GSR reactions occurred as a monotonic function of amount of change. Lengthened RTs were also observed; the amount of such lengthening did not appear to be simply related either to evoked GSR or to amount of stimulus change.

reaction time performance colored light stimuli orienting response arousal

7   Haywood, H.C.: Novelty seeking behavior as a function of manifest anxiety and physiological arousal. *J Pers, 30:*63, 1962.

Twenty Ss, at each of three levels of manifest anxiety (high, moderate and low) had to choose between the novel and familiar members of fifteen pairs of stimulus cards before and after a taped presentation of an incomprehensible message. Measures of palmar sweating were taken immediately following each of the two novelty-seeking tests. A control group (30 Ss) went through the same procedure except that the arousal message was omitted. Novelty-seeking scores

task performance anxiety novelty arousal

were: (1) number of novel cards chosen out of fifteen choices; (2) mean number of seconds spent viewing novel cards. The groups differing in manifest anxiety did not differ significantly in either measure of novelty-seeking, in initial palmer-sweat level, or in magnitude of palmar-sweat change following the arousal message. All three experimental groups exhibited a decrease (p < .01) in mean number of novel stimulus cards chosen for viewing following the arousal message, while the control group actually increased in this measure of novelty-seeking. All three groups also exhibited a decrease in the time spent viewing novel stimulus cards following the arousal message, but the amount of decrease was not significantly larger than that observed in a control group that merely waited ten minutes instead of listening to the arousal message. Palmar sweating increased significantly (p < .005) with the imposition of the arousal message. Manifest-anxiety scores failed to predict the magnitude of the decreases in novelty-seeking or the increases in palmar sweating following the arousal message.

G 8   Kleinman, Kenneth M., and Stern, John A.: Task complexity, electrodermal activity and reaction time. *Psychophysiology, 5:51, 1968.*

The influence of task complexity upon the relationship between electrodermal activity and reaction time was studied. Subjects performed either a simple or complex fixed foreperiod reaction time task. Various measures of skin resistance were taken before and during performance of the task. Only on the more complex task were electrodermal measures related to reaction time. However, the sign of the relationship was opposite to that found in other investigations; subjects with many spontaneous fluctuations and orienting responses reacted slowly. The results were interpreted in terms of the influence of both task complexity and foreperiod characteristics.

reaction time performance task complexity spontaneous GSRs orienting responses preparatory interval

G 9   Lieblich, Israel: Manipulation of contrast between GSRs in very young children. *Psychophysiology, 7:436, 1970.*

Each one of twenty-six children, aged three and four, was tested in six ordered information detection sequences. Physiological responsiveness was observed in the GSR. It was found that short-term physiological activation (STPA) could be manipulated in the predicted order using combinations of the following facets: (1) frequency of usage of the stimulus by the organism, (2) relevance of the stimulus to the organism, (3) whether or not a verbal response to the stimulus was required. The results were similar to those observed previously in an adult sample.

activation
children
verbal
 responses

G 10 Obrist, Paul A., Hallman, Shannon I., and Wood, Donald M.: Autonomic levels and lability and performance time on a perceptual task and a sensory-motor task. *Percept Mot Skills, 18:753,* 1964.

This experiment was intended to evaluate further an hypothesis in which perceptual and sensory-motor performances were considered to be influenced by autonomic processes via autonomic regulation of cortical activity. For this purpose, lability and level measures of sudomotor activity and heart rate were obtained during rest and performance in fifty-four male Ss. The hypothesis was consistently supported in seven significant or near-significant correlations out of a possible fourteen. Faster performance time on the sensory-motor task was found with Ss having low resting heart rate, increased heart rate variability during performance, and low levels of skin resistance. Faster performance time on the perceptual task was found in Ss with a high frequency of GSR activity during performance. Also, an interaction effect was suggested between some of the autonomic measures, being most pronounced in the perceptual task.

task per-
 formance
perceptual
 tasks
sensory-
 motor tasks
GSR
HR

G 11 Snider, Irving J., and Bregman, Albert S.: The effect of GSR confirmed perception of bisensory input on immediate verbal memory. *Psychophysiology, 7:169,* 1971.

Following adaptation, Ss learned visually presented paired associate (PA) word lists, while "distracting" verbal material was read aloud to them. Skin resistance was recorded. Ss who received auditory "interference" containing words present

learning
distraction
bisensory
 stimuli

in the PA task made fewer errors than controls. An objective scoring method showed that GSR peaks following the onset of relevant words in the "interference" were more frequent than those following control words, confirming Ss' verbal reports of perception of an attention to relevant stimuli. The improved learning could not be accounted for by changes in the tonic level of skin resistance, but seemed to be a direct result of the bimodal input.

spontaneous GSRs

G 12   Surwillo, Walter W.: The influence of some psychological factors on latency of the galvanic skin reflex. *Psychophysiology, 4:223, 1967.*

The purpose of this study was to examine the effect of differences in motivation and in attention on latency of the endosomatic GSR. Using verbal instructions, two different levels of motivation were induced in a group of thirty-seven Ss who performed a simple reaction task in which they pressed a button whenever a 250 cycle tone was presented. The same tone also served as a stimulus for eliciting the GSR. In a second experiment, forty-two different Ss performed a similar reaction task, but in this case the stimulus was the 250 cycle tone or a 1,000 cycle tone of equal subjective intensity. Ss were asked to give a voluntary response to all tones irrespective of frequency and then, later on, to respond only when the 1,000 cycle tone was presented. Although voluntary reaction times were significantly shorter under conditions of high as compared with low motivation, latency of the GSR did not differ for the two conditions. In the second experiment, significantly shorter GSR latencies were recorded under the condition where Ss were required to pay closer attention to the stimulus.

reaction time performance
motivation
attention
GSR latency
verbal stimuli
instructional set
subjective reports

:ORRELATES
)F PERSONALITY

1   Burdick, J.A.: Autonomic lability and neuroticism. *J Psychosom Res, 9:*339, 1966.

The frequency of nonspecific GSR "bursts" during fifteen minutes of rest by twenty-seven male Ss was not correlated significantly to either neuroticism or extraversion as measured by the MPI.

neuroticism
extraversion
GSR frequency

2   Coles, Michael G.H., Gale, Anthony, and Kline, Paul: Personality and habituation of the orienting reaction: Tonic and response measures of electrodermal activity. *Psychophysiology, 8:*54, 1971.

Eysenck's (1967) hypotheses concerning extraversion, neuroticism, and physiological reactivity were tested in relation to habituation. A factorial design, varying extraversion (three levels) and neuroticism (two levels) was employed: sixty subjects, ten per cell. Both tonic and response measures of electrodermal activity (skin conductance) were recorded. The results showed (1) high neurotics were more reactive than low neurotics (for two measures of habituation and total number of responses), (2) extraversion was inversely related to spontaneous activity, (3) latency of first response was moderately related (10% level only) both to neuroticism (inversely) and to extraversion (directly), (4) tonic conductance measures failed to discriminate between groups, (5) measures which discriminated between personality groups were intercorrelated. Since the measures taken were related to both extraversion and neuroticism, the findings do not support Eysenck's prediction that these measures are related to extraversion alone.

neuroticism
extraversion
orienting response
habituation
response components

H 3   Eysenck, H.J.: Extraversion and the acquisition of eyeblink and GSR conditioned responses. *Psychol Bull, 63*:258, 1965.

A summary is given of studies relating eyeblink and GSR conditioning to the personality dimension of extraversion (E). It is found that extraverts are poorer in eyeblink conditioning when conditions favor the development of inhibition, as by the use of partial reinforcement; they do not differ from introverts when conditions are such as to preclude the development of inhibition. Extraverts are poorer in GSR conditioning when relatively mild stimuli are used, but do not differ from introverts when very strong stimuli are used, making impossible the development of cortical inhibition. They are also poorer than introverts when discrimination learning is involved facilitating the growth of inhibition. Correlations between conditioning and personality appear to be dependent on the suitability of experimental conditions to evoke cortical inhibition; correlations are process and not status functions. These findings have implications for the problem of the generality of the hypothetical factor of conditionability.

extraversic
condition-
ability

H 4   Roessler, Robert, Burch, Neil R., and Childers, Harold E.: Personality and arousal correlates of specific galvanic skin responses. *Psychophysiology, 3*:115, 1966.

Basal skin resistance (BSR) and galvanic skin responses (GSR) to five intensities of sound and light were recorded on four occasions in thirty-two student subjects (Ss). These occasions were assumed to include unfamiliarity and basal and real life stress conditions. All Ss completed the MMPI, California Personality Inventory, Wechsler Adult Intelligence Scale, Clyde Mood Scale, and Examination Anxiety Scale. GSR amplitude was greater under conditions of unfamiliarity, alertness (by electroencephalographic criteria), and higher intensities of stimulation in both stimulus modalities. It was not greater during the presumed stress period. High ego strength high Barrier score Ss showed a greater GSR amplitude than low ego strength-low Barrier Ss. Test indices of anxiety generally were not related to GSR amplitude, nor were other personality and mood variables.

personality
stimulus
intensity
familiarity
intelligenc
anxiety
stress
habituatio
ego-strengt

5   Sadler, Timothy G., Mefferd, Roy B. Jr., and Houck, Robert
L.: The interaction of extraversion and neuroticism in
orienting response habituation. *Psychophysiology, 8:*312,
1971.

Twenty different consonant trigrams were presented individually to thirty-eight observers in a standard OR habituation paradigm while the GSRs and BSRs were recorded.
The observers were later categorized according to extraversion and neuroticism (anxiety) scores. All observers evidenced habituation in varying degrees to these dissimilar
stimuli; however, the stable observers responded to more of
the stimuli than did the neurotics. This basic neuroticism
effect was modified by the extraversion factor as shown by
response magnitudes: stable introverts and neurotic extraverts habituated differently than did the stable extraverts
and neurotic introverts. This significant extraversion × neuroticism interaction was also present, in the same form, in
the BSR values, while with stable extraverts and neurotic
introverts, the BSRs increased (i.e. they became less attentive).

extraversion
neuroticism
orienting
 response
anxiety
habituation
GSR
BSR

CORRELATES OF CONSTITUTIONAL AND SOCIAL FACTORS

I 1   Ax, Albert F., and Bamford, Jacqueline L.: Validation of a psychophysiological test of aptitude for learning social motives. *Psychophysiology, 5:*316, 1968.

This study was based on two assumptions. The first is that the hierarchy of motives is learned. "Hierarchy of Motives" is a concept denoting those largely unconscious systems which enable the selection of alternative behavior. The second assumption is that learning the hierarchy of motives requires an aptitude which varies widely in the population. The working hypotheses were: (1) presently measured aptitudes and environmental influences are insufficient to account for the observed variance in performance, and (2) that a discriminative learning task which requires a differential physiological response of the autonomic nervous system can measure the aptitude for learning social motives. Sixty-three Negro subjects were classified into two relatively higher and lower motivation groups based on their history of employment (from interview data) or on vocational training school teachers' ratings. They were subjected to a single session of discriminative classical autonomic conditioning involving tones and pain, and given intelligence, personality, and level of aspiration tests. It was found that eighteen variables, each individually statistically significant, when combined by means of a discriminant function analysis, classified 92 percent of the subjects into their correct criterion (motivation) groups. It was concluded that the working hypotheses were strongly confirmed and that the two assumptions were supported. Implications of these findings if confirmed by replication are (1) that a fundamental human aptitude for learning motives exists and can be measured; (2) having measures of

aptitudes
motivation
condition-
ability
contingenc
awareness
intelligenc

the aptitude enables exploration of its relationships to other aptitudes and characteristics; (3) knowledge of these relationships will make it possible (a) to more accurately predict human performance involving motivation, (b) to more appropriately select and place personnel, (c) to devise more practicable training procedures for developing socially desirable motives, and (d) to provide persons unprepared for self-support with more appropriate vocational training.

2 Dickson, Hollida W., and McGinnies, Elliott: Affectivity in the arousal of attitudes as measured by galvanic skin response. *Am J Psychol, 79*:584, 1966.

This experiment investigated the assumption that attitudes are emotionally supported. On the basis of scores on an attitude scale, twenty pro-church, twenty anti-church, and twenty neutral Ss were chosen. They were presented with twelve tape-recorded statements, four favorable, four neutral, and four critical with respect to the church, and their GSRs to each statement were recorded. It was found that both the pro- and anti-church Ss demonstrated proportionately higher GSRs to those statements which contradicted their measured attitudes. The results support the hypothesis that both extremes on an attitudinal continuum have an affective component and that autonomic response is elicited more strongly when the attitude is challenged than when it is reinforced.

attitudes
emotional reactivity
spontaneous GSRs

3 Fisher, L.E., Kotses, H., and Christie, D.J.: Negro-white differences in GSR response components and experimenter race effects. *Psychophysiology, 9*:279, 1971 (abstr.).

The present study was designed to ascertain whether or not racial differences exist in the several components of the skin resistance response and to assess the importance of the role of the experimenter's race in determining the S's responsiveness. Basal measures (base resistance, base conductance, log base conductance), GSR magnitude, and frequency of spontaneous fluctuations of twelve Negro and twelve Caucasian Ss were recorded by two Negro and two Caucasian experimental assistants matched as closely as possible for age, physical stature, and dress. Following a fifteen-minute resting

response compon- ents
experimen- ter race effects
spontaneous GSRs
GSR magni- tude

phase, all Ss received fourteen 1-second bursts of 75 dB white noise. Variable stimulus intervals with a mean of forty-five seconds were employed. Significant subject race effects, but no experimenter race effects, were found for all base level measures. Negro Ss had significantly higher base resistance levels. Conversely, experimenter race effects, but no subject race effects were apparent in the GSR magnitude data. Response magnitude decreased for all Ss over trials. However, differential rates of decrease were noted such that white Ss showed a much slower rate of decrease when paired with black Es. Finally, a significant decrease in the production of spontaneous fluctuations over trials for all Ss was observed. Ss produced fewer spontaneous fluctuations with same-race Es than they did with other-race Es.

I 4   Johnson, Laverne C., and Landon, Marvin M.: Eccrine sweat gland activity and racial differences in resting skin conductance. *Psychophysiology, 1*:322, 1965.

Active eccrine sweat gland activity was measured in thirty Negro and twenty-nine Caucasian male subjects to determine whether sweat gland activity was a possible factor in racial differences in skin conductance. Basal skin conductance, heart rate, respiratory rate, finger skin temperature, and blood pressure were also obtained. Negro Ss had significantly lower skin conductance, but no other significant physiological differences were found. While there was no significant difference in number of active sweat glands between the races, the intragroup relationship between sweat gland count and skin conductance was significantly higher for the Negro Ss. The two groups did not differ in number of nonspecific galvanic skin responses (GSRs), but the Caucasian Ss showed greater change in skin conductance to an initial tone stimulus. When differences in prestimulus levels were taken into account, the group differences in response to stimuli were no longer significant.

*sweat glan
racial
  differenc
SC*

I 5   Juniper, Kerrison Jr., and Dykman, Roscoe A.: Skin resistance, sweat gland counts, salivary flow, and gastric secretion: Age, race, and sex differences, and intercorrelations. *Psychophysiology, 4*:216, 1967.

Skin resistance, sweat gland counts, salivary flow, gastric secretion, and pH were measured in volunteers and patients of both sexes, Negroes and Caucasians. Correlational analysis suggested two negatively related clusters: (1) salivary flow, sweat gland counts, and gastric secretion; and (2) age, skin resistance, and pH. Skin resistance was higher in Negroes than Caucasians, and in females than males, increasing irregularly with age.

constitutional factors
age
sex differences
race differences
sweat glands
gastric secretion

6   Lieblich, Israel, Kugelmass, Sol, and Ben-Shakhar, Gershon: Psychophysiological baselines as a function of race and ethnic origin. *Psychophysiology, 10:* 1973.

Basic skin conductance and pulse rate measurements were obtained from groups differing in race and ethnic origin in Israel. The results suggest higher skin conductance in Caucasians than in Negroes, and in Bedouins than in non-Bedouins. There is some suggestion of an interaction between race and ethnic origin in relation to skin conductance. Both Caucasian and Negroid Bedouin tend to have lower pulse rates than the Jewish sample.

race differences
ethnic differences
HR
SC

7   Silverman, A.J., Cohen, S.I., and Shmavonian, B.M.: Psychophysiologic response specificity in the elderly. *J Gerontol, 13:*443, 1958.

The suggestion that the elderly have a reduced C.N.S. response capacity prompted this study, which was designed to explore sympathetic activity and C.N.S. arousal. Ten male college students (ages twenty to twenty-four and ten male elderly subjects (age sixty to sixty-five) were matched for physical and mental health, I.Q., and educational level. After a baseline period of galvanic skin reflex recording, a series of eighty-four auditory stimuli were presented at twenty-second intervals. Stimuli included tones, neutral phrases, phrases "charged" for the young, and other phrases "charged" for the elderly. Results: (1) No differences between groups were noted in latency time or in number of stimuli to which responses were given. (2) The elderly group showed decreased mean amplitude of G.S.R. as well as decreased numbers of

age
arousal
sensory stimuli
emotional stimuli
autonomic responsivity
recall
socio-psychologic factors

"spontaneous" G.S.R. fluctuations. Previous as well as the present study has related this finding to decreased C.N.S. arousal, which also correlated with decreased ability to recall. (3) In spite of the overall decreased responsivity in the elderly group, analysis of their responses to "charged" phrases suggests that they are capable of responding. Not only did the elderly respond more to statements about the old (and the young group to phrases about the young) : the elderly also responded more in absolute terms to those statements than did the young subjects. In other words, when the stimulus was appropriate the apparent lowered responsivity disappeared. Lack of interest, communication problems, sociocultural problems, low motivation, and emotional difficulties could all be factors resulting in decreased responsivity and decreased C.N.S. arousal with its concomitants of reduced psychomotor efficiency and impaired recall. In the absence of C.N.S. disease decreased C.N.S. functioning seen in the elderly may well be more a function of the above than of minute and subclinical pathological changes.

I 8   Sternbach, Richard A., and Tursky, Bernard: Ethnic differences among housewives in psychophysical and skin potential responses to electric shock. *Psychophysiology, 1*:241, 1965.

From earlier work on the effects of instructional sets, it was hypothesized that subcultural differences in attitudes toward pain should be reflected in psychophysiological correlates. Yankee, Irish, Jewish and Italian housewives participated in threshold and magnitude estimation studies of electrical shock, and their skin potential responses to repetitive electrical stimulation were recorded. Significant differences in upper thresholds and in the adaptation of diphasic palmar skin potentials are consonant with attitudinal differences, and such differences support earlier findings on the influence of sets on psychophysiological functioning.

response threshold electric shock ethnic difference attitudes adaptation SP

I 9   Tursky, Bernard, and Sternbach, Richard A.: Further physiological correlates of ethnic differences in responses to shock. *Psychophysiology, 4*:67, 1967.

The effects of subjects' sets on autonomic functioning had previously been demonstrated when the sets were induced

ethnic differences

by explicit experimental procedure. It was hypothesized that implicit (nonverbalized) sets should likewise have physiological correlates. The hypothesis was tested by exposing subjects of four different ethnic groups, whose attitudes toward pain and pain expression are different, to an experimental procedure involving electric shock. Differences were found in resting mean heart rate and palmar skin resistance and face temperature levels, in palmar skin potential responses to repetitive shocks, and in correlations between thresholds and heart rate, skin resistance and skin potential levels. These results closely parallel the attitudinal differences, and together with previously reported findings of differences in upper thresholds and adaptation of the diphasic skin potential, strongly confirm the hypothesis that subjects' implicit sets influence their patterns of autonomic responses.

attitudes
response
 thresholds
electric
 shock
HR
T°
GSR
SP

CORRELATES OF
COGNITIVE ACTIVITY

J 1   Andreassi, J.L.: Some physiological correlates of verbal learn-
       ing task difficulty. *Psychon Sci, 6:*69, 1966.

       Subjects learned three lists of nonsense syllables on three suc-   *verbal*
       cessive days while physiological variables were recorded. Sub-   *learning*
       jects showed significant increases in palmar conductance and   *SC*
       heart rate with the list of words having high associative value.   *HR*

J 2   Andreassi, J.L., and Whalen, P.M.: Some physiological corre-
       lates of learning and overlearning. *Psychophysiology, 3:*406,
       1967.

       Two experiments were conducted to investigate physiologic   *learning*
       activity associated with original learning and overlearning of   *overlearnin*
       verbal materials (nonsense syllables). In Experiment I, the   *verbal*
       physiologic responses measured were heart rate (HR), pal-   *stimuli*
       mar skin conductance (PSC), and galvanic skin responses   *habituatior*
       (GSRs) during original learning, overlearning, and new   *GSR*
       learning. In Experiment II, the same physiologic responses   *PSC*
       were recorded, but original learning was followed by two   *HR*
       overlearning phases. The results showed that there were de-
       creases in all of the physiologic measures with overlearning;
       there were increases in all of the measures with new learning;
       and further decreases in physiologic activity occurred with
       "double overlearning." It was concluded that the drop in
       physiologic activity which occurred with overlearning was
       due to an habituation of physiologic responses when subjects
       were no longer required to assimilate novel materials and a
       reduction in apprehensiveness as the experiment progressed.

J 3   Cauthern, Nelson: GSR and varying levels of information.
       *Psychophysiology, 10:*204, 1973.

The GSR has been conceptualized as a stimulus specific response with little information value (Averill and Opton, 1968). However, the present study demonstrates that the GSR is sensitive to varying amounts of information. In the present study Ss were asked to predict before each trial which one of three equally likely sequences of numbers was to be presented. The sequences were taped and played through earphones. Sequence I consisted of the number 1, followed by sixty seconds of silence; sequence II consisted of the number 1, followed by thirty seconds of silence, the number 2, followed by sixty seconds of silence. Sequence III consisted of the number 1, followed by thirty seconds of silence, the number 2, followed by thirty seconds of silence, the number 3, followed by thirty seconds of silence. The information supplied by the numbers in the sequence was determined by the prediction made; e.g. if sequence I were predicted and sequence III followed, the S would know that he had predicted incorrectly when the number 2 was presented. When the number 3 was presented, its information value would be low since the prediction had already been disconfirmed. Motivation was introduced by offering $.25 for each correct prediction. To keep the physical stimulus situation constant, only the predictions to sequence III were analyzed. It was hypothesized that the GSR would be greater for the numbers that supplied more information about the prediction; the response to the last number in sequence III should be less if sequence I were predicted than if sequence II were predicted since I would have already been disconfirmed. Although for both sequence II and III the final number supplied definitive information about the correctness of the prediction, it was hypothesized that the response to the final number would be greater if sequence III were predicted since it had the additional motivational component of gain. The results confirmed the hypotheses.

information value prediction GSR responses cognitive elaboration motivation

4   Corteen, R.S.: Skin conductance changes and word recall. *Brit J Psychol, 60*:81, 1969.

Tested the hypothesis that size of phasic conductance response to an item is positively related to later recall of that item. Results confirmed the hypothesis with the additional

recall SC magnitude

finding that the positive relation increases with increasing delay in recall. The findings are examined in terms of a simple memory process.

J 5   Courter, R.J., Wattenmaker, R.A., and Ax, A.F.: Physiological concomitants of psychological differentiation. *Psychophysiology, 1:*282, 1965.

Thirty-two male college students who scored above 50 (standard score) on the Closure Flexibility (CF) test were designated field independent (FI), and eight who scored below 50 were designated field dependent (FD). It was found that FI subjects were able to discriminate between the conditioned tone (CS) and the unreinforced generalization tones by the amplitude of their GSR significantly better (p < 0.01) than were FD persons. Although it cannot be asserted that this relationship is dependent on the autonomic response system, there is tentative support for this position. It seems probable that even the FD subjects could distinguish between the two most different pitched tones; yet they failed to make this distinction by their GSR responses. This lack of differentiation by the FD subject appears to be a function of a less well-differentiated autonomic nervous system. This study demonstrates that the stimulus generalization gradient involves an interaction between the cognitive style of the organism and the impinging stimuli, not merely the quantitative physical characteristics of the stimuli.

field dependency
cognitive tasks
stimulus discrimination
stimulus generalization
cognitive style

J 6   Cowles, M.P.: Skin conductance and reaction time with and without knowledge of results. *Psychon Sci, 20:*117, 1970.

Skin resistance was monitored during a simple RT task carried out by two groups of Ss (N = 37). Both groups were rewarded, but only one group was given knowledge of results. Mean log basal conductance level was negatively and significantly related to RT in the no-knowledge-of-results group. No such relationship was found for the knowledge-of-results group, which had significantly faster RTs. There was no significant difference between mean log basal conductance level in the two groups. Results suggest that basal skin conductance level does not reflect activity in a postulated reinforcement system.

knowledge of results
reaction time tasks
BSC

7   Edelberg, R.: Response of cutaneous water barrier to idea-
     tional stimulation: A GSR component. *J Comp Physiol
     Psychol, 61:*28, 1966.

Artificially increasing the local surface humidity of human   *ideational
skin produced sudden inward passage of water in response to   stimuli*
various alerting or ideational stimuli often with an electro-   *surface
dermal skin potential response and was associated with the   humidity*
apositive wave of producing sweat. It is interpreted as an   *sweating
indication of transient increase in epidermal permeability to   epidermal
water. One of two independent reflexes comprise the GSR.   permeabil-
The increase in cutaneous permeability demonstrated here   ity*
by absorption of water from humid air would also result in   *SP*
an outward movement of water into drier air and constitutes
a likely source of error in studies of sweat gland-GSR relations.

8   Elias, Marjorie F.: Heart rate, skin potential response, and
     latency of overt response, as indicators of problem recogni-
     tion and solution. *Psychon Sci, 18:*337, 1970.

Studied heart rate, skin potential, and response latency in re- *problem
lation to the recognition and solution of problems by eight-   recognition*
een high-school students. A continuous series of rule-induc-   *problem
tion problems was presented without any pause between   solving*
problems. The problems were sequentially related in that   *task
each new problem demanded a refinement of the rule just   complexity*
induced for the preceding problem. Increases in skin poten-   *feedback*
tial and response latency occurred when new problems were   *HR*
introduced, and decreases in the same measures were found   *SP*
when they were solved. Heart rate was not indicative of
recognition or solution of problems. When events during
trials—stimulus, response, feedback—were looked at separately, the events of stimulus onset and response were associated with significant increases at recognition. Only the feedback event was associated with a significant decrease at solution. It is suggested that these changes indicate a labile state
during which problem-solving occurs.

9   Kaplan, Stephen, Kaplan, Rachel, and Sampson, Jeffrey R.:
     Encoding and arousal factors in free recall of verbal and
     visual material. *Psychon Sci, 12:*73, 1968.

Forty male Ss were presented twenty-four items, half as words *free recall*
and half as simple line drawings with the instruction to try *verbal*
to remember them. Free recall was tested immediately after   *stimuli*
presentation and thirty minutes later. Picture recall was   *pictorial*
significantly greater than word recall (p < .001). Mean GSRs *stimuli*
based on items presented as words predicted both word and   *encoding*
picture recall (p < .001). It was suggested that the GSR   *arousal*
findings point to a verbal encoding both for words and pic-   *GSR*
tures. Since pictures appear to be coded visually as well, their
double coding might provide an explanation for superior
memory of these items.

J 10   Levonian, E.: Attention and consolidation as factors in re-
        tention. *Psychon Sci, 6:275,* 1966.

The skin resistance of subjects was recorded during an in-   *information*
structional film. Subjects were tested immediately after, and *memory*
one week after. The retention decrement preceding the in-   *attention*
formation presentation led to short-term and long-term retention.

J 11   Lieblich, Israel: Manipulation of contrast between differ-
        ential GSRs in very young children. *Psychophysiology, 7:436,*
        1971.

Each one of twenty-six children, aged three and four, was   *information*
tested in six ordered information detection sequences. Phy-   *detection*
siological responsiveness was observed in the GSR. It was   *children*
found that Short-term Physiological Activation (STPA) could   *verbal*
be manipulated in the predicted order using combinations of   *behavior*
the following facets: (1) frequency of usage of the stimulus *autonomic*
by the organism, (2) relevance of the stimulus to the organ- *reactivity*
ism, and (3) whether or not a verbal response to the stimulus
was required. The results were similar to those observed previously in an adult sample (Lieblich, 1969).

J 12   Lykken, D.T., Macindoe, I., and Tellegen, A.: Perception:
        Autonomic response to shock as a function of predictability
        in time and locus. *Psychophysiology, 9:*318, 1972.

Signals were used to manipulate S's ability to predict when and where (i.e. on which limb) he would receive each of forty-eight painful shocks. Two groups of 24 S's received twelve shocks in each of four predictability conditions. Heart rate and palmar SC were monitored throughout. Both HR and SC responses to shock were consistently reduced when shock was preceded by a warning signal; predictability of locus had no effect on HRR and a weak effect on SCR. More anxious Ss showed greater postshock HR acceleration under all conditions; less anxious Ss showed greater anticipatory HR acceleration. In a separate experiment, 9 Ss in whom the later components of the vertex AER increased systematically with shock intensity showed a decrease in these same components when shock was made predictable in time.

electric shock perception prediction response characteristics HR SC

13   Mefferd, Roy B. Jr., and Wieland, Betty A.: Modification in autonomically mediated physiological responses to cold pressor by word associations. *Psychophysiology,* 2:1, 1965.

Physiological measures—basal skin resistance (BSR), galvanic skin resistance (GSR), electrocardiogram (EKG), and skin temperatures—were made on 120 consecutive days on three male subjects during rest, a twenty-item word association test, recovery, a cold-pressor test, a combination of cold-pressor, and a second similar word-association test, and final recovery. Each stimulus alone induced increased sympathetic activity. Ongoing stress (cold pressor) responses, however, were depressed during the word-association test. Furthermore, the nature, reaction times, and commonalities of the associations were influenced by the stress. The inhibition was not due to order, threshold, adaptation, or conditioning effects.

word association stress cognitive factors BSR GSR

14   Pishkin, Vladimir, and Shurley, Jay T.: Electrodermal and electromyographic parameters in concept identification. *Psychophysiology,* 5:112, 1968.

This study examined concept identification (CI) performance as a function of physiological arousal and physiological activity as a function of task complexity and expectation of success or failure. The development of an unsolvable set

concept identification performance

constituted stresses used to manipulate arousal. Results *task com-*
showed the following: (1) a positive correlation between CI *plexity*
errors and muscle action potential (MAP), (2) a negative *stress*
correlation between spontaneous GSRs and MAP, (3) a *arousal*
greater number of spontaneous GSRs in low complexity- *EMG*
solvable set CI as compared with high complexity problems,
(4) progressively improving CI performance in low com-
plexity-solvable set problems, (5) increase in MAPs with
high complexity-unsolvable set CI. These findings were interpreted as indicating that MAP reflects internal disturbance associated with inability to process information while
spontaneous GSRs reflect successful information intake.

J 15   Tursky, B., Schwartz, G.E., and Crider, A.: Differential patterns of heart rate and skin resistance during a digit transformation task. *J Exp Psychol, 83:*451, 1970.

Fifteen undergraduates performed a paced digit-transforma- *task per-*
tion task at two levels of difficulty under an overt or covert   *formance*
response requirement. Time-locked recordings of heart rate *task diffi-*
and skin resistance showed heart rate deceleration during the   *culty*
information intake phase of the task and acceleration during *information*
cognitive processing. Skin resistance showed a generalized   *intake*
arousal pattern during both information intake and process- *cognitive*
ing. Response magnitudes in both measures were generally   *processing*
enhanced in the more difficult condition and under the re- *arousal*
quirement to make an overt response indicating task fulfill- *directional*
ment. Results support J.I. Lacey's hypothesis of directional   *fractiona-*
fractionation of autonomic response as a function of the in-   *tion*
ternal-external attention demands of imposed tasks. *attention*

J 16   Zimbardo, P.G., Cohen, A.R., Weisenberg, M., Dworkin, L.,
and Firestone, I.: Control of pain motivation by cognitive
dissonance. *Science, 151:*217, 1966. (Copyright 1966 by the
American Association for the Advancement of Science.)

Responses by humans to painful electric shocks are signifi- *cognitive*
cantly modified at subjective, behavioral and physiological   *dissonanc*
levels by verbal manipulation of degree of choice and justi- *pain perce*
     tion

fication for further exposure to the aversive stimuli. Pain perception, learning, and galvanic skin response are altered under these conditions of "cognitive dissonance" as they are by reductions in voltage intensity.

electric shock
learning
GSR

SECTION K

STRESS

K 1 Costell, R.M., and Leiderman, P.H.: Psychophysiological concomitants of social stress: The effects of conformity pressure. *Psychosom Med, 30*:298, 1968.

Skin potential concomitants of social conformity and independence studied on modified Asch situation utilizing naive subjects in minimum and major roles. Behavior and skin potential data for both roles demonstrate increased autonomic arousal for minimum subjects remaining independent during conformist pressure. Minimum subjects yielding to conformist pressures had lower levels of arousal, similar to habit pattern of control S's. Major role S's confronting independent minimum role S's exhibit increased habit utilization of skin potential when contrasted with major role S's facing yielding minimum role S's.

stress
social
 behavior
autonomic
 arousal
SP

K 2 Kilpatrick, Dean G.: Differential responsiveness of two electrodermal indices to psychological stress and performance of a complex cognitive task. *Psychophysiology, 9*:318, 1972.

Sixteen high trait anxious and sixteen low trait anxious male Ss were assigned to a high stress (HS) or a low stress (LS) condition and were given differentially stressful instructions. All Ss were then required to perform a complex cognitive task, the Halstead Category Test. Adjusted indices of tonic and phasic exosomatic electrodermal activity were monitored throughout the experiment. Level of tonic skin conductance (SC) was only minimally responsive to the manipulation of psychological stress but increased greatly during cognitive and perceptual activity. Phasic activity increased significantly following psychological stress but not following cognitive and perceptual activity. It was concluded that these results support a multiple component theory of electrodermal activity. Phasic electrodermal activity appears to increase with

stress
anxiety
cognitive
 tasks
spontaneou.
 GSRs
response
 compon-
 ents

psychological as well as physical threat and was suggested to be a good index of autonomic emotional arousal. Tonic SC appears to change mainly as a function of cognitive activity.

3 Kopacz, Frederick M. II, and Smith, Barry D.: Sex differences in skin conductance measures as a function of shock threat. *Psychophysiology, 8:293, 1971.*

Investigations of sex differences in various electrodermal measures have yielded inconsistent results. The present investigation attempted to examine sex differences primarily as a function of varied conditions of threat (stated probability of receiving electric shock). Thirty males and thirty females were randomly assigned to three conditions: High Threat Probability (HTP), Moderate Threat Probability (MTP), or No Threat Probability (NTP). All Ss heard, under assigned threat instructions, two sets of eleven tones, preceded by a nonstimulation period and followed by eleven tones with shock threat removed. Results indicated that the threat conditions did affect electrodermal measures as expected. In addition, males exhibited higher tonic (basal conductance) levels throughout, while females displayed greater phasic reactivity (GSR magnitude) and a larger number of nonspecific GSRs. In addition, nonspecific frequency was affected by the interaction of sex with treatment (threat), such that females displayed higher frequencies under moderate threat, while males increased linearly with increased threat. Degree of stress or threat, the possibility of differential perceptions, and a theory of differential hormonal functioning were applied in interpreting results.

stress
threat
sex differ-
* ences*
spontaneous
* GSR*
habituation
response
* compon-*
* ents*
BC

4 Lykken, D.T., Miller, R.D., and Strahan, R.F.: Some properties of skin conductance and potential. *Psychophysiology, 5: 253, 1968.*

Skin conductance (SC) and skin potential (SP) were measured simultaneously from opposite hands during a stress period and a subsequent prolonged relaxation in nineteen undergraduates. With the Ss relaxed toward the end of the session, simultaneous measures of SC and SP were taken between various combinations of two active and two drilled

stress
relaxation
polarity
model
arousal
sleep

reference electrodes on both hands. SC measured with the external voltage connected in series-adding with the endogenous SP (i.e. positive pole to the active electrode) was 13 percent higher than when measured in reverse polarity. Supplementary experiment showed that this "rectification effect" could be entirely attributed to the effect of the endogenous potential. A method of estimating SC from SP readings with no external current source was shown to give results equivalent to values measured in the usual way. These and other findings support the claim that steady-state electrodermal properties fit a simple model of a variable voltage and a variable resistance in series. Within-S correlations of SC and SP were high for Ss with low average SCs, lower for high-SC Ss who seemed less able to relax. The data suggest that SP may be an inverted U-shaped function of arousal and perhaps that the "beta process," which drives the tonic SP downward with increasing arousal, may begin to function at much lower levels of arousal for some Ss than for others. Phasic responses obtained at the end of the session when some Ss were apparently asleep suggest that, when S is drowsy or in light sleep, both the phasic SC changes and the SP responses (SPR) have lengthened and variable latencies, and the SPR is uniformly a large, negative going (alpha) response. Uniphasic beta SPRs were rather consistently obtained when the prestimulus tonic SP was already high.

K 5   McDaniel, C. Douglas, Mefferd, Roy B. Jr., Wieland, Betty A., Sadler, Timothy G., and Benton, Richard G.: Modification of galvanic skin responses by reaction time measurements. *Psychophysiology, 4*:340, 1968.

Galvanic skin responses (GSRs) were measured on twelve male Ss under four conditions: rest, reaction time measurements, a cold pressor, and a combination of cold pressor and reaction time measurements. Both reaction time measurements alone and cold pressor alone caused increased sympathetic activity, but when the former was combined with cold pressor, the ongoing autonomic activity was depressed.

stress
reaction
  time
pain
autonomic
  reactivity
GSR
  responses

K 6   Miller, L.H., and Shmavonian, B.M.: Replicability of two GSR indices as a function of stress and cognitive activity. *J Pers Soc Psychol, 2*:753, 1965.

A replication of an experiment by Katkin in which 2 GSR indices, nonspecific activity, and basal skin resistance were found to vary independently as a function of experimental conditions was conducted. An attempt to explicate the nature of the psychological dimensions underlying the phenomena was made by adding a noninterview control group to Katkin's design. The four groups in the 2 × 2 factorial design were: stress/interview, nonstress/interview, stress/noninterview, and nonstress/noninterview. The divergence of GSR nonspecifics and basal skin resistance previously reported by Katkin was reproduced for the stress groups. There were no significant differences between interview and noninterview groups. It was concluded that the changes following the interview could not be attributed solely to the interview.

*stress
cognitive
    activity
spontaneous
    GSRs
measure-
    ment
    indices*

K 7   Roessler, Robert, and Collins, Forrest: Personality correlates of physiological responses to motion pictures. *Psychophysiology, 6:732,* 1970.

Skin conductance (SC) and heart rate (HR) responses to rest, to a bland and to a stressor motion picture film were examined in twenty student subjects (Ss). Ss were divided equally into a high ego strength (Es) and a low Es group on the basis of their scores on the Barron scale of the MMPI. These groups were balanced for film presentation order and did not differ significantly on trait anxiety as measured by the Taylor Manifest Anxiety Scale. The Zuckerman Multiple Affect Adjective Check List was administered before and after both the stressor and the bland film. High Es Ss were more responsive in SC and HR under all three conditions and showed a greater range of SC values than did low Es Ss. Subjective states paralleled physiological states. High Es Ss reported significantly greater state anxiety than did low Es Ss.

*stress
anxiety
personality
ego strength
motion
    pictures
subjective
    states
HR
SC*

K 8   Zuckerman, Marvin, Persky, Harold, and Link, Kathryn E.: The influence of set and diurnal factors on autonomic responses to sensory deprivation. *Psychophysiology, 5:612,* 1969.

This study was designed to test the hypothesis that a stress set or no set (uncertainty) would produce greater arousal in

*stress
uncertainty*

sensory deprivation (SD) than a relaxation set. The role of a
diurnal (AM vs PM) factor was also evaluated. Eighteen male
subjects were run in a three-hour SD condition in the morning, and eighteen were run in the afternoon. One third of the
subjects were given a stress set emphasizing the stressful and
peculiar effects of SD, one-third were told nothing, and one-
third were told that the study was on the effects of "relaxation." Heart Rate, Breathing Rate (BR), Skin Conductance,
and Nonspecific GSR fluctuations (NS-GSRs) were measured before and during the SD condition. BR was higher in
the stress set group than in the other set groups. NS-GSRs
were higher in the stress set and no set groups than in the relaxation set group. Subjects showed more reaction on both
of these measures in the afternoon than in the morning.

*sensory
   depriva-
   tion
arousal
diurnal
   factors
set
HR
SC
respiration*

ANXIETY, FEAR, DEPRESSION

ANXIETY

1 Brandt, K., and Fenz, W.D.: Specificity in verbal and physiological indicants of anxiety. *Percept Mot Skills, 29:*663, 1969.

Studied relationships between subjective self-reports of anxiety and objective recordings of comparable physiological indices with twenty-four female undergraduates. A modification of the Taylor Manifest Anxiety Scales for autonomic arousal (AA) and striated muscle tension (MT) provides self-reports of anxiety. Group 1 S's scores showed AA<MT and Group 2 MT>AA. Skin resistance, basal conductance, heart rate, eyeblinks, and number of EMG's showed consistent group differences. Heart rate indicated that differences between groups were related to the level of induced stress, the higher levels being associated with greater group differences. Most measures showed successive increases in activity across conditions, indicating that Ss were responsive to them. EMG showed a peak in the condition of mild stress which might reflect inhibitory control.

anxiety
stress
autonomic response patterns
self-reports
HR
EMG

2 Fenz, Walter D., and Dronsejko, Krystyna: Effects of real and imagined threat of shock on GSR and heart rate as a function of trait anxiety. *J Exp Res Pers, 3:*187, 1969.

The study raised the question: What makes for an effective control of autonomic arousal, namely, for the ability to modulate involuntary, autonomic behavior? Individual differences in trait anxiety were found to be a relevant variable. Medium anxious Ss were able to emit GSRs and show heart rate acceleration by merely thinking about a painful event, and to inhibit GSRs and show heart rate deceleration in actual anticipation of the painful event. High anxious Ss

anxiety
imaginal stimuli
stress
anticipation
electric shock
response fractionation

99

showed autonomic excitation and low anxious Ss autonomic   *GSR fre-*
inhibition under both conditions.   *quency*
                                                             HR

L 3   Fried, Robert, Friedman, Miriam, and Welch, Livingston:
       High and low anxiety and GSR adaptation. *Psychon Sci,*
       *9:*635, 1967.

       GSR records were obtained for two groups of 20 Ss differing   *anxiety*
       in score on the Eysenck Personality Inventory (high and low   *personality*
       scores) while they were presented with a series of eighty   *visual*
       stimuli (four different lights alternating in apparent random   *stimuli*
       sequence). Typical adaptation phenomena were observed   *conditionec*
       for the high-N group while no adaptation was evident in the   *inhibition*
       low-N group. It is concluded that the observed relationship   *adaptation*
       between anxiety and adaptation supports the contention that
       adaptation of the GSR is a form of conditioned inhibition.

L 4   Gilberstadt, Harold, and Maley, Michael: GSR, clinical state
       and psychiatric diagnosis. *J Clin Psychol, 21:*235, 1965.

       Analysis of the psychogalvanic activity of seventy-three psy-   *anxiety*
       chiatric admissions to a general hospital indicated that (1)   *depression*
       presence of anxiety is associated with higher levels of activity; *psychiatric*
       (2) presence of depression is associated with lower levels of   *diagnosis*
       activity; (3) the majority of patients show a mixture of   *GSR*
       anxiety and depression with the balance between these states
       being reflected in levels of activity; and (4) there are few
       differences between psychiatric diagnosis groups in activity
       levels apparently because such groups include cases with
       mixtures of anxiety and depression as well as combinations
       of cases showing anxiety, depression, and neither anxiety nor
       depression.

L 5   Katkin, Edward S.: The relationship between a measure of
       transitory anxiety and spontaneous autonomic activity. *J*
       *Abnorm Psychol, 71:*142, 1966.

       The effects of stress (threat of shock) on GSR nonspecific   *anxiety*
       responses were evaluated for Ss who differed in transitory   *stress*
       anxiety as measured by the Affect Adjective Check List   *recovery*
                                                                      rate

(AACL). Fifty-two Ss were equally divided among four groups: Hi AACL stress, Lo AACL stress, Hi AACL nonstress, Lo AACL nonstress. First, all Ss rested, then both stress groups were threatened with shock while both nonstress groups continued resting; finally all Ss rested again. During the second period GSR nonspecifics increased for both stress groups; however, during the final period, after the cessation of stress, GSR nonspecifics decreased more for the Lo AACL Ss than for the Hi AACL Ss. It was concluded that the AACL may be related to "Autonomic Recovery Rate."

spontaneous GSRs

6   Katkin, Edward S.: Relationship between manifest anxiety and two indices of autonomic response to stress. *J Pers Soc Psychol, 2:*324, 1965.

The effects of stress (threat of shock) on the basal skin resistance and the GSR nonspecific responses were investigated for Ss who differed in anxiety levels on the Taylor anxiety MA scale. Twenty-six high anxious (HA) and twenty-six low anxious (LA) Ss were randomly assigned to stress and nonstress conditions, yielding four groups. First, all Ss rested, then both stress groups were threatened with shock (electric) while both nonstress groups continued resting. Finally all Ss were tested again. During the second period, GSR nonspecifics increased and basal resistance decreased for the shock-threatened groups, only as expected; however, during the final period (after a fifteen-minute interview), GSR nonspecifics decreased to the prethreat level for the shock threat groups but basal resistance continued to decrease for all groups. Both GSR indices were unrelated to individual differences in anxiety level. The 2 GSR indices reflect different phenomena.

anxiety stress spontaneous GSRs electric shock BSR

7   Katkin, Edward S., and Rappaport, Herbert: Relationship among manifest anxiety, response to stress, and the perception of autonomic activity. *Psychophysiology, 6:*646, 1970.

Subjects were forty-eight male undergraduates who scored in the upper and lower 20 percent on the Taylor MA scale. All Ss rested for eight minutes and then half of each group was given instructions designed to induce a mild state of stress,

anxiety stress spontaneous GSRs

while the other half of each group was told to continue resting. The "stress" instructions consisted of telling Ss that we
had them connected to a "lie detector" apparatus that was
capable of identifying their emotional responses; furthermore, we wanted them to signal us by pressing a micro-
switch each time they felt such a response. We would be
testing them for accuracy of report and honesty about themselves. Thus, Ss were placed in a situation of competing with
a "sophisticated" machine. Analysis of variance confirmed
that among the anxious Ss, there was a significant elevation
in rate of GSR during the second period, and that for low
anxious subjects there was no significant change in rate. Both
high and low anxious Ss in the control group showed a
modest decline in rate during the second period. The second
alternative hypothesis was rejected completely. Not only were
there real differences in the response tendencies of high and
low anxious Ss, there was also no evidence that these Ss could
differentially identify their responses; the mean number of
reported "emotional responses" was almost identical for the
high and low anxious Ss.

*autonomic
perceptio[n]
instruction[s]
subjective
reports*

L 8 Lader, Malcolm, and Mathews, Andrew: Physiological
changes during spontaneous panic attacks. *J Psychosom Res,
14*:377, 1970.

Spontaneous panic attacks occurred in three anxious female
patients during the course of polygraphic recording in a
laboratory situation. The concomitant physiological changes
are described. Cardiovascular measures and skin conductance
showed parallel effects, whereas the electromyogram correlated poorly with the other measures. The panic attacks were
self-limiting.

*anxiety
panic
SC
HR
EMG*

L 9 Pillard, Richard C., Carpenter, James, Atkinson, Kim Wells,
and Fisher, Seymour: Palmar sweat prints and self-ratings as
measures of film-induced anxiety. *Percept Mot Skills, 23*:771,
1966.

To observe the response to an affect-arousing film, a palmar
sweat print and self-ratings of anxiety and sweat-output were
taken from 14 Ss, once before and once during a film be-

*anxiety
movies
sweat prints*

lieved to induce "anxiety." Ss showed significantly darker sweat prints and reported more anxiety during the film. The increase in palmar sweat appears to correlate moderately with both of the self-ratings. This finding is compared with similar relationships obtained by Lazarus and his co-workers. Some difficulties in the measurement of psychophysiologic variables are discussed.

L 10   Rappaport, Herbert, and Katkin, Edward S.: Relationships among manifest anxiety, response to stress, and the perception of autonomic activity. *J Consult Clin Psychol, 38*:219, 1972.

The effects of a mild ego-involving stress on nonspecific galvanic skin responses (GSRs) were evaluated for Ss who differed in anxiety level as measured by the Taylor Manifest Anxiety Scale. Forty-eight Ss were divided among four groups: high-anxiety stress, low-anxiety stress, high-anxiety nonstress, low-anxiety nonstress. After an initial rest period, Ss in the stress condition were asked to identify their own "emotional responses" while monitored by a "lie detector." They were competing with the machine for accuracy of report and were instructed that the machine could detect mistakes or false reports. The Ss in the nonstress condition continued to rest. The results indicated that high-anxiety Ss showed a significant increase in GSR rate in the stress period when compared with low-anxiety Ss. The control groups showed no difference as a function of anxiety level. It was concluded that scores on the Manifest Anxiety Scale reflect "reactive" anxiety, the autonomic components of which are differentially elicited by ego-involving stress situations.

anxiety
stress
ego-involv-
ing
autonomic
perception
subjective
reports

FEAR

L 11   Geer, J.H.: Fear and autonomic arousal. *J Abnorm Psychol, 71*:253, 1966.

Thirty-two female undergraduates were classified into (H.F.) high fear or (L.F.) low fear of spiders. After reducing orienting responses by neutral animals, subjects in the experimental condition were shown spider pictures, subjects in

fear
desensitiza-
tion
GSR

the control group were shown pictures of snakes. Responses to the last neutral stimuli was used as a baseline. H.F.'s subjects, when first shown spider, yielded greater GSR's than others. Also GSR's were of greater duration.

L 12   Grossberg J.M., and Wilson, H.K.: Physiological changes accompanying the visualization of fearful and neutral situations. *J Pers Soc Psychol, 10:*124, 1968.

To test an assumption of Wolpe's systematic desensitization therapy that imagining fearful scenes produces physical arousal, eighteen high-anxiety and eighteen low-anxiety girls first read and then were told to imagine fearful and neutral scenes four times. Heart rate, skin conductance, and forehead EMG were recorded during the reading and imagining. For heart rate and skin conductance, (1) there were no significant differences between fearful high-anxiety and low-anxiety, (2) during the reading there were no significant differences between fearful and neutral scenes, (3) during imagining fearful scenes produces significantly more arousal, (4) both measures declined significantly over trials. EMG failed to differentiate fearful and neutral scenes, but low-anxiety subjects showed significantly more EMG than the high-anxiety subjects. To assess possible biases in scene presentations, ten matched control subjects, neutral to both fearful and neutral scenes, were presented tapes of the experimental groups procedure. Persistence of significant heart rate and skin conductance differences for fearful versus neutral scenes suggested a confounding of extraneous factors with self-rated fear in producing greater arousal during fearful scenes.

fear
desensitization
arousal
anxiety
imagery
HR
EMG
SC

L 13   Wilson, Glenn D.: GSR responses to fear-related stimuli. *Percept Mot Skills, 24:*401, 1967.

GSR responses to a set of tachistoscopically presented color slides were compared for 10 Ss who reported intense fear of spiders and 10 Ss admitting no unreasonable fears. Employing the index, ratio of response to spider-pictures over response to neutral stimuli (landscapes), perfect discrimination between the two groups of Ss was obtained.

fear
pictorial
stimuli
stimulus dis-
crimina-
tion

DEPRESSION

L 14 Bagg, C.E., and Crookes, T.G.: Palmar digital sweating in women suffering from depression. *Brit J Psychiatry, 112:*1251, 1966.

Measurements of palmar digital sweating, by a plastic paint technique, were made on a group of eighteen female patients suffering from depression. Readings were taken on three occasions within the compass of a week, while they were ill, the middle one of these while they were awaiting E.C.T., and on a further occasion when they were recovered. Sweating was significantly reduced during the illness, compared with the recovered values. On the E.C.T. occasion, the mean sweat count of the group was not different from the other depressed occasions, but the changes shown by individuals on the E.C.T. day were significantly correlated with their neuroticism score on the M.P.I., the more neurotic showing a decrease, the less neurotic an increase, in sweating. Pulse rate was taken on each occasion that the sweating was measured. There was no significant difference between depressed and recovered readings, but there was a significant decrease on the E.C.T. day. There was also a correlation between changes in pulse rate and changes in sweating. Discussion was mainly in terms of the similarity, in this and other studies, of autonomic changes found in depression with those in states of anxiety. Emphasis was placed on the distinction between "background" autonomic measurements and changes in response to specific stimuli, and on the reasons why patterns in the two types of measurement would not be expected to be the same.

depression
sweating
E.C.T.
autonomic
response
patterns
HR

L 15 McCarron, Lawrence T.: Psychophysiological discriminants of reactive depression. *Psychophysiology, 10:*223, 1973.

Physiological measures of skin resistance response, heart rate, respiration rate, and electroencephalogram (EEG) were used in a multiple discriminant analysis to differentiate a group of ten questionnaire-abnormal Ss from a group of thirty normal Ss. The questionnaire-abnormal Ss were operationally defined as reactively depressed from specified Minnesota Multiphasic Personality Inventory (MMPI) profiles of the 2-4,

depression
personality
discriminant
analysis
GSR
HR

2-4-7 code types. The control group was operationally defined   *respiration*
by a clinically normal MMPI profile. The method of period   *EEG*
analysis was used to electronically transcribe the analog
physiological data to digital data for computer manipulation.
The depressed group was differentiated from the control
group by decreased skin resistance responses, a rapid heart
rate, increased respiration rate, and greater activation-com-
plexity of EEG.

L 16   Noble, Peter, and Lader, Malcolm: The symptomatic corre-
       lates of the skin conductance changes in depression. *J Psy-
       chiatr Res, 9:*61, 1971.

Psychometric and skin conductance data were recorded on   *depression*
thirty-four depressed inpatients prior to a course of ECT.   *anxiety*
Thirty-one subjects were retested when clinically improved   *arousal*
two weeks subsequent to the ECT. Mean physiological levels   *SC*
did not alter significantly subsequent to ECT. However, in
the depressed state there was a tendency for low skin conductance and reduced fluctuations to be associated with depressive symptomatology of a biological type. The relationship
found between reduced sweat gland activity and weight loss
may suggest hypothalamic dysfunction in these patients. A
correlation was found between reduced sweat gland activity
and retardation which is in line with other studies on the
physiology of depression. Basal physiological levels were unrelated to anxiety; however, anxiety increase was associated
with marked physiological change. Skin conductance and
fluctuation levels may thus be used as indices of change in
arousal in depressed patients.

L 17   Peck, R.E.: Observations on salivation and palmar sweating
       in anxiety and other psychiatric conditions. *Psychosomatics,
       7/6:*343, 1966.

A precise technique for measuring salivary excretion rate   *depression*
and palmar sweating is described. Parameters based on   *alcoholism*
seventy-one controls and eighty-five patients are established. *age*
There is great inter- and intra-individual variability. There *psychotropic*
is no difference between sexes, but both salivation and   *drugs*
palmar sweating decrease with increasing age. Depression   *mood*
                                                              salivation

lowers both measures and alcoholics tend to lie at the other end of the continuum. Both weekly and diurnal variations occur. Psychotropic drugs depress salivation, but not sweating. Both measures can mirror changes in mood, clinically and experimentally.

SECTION M

CORRELATES OF PSYCHOPATHOLOGY

PHOBIAS

M 1   Hoenig, J., and Reed, G.F.: The objective assessment of desensitization. *Brt J Psychiatry, 112:*1279, 1966.

Four patients with monosymptomatic phobias were treated   *phobias*
by systematic desensitization as recommended by Wolpe   *desensitiza-*
(1958). The outcome of the treatment was tested by record-   *tion*
ing anxiety responses by the psychogalvanic response (P.G.   *anxiety*
R.) to the stimulus word in a word association test, to   *verbal*
imagery and to real stimuli. It was shown that the findings   *stimuli*
obtained by this method need not conform to the results   *imagery*
assessed by the usual clinical methods, which alone have
limited reliability, and that in controlled trials the objective
method described here might help to eliminate some of the
contradictory results reported in the past.

M 2   Lader, M.H.: Palmer skin conductance measures in anxiety
and phobic states. *J Psychosom Res, 11:*271, 1967.

Ninety patients consisting of five groups—anxiety-with-de-   *phobias*
pression, anxiety state, agoraphobia, social phobia, and spe-   *anxiety*
cific monosymptomatic phobia—were physiologically and   *depression*
clinically studied in an effort to link psychiatric syndromes   *arousal*
more firmly to biological foundations. The physiological   *sedatives*
study consisted of a standardized laboratory procedure in   *application*
which the palmar skin conductance was recorded during the
presentation of twenty identical 1-kHz auditory stimuli of
100-db intensity and one-second duration applied at intervals of forty-five to eighty seconds. Clinical variables rated
included levels of general and situational anxiety, assessments of overt anxiety, frequency of panic attacks, and re-

sponse to treatment with sedatives. It was found that specific phobics are different in terms of arousal from other phobic patients.

3   Wilson, G.D.: An electrodermal technique for the study of phobias. *NZ Med J, 65:*696, 1966.

An outline is given of some preliminary attempts to observe phobias by measuring galvanic skin responses to pictorial representations of the phobic target presented tachistoscopically through a translucent screen. A control experiment on nonphobic subjects is described, and the responses of two phobic subjects used to illustrate the procedure.

phobias
fear
pictorial
 stimuli
applications

SCHIZOPHRENIA

4   Ax, A.F., and Bamford, J.L.: The GSR recovery limb in chronic schizophrenia. *Psychophysiology, 7:*145, 1970.

Recently, Edelberg (1970) has described a method for scoring the recovery limb of the GSR and reported more rapid recovery with greater signal significance to the subject. Mednick and Schulsinger have reported (1968) that the GSR recovery rate is significantly faster for their young subjects who have high risk for schizophrenia. These reports stimulated us to review our data on twenty-eight chronic schizophrenic patients and eighteen healthy control subjects (Ax, Bamford, Beckett, Fetz, and Gottlieb, 1970).

schizo-
 phrenia
recovery
 time
comment

5   Ax, A.F., Bamford, J.L., Beckett, P.G.S., Fetz, N.F., and Gottlieb, J.S.: Autonomic conditioning in chronic schizophrenia. *J Abnorm Psychol, 76:*140, 1970.

Studied classical conditioning of autonomic responses of twenty-eight chronic schizophrenic and eighteen healthy Ss by means of a discrimination paradigm employing three tones differing in pitch as CSs, and two intensities of DC produced pain as UCSs. It was found that patients, as compared with the healthy control group, had normal resting physiological levels and UCRs, but significantly impaired CR amplitudes, reduced discrimination scores, and smaller

schizo-
 phrenia
condition-
 ing
emotions
learning
social
 motivation

orienting responses. Results suggest an impaired aptitude for emotional learning which might account for the severe impairment in social motivation and emotional maturity observed in these chronic schizophrenic patients.

M 6   Ax, Albert F., Bamford, Jacqueline L., Beckett, Peter G.S., Domino, Edward F., and Gottlieb, Jacques S.: *Psychosom Med, 31*:353, 1969.

Physiologic response patterns during infusions of epinephrine and norepinephrine were examined with regard to their relationships to those of fear and anger. A similarity was found between responses to fear and epinephrine on the one hand, and to anger and norepinephrine on the other. Experiments were done to compare physiologic response patterns of chronic schizophrenic patients with those of nonschizophrenic subjects during the cold pressor test. The majority of schizophrenic patients reacted with a norepinephrine-like (anger) pattern, whereas control subjects most often reacted with an epinephrine-like (fear) pattern. The question was raised whether these patterns may have been present before the onset of schizophrenia and hence could play a diagnostic or etiologic role.

schizophrenia epinephrin fear anger autonomic response patterns stress

M 7   Baer, Paul E., and Fuhrer, Marcus J.: Cognitive factors in differential conditioning of the GSR: Use of a reaction time task as the UCS with normals and schizophrenics. *J Abnorm Psychol, 74*:544, 1969.

Twenty-two normals and twenty-two schizophrenics underwent differential conditioning of the GSR, using eight-second tones of differing frequencies as the CSs, an eight-second CS-UCS interval, and a UCS comprised of an RT task signaled by a low-intensity light. Both inertial reports and postconditioning interviews were obtained. Twelve Ss in the normal group verbalized the conditional stimulus relations accurately, compared to 3 Ss in the schizophrenic group. The normal group showed significant GSR differentiation, though conditioning was limited to the group of accurately verbalizing Ss. No evidence for conditioning was obtained in the schizophrenic group. Normal Ss had faster RTs than schizophrenic

schizophrenia reaction time task differential conditioning verbal behavior

Ss. The RT of accurately verbalizing normals was shorter than that of inaccurately verbalizing normals, and the degree of GSR differentiation was significantly correlated with RT.

8   Bernal, Martha E., and Miller, William Hansford: Electrodermal and cardiac responses of schizophrenic children. *Psychophysiology, 7:*155, 1970.

The reactivity and habituation of autistic schizophrenic and normal children were compared using a variety of stimuli. The first two stimulation conditions were fifteen tone trials followed by a novel tone stimulus, and fifteen periods of darkness followed by a single period of partial illumination. Order of these stimulation conditions was counterbalanced in a groups X order X trials anova factorial design. Other stimuli were tones varying in intensity and photic flashes presented in fixed order following the first two conditions. The two groups differed in magnitude of response to the first three tone and illumination change trials, and thereafter showed no differences in habituation or reinstatement to the novel stimulus. This difference consisted of greater responsivity for the normals and was independent of base level, spontaneous activity, order of condition, and type of stimulus. The schizophrenics showed a relationship between GSR magnitude and tone intensity that was similar to the normals' physiological tracking of changing intensity. Results for photic stimulation were the same as for the first two stimulus conditions. The peak-to-valley cardiac measure failed to yield any reliable group differences under any stimulation condition.

*schizo-
phrenia
orienting
response
children
habituation
GSR
HR*

9   Bernstein, A.S.: Phasic electrodermal orienting response in chronic schizophrenics: II. Response to auditory signals of varying intensity. *J Abnorm Psychol, 75:*146, 1970.

Phasic electrodermal orienting response (OR) to brief tones was studied at 60, 75, or 90 db. Results supported earlier findings obtained with brief visual stimuli both in retest and in newly recruited subjects among clear and confused chronic schizophrenics and normal controls. Confused patients in

*schizo-
phrenia
information
intake
orienting
response*

particular showed diminished reactivity to stimuli of low to
moderate intensity. A moderate increase in stimulus intensity
significantly improved initial OR frequency among confused
patients without affecting response amplitude. Further increase in stimulus intensity brought initial OR amplitude as
well to normal levels. Chronic schizophrenics again showed
consistently faster habituation than controls. Results are not
attributable to particular diagnostic subgroupings or total
time in hospital. While long hospitalized patients with a
hebephrenic diagnosis are more likely to be confused, it is
the fact of confusion itself that is significant in determining
OR. Results suggest faster but less detailed assimilation of
information among chronic schizophrenics in general,
coupled with a defensive attenuation of specific input among
confused patients in particular.

*response
compon-
ents
habituation*

M 10   Goldstein, Michael J., Rodnick, Eliot H., Jackson, Newton
P., Evans, Jerome R., and Bates, John E.: The stability and
sensitivity of measures of thought, perception and emotional
arousal. *Psychopharmacologia, 24:*107, 1972.

The paper presents evidence concerning the stability and
sensitivity of three classes of behavioral measures: (1) word
association quality, (2) perceptual coping style, and (3) skin
resistance level and reactivity across a twenty-one-day interval. Acute schizophrenic males were administered these
measures seven and twenty-eight days following admission to
a state hospital. Half of the patients were assigned to active
phenothiazine medication at seven days and half continued
on placebo. Comparison of correlations between seven- and
twenty-eight-day data for drug and placebo groups revealed
different patterns of stability across time and sensitivity to
drug ingestion for each of these three classes of measures.

*schizo-
phrenia
word associ
ation
perceptual
style
GSR reac-
tivity
drugs*

BRAIN DAMAGE

M 11   Holloway, Frank A., and Parsons, Oscar A.: Physiological
concomitants of reaction time performance in normal and
brain-damaged subjects. *Psychophysiology, 9:*189, 1972.

Autonomic and somatic concomitants of simple reaction
time performance were examined in normal and brain-

*brain
damage*

damaged patients. The reaction time task involved a warning stimulus preceding the execution stimulus by a variable foreperiod. The normal Ss displayed the expected relationships between performance and physiological activity, such that fast reaction times were associated with greater HR deceleration, larger electrodermal response magnitudes, and less EMG activity during the preparatory foreperiod of the task. BD Ss, however, generally displayed either no relationships between autonomic or somatic activity and reaction time or a relationship opposite to that seen in normals, namely, that slower reaction times were associated with larger autonomic responses to the warning stimulus. The results were discussed in terms of two possible mechanisms which may be operative in the BD Ss: (1) that their autonomic responsivity becomes "dissociated" from changes in the external environment, and (2) that such "dissociated" activity may represent or reflect an active source of interference with the S's ability to attend to or to efficiently execute the task.

reaction time performance
HR
EMG

1 12   Holloway, Frank A., and Parsons, Oscar A.: Unilateral brain damage and bilateral skin conductance levels in humans. *Psychophysiology,* 6:138, 1969.

Left and right, palmar, and dorsal skin conductance levels (SCLs) were obtained from hospital controls, left hemisphere lesion Ss, right hemisphere lesion Ss, and diffuse or bilateral lesion Ss during several experimental conditions involving rest, passive auditory stimulation, motor reactions, and simple "perception." The unilateral lesion groups generally displayed significantly higher palmar SCLs on the side contralateral to their lesion. Such "laterality" was not demonstrated in dorsal recordings or in the hospital controls or diffuse lesion group. These unilateral lesion groups had higher palmar SCLs during passive stimulation than during rest, motor or perception phases. Results were discussed in terms of possible neural mechanisms underlying the phenomena.

brain damage
bilateral responses
sensory stimuli
motor stimuli
mechanisms

1 13   Parsons, Oscar A., and Chandler, Peter J.: Electrodermal indicants of arousal in brain damage: Cross-validated findings. *Psychophysiology,* 5:644, 1969.

Two independent experiments were performed in which skin resistance levels, transformed to log skin conductance levels (SCLs), and GSRs of brain-damaged (BD) and nonbrain-damaged (NBD) patients were measured under varying task demands. Cross-validated results indicate that BD had significantly higher log SCLs and GSRs than NBD over conditions. Patterns of correlations between and within measures of arousal and performance were similar in both experiments and tended to differ for BD compared to NBD. Positive correlations between arousal measures and performance in the BD suggest that their impaired performance cannot be ascribed to nonoptimal levels of arousal, at least as measured electrodermally. A group of schizophrenics subjected to the same experimental conditions had levels of electrodermal activity and performance which were intermediate to those of BD and NBD. Other results suggest that different psycho-physiological relationships exist in BD and schizophrenic patients. The hypothesis that brain damage leads to release of inhibitory control over systems involved in electrodermal activity seems worthy of further investigation.

brain damage schizo-phrenia performance tasks arousal mechanisms

MENTAL RETARDATION

M 14   Lader, M.H., and Wing, L.: Physiological measures in agitated and retarded depressed patients. *J Psychiatr Res, 7:*89, 1969.

Thirty-five patients of primary depression of moderate or severe degree were compared to normal subjects. Palmar skin conductance, P.R., and forearm E.M.G. were recorded during the presentation of twenty 1 KHZ auditory stimuli of 100 db intensity and one second duration. There were clear-cut differences between agitated depressives (more sweat gland activity and more skin conductance fluctuations) than the retarded depressive type. The results compared with views that retardation and agitation are independent, not mutually exclusive.

mental retardation depression agitation auditory stimuli SC repsonse EMG

M 15   McCabe, Michael W., and Fenz, Walter D.: Habituation of the GSR to tones in retarded children and normal controls. *Psychophysiology, 6:*5, 1970.

Habituation of the galvanic skin response to 1000 Hz tones was studied in thirty normal, grade 8 children (mean age, 13.6 years) and thirty retarded children (mean age, 14.2 years). Fifteen trials at each of 35, 70 and 100 db levels were presented to all Ss in a Latin Square design. Tone duration for half the Ss in each group was 3.0 sec, for the other, 0.5 sec, with a constant intertrial interval of ten seconds for both groups. The major results were as follows: All Ss, retardates and normal controls, habituated to the 100 db and the 70 db tones, but showed little change in response to the 35 db tones. The response pattern of the two groups nevertheless differed: at the 70 db intensity, control Ss had a greater initial response and responded throughout more strongly than retardates, $F(14,784) = 2.02$, $p < .01$; a significant opposite effect was found in responses to the 100 db tones, $F(14,784) = 2.98$, $p < .001$. The F values represent interactions between Groups and Tone Sequence, combining the responses to the .5- and the 3.0-second durations. There was a significant Group X Duration interaction, $F(14,784) = 2.00$, $p < .01$, control Ss responding more strongly to the tones with a .5-second duration, while retardates to the tones with the 3.0-second duration. This interaction was significant only at the 100 db level. No significant order effects were found.

mental retardation children habituation

16 Tizard, Barbara: Habituation of EEG and skin potential changes in normal and severely subnormal children. *Am J Ment Defic, 73*:34, 1968.

Changes in skin potential and EEG in response to sounds were recorded from three groups of children aged eight to ten years—a normal group, a group of overactive imbeciles, and a control imbecile group—during the waking and sleeping states. Only the normal children showed habituation of the skin potential response while awake; while asleep no habituation occurred in any group. There was no difference in the frequency of EEG and skin potential changes in response to sound in the three groups. A difference in alertness between the groups while awake was a confounding variable.

mental retardation children habituation

17 Wolfensberger, Wolf, and O'Connor, Neil: Relative effectiveness of galvanic skin response latency, amplitude and

duration scores as measures of arousal and habituation in normal and retarded adults. *Psychophysiology, 3:*345, 1967.

The comparability of latency, duration and amplitude scores of the first derivative of the GSR in normal and retarded young adults was studied under various conditions of stimulus intensity, duration and repetition. Duration scores were a measure of the onset-to-peak time of the primary wave and were found to be most sensitive to changes in stimulus conditions, least subject to measurement errors, and least cumbersome to handle statistically. Latency scores were found to be least sensitive, with amplitude scores occupying an intermediate position. The correlations between the three types of responses were low and showed no substantial or meaningful differences between stimulus conditions and S groups. It is concluded that for some types of GSR measurement, duration scores can replace the more commonly used amplitude scores.

mental retardatio response components arousal habituation

ALCOHOLISM

M 18   Gross, K., and Stern, J.A.: Habituation of orienting responses as a function of "instructional set." *Cond Reflex, 2:* 291, 1967.

Electrodermal and plethysmographic recordings were obtained from three groups of alcoholic patients. The groups differed in terms of instruction given for responses in a series of words spoken by E. Instructions did not have predicted effects on the rate of electrodermal response habituation. The amplitudes for group B was lower than A or C. Relative importance of associative and verbal responses to a stimulus word for eliciting alcoholic responses was considered.

alcoholism instruction verbal stimuli habituation

PSYCHOSES

M 19   Chambers, D.A.: Conditioning in psychotics. *Acta Psychiatr Scand, 41:*1, 1965.

Theoretical attempts, notably by Pavlov, were made under an assumption of constitutional deficit to explain behavior pathology in conditioning terms. The evidence produced

psychoses conditionability

established that psychotics can be conditioned, but it is equivocal concerning the conditioning ability of psychotics relative to normal subjects. The present study tested the theory that the conditioning performance of psychotics differs from that of nonpsychotics. Normal subjects, jail inmates, acute psychotics, were studied with galvanic skin responses and verbal and salivation conditioning procedures, and the performance of the chronic subjects was cross-validated. The psychiatric differentiation of the psychotic and nonpsychotic subjects was supported by the results of objective performance tests, on which the psychotics demonstrated a performance deficit. The conditioning findings failed to confirm the theoretical effects of psychosis, but indicated that institutionalization was an important factor influencing performance, irrespective of whether or not the subject was psychotic. The effects of institutionalization were interpreted in terms of reinforcement history.

verbal stimuli applications

20 Hare, Robert D.: Temporal gradient of fear arousal in psychopaths. *J Abnorm Psychol, 70:*442, 1965.

Skin conductance of psychopathic (P) and non-psychopathic (NP) criminals and noncriminal controls (N = 11 each group) was monitored while the numbers 1 through 12 were consecutively presented on a memory drum. After the first trial, Ss were informed that on each of the remaining five trials they would receive a strong electric shock when Number 8 appeared. Log conductance increases in the interval prior to shock were significantly smaller and began later for the P than for the NP Ss. The psychopaths were less responsive to shock than were the NP criminals but did not differ significantly from the noncriminal controls. There were no significant differences among groups in the rate of recovery from the effects of shock. The results were consistent with the hypothesis that the temporal gradient of fear arousal and response inhibition is steeper for psychopaths than for normal persons.

psychopathic criminals fear arousal responsivity recovery SC

21 Zuckerman, M., Persky, H., and Curtis, G.C.: Relationships among anxiety, depression, hostility and autonomic variables. *J Nerv Ment Dis, 146:*481, 1968. (Copyright 1968 by the Williams & Wilkens, Co., Baltimore.)

Describes correlation between interview-based ratings of affects and autonomic measures made in a cold pressor test and in blood pressure and pulse in physical exam. Ss were twenty-nine male psychotic patients and twenty-five normal males. Spontaneous GSR fluctuations were correlated with anxiety and depression ratings in patients and combined groups. BP increases in response to cold pressor were higher in the pattern than the control and tended to correlate with other than anxiety measures.

psychoses
spontaneou
  GSR
physical
  stimuli
anxiety
depression

CLASSICAL
CONDITIONING

RESPONSE CHARACTERISTICS

N 1 Badia, P., and Defran, R.H.: Orienting responses and GSR conditioning: A dilemma. *Psychol Rev, 77*:171, 1970.

An orienting response (OR) analysis was applied to galvanic skin response (GSR) conditioning phenomena of CR acquisition and UCR diminution. The analysis focused on the stimulus properties of CS and UCS omission. A hypothetical response to UCS omission was suggested to affect CR measurement with short but not long interstimulus intervals (ISIs) thus contributing to the shape of the conventional ISI function. Data were presented supporting the assertion that responses to UCS omission appear to be ORs, not CRs. The question was raised whether it is possible to determine an ISI function for GSR conditioning using current testing methods. In the second portion of the paper, a theoretical account of UCR diminution based on conditioning is critically analyzed. Evidence is cited supporting an OR analysis of diminution, and new data are presented which show that ORs occur to omission of the first of two paired stimuli.

orienting response stimulus characteristics theory review

N 2 Burstein, Kenneth R., and Smith, Barry D.: The latency distribution of the skin conductance response as a function of the CS-UCS interval. *Psychophysiology, 9*:14, 1972.

Latency distributions were obtained for the skin conductance response, by blocks of five trials, for groups (N = 13) conditioned with CS-UCS intervals of 3.5, 5.5, 7.5, 10.5, 15.5, and 20.5 seconds. Another group (N = 13) received five, ten, fifteen, twenty, twenty-five and thirty trials respectively with a .5-second CS-UCS interval. For all blocks of five trials in

latency orienting response SC

the extended CS-UCS groups, the modal response occurred in the two to three second latency range characteristic of the orienting response (OR). There was no significant difference in OR frequency as a function of the CS-UCS interval. There was no systematic increase in response frequency with repeated trials in any of the latency ranges scored. No significant difference in acquisition was obtained as a function of the CS-UCS interval in the extended CS-UCS groups for either frequency or for magnitude. Performance of the (composite) .5-second CS-UCS group was superior to that of the extended groups. This difference was not attributable to differential OR frequency. The PC group also exhibited a modal response in the two to three second (OR) latency range. Response frequency in the OR latency range was lower in the PC group than in the conditioned groups, but response frequency outside of the OR range was higher in the PC groups than in the conditioned groups.

N 3   Corah, Norman L., and Tomkiewicz, Robert L.: Classical conditioning of the electrodermal response with novel stimuli. *Psychophysiology, 8*:143, 1971.

Most attempts to classically condition the GSR have used aversive stimuli. A series of twenty novel slides were used as UCS in a delayed differential conditioning paradigm involving reinforced and unreinforced CS. Thirty female undergraduates were given ten habituation trials, forty conditioning trials of which one-half were reinforced, and ten extinction trials. Orienting response, anticipatory response, and postconditional stimulus response components were analyzed separately for the different series. Differential conditioning was obtained for two of the responses during the conditioning and extinction series. Results indicate that a relatively mild novel stimulus can also effectively condition the GSR.

novel stimuli stimulus discrimination response components

N 4   Dengerink, H.A., and Taylor, S.P.: Multiple responses with differential properties in delayed galvanic skin response conditioning: A review. *Psychophysiology, 8*:348, 1971.

Studies of delayed GSR conditioning have shown that when an interstimulus interval (ISI) of sufficient duration is em-

response characteristics

ployed, multiple responses may occur within that interval. *delayed con-*
The studies reviewed indicate that GSRs which occur early *ditioning*
in the interval are present by the second conditioning trial. *multiple*
They tend to habituate, appear to be orienting responses, *responses*
and, under certain circumstances, they are conditional. *review*
Those responses which occur during the later portion of the
interval are minimal, if at all present, when conditioning is
initiated but show a negatively accelerated growth curve
across trials. These second responses are conditional and may
be protective reflexes which prevent damage to the skin. It
is concluded that in GSR conditioning the choice of an ISI
and the specification of ISI responses may seriously affect the
nature of the behavior observed and may have serious implications for other areas of psychological investigation.

N 5 Epstein, Seymour, Burstein, Kenneth, and Smith, Barry:
Stimulus generalization of the GSR following a variety of
conditioning and pseudoconditioning procedures. *Psychophysiology, 8:*714, 1971.

Seven groups of 12 Ss were exposed to various conditioning *delayed con-*
and control procedures in a delayed conditioning paradigm. *ditioning*
The conditioning groups included a group that labeled the *stimulus*
CS before presentation of the UCS, a group that labeled the *generaliza-*
CS after presentation of the UCS, and a group that did not *tion*
label at all. The control groups included a backward conditioning group, a CS-only group, a UCS-only group, and a
random, unpaired CS-UCS group. All conditioning groups
and no control group exhibited the inverted U-shaped acquisition curve which is typically reported in studies of GSR
conditioning. There was evidence that UCRs, ORs, and their
interaction can interfere with delayed as well as with non-
delayed CRs. With initial OR reactivity controlled, there was
equivocal evidence for a monotonic generalization gradient.

N 6 Grings, William W., and Lockhart, Russell A.: Problems of
magnitude measurement with multiple GSRs. *Psychol Rep,
17:*979, 1965.

In long delay or trace conditioning more than one maximum *delayed con-*
for the GSR response curve is obtained. CRs expressed as *ditioning*

magnitudes of response may employ either stimulus onset points or response onset points as base levels from which to measure changes (GSRs). Data are presented to demonstrate that different magnitude measures (those from CS onset and from CR onset) may yield different sensitivity to independent variation and different values for empirically defined conditioning phenomena. Further data show that responses occurring in close succession during a trial may be independent.

trace conditioning
GSR magnitude measurements

N 7   Grings, William W.: Anticipatory and preparatory electrodermal behavior in paired stimulation situations. *Psychophysiology, 5:*597, 1969.

Electrodermal indicators of anticipation and preparation accompanying paired stimulation are divided into three classes: (1) features of responding between onsets of the stimuli; (2) changes in response to the second stimulus which occur only when the first stimulus is present; and (3) responses at the point where the response to the second stimulus would occur, but which are observed in the absence of the second stimulus. The first two classes are elaborated here. Two experiments explore responses in the interstimulus interval. The number of such responses, their probability of occurrence, and the magnitudes of changes, identified either by ordinal number of occurrence or latency, all show differential behavior in the form of reinforcement effects (pairing versus nonpairing) and trace-delay conditioning differences. Preparatory responses of the second class are illustrated by phenomena from conditioning studies, namely UCR diminution and perceptual disparity responding. The data are interpreted as demonstrating the signal character of the first stimulus which sets or prepares the individual for receipt of the second stimulus.

stimulus characteristics
paired stimuli
anticipatory responses
preparatory set

N 8   Kimmel, E.: Judgments of UCS intensity and diminution of the UCR in classical GSR conditioning. *J Exp Psychol, 73:* 532, 1967.

This GSR conditioning study evaluated a conditioned inhibition explanation of UCR diminution and recovery in

conditioned inhibition

classical conditioning. Ss were randomly assigned to nine groups of eighteen Ss each, with six groups comprising the main experiment and three for control purposes. All Ss had sixteen trials of CS-UCS either paired or unpaired and two trials of UCS alone. The GSR to the CS (light), the GSR to the UCS (shock), and the intensity judgments of the shock were obtained. A comparison of the CRs in the paired and unpaired groups showed that conditioning occurred and was a positive function of CS duration. Diminution of the UCR and its recovery on test trials was greater in the paired groups than the unpaired groups. Although CS duration failed to produce significant difference in this effect, the five-second group demonstrated the greatest degree of it. The judgment data paralleled the UCRs during training in the three and one second paired groups, but on the test trials the judgment dropped while the UCRs increased. The results were interpreted to mean that a simple associative explanation of UCR diminution was more or less compatible with the data.

shock intensity subjective judgments

9 Mordkoff, Arnold M.: Palmar-dorsal skin conductance differences during classical conditioning. *Psychophysiology*, 5:61, 1968.

Investigated the sweat gland-epidermis basis of the skin conductance response in a study in which measurements were obtained from both the palmar and dorsal surfaces of the hand during classical conditioning. In a previous study using a long CS-UCS interval, palmar measurements, representing mainly the sweat gland component, gave rise to larger anticipatory CRs. In this study (CS-UCS interval = .5 sec.) it was predicted and confirmed on the basis of an adaptation theory that the epidermal component (dorsal measurement) would predominate and be equal to or greater than that of the sweat gland (palmar measurement). Ss were ten 17 to 27-year-old males.

response components sweat glands mechanisms

10 Prokasy, W.F., and Ebel, H.C.: Three components of the classically conditioned GSR in human subjects. *J Exp Psychol,* 73:247, 1967.

Three responses were defined by a latency criterion in human GSR conditioning conducted with an eight-second interstimulus interval: 1.35 to 4.95, 4.95 to 9.53, and 9.53 to 14.55 seconds after CS onset for the first, second, and third responses. It was found that (1) the first and second responses were statistically independent; (2) increasing the CS intensity increased first response frequency (but not amplitude) and did not affect the second response at all; (3) of the three responses, only the second did not show a postasymptotic decrement; (4) the second response was essentially probabilistic, no amplitude changes were observed; (5) the first response was similar in many respects to the alpha response in eyelid conditioning; and (6) the third response, though not statistically independent of the second, was sufficiently distinct to merit further study.

response compon- ents stimulus character- istics

N 11 Schell, Anne M., and Grings, William W.: Judgments of UCS intensity and diminution of the unconditioned GSR. *Psychophysiology, 8:*427, 1971.

Perceptions of UCS intensity associated with UCR diminution in a classical conditioning situation were investigated using a procedure in which S matched the loudness of a tone of variable intensity to that of a white noise UCS. Changes in the subjective loudness of the UCS paralleling the changes in UCR magnitude observed with CS-UCS pairings were found.

stimulus intensity subjective judgment

N 12 Wickens, D.D., and Harding, G.B.: Effect of UCS strength on GSR conditioning: A within subject design. *J Exp Psychol, 70:*151, 1965.

Using a within-S design, 20 Ss had one CS (light or tone) associated with a stronger UCS (2.5 ma shock) for ten trials and the other CS (tone or light) associated with a weaker UCS of 1.5 ma. The ISI was one second and the response measured was GSR. The data during training and extinction indicate a clear superiority of the strong over the weak UCS-associated CS. Results are contrasted with a comparable within-subject design where differences failed to reach significance and use of a within-subject design for GSR is recommended wherever possible.

stimulus character- istics method- ology

N 13 Wittig, A.F., and Wickens, D.D.: Latency and magnitude of GSR as a function of interstimulus interval. *J Exp Psychol, 71:*466, 1966.

The relationship between latency and magnitude was studied as a function of ISI. The correlations between the two measures varied between —.68 and —.85 on the extinction trials. Significant differences among groups as a function of ISI were found only for the latency measure, but both measures showed maximal conditioning in the 450 to 1250 msec. range.

response character- istics
stimulus character- istics
GSR latency
GSR magni- tude

CONDITIONING PROCEDURES

N 14 Baer, Paul E., and Fuhrer, Marcus J.: Cognitive processes in the differential trace conditioning of electrodermal and vaso- motor activity. *J Exp Psychol, 84:*176, 1970.

Postconditioning interviews of 20 Ss who underwent differ- ent trace conditioning of concurrently recorded electro- dermal and vasomotor responses were assessed for S's ability to conceptualize the differential stimulus relations accurately. Confirming the results of Baer and Fuhrer, who used both intertrial verbal reports and postconditioning interviews, it was found that electrodermal differentiation occurred only among accurately verbalizing Ss (N = 11). Concordance be- tween accuracy of verbalization and the extent of differential conditioning was also demonstrated for vasomotor responses, though the extent of vasomotor and electrodermal condition- ing was not significantly correlated.

trace condi- tioning
cognitive processes
vasomotor responses
verbal behavior

N 15 Baxter, R.: Diminution and recovery of the UCR in delayed and trace classical GSR conditioning. *J Exp Psychol, 71:*447, 1966.

A study of the effects of CS duration on UCR decrement. Four groups of sixteen Ss received sixteen paired and un- paired tone-shock presentations with either a short or a long CS followed by four UCS-only test trials. The dependent variable was the GSR measured within four seconds follow- ing stimulus onset. The results showed a significantly greater

delayed con- ditioning
trace con- ditioning
stimulus character- istics

degree of UCR decrement during acquisition for the Ss in paired groups. Also Ss in the paired groups differed significantly (in favor of delayed CS) in amount of UCR recovery as a function of CS duration during acquisition. It was concluded that a conditioned inhibition process under control of the CS was one of the factors responsible for UCR decrement in classical conditioning.

conditioned inhibition

N 16   Burstein, Kenneth R., and Epstein, Seymour: Procedure for reducing orienting reactions in GSR conditioning. *J Exp Psychol, 78:*369, 1968.

Fifteen Ss received sixteen adaptation, sixteen conditioning, and sixteen extinction trials with an apparatus designed to eliminate reflex ORs to stimulus onset. The apparatus consisted of a dial with markings for CS intervals and a moving pointer. The UCS, an electric shock, occurred at CS offset. That the procedure effectively eliminated reflex ORs was exhibited by an extremely low rate of responses in the absence of threat of shock. Threat of shock increased responses to stimulus onset. During conditioning there was an early rise in response for the conditioning interval only followed by a protracted decline. It was concluded that habituation of the CR during conditioning and implicit expectancies associated with the stimulus situation continue to complicate GSR conditioning when reflex ORs to the CS are eliminated.

*classical conditioning
orienting response
procedures
threat
expectancy
habituation*

N 17   Corah, N.L.: "Trialess" conditioning of the electrodermal response. *Psychophysiology, 9:*266, 1972.

Conditioning of the EDR was attempted in a context approaching real life situations, i.e. in a fluid context without discrete trials. A differential paradigm was used with a dental film as the CS+ and a training film as the CS−. Ten different points in CS+ were programmed for shock UCS presentation. The same intervals in CS− were keyed for comparison. Ss viewed the training film and then the dental film. This sequence was repeated. Three groups of 10 Ss each participated: a no-shock control group, a group shocked ten times during the first presentation of CS+, and a group shocked during the first CS+ and three times during the second pre-

*trialess conditioning
pictorial
stimuli
anticipatory
responses
EDR*

sentation. Analysis of EDRs following the seven no-shock points during the second presentation gave no significant result. Analysis of the responses occurring in the five seconds preceding each point ("anticipatory responses") yielded significant differences between the dental and training films for the two reinforcement groups but not for the control group. There were no differences between the two reinforced groups. It was concluded that a specific anticipatory response was conditioned.

18 Furedy, John J.: Explicitly-unpaired and truly random CS-controls in human classical differential autonomic conditioning. *Psychophysiology, 8:*497, 1971.

The conventionally used explicitly-unpaired CS- (euCS-) of the differential conditioning paradigm, a stimulus which is negatively correlated with the US, may generate inhibition and hence be an inappropriate control for CS+ conditioning. An implication of this possibility is that the CS+-euCS— performance difference should exceed the difference between CS+ performance and performance to a truly random CS— (trCS—) , a stimulus which is uncorrelated with US occurrence. This implication was tested in a five-second delay conditioning skin resistance response study (Experiment I, N = 32) and an 8-second delay conditioning plethysmographic digital pulse volume response study (Experiment II, N = 48) . While highly reliable discrimination between CS+ and the two control CSs (euCS— and trCS—) was obtained in both experiments, neither experiment yielded the outcome expected from the position that euCS— generates inhibition.

control procedures finger pulse volume vasomotor response

19 Furedy, J.J., and Schiffman, K.: Tests of the propriety and traditional discriminative control procedure in Pavlovian electrodermal and plethysmographic conditioning. *J Exp Psychol, 91:*161, 1971.

According to R. Rescorla's contingency position, the traditionally used explicitly unpaired CS of the differential conditioning paradigm is an inappropriate control for CS+ conditioning. It follows that the CS+:euCS— performance difference should exceed the difference between CS+ per-

classical conditioning delayed conditioning

formance and performance to a truly random CS— (trCS), *condition-*
a stimulus which is uncorrelated with UCS occurrence. This *ing per-*
implication was tested on thirty-two undergraduates in a .75- *formance*
second delay conditioning study with GSR and digital *controls*
volume pulse change as dependent autonomic variables. Re- *autonomic*
liable autonomic discrimination between CS+ and the two *response*
control CSs (euCS— and trCS) was obtained, but the impli- *discrimina-*
cation derived from the contingency position was not con- *tion*
firmed in either autonomic measure, even though Ss were
shown to be aware of the contingency differences considered
important by Rescorla.

N 20   Geer, J.H.: A test of the classical conditioning model of emotion: The use of nonpainful aversive stimuli as unconditioned stimuli in a conditioning procedure. *J Pers Soc
Psychol, 10:*148, 1968.

A test of classical conditioning model of human emotions *aversive con-*
was conducted using aversive, but not painful stimuli. Forty- *ditioning*
eight subjects equally divided between sexes, assigned to *model test-*
groups having either forward, backward or random associa- *ing*
tion between CS's (tones) and UCS (color photos of victims *emotion*
of violent deaths). Results using GSR as the P.V. indicate
that whenever comparing forward with backward conditioning, model held quite well. Conditioning of random association between CS and UCS produced the greatest effect. Subjects were more reactive in that condition than in either
forward or backward conditioning. Data were interpreted to
indicate that subjects were sensitive to conditioning of random association between stimuli and that conditioning has
powerful effects. Further, when conditions for the conditioning model are met, the model appears to predict outcome.

N 21   Grings, William W., and Lockhart, Russell A.: Galvanic
skin response during avoidance learning. *Psychophysiology,
3:*29, 1966.

Relations between galvanic skin response (GSR) and other *avoidance*
variables during learning of a shock-avoidance task were *instruction*
observed. Ss operated a four-position switch as cued by visual *expectancy*
stimuli: one always shocked, one never shocked, and two *GSR*

associated with switch positions which avoided the shock. Forty-eight Ss formed successive subgroups which exhibited: (1) progressively better avoidance learning with increased awareness instruction and (2) significantly decreased GSR when the correct avoidance had been learned. Analyses were made to differentiate autonomic responding due to reinforcement (i.e. number of shocks received) from that due to expectancy (anticipation of avoidance).

22 Grings, William W., and Uno, Tadao: Counterconditioning: Fear and relaxation. *Psychophysiology, 4:*479, 1968.

Counterconditioning of autonomic responses was evaluated by means of a compound stimulus transfer paradigm. During three sessions on different days Ss were conditioned to give a GSR to a visual stimulus (colored light) and further trained to relax on presentation of a visually projected stimulus word. After training on both experiences had progressed, test trials were introduced to assess the magnitude of response to the fear cue alone and to the compound stimulus created by simultaneous presentation of both cues (the word superimposed on the colored light background). Significant inhibitory transfer effects were observed with the GSR. On the last test trials the digital pulse volume showed less constriction to the compound of fear and relaxation stimuli than to the fear stimulus alone.

countercon- ditioning stimulus transfer color visual signals fear finger pulse volume

23 Kimmel, H.D., Sternthal, H.S., and Strub, H.: Two replications of avoidance conditioning of the GSR. *J Exp Psychol,* 72:151, 1966.

Two replications of an earlier study of avoidance conditioning of the GSR were done. The first involved twenty-two pairs of Ss who received a visual CS and the second used twenty-one pairs of Ss who received an auditory CS. The CS-US interval was five seconds in both studies. Following a series of CS-only trials, paired acquisition trials were run in which the avoidance S of a pair could make a criterion GSR that resulted in both Ss of the pair avoiding the shock. Following acquisition all Ss were given ten extinction trials. The results of both studies showed that the avoidance Ss made

avoidance condition- ing GSR

larger GSRs than the control Ss during acquisition and extinction, but the only significant effect was that of the combined extinction differences. It was concluded that these results provided further support for the assertion that the GSR
can be conditioned with an avoidance procedure.

N 24   Kimmel, H.D., and Sternthal, H.S.: Replication of GSR
       avoidance conditioning with concomitant EMG measure-
       ment and subjects matched in responsivity and condition-
       ability. *J Exp Psychol*, 74:144, 1967.

This study replicated Kimmel and Baxter's (1964) on avoid-   *avoidance*
ance conditioning of the GSR with yoked pairs of avoidance   *GSR magni*
and control Ss matched in responsivity and conditionability   *tude*
and with concomitant EMG measurement. The nineteen   *GSR re-*
pairs of Ss (of a total of twenty-four) who were most closely   *sponsivity*
matched in responsivity and conditionability differed in ad- *condition-*
justed GSR magnitude during acquisition (but not quite   *ability*
significantly), and the difference vanished during extinction. *EMG*
It was concluded that the use of a yoked control design without matching Ss in responsivity and conditionability may
tend to exaggerate the observed avoidance conditioning effect
spuriously. The EMG measures were found to be unrelated
to GSR responses and not capable of explaining the differences that were observed.

N 25   Lockhart, R.A.: Temporal conditioning of GSR. *J Exp
       Psychol*, 71:438, 1966.

Temporal conditioning (time as CS, shock as UCS) of the   *temporal*
GSR was demonstrated in a situation where spontaneous re-   *condition-*
sponding sensitization, reactive inhibition, and time-estima-   *ing*
tion processes were properly controlled. The nature of   *theory*
"Time" as an elicitive stimulus is discussed in terms of
stimulus trace and response-produced stimulus cycle, both of
which are considered inadequate explanations of temporal
conditioning. The acquisitioning and the failure to extinguish the temporal CR pose theoretical problems.

N 26   McDonald, David G.: A re-analysis of GSR conditioning.
       Psychophysiology, 1:291, 1965.

Lockhart and Grings (1963) have suggested that a previous analysis of galvanic skin response (GSR) conditioning by Stewart, Stern, Winokur and Fredman (1961) failed to establish its major point since it neglected to include a pseudoconditioning control for sensitization effects. In the present paper an experiment is reported in which this control was included, and it was found that the initial report of Stewart, et al. was supported. That is, there was significant evidence of a conditional anticipatory GSR which was not due to sensitization effects.

classical conditioning
controls
conditioning procedures
anticipatory responses

N 27 Mordkoff, Arnold M., Edelberg, Robert, and Ustick, Michael: The differential conditionability of two components of the skin conductance response. *Psychophysiology, 4:*40, 1967.

The dual effector basis of the skin conductance response (SCR) was investigated in an experiment in which responses from both the dorsal and palmar surfaces of the hand were classically conditioned using a delayed discrimination conditioning paradigm. Orienting (OR), anticipatory (AR) and unconditional responses (UCR) were distinguished on the basis of latency. Both the anticipatory response and the response which occurred when the unconditional stimulus (UCS) was omitted (CR) were conditional. The magnitude of the response from the dorsal and palmar placements was similar for the ORs, UCRs and CRs, but the palmar ARs were significantly greater than the dorsal. A conditioning index which took into account the magnitude of the UCR, revealed that the palmar AR differentiated between reinforced and nonreinforced conditional stimuli to a greater degree than the dorsal response. These results are consistent with the hypothesis that the epidermal component of the SCR, reflected in measurements from the dorsum of the hand, accompanies the alerting or orienting response of the organism, whereas the sweat gland component of the SCR, represented largely in measurements from palmar sites is primarily associated with a defensive, anxiety-like response.

differential conditioning
orienting response
anticipatory responses
sweat glands
mechanisms

N 28 Morrow, M.C., Seiffert, P.D., and Kramer, Lorr L.: GSR conditioning and pseudoconditioning with prolonged practice. *Psychol Rep, 27:*39, 1970.

Gave two groups of fourteen undergraduate Ss each, sixteen
conditioning or pseudoconditioning trials/day for five days.
The compound (light-tone) CS was paired with a 3.5 ma
electric shock (interstimulus interval = .5 sec.) in the conditioning group, but the stimuli were not paired in the pseudoconditioning group. On day six both groups received two
counterbalanced CS-element test trials and then eighteen
CS-compound extinction trials. During acquisition, the conditioning group produced significantly larger GSRs overall
than the pseudoconditioning group, and the former's responses generally increased over test trials on each day while
the latter's responses declined. There was an overall decrease
in GSR magnitude overnight in the conditioning group and
an overall rise in the pseudoconditioning group. The GSR
was significantly smaller in the conditioning group on the
first element test trial than it was on the first compound trial
on day five, but it was not significantly different from the
final compound trial on day five, or from the mean of the
first two compound trials on day six. There was a sustained,
statistically significant difference in mean magnitude between the two groups across the extinction trials with very
little evidence of any extinction effects.

*practice
pseudocon-
ditioning
GSR magni-
tude*

N 29   Ohman, Arne: Interaction between instruction-induced expectance and strength of unconditioned stimulus in GSR
conditioning. *J Exp Psychol, 88*:384, 1971.

After twelve long interstimulus interval GSR conditioning
trials, four groups of Ss were instructed about increases or
decreases in the intensity of the shock that was used as the
UCS. The actual shock was then increased or decreased in
strength. For a control group, the shock was not mentioned
in the instruction, and the actual shock was not changed. On
the trial immediately following instruction, the magnitude
of the CS and pre-UCS responses were found to be manipula-
ble in an upward but not in a downward direction through
the instruction. On the second and third trials following instruction, the pre-UCS response was biggest when there was
a conflict between the instruction and the actual shocks,
whereas the CS response was primarily determined by shock
intensity. The UCR was found to be smallest when the in-

*classical con
ditioning
condition-
ing proce-
dures
instructions
expectancy*

struction about changes in shock intensity was in agreement with the actual changes.

30 Orlebeke, J.F., and Van Olst, E.H.: Learning and performance as a function of CS-intensity in a delayed GSR conditioning situation. *J Exp Psychol, 77*:483, 1968.

Refutes Razran's prediction that the amount of conditioning is a function of the intensity of the CS. A difficulty in testing Razran's statement is how to distinguish in experimental operations the learning component and the performance component of a GSR. These components were recorded separately in a delayed GSR-conditioning procedure, with a ten-second CS. The results showed that the conditioned anticipatory responses (latency 3 to 11 sec.) did not vary with CS intensity; however, sensitization responses, occurring with shorter latencies, showed the expected intensity effect. In the data treatment, GSRs were expressed as △log C only. If, however, GSRs expressed as △log C were corrected for conductance changes on adaptation trials, dissimilar results were to be expected. It was shown that such methods of correction are inappropriate in comparisons of effects of different stimulus-intensity conditions.

delayed conditioning
response components
stimulus intensity

31 Pendergrass, Virginia E., and Kimmel, H.D.: UCR diminution in temporal conditioning and habituation. *J Exp Psychol, 77*:1, 1968.

A study was done to compare diminution of the GSR to a 1,000-cps tone during regular and irregular temporal spacing of the tones and to determine the influence of a judgment task on the GSR under these conditions. One group received a 90-db tone every forty seconds for forty trials, while one group received the series of forty tones at irregular temporal intervals of twenty, thirty, forty, fifty, or sixty seconds. In addition, half of the Ss in each group were required to judge the intensity of the UCS after each stimulus presentation. No evidence was found for temporal conditioning in the non-judgment groups, although there did appear to be anticipatory conditioned responding in the judgment groups. It was suggested that the task facilitated the development of antici-

reinforcement schedule
judgment task
anticipatory responses
habituation

patory responding in temporal conditioning, and as a consequence also resulted in smaller GSRs to the tone. In habituation, however, the task appeared to disrupt the ongoing process and eliminated response attenuation. Increased arousal
or attention induced by the task and/or by S's perception of
regular spacing was proposed as a possible explanation of
these effects.

N 32   Prescott, James W.: Neural timing mechanisms, conditioning, and the CS-UCS interval. *Psychophysiology*, 2:125, 1966.

The history of GSR classical conditioning studies on the op-   *delayed con-*
timal CS-UCS interval has been evaluated in the context of   *ditioning*
the phenomena of internal inhibition of delay (IID), an   *neural tim-*
effect of delayed reinforcement. It was concluded from this   *ing mecha-*
review that nearly all GSR studies concerned with this theor- *nisms*
etical issue lack validity, since responses to stimulus onset *review*
(orienting and unconditioned responses) and not delayed
conditioned responses have been the subject of measurement.
The existence of an "optimal" CS-UCS interval is questionable, however, and appropriate experimental methodology is
suggested for the solution of this problem. The role of
temporal processes in classical conditioning has been emphasized, and the concept of "precision" in neural timing
mechanisms mediating delayed CRs has been advanced. It
is suggested that the neural temporal properties of the conditioning process have greater heuristic value than the intensity
properties of the conditioned response.

N 33   Schell, Anne M., and Grings, William W.: Avoidance conditioning of the GSR: Nature of the response. *Psychophysiology,* 7:402, 1971.

The effects of avoidance conditioning of the GSR on HR re-   *avoidance*
sponses were investigated. Seven Ss were allowed to avoid a   *condition-*
shock if their GSR during a preceding 5.0 second light was   *ing*
greater than a criterion magnitude. Each avoidance S had a   *contingency*
yoked-control partner who received exactly the same series   *awareness*
of shocked and nonshocked trials, regardless of his own GSR   *HR*
behavior. Sixty trials were given. Avoidance Ss gave significantly larger GSRs and cardiac deceleration took place at a

significantly greater rate in the avoidance group. The results were interpreted as supporting the conclusion that when an avoidance paradigm is used to modify a particular autonomic response, the effects extend to other autonomic arousal or anticipatory responses. Each S was questioned in a posttraining interview about his awareness of means of avoiding the shock. No S was able to verbalize any method that could be used to prevent shock from occurring.

N 34   Shnidman, Susan R.: Avoidance conditioning of skin potential responses. *Psychophysiology, 6:*38, 1969.

Avoidance of electric shock was used to manipulate skin potential changes elicited by a simple visual stimulus. Experimental and control Ss were matched on habituation trials and yoked for forty acquisition and ten extinction trials. During acquisition the avoidance Ss differentiated between stimulus and nonstimulus periods more reliably than the controls. During extinction the avoidance group produced significantly more criterion electrodermal responses with greater magnitude of positive wave components than the control group. Some of the problems of appropriate control procedures inherent in this design are examined in relation to these results.

avoidance conditioning
response rate
SPR

COGNITIVE PROCESSES

N 35   Baer, Paul E., and Fuhrer, Marcus J.: Cognitive processes during differential trace and delayed conditioning of the GSR. *J Exp Psychol, 78:*81, 1968.

The concordance between conditional GSR differentiation and ability to verbalize conditional stimulus relations accurately was assessed in twenty-six trace conditioned Ss. The CSs were 1.5-second tones of differing frequencies, the UCS was a shock, and the CS-UCS interval was eight seconds. Division of the ISI and the post-UCS period into three intervals permitted the analyses of multiple GSRs. Both intertrial reports and postconditioning interviews were obtained. Conditional differentiation was limited to a group of 10 Ss who accurately verbalized the stimulus contingencies during postconditioning interviews. In a comparison group of

trace conditioning
delayed conditioning
stimulus schedules
contingency awareness
verbal behavior
GSR differentiation

twenty-six delayed conditioned Ss, more Ss (eighteen) verbalized accurately. Both the trace and delayed groups showed
significant first interval GSR differentiation during acquisition. The trace group did not differentiate in the second
interval during acquisition, nor in any of the three intervals
during extinction, but the delayed group did. Assessing GSR
differentiation in accurately verbalizing Ss only, trace Ss did
not condition in the second interval during acquisition nor
in the first two intervals during extinction; delayed Ss conditioned in all relevant intervals.

N 36   Bridger, W.H., and Mandel, I.J.: Abolition of the PRE by
       instructions in GSR conditioning. *J Exp Psychol, 69:*476,
       1965.

Eighty human Ss divided into two groups of CRF and two   *information*
groups of 25 percent PRF were used in a GSR classical condi-   *stimulus dis-*
tioning paradigm to test the discrimination hypothesis as an   *crimina-*
explanation of the PRE. Removal of the shock electrodes   *tion*
and instructions as to the onset of extinction was assumed to   *GSR*
provide equalization of discriminability between the acquisition and extinction series for one PRF and one CRF group.
A postexperimental inquiry for these informed groups provided a test of discriminability independent of resistance to
extinction. The results demonstrated the presence of the
PRE in the noninformed groups and its abolition in the informed. The presence of a conditioned GSR during extinction in the informed groups combined with the abolition of
the PRE suggests a two-component CR characterized as a
simple conditioned CR and a mediated CR.

N 37   Brotsky, S. Joyce: Classical conditioning of the galvanic skin
       response to verbal concepts. *J Exp Psychol, 76:*250, 1968.

Semantic conditioning of the GSR in 200 undergraduates   *verbal*
was established through the auditory presentation of neutral   *stimuli*
words, with interspersed CS-UCS pairings. The CSs were   *concept gen-*
verbal stimuli (concept instances) to which a common re-   *eralization*
sponse (concept name) could be given. The number of dif-   *condition-*
ferent reinforced CSs and the number of reinforcements of   *ability*
each CS were systematically varied. The UCS, one second of   *GSR magni-*
                                                                tude

white noise, followed the CS by ten seconds. Reliable generalization of the GSR from a concept instance to the concept name was demonstrated. Ss who showed strong conditioning and generalization were better able to verbalize the experimental contingencies and showed greater negative shifts on semantic differential ratings of the test words. Although Ss who produced large GSRs to the first UCS produced large GSRs to other auditory stimuli, they showed neither stronger conditioning, generalization, nor more adequate verbal reports than Ss with low orienting reflexes.

verbalization
orienting response

N 38 Carey, C.A., Schell, A.M., and Grings, W.W.: Effect of ISI and reversal manipulation on cognitive control of the conditioned GSR. *Psychophysiology, 9:*266, 1972.

This study was designed to test the effects of basic parameters on the cognitive control of the classically conditioned GSR. Forty-eight undergraduates received initial and transfer training trials with colored lights as the CSs and an electric shock as the UCS. All Ss were informed of the CS-UCS relationship before both initial and transfer trials. During the initial phase, half of the Ss received pseudoconditioning trials and half discrimination conditioning trials, and for half of *these* groups the interstimulus interval (ISI) (or CS duration for pseudoconditioning groups) was 0.5 seconds and for half 7.0 seconds. In transfer trials, the conditioning groups received a reversal task while the pseudoconditioning groups received their first discrimination problem. Both conditioning groups discriminated on initial trials. On transfer trials all four groups showed significant overall and first trial discrimination with no between-group differences. It appears that the instructional variable overrides any ISI or transfer from initial learning effects.

cognitive control
colored visual signals
instructions
pseudoconditioning
stimulus discrimination
learning transfer

N 39 Cole, Spurgeon N., and Sipprelle, Carl N.: Extinction of a classically conditioned GSR as a function of awareness. *Behav Res Ther, 5:*331, 1967.

Insight, defined as the ability to verbalize the stimulus-response contingency of acquisition, has been found to be unrelated to the extinction of an operantly conditioned verbal

contingency awareness
verbalization

response. A GSR response was classically conditioned in
thirty 18-year-old male college students. Ss were divided into
insight and no-insight groups following acquisition, and extinction trials were run which demonstrated a positive relationship (p < .001) under these particular conditions. It was
concluded that the role of insight in extinction is a complex
function of mode of conditioning (classical versus operant)
and/or mode of response (voluntary versus involuntary), and
that further studies utilizing the classical-voluntary and oper-
ant-involuntary combinations will be needed to define that
function.

insight
extinction
GSR

N 40   Courter, R.J., Wattenmaker, R.A., and Ax, A.F.: Physio-
        logical concomitants of psychological differentiation. *Psycho-
        physiology, 1:*282, 1965.

Thirty-two male college students who scored above 50 (standard score) on the Closure Flexibility (CF) test were designated field independent (FI), and eight who scored below 50
were designated field dependent (FD). It was found that FI
subjects were able to discriminate between the conditioned
tone (CS) and the unreinforced generalization tones by the
amplitude of their GSR significantly better (p < 0.01) than
were FD persons. Although it cannot be asserted with certainty that this relationship is dependent on the autonomic
response system, there is tentative support for this position.
It seems probable that even the FD subjects could distinguish
between the two most differently pitched tones; yet they
failed to make this distinction by their GSR responses. This
lack of differentiation by the FD subject appears to be a function of a less well-differentiated autonomic nervous system.
This study demonstrates that the stimulus generalization
gradient involves an interaction between the cognitive style
of the organism and the impinging stimuli, not merely the
quantitative physical characteristics of the stimuli.

field de-
pendency
stimulus di
crimina-
tion
cognitive
style
closure

N 41   Dawson, M.E., and Grings, W.W.: Comparison of classical
        conditioning and relational learning. *J Exp Psychol, 76:*227,
        1968.

Classical conditioning and relational learning were compared
with the human GSR using fifty-four undergraduates as Ss.

masking tas
relational
learning

The experiment consisted of four parts: (1) adaptation in which all Ss were presented CS alone; (2) acquisition I in which the CC group was presented CS-UCS pairings but was prevented from learning the CS-UCS relation by masking task, and the RL group was presented a pseudoconditioning paradigm; (3) acquisition II in which all Ss terminated the masking task, the RL group was informed of a CS-UCS relation and all Ss were presented 1 CS-UCS pairing in the middle of four pairs of test trials; and (4) extinction instructions and all Ss were administered extinction trials. Results indicate that: (1) masked CS-UCS pairings were not sufficient to establish conditioned GSRs, (2) information of a CS-UCS relation was sufficient to establish condition-like GSRs, and (3) extinction instructions were sufficient to abolish conditioned-like GSRs.

42 Dawson, Michael E., and Satterfield, James H.: Can human GSR conditioning occur without relational learning? *Proceedings of the 77th Annual Convention of APA, 4*:69, 1969.

Twenty-five paid college students were presented a series of CS-UCS pairings embedded in a masking task. One group was and one group was not informed of the CS-UCS relation. The informed group demonstrated conditioning while the noninformed group did not. Within the limiting conditions of the experiment, these findings suggest that relational learning is a necessary condition for human GSR classical conditioning.

contingency awareness

43 Dawson, Michael E.: Cognition and conditioning: Effects of masking the CS-UCS contingency on human GSR classical conditioning. *J Exp Psychol, 85*:389, 1970.

A discrimination classical conditioning paradigm was embedded in a masking task and presented to seventy-five undergraduates to attenuate learning of the CS-UCS contingency without affecting perception of the individual CSs. One half of the Ss were instructed about the CS-UCS contingency, while the other one-half were not. Results were that instructed Ss conditioned, while the noninstructed Ss failed to condition. Results were confirmed whether the CS-UCS in-

contingency awareness stimulus discrimination

terval was one or eight seconds and whether the number of trials was thirty or sixty. These findings, in conjunction with other reports, suggest that the ability to verbalize the CS-UCS contingency is an important, perhaps even essential, variable in human GSR classical conditioning.

N 44   Dawson, Michael E., and Biferno, Michael A.: Concurrent measurement of awareness and electrodermal classical conditioning. *Psychophysiology, 10:*197, 1973.

The purpose of this experiment was three-fold: (1) to devise a method of measuring awareness of the CS-UCS contingency concurrently with electrodermal classical conditioning, (2) to test the validity of the measuring device and, (3) to relate the temporal development of awareness with that of electrodermal classical conditioning. The Ss, fifty-six paid volunteer college students, were administered a discrimination delay classical conditioning paradigm embedded in a masking task. The CSs were tones of eight seconds duration, the UCS was a shock of .5 second duration, and the CS-UCS interval was eight seconds. All Ss were instructed to push buttons during the experiment so as to express their expectancy of the shock (UCS). The five buttons were arranged in a row and labeled "certain no shock," "uncertain no shock," "completely uncertain," "uncertain shock," "certain shock." Activation of each button controlled varying magnitudes of pen deflections on one channel of the polygraph. Thus, on each conditioning trial, S's expectancy of shock as well as the GSR was recorded. Awareness of the correct CS-UCS contingency was inferred if S made three consecutive predictions of greater probability of shock to CS+ than to CS−. It was shown that this method of measuring awareness of the CS-UCS relationship is valid. It was also shown that GSR classical conditioning (in both the "orienting response" interval as well as in the "anticipatory response" interval) occurred only at the time that awareness had developed. There was no GSR conditioning prior to the development of awareness. These results support the hypothesis that awareness of the CS-UCS contingency is an essential factor in human GSR classical conditioning.

contingency
awareness
electric
shock
anticipatory
responses

45 Erlebacher, Albert: Differential GSR conditioning with a complex CS. *Psychon Sci, 12:*129, 1968.

Investigated the effect of stimulus information on differential conditioning by using geometrical figures with one relevant and one irrelevant piece of information as CSs. Ss were forty undergraduates. Differential conditioning was possible. Conditioning was rapid, indicating the influence of concept formation or language. The effect of control variables had minimal influence on conditioning.

cognitive informa-tion

stimulus dis-crimina-tion

concept formation

46 Fuhrer, M.J., and Baer, P.E.: Differential classical conditioning: Verbalization of stimulus contingencies. *Science, 150:*1479, 1965. (Copyright 1965 by the American Association for the Advancement of Science.)

The verbal activity of female subjects undergoing differential classical conditioning was investigated through their verbal reports between conditioning trials and interviews with them after conditioning. Conditional differentiation in galvanic skin responses occurred only in the group of subjects who accurately verbalized the stimulus contingencies.

contingency awareness

verbal behavior

47 Fuhrer, Marcus J., and Baer, Paul E.: Cognitive processes in differential GSR conditioning: Effects of a masking task. *Am J Psychol, 82:*168, 1969.

Differential GSR conditioning was assessed in a group (N = 43) which had the conditioning procedure embedded in a probability-learning task (Group M) and in a comparison group (N = 24) which underwent a conventional differential-conditioning procedure (Group C). The CSs were eight-second tones of differing frequencies, the UCS was a shock, and the CS-UCS interval was eight seconds. Division of the CS-UCS and the post-UCS period into three 4-second intervals permitted the analysis of multipile GSRs. Content analyses of postconditioning interviews indicated that 62 percent of the Ss in Group C verbalized the stimulus relations accurately, while only 30 percent of the Ss in Group M did so. As expected from a cognitive viewpoint, Group M showed

cognitive awareness

masking

verbaliza-tion

significantly less conditional differentiation of GSRs in all three intervals. Significant GSR conditioning was observed in the three intervals for the fifteen accurate verbalizers in Group C, but there was no evidence of conditioning in any interval for the nine inaccurate verbalizers. The thirteen accurate verbalizers in Group M showed significant second-interval differentiation while the thirty inaccurate verbalizers did not. However, both accurate and inaccurate verbalizers in Group M showed significant first-interval conditioning during the late acquisition trials.

N 48   Furedy, John J., and Ginsberg, Stanley: Effects of varying signaling and intensity of shock on an unconfounded and novel electrodermal autonomic index in a variable and long-interval classical trace conditioning paradigm. *Psychophysiology, 10:*328, 1973.

After a review of the evidence against the role of autonomic responses in the mediation of informational cognitive control, which occurs when merely signaling an inescapable shock reduces perceived aversiveness, it was noted that verbal indices of aversiveness had yielded results which were contrary to the informational control notion itself. On the other hand, the fact that signaled shocks elicit smaller autonomic responding than unsignaled shocks still does not support the notion, because of confounding through response interference. In the present experiment with 48 Ss, electrodermal recovery time was examined as an unconfounded and novel autonomic index of the relative aversiveness of signaled and unsignaled shocks in a specially adapted form of the differential conditioning paradigm. This autonomic index was sensitive to the UCS-intensity manipulation, but despite this sensitivity, both this autonomic index and other verbal indices showed that, contrary to the informational-control notion, signaling does not reduce shock aversiveness.

aversive stimuli non-signal stimuli differential conditioning stimulus intensity verbal behavior informational cognitive control

N 49   Gruber, Ronald P., Reed, David R., and Block, James D.: Transfer of the conditioned GSR from drug to nondrug state without awareness. *J Psychol, 70:*149, 1968.

Conditioning of the GSR was carried out in human subjects during and after light planes of general anesthesia. During

non-awareness

the anesthetic (drug) state, subjects showed no evidence of a GSR to the experimental stimuli. However, the testing twenty-four hours later (in nondrug state) indicated that (1) subjects had no awareness of events occurring during the drug state, and (2) subjects demonstrated a residual conditioned GSR. Awareness, as well as the conditioned GSR, was discussed in terms of a learning process that may transfer from a drug to a nondrug state. Factors which influence the transfer of learning were implicated as the means by which the conditioned GSR but not awareness was evident in the nondrug state.

anesthesia
condition-
ability
state
dependent
learning
memory
GSR

50 Mandel, I.J., and Bridger, W.H.: Interaction between instructions and ISI in conditioning and extinction of the GSR. *J Exp Psychol, 74:*36, 1967.

Ninety human Ss acquired a differentially conditioned GSR with an instructed acquisition procedure under three different interstimulus intervals (ISIs): backward (UCS-CS), and 500 msec and five seconds forward. At the onset of extinction each ISI group was divided into informed and noninformed halves. A postexperimental inquiry eliminated those informed Ss who did not believe the extinction instructions. The backward conditioned GSR group did not demonstrate resistance to extinction under either extinction condition. Among the two forward ISI groups during extinction the five seconds group demonstrated a larger differential response under the noninformed condition while the 500 msec group had a larger differential response under the informed condition. Both forward ISI groups demonstrated differential extinction responses under the informed condition contrary to their cognitive expectancy. Alternative theories are presented to account for the results.

differential
condition-
ing
instructions
extinction
cognitive
expectancy

51 Prokasy, William F., Williams, William C., Kumpfer, Karol L., Lee, William Yu-Ming, and Jenson, William R.: Differential SCR conditioning with two control baselines: Random signal and signal absent. *Psychophysiology, 10:*145, 1973.

Thirty-six Ss, informed about the contingencies, were given differential SCR training with three different signals: CS+,

contingency
awareness

CS—, and a signal which was random with respect to UCS *differential* occurrence. UCSs occurred randomly between trials, and *condition-* during random signal trials were correlated with CS— pres- *ing* ence and were absent during CS—. Employing nonspecific re- *mechanism* sponse frequency and amplitude, as well as responding dur- ing random signal trials as baselines for comparison, evidence for both inhibitory and excitatory influences was obtained. The pattern of these influences was such as to question the proposition that a CS+ acquires general excitatory properties and a CS— acquires general inhibitory properties.

N 52   Shean, Glenn D.: The relationship between ability to verbalize stimulus contingencies and GSR conditioning. *J Psychosom Res, 12:*245, 1968.

The results of this investigation indicate that cognitive dif- *contingenc* ferentiation of conditional stimulus contingencies resulted in *awareness* autonomic behavior change similar to that observed to result *verbaliza-* from traditional classical conditioning procedures. Condi- *tion* tioned autonomic activity occurred only in those Ss who *condition-* were able to accurately verbalize stimulus contingencies. *ability* When verbalization of stimulus contingencies was inaccurate or omitted, no evidence of conditioned GSR differentiation was elicited, even after repeated CS-US pairing. The results of this experiment are interpreted as being consistent with an approach which maintains that repeated pairing of stimuli is not a necessary and sufficient condition for the acquisition of a conditioned autonomic response. This viewpoint in- cludes verbal-perceptual variables as relevant determiners of the conditioning process and maintains that much of human learning may result from the mediated association of work symbols, rather than through actual stimulus pairing.

N 53   Shean, Glenn D.: Instrumental modification of the galvanic
skin response: Conditioning or control? *J Psychosom Res,
14:*155, 1970.

The present experiment represents an attempt to determine *instruction-* the effect of instrumental contingencies upon the Galvanic *al set* Skin Response (GSR) under conditions in which cognitive *cognitive* and skeletal mediators are experimentally controlled through *mediation* differential preconditioning instructions. The results of this experiment indicate that GSR magnitude can be both increased and decreased by appropriate instrumental contingencies. However, these results do not appear to have resulted from direct instrumental conditioning of the GSR; but rather from S's controlling autonomic activity through cognitive and respiratory mediators serving as conditioned or unconditioned stimuli which in turn elicit the GSR. Cognitive and skeletal mediators appear to have been effectively eliminated in most Group II S's, thus providing conditions appropriate for unequivocal evidence of instrumental GSR conditioning. Group II S's however did not evidence GSR conditioning as a result of the application of instrumental contingencies. The greater magnitude of Group II classically conditioned GSR's appears to have resulted from the rather disconcerting instructions given to this group prior to beginning the conditioning procedure.

voluntary operants skeletal mediators

54 Streiner, David L., and Dean, Sanford J.: Expectancy, anxiety, and the GSR. *Psychon Sci, 10:*293, 1968.

Traditionally, CR magnitude in classical conditioning was thought to be dependent only upon properties of the CS and UCS. This study investigated the cognitive factor of S's expectancy of shock and his anxiety on GSR amplitude. Each of twenty-six high-anxious and thirty low-anxious males received twenty conditioning trials on a 50 percent random reinforcement schedule and had to state his expectation of shock before each trial. There was a significant correlation between verbalized expectancy and CR amplitude. High-anxious Ss extinguished more slowly than low-anxious Ss and had greater mean shock expectancies during acquisition.

expectancy anxiety cognitive influences

55 Swenson, Richard P., and Hill, Frances A.: Effects of instruction and interstimulus interval in human GSR conditioning. *Psychon Sci, 21:*369, 1970.

Administered facilitating and inhibiting sets to seventy-two undergraduates in a classical GSR conditioning situation employing a within-S design. Three groups of 24 Ss each were given four UCS adaptation trials followed by ten acquisition

instructional set stimulus characteristics

and sixteen extinction trials. Three different interstimulus intervals were included as a between-S variable. Both acquisition and extinction data reveal that GSR magnitude on facilitatory trials was significantly larger than on inhibitory trials (p < .01). Results further indicate that differential responding in accord with instructional set was not dependent upon an extended CS-UCS interval.

N 56   Uno, Tadao: The effects of awareness and successive inhibition on interoceptive and exteroceptive conditioning of the galvanic skin response. *Psychophysiology, 7:27*, 1970.

The general conclusion from Soviet studies of interoceptive conditioning has been that interoceptive conditioning is unconscious, established at a slower rate, and is more resistant to extinction than exteroceptive conditioning. Forty-eight paid volunteer subjects were classically conditioned to both interoceptive (zero and fifty degree C water in an intubated balloon located between the bronchial and diaphragmatic constrictions of the esophagus) and exteroceptive CSs (256 and 512 Hz tones at 60 db). Significant interoceptive and exteroceptive conditioning of the GSR was obtained using responses occurring within the interstimulus or first interval (FIR) as well as the post-UCS or second interval (SIR). FIR conditioning progressed at a slower rate to interoceptive than to exteroceptive stimulation whereas SIR conditioning was equally effective to both modes of stimulation. Unawareness of interoceptive stimulation or their reinforcement contingencies tended to eliminate FIR but not SIR conditioning. Although not statistically supported, successive inhibitory-excitatory compounding of interoceptive and exteroceptive CSs indicated stronger response tendencies to the interoceptive CSs when equated to exteroceptive conditioning strength. These results demonstrate the complexity of GSR conditioning when CS modality, response types, and awareness of CS-UCS contingencies are considered.

contingenc awareness internal stimuli external stimuli verbalization

N 57   Wilson, Glenn D.: Reversal of differential GSR conditioning by instructions. *J Exp Psychol, 76:*491, 1968.

GSR was conditioned to a blue light (CS+) using mild shock as UCS and a 50 percent reinforcement schedule, while

conditioning rever.

a yellow light (CS−) was presented an equal number of times without reinforcement. After conditioning was established, instructions designed to reverse the significance of CS+ and CS− were given, followed by a test series with both stimuli unreinforced. Results showed a sudden reversal of the differential conditioning, GSRs of greater magnitude being evoked by CS−. These new CRs did not extinguish but tended to increase in magnitude over nonreinforced test trials. A two-component theory of autonomic conditioning was not supported; the CR appeared to be fully ascribable to Ss' anticipation of shock.

instruction-al set
anticipatory responses
theory

PERSONALITY AND CONSTITUTIONAL FACTORS

N 58   Marton, L., and Urban, J.: Electrographical tests of individual differences in elementary learning processes. *Magyar Psyichologiai Szemle, 24:33*, 1967.

Correlations were found between various indices of conditioning EEG responses and GSR to optical and auditory stimuli and the introversion-extroversion scores of Ss.

personality
GSR
EEG response

N 59   Morgenson, D.F., and Martin, Irene: Personality, awareness and autonomic conditioning. *Psychophysiology, 5:536*, 1969.

The relationship between extraversion and autonomic conditioning was examined in three response systems: skin resistance, pulse rate, and pulse volume. A discrimination schedule was employed as suggested by Eysenck (1965), and also as a means of differentiating conditioning effects from pseudoconditioning. Ss were afterwards interviewed to assess whether or not they were aware of the CS-UCS contingency. Most of the Ss (ninety-three out of 115) could verbalize the contingency, and evidence of conditioning was clear-cut in this group and virtually nonexistent in the unaware group. There were no significant correlations between conditioning and personality in any of the response systems, a finding considered in the light of the overwhelming effect of cognitive factors on the acquisition curve.

personality
condition-ability
contingency awareness
verbaliza-tion

N 60   Purohit, Arjun P.: Personality variables, sex-difference, GSR responsiveness and GSR conditioning. *J Exp Res Pers, 1:166*, 1966.

The frequencies of conditioned GSRs during conditioning
and extinction were correlated with scores on the Maudsley
Personality Inventory's E and N scales. Manifest Anxiety
Scale, kinesthetic after-effect test, spiral after-effect test, serial
reaction-time test, GSR lability, heart-rate lability, spontaneous GSRs, and resistance to GSR adaptation in sixty-four
males and sixty-four females. Only the scores of resistance to
GSR adaptation, spontaneous GSRs, GSR lability, and serial
reaction-time test were significantly related. Males gave significantly more conditioned GSRs and scored significantly
higher in all the four correlates of conditioned GSRs. Implications of these findings are discussed.

*response
character-
istics
personality
sex differ-
ences
HR*

N 61   Shmavonian, B.M., Miller, L.H., and Cohen, S.I.: Differences among age and sex groups in electrodermal conditioning. *Psychophysiology, 5:*119, 1968.

Four groups—Young Males, Young Females, Aged Males, and
Aged Females—were run in a discrimination conditioning
paradigm with a variety of autonomic and central measures.
This paper deals primarily with Electrodermal Responses.
The findings indicate that in all measures the Young Males
and Young Females show the best discriminated conditioning, followed by Aged Females and Aged Males. In the GSP
there are hints that the negative wave of the response might
be related to the orienting phenomena whereas the positive
wave is what becomes discriminately conditioned in the experiment. A cognitive questionnaire was accurately answered
in the same rank order as the conditioning, that is, Young
Males, Young Females, Aged Females and Aged Males.

*age
sex differ-
ences
condition-
ability
cognitive
influences
GSR*

N 62   Wilson, Glenn D.: Personality, GSR conditioning and response to instructional set. *Psychol Rep, 22:*618, 1968.

Much controversy concerns the relationship between personality and the hypothesized factor of "conditionability."
Spence (2) argues for a positive association between "drive,"
operationalized as questionnaire anxiety and the ease with
which autonomic conditioning can be established, while
Eysenck (1) reviews evidence that introverts acquire CRs
more readily than extraverts. This note further presents re-

*personality
instruction
al set
color signal*

sults concerning the personality factor in GSR conditioning and also opens the question of individual differences in the extent to which CRs can be influenced by instructions. GSR was conditioned to a blue light (CS+), using mild shock as UCS and a 50 percent reinforcement schedule, while a yellow light (CS—) was presented an equal number of times unreinforced. After conditioning, instructions designed to reverse the significance of CS+ and CS— were given (3), followed by a test series with both stimuli unreinforced. Ss then rated the extent to which they had believed the instructions. Personality information on the 15 Ss (high school students aged fifteen to seventeen) was obtained using the EPI, and the Conservatism Scale (4). A conditioning index was calculated for each S by dividing the mean GSR to unreinforced CS+ trials during conditioning by the mean GSR to appropriate CS— comparison stimuli. An index of instruction effect was obtained by adding the conditioning score to a similarly computed index of reversal of the original conditioning. Neuroticism did not relate significantly to conditioning while contrary to the findings of Eysenck, extra-version related positively ($p = .45$, $p < .05$). Furthermore, of the three experimental conditions listed by Eysenck as being favorable to the development of "cortical inhibition" and hence to an inverse relationship between extraversion and conditionability, at least two of these (partial reinforcement and discriminative as opposed to single-stimulus conditioning) applied clearly in this experiment. The personality variable which related most strongly to conditioning was, however, conservatism ($p = -.57$, $p < .05$). Though interpretation of this result is premature, it is likely that the relationship was mediated by Ss' attitude toward the punishment implied by electric shock and may be taken as further evidence for a cognitive interpretation of GSR conditioning. Finally, there was strong evidence that extraversion was important in determining S's acceptance of the instructions concerning the light-shock contingency, the effect being apparent in both self-report and GSR measures. E-scores were positively related to the index of instruction effect ($p = .56$, $p < .05$) and inversely related to Ss' ratings of the extent to which they were suspicious of the instructions ($p = .70$, $p < .01$).

SECTION O

OPERANT CONDITIONING

REINFORCEMENT TECHNIQUES

O 1   Crider, Andrew, Shapiro, David, and Tursky, Bernard: Reinforcement of spontaneous electrodermal activity. *J Comp Physiol Psychol, 61:*20, 1966.

Contingent stimulation of spontaneous electrodermal fluctuations in human Ss increased their frequency of occurrence relative to a noncontingent stimulation control. The effect was facilitated by, but not dependent on, pseudoinstructions to produce emotional behavior. It was independent of time trends in electrodermal level, heart rate, respiration rate, and gross skeletal activity. The similarity of this phenomenon to Sokolov's conditioned orienting reflex is discussed.

instruction
SP
HR
muscle
  activity

O 2   Dean, Sanford J., Martin, R.B., and Streiner, D.: Meditational control of the GSR. *J Exp Res Pers, 3:*71, 1968.

Female undergraduates given training involving the overt and implicit verbalization of differential verbal stimuli associated with the onset and cessation of shock were tested on subsequent ability to control the GSR in an instrumental situation where the production and inhibition of the GSR were contingencies for shock avoidance. The major effects of the training were to increase the ability to inhibit, but not to increase the ability to produce a GSR. Control conditions suggested that the observed training effects were not due to shock adaptation and, further, that GSR control did not occur in the absence of such training or in the absence of cognitive mediation.

operant con-
  ditioning
information
training
GSR sup-
  pression
cognitive
  mediation

O 3   Defran, R.H., Badia, Pietro, and Lewis, Paul: Stimulus control over operant galvanic skin responses. *Psychophysiology, 6:*101, 1969.

Operant conditioning of the galvanic skin response (GSR) using a discrimination procedure was attempted in both acquisition and extinction. During acquisition male Ss were given contingent reinforcement during S+ intervals and noncontingent reinforcement during S— intervals. All reinforcement was withheld during extinction. A criterion response was defined as a .5 percent increase in skin resistance occurring in the absence of electromyogram (EMG) or respiration irregularities. A frequency analysis of GSRs showed that stimulus control was obtained in extinction but not in acquisition. Interpretations based upon skeletal mediation and adaptation were not supported.

stimulus discrimination
EMG
respiration

) 4   Edelman, Robert I.: Effects of differential afferent feedback on instrumental GSR conditioning. *J Psychol, 74:3,* 1970.

Three levels of electric shock (pain, medium and threshold) were utilized across groups to produce differential skin conductance. After each of twelve shocks, Ss (fifty-five undergraduates) were reinforced by light onset (exchangeable for money) for each five-second period that the GSR was above its preshock level (acquisition). Four extinction trials followed during which no reinforcement was forthcoming. Control groups were provided for habituation to shock and for effects of light onset. Possible somatic mediation was assessed by questionnaire and by measurement of respiration rate, respiration amplitude, and EMG amplitude. Additionally, 5 Ss were exposed to reinforcement withdrawal after shock when major increases in skeletal activity were observed. Results indicate successful conditioning in the medium and pain shock-intensity groups. Except for EMG data, all indices of skeletal activity suggested that somatic mediation occurred. Further, it was demonstrated that spontaneous fluctuations in skin conductance, which constituted the dependent measure of virtually all previous studies, were also associated with somatic mediation.

feedback
shock
  intensity
somatic
  responses
SC
EMG

) 5   Gavalas, Rochelle Johnson: Operant reinforcement of an autonomic response: Two studies. *J Exp Anal Behav, 10:* 119, 1967. (copyright 1967 by the Soicety for the Experimental Analysis of Behavior, Inc.)

Two successive studies were conducted to determine the possibility of operant reinforcement of nonspecific galvanic skin resistance responses. In the first study, with five experimental and three control subjects who served for twenty to thirty minutes a day for ten days, all experimental subjects learned to emit more nonspecific galvanic skin resistance responses than their *ad hoc* matched controls. In a second study, nine experimental and nine control subjects were matched for first-day levels of reactivity and yoked for operant reinforcement schedules. Significant differences between the two groups were found on the last day of conditioning and during extinction. Six of the nine experimental subjects showed higher cumulative rate curves than their matched and yoked controls. The concomitant measures (basal resistance, heart rate, etc.) all supported this finding. It was suggested that operant reinforcement of autonomic response tends to maintain a certain level of responding in contrast to persistent adaptation in the control group.

GSR frequency
spontaneous GSR
adaptation
HR

O 6   Greene, William A., and Nielsen, Thomas C.: Operant GSR conditioning of high and low autonomic perceivers. *Psychon Sci, 6:*359, 1966.

The effect of contingent and noncontingent reinforcement on unelicited GSRs was assessed for High and Low Autonomic Perceivers. From a group of 160 Ss, the 20 Ss who scored highest and the 20 Ss who scored lowest on Mandler's Autonomic Perceptibility Questionnaire were given ten minutes of rest, sixteen minutes of reinforcement, and ten minutes of extinction. The effect of the reinforcer was limited to the Low Autonomic Perceivers.

autonomic perception
instructions
GSR

O 7   Greene, William A.: Operant conditioning of the GSR using partial reinforcement. *Psychol Rep, 19:*571, 1966.

This study was designed to determine the influence of partial reinforcement upon the rate of emission of unelicited GSRs. Ninety college students were divided into two groups with respect to delivery of visual reinforcement. Contingent (C) and Noncontingent (NC). The Contingent group was divided further into three subgroups, each of which received

reinforcement technique
partial reinforcement
GSR frequency

a different schedule of partial reinforcement; each contingent group had a yoked Noncontingent control. The overall rate of responding was greater during Contingent reinforcement than Noncontingent reinforcement. Among the Contingent groups the effect of partial reinforcement was maximal during the initial minute of acquisition and the initial minutes of extinction. During the extinction period the Contingent and the Noncontingent groups tended to converge. A no-stimulation control group showed fairly steady responding during the last thirty-two minutes.

) 8   Grings, William W., and Carlin, Sidney: Instrumental modification of autonomic behavior. *Psychol Rec, 16:*153, 1966.

The GSR to a signal light was observed as a function of contingent receipt or avoidance of shock. An "avoidance" paradigm appears to increase frequency of response to the CS and to reduce average response magnitude. A "punishment" paradigm appears to decrease frequency of responding and to reduce average magnitude of response even more than the avoidance paradigm.

avoidance response frequency GSR magnitude

) 9   Helmer, J. Eric, and Furedy, John J.: Operant conditioning of GSR amplitude. *J Exp Psychol, 78:*463, 1968.

Forty undergraduates were given a five cent-associated light as positive reinforcement contingent on the amplitude of a GSR following a lever press. Forty controls had their reinforcement schedules yoked to that of their experimental partners. Ss were told that reinforcement was dependent on the accuracy of their estimate of the conclusion of a one-minute interval, as indicated by their lever press. Mean GSR amplitude following the lever press was significantly greater for the experimental (contingent-reinforcement) Ss than for the noncontingent controls, indicating successful operant conditioning of a nonspontaneous autonomic response.

GSR amplitude time estimates instructions

) 10   Martin, Randall B., and Dean, Sanford J.: Instrumental modification of the GSR. *Psychophysiology, 7:*178, 1970.

Four experiments investigated the effects of instructions, response-contingent shock, and the latency of the critical re-

sponse on the GSR. Using a discrimination procedure, in
which responding in the presence of one stimulus avoided
shock while responding in the presence of another led to
shock, it was found that relative to noninstructed, yoked-
noncontingent conditions, instructed subjects responded at
higher levels to the respond stimuli and at lower levels to
inhibit stimuli. The effects of instructions appeared stronger
than the effects of the shock contingencies. Only when the
"contingent" GSR was of the "anticipatory" latency were
differential effects obtained, however, no effects were observed in the absence of cognitive mediation.

*contingency
awareness
instructions
anticipatory
responses*

O 11   Schwartz, Gary E., and Johnson, Harold J.: Affective visual
        stimuli as operant reinforcers of the GSR. *J Exp Psychol, 80:*
        28, 1969.

The present study was undertaken to determine whether
affective stimuli could act as more potent reinforcers of spontaneous GSR activity than those previously employed. Contingent (C) Ss were shown slides of nude females taken from
a popular magazine each time they produced a spontaneous
GSR. Noncontingent (NC) Ss were matched on resting GSRs
with C Ss and received the same number of reinforcers per
minute as C Ss except at times when no GSRs were present.
During conditioning the C group showed a substantial increase in frequency of GSRs, while the NC group showed a
marked decrease. These differences were maintained during
an extinction period. No differences were obtained for either
heart rate or respiration rate during conditioning or extinction, although GSR level evidenced Group x Time interactions. It was concluded that the strength of a reinforcer is an
important parameter which must be considered in operant
studies of autonomic responding.

*affective
stimuli
reinforce-
ment
strength
respiration
HR*

O 12   Shnidman, Susan R., and Shapiro, David: Instrumental
        modification of elicited autonomic responses. *Psychophysiol-
        ogy, 7:*395, 1970.

Discrete trials methodology was used to study the instrumental modification of elicited palmar skin potential responses in
humans. Simple auditory stimuli defined the trials for a

*discrete
trials
elicited
responses*

number of different reinforcement conditions. Data indicate that autonomic responses elicited by discrete stimuli can be facilitated by operant reinforcement, but there is no evidence for an inhibitory or suppressive effect. The specific contingency of reinforcement and response appears necessary to show the effect.

SPR

) 13 Stern, Robert M.: Operant conditioning of spontaneous GSRs: Negative results. *J Exp Psychol, 75:*128, 1967.

Operant conditioning of unelicited GSRs was attempted in a study that added two new control groups and reinterpreted the role of the usual control group in experiments of this type. Postsession questionnaire replies supported this reinterpretation; however, GSR data showed no separation of the groups during either conditioning or extinction.

negative results subjective reports

) 14 Whittome, V.J., and Lader, M.H.: Operant GSR conditioning: An attempt to condition differentially the two sides of the body. *J Psychosom Res, 16:*421, 1972.

An attempt was made to condition instrumentally the galvanic skin responses of ten human subjects. Each subject took part in four sessions, each consisting of sixty presentations of an auditory stimulus. Galvanic skin responses were recorded simultaneously from both hands. The crucial variable was the ratio of the two responses: each time the ratio following a stimulus presentation was greater than that which had followed the previous stimulus, the subject received a small monetary reward. No consistent conditioning effects were detected and the reasons for this are discussed.

operant conditioning bilateral responses differential conditioning

REINFORCEMENT SCHEDULES

) 15 Greene, William A., and Sutor, Linda T.: Stimulus control of skin resistance responses on an escape-avoidance schedule. *J Exp Anal Behav, 16:*269, 1971. (copyright 1971 by the Society for the Experimental Analysis of Behavior, Inc.)

The effects of discrimination and avoidance training on the skin resistance response were studied in eight humans. Re-

avoidance

sponses occurring during one stimulus delayed the interruption of music for thirty seconds; responses during a second stimulus either had no effect or interrupted the music for fifteen seconds. The results showed stimulus control in all subjects and an increased discrimination between the first one half and last one half of the sessions for seven of the eight subjects.

stimulus discrimination
contingency awareness
arousal
individual variation

O 16 McMullin, William E., and Greene, William A.: Operant conditioning of the skin resistance response on a multiple schedule. *Psychophysiology, 6:*640, 1970.

The purpose of this study was to determine if the characteristic fixed-ratio (FR) pattern of behavior could be obtained with the Skin Resistance Response (SRR) after operant conditioning. Four college, male, sophomore students served as subjects for twenty sessions in an experiment designed to assess the influence of a fixed-ratio schedule of reinforcement on the unelicited SRR. Within each of the twenty sessions the subject's SRRs and respiratory activity was monitored. Under discriminative stimulus I (S^{DI}), SRRs were reinforced with points on a counter by a FR schedule. Under discriminative stimulus II (S^{DII}), points were delivered on the counter for each period twenty-five seconds during which no SRRs occurred. During each session respiration responses were monitored, and whenever it was determined that a change in respiration elicited a SRR, that SRR was neither counted nor reinforced. The results of the study indicated that for three of the four subjects, (1) a discrimination was formed between S^{DI} and S^{DII}, (2) SRRs increased with increasing FR requirements, and (3) typical FR performance was not obtained on the cumulative records. The results are discussed in terms of the relative "power" of the reinforcer used in operant autonomic conditioning and in terms of the balance of control exerted on autonomically mediated responses from homeostatic-reflexive mechanisms on the one hand and firm stimulus control resulting from operant conditioning on the other.

reinforcement schedule
stimulus discrimination
SRR

O 17 Shapiro, David, and Crider, Andrew: Operant electrodermal conditioning under multiple schedules of reinforcement. *Psychophysiology, 4:*168, 1967.

An operant discrimination procedure was used to determine whether human subjects show shifts in palmar skin potential response rate under varying schedules of reinforcement. In Experiment I, a monetary reinforcer was either given or subtracted on a short fixed ratio schedule during alternating five-minute periods. In Experiment II, the schedules alternated between ten-minute periods in which either a variable number of responses or long inter-response times were reinforced. Each experiment consisted of seven subjects tested over several sessions. The results indicated differences in response rates consonant with changes in the scheduling of reinforcement. Concurrent recordings of respiration, heart rate, and skin potential level showed that the reinforcement effects were generally specific to the skin potential response variable.

stimulus discrimination
instructions
motivation
response strategies
cognitive influences
HR
SPR

) 18   Shapiro, David, and Watanabe, Takami: Timing characteristics of operant electrodermal modification: fixed-interval effects. *Jap Psychol Res, 13*:123, 1971.

Palmar skin potential responses in human subjects were reinforced under several fixed-interval schedules of reinforcement varying from fifty to 150 seconds. With the exception of an initial response burst immediately after reinforcement, the response characteristics appear to be comparable to those observed for skeletal operants. Data are also presented showing that efficiency of performance is improved when subjects are provided an external clock. Concomitant changes in other physiological variables recorded do not show any consistent evidence for somatic mediation of the learned patterns of skin potential activity.

skeletal operants
feedback
SPR

SOMATIC RESPONSES

O 19   Birk, Lee, Crider, Andrew, Shapiro, David, and Tursky, Bernard: Operant electrodermal conditioning under partial curarization. *J Comp Physiol Psychol, 62*:165, 1966.

An immobilizing but subparalytic dose of d-tubocurarine administered to a volunteer S prior to reinforcement for emission of electrodermal responses produced no diminution of response frequency in comparison with a control session.

somatic responses
curare
response rate

This is consistent with previous findings of independence between somatic activity and operantly conditioned electrodermal activity.

O 20   Gavalas, R.J.: Operant reinforcement of a skeletally mediated autonomic response: Uncoupling of the two responses. *Psychon Sci, 11*:195, 1968.

The mediation explanation of the effect of operant reinforcement of autonomic responses assumes that skeletally mediated autonomic responses can be easily and fortuitously conditioned. GSR deflections elicited by deep respirations were operantly reinforced. The two responses became uncoupled: the skeletal (deep respiration) response showed a classic instrumental learning curve; the autonomic response showed great variability and only marginal (E-C) gains during extinction. It is possible that these marginal gains were artifactual since the percent of deep respirations eliciting GSRs showed a marked habituation to increasing repetitions of the respiration response.

*elicited
  GSRs
skeletal
  mediation
mechanisms
habituation
respiration*

O 21   Rice, David G.: Operant conditioning and associated electromyogram responses. *J Exp Psychol, 71*:908, 1966.

Operant GSR conditioning was attempted with Ss seated in a dark room and unelicited GSRs reinforced with a white light. Electromyographic (EMG) monitoring of the fingers holding the GSR electrodes indicated preceding muscle-tension changes (which can often lead to a GSR). Response frequency for contingent reinforcement and yoked noncontingent reinforcement control groups differed significantly over the reinforcement period when all criterion unelicited GSRs were reinforced. Separate analyses of GSRs preceded and not preceded by EMG changes within the same S gave no indication that movement-related GSRs were significantly responsible for the experimental and control group difference during reinforcement. Additional Ss were reinforced for only those criterion GSRs given in the absence of preceding EMG changes. Evidence for operant conditioning in these Ss was equivocal. A complicating factor was the greater average number of GSRs necessary for reinforcement, compared to Ss

*somatic
  responses
EMG
spontaneous
  GSRs*

in the condition where all criterion GSRs were reinforced. The present findings do not support the hypothesis that a skeletal (rather than an autonomic) response is acquired in operant GSR conditioning.

O 22   Van Twyver, H.B., and Kimmel, H.D.: Operant conditioning of the GSR with concomitant measurement of two somatic variables. *J Exp Psychol, 72*:841, 1966.

An attempt was made to determine whether operant GSR conditioning depends upon changes in somatic responses. The Ss were twenty-one pairs of college students who received either contingent or noncontingent reinforcement during a reinforcement period. A ten-minute rest period was followed by sixteen minutes of reinforcement and then ten minutes of extinction. In addition to the GSR, respiration rates and EMGs were recorded. Ss receiving contingent reinforcement increased significantly in GSR rates during acquisition while a noncontingent group declined slightly. A significant Contingency x Minutes interaction was also found for GSR rates during this period. During reinforcement, there were no statistically significant differences between groups in respiration rate, forearm movements, or frequency of breathing irregularities. Subtraction of all somatic associated GSRs resulted in no attenuation of the conditioning effect. During extinction the contingency effect reached significance only after subtraction of all movement associated GSRs. The results were interpreted as evidence that the GSR may be operantly conditioned in the absence of somatic mediation.

somatic responses
respiration
EMG

OPERANT SUPPRESSION

O 23   Crider, Andrew, Schwartz, Gary E., and Shapiro, David: Operant suppression of electrodermal response rate as a function of punishment schedule. *J Exp Psychol, 83*:333, 1970.

Replicated the H.J. Johnson and G.E. Schwartz finding that a brief period of continuous punishment of the spontaneous electrodermal response with an aversive tone reduces response frequency to approximately 50 percent of operant level. Less suppression was found under a partial schedule in

aversive stimuli
response rate
extinction

which every second response was punished. The experiment, using twenty university students and employees, employed a 2 × 2 factorial design with continuous versus partial punishment and contingent versus yoked aversive stimulation as the factors. The analysis was based on response frequencies during a twenty-minute extinction test period following a twenty-minute treatment period. Results showed contingent-yoked differences to be greater under the continuous than under the partial schedule. No recovery from suppression was observed during extinction in either condition.

O 24 Johnson, Harold J., and Schwartz, Gary E.: Suppression of GSR activity through operant reinforcement. *J Exp Psychol, 75:*307, 1967.

Aversive stimulation was applied differentially to spontaneous GSR activity in four groups of Ss. Two groups (C groups) were exposed to a loud tone each time they showed spontaneous GSRs, and two groups (NC groups) were given the same number of tones, but at times when there were no GSRs. In addition, Ss in 1 C and 1 NC group were instructed that their behavior had something to do with the number of tones received during the experiment. The C groups showed significant decreases in GSR activity while the NC groups showed little change. The instruction variable did not significantly affect GSR activity.

aversive stimulation instructions response suppression

O 25 Senter, R.J., and Hummel, William F. Jr.: Suppression of an autonomic response through operant conditioning. *Psychol Rec, 15:*1, 1965.

Eight college-age Ss were subjected to a brief shock administered contiguously with the emission of spontaneous GSRs. A yoke-control group received shocks uncorrelated with GSR. When GSRs were consistently associated with shock punishment, a decrease in their frequency was observed. It is concluded that the aspect of GSR activity examined in this study is a conditionable operant and is associated with a sensory correlate.

avoidance response suppression

INFLUENCE OF OTHER VARIABLES

) 26   Baron, Jonathan: An EEG correlate of autonomic discrimination. *Psychon Sci, 4:*255, 1966.

In a forced choice procedure, Ss can identify the presence or absence of their own spontaneous GSRs. Correctly and incorrectly discriminated GSRs are preceded by opposing patterns of 5 cps EEG activity. It is suggested that discriminable GSRs are produced by the same central events which serve as cues for the discrimination.

emotional stimuli
reinforcement
response discrimination
EEG correlate

) 27   Graham, L.A., Cohen, S.I., and Shmavonian, B.M.: Sex differences in autonomic responses during instrumental conditioning. *Psychosom Med, 28:*264, 1966.

Behavior of twenty-one women in an instrumental conditioning experiment using a push-avoidance response was quite similar to previous study of men. Women had lower levels of galvanic skin response activity and higher heart rates. GSR discriminition during avoidance learning was less pronounced for women than for men. Both groups had a tendency for the HR to slow when behavior was inhibited by instruction.

avoidance
sex differences
HR

O 28   Shapiro, D., Schwartz, G.E., Shnidman, S., Nelson, S., and Silverman, S.: Operant control of fear-related electrodermal responses in snake-phobic subjects. *Psychophysiology, 9:*271, 1972.

Twenty volunteer women with snake phobias were shown eighty slides of snakes, arranged in order of increasing fear (five seconds each, two per minute) . Slides 1 through 10 were used for baseline. On slides 11 through 70, 10 Ss were reinforced with a tone (monetary bonus) if the GSR elicited by the slide was larger than the GSR to the preceding slide. Ten Ss were similarly reinforced but only when the GSR was smaller in amplitude. A shaping procedure was used to determine criterion GSR amplitudes. Slides 71 through 80

phobias
desensitization
motivation
shaping
subjective reports
pictorial stimuli
GSRs

were used for extinction, with no reinforcement. Although both groups showed smaller GSRs over the slides, the change was larger in the decrease group, this difference being significant during extinction. Subjective reports obtained by a snake and spider fear questionnaire given before and after the session suggested that a greater reduction of fear of snakes, but not spiders, occurred in the decrease group. Implications for desensitization and behavior control will be discussed.

O 29 Martin, Randall B., Dean, Sanford J., and Shean, Glenn: Selective attention and instrumental modification of the GSR. *Psychophysiology, 4:*460, 1968.

A series of experiments were conducted on instrumental modification of the Galvanic Skin Response (GSR) in a discrimination procedure where preparatory signals indicated which discriminative stimulus was to occur. When shock avoidance was contingent upon the presence of a response the GSR was enhanced; when shock avoidance was contingent upon the inhibition of a response there was a decrement in reactivity. Heart rate acceleration occurred to Respond stimuli while deceleration occurred to Inhibit stimuli. Various types of cognitive strategies were reported by the subjects from attempts to control attention by attending less to stimuli associated with inhibition to attempts to arouse a response by thinking of exciting events and to inhibit by thinking of calming events. Post-experimental recognition of words tended to be negatively related to magnitude of response. When the verbal stimuli served directly as discriminative stimuli, however, these relationships tended to be reversed.

avoidance cognitive strategies stimulus discrimination preparatory signals verbal stimuli attention autonomic reactivity sex differences GSR

O 30 Shapiro, David and Watanabe, Takami: Reinforcement of spontaneous electrodermal activity: A cross-cultural study in Japan. *Psychophysiology, 9:*340, 1972.

A within-subjects experimental design was used to examine the effects of contingent versus noncontingent reinforcement of spontaneous skin potential responses in Japanese subjects, and the results were compared with previous data obtained

stimulus discrimination cultural differences

from a comparable sample of American subjects. The same overall pattern of differentiation between the two conditions of reinforcement was observed in both national groups, contingent reinforcement producing heightened rates of skin potential response relative to noncontingent reinforcement. Compared to the Americans, the Japanese showed more immediate differentiation between contingent and noncontingent reinforcement. The results are discussed in terms of previous cross-cultural psychophysiological research.

SECTION P

BIOFEEDBACK

P 1   Archer, James Jr., Fiester, Thomas, Kagan, Norman, Rate, Lyman, Spierling, Thomas, and Van Noord, Robert: New method for education, treatment and research in human interaction. *J Counseling Psychol, 19*:275, 1971.

Initial exploration using physiological feedback as part of a videotaped feedback, simulation film, training and treatment method is described. In the first phase of the research a graphic representation of a subject's eccrine sweat rate was videotaped with one camera, while another camera simultaneously videotaped the subject's face and torso. Recall was then conducted with a split-screen replay of these two recordings. Subject reactions to the physiological feedback are evaluated and described. A cardiac measure was added to the process to provide a comparison of the two different physiological feedbacks. Hypotheses explaining the effect of this feedback on subjects and the relationship between the two feedbacks are presented.

feedback
subjective
  responses
sweating
HR
theory
application

P 2   Hughes, W.G., and Shean, G.D.: Personality and ability to control the galvanic skin response. *Psychophysiology, 8*:247, 1971.

The effects of external feedback and awareness of reward contingency upon the ability to voluntarily suppress a conditioned GSR were studied in twenty-one highly neurotic introverted and twenty-one low neurotic extraverted Ss selected on the basis of the Maudsley Personality Inventory. A conditioned GSR was established by five classical pairings of a CS (signal lamp) and a UCS (aversive electric shock). On subsequent presentations of the CS Ss were required to maintain their GSR below 500 ohms change on five consecutive trials in order to receive reward (cessation of shock). Ss were instructed to suppress their GSR by employing cognitive ma-

personality
voluntary
  control
conditioning
contingency
  awareness

nipulations such as "thinking relaxing thoughts." Results showed that Ss who were aware of the reward contingency and who received appropriate positive or negative feedback after each trial were able to reduce their GSR over twenty test trials significantly more than the control group and a group which was aware of the reward contingency but received no feedback. High neurotic introverts were significantly more successful on this task than low neurotic extraverts.

P 3 Klinge, Valerie: Effects of exteroceptive feedback and instructions on control of spontaneous galvanic skin responses. *Psychophysiology, 9:*305, 1972.

To more fully explore the possibility of control of the autonomic nervous system (ANS) in the human S, this study investigated the effects of instructions and exteroceptive feedback on the control of spontaneous galvanic skin responsivity (GSR). Two sets of instructions ("Relax" and "Think") were alternately presented to Ss under four types of meter feedback: accurate, positive, negative and control. In addition to GSR activity, respiration and cardiac rates were recorded. The results indicated that Ss receiving accurate feedback were significantly better able to comply with the "Relax"-"Think" instructions; next most effective was positive feedback, while negative and control feedback were least effective. No within-subject relationships were found between control of spontaneous GSRs and respiration or cardiac activity. The results suggest that Ss are responsive to the consequences of their autonomic behavior in much the same manner as they are responsive to the consequences of other learned behaviors.

feedback
voluntary
control
instructions
response
specificity
response
rate
respiration
HR

P 4 Simonov, P.V., and Valueva, M.N.: On physiological mechanisms of conditioned switching in man. *EPEBAH,* 387, 1966.

Subjects can learn to control their GSR well enough to send Morse code (Simonov and Velueva, 1966) if they receive GSR feedback.

feedback
voluntary
control

P 5 Stern, R.M., and Kaplan, B.E.: Galvanic skin response: Voluntary control and externalization. *J Psychosom Res, 10:*349, 1967.

A study was conducted to determine the extent to which college students could control their GSRs through the use of ideational stimuli both with and without externalization. An experimental group of forty subjects were provided with continuous visual feedback (externalization) of their own GSR records during a ten-minute rest period and a ten-minute respond period. During the former period, subjects were instructed to increase their skin resistance by relaxing; during the latter they were to produce decreases in resistance (GSRs) by thinking about emotional situations. A control group received the same instructions but no externalization. The results indicated that during the ten-minute respond period, the experimental subjects showed a slight increase in rate of GSRs emitted, while the control group showed a marked decrease. During the rest period, both groups maintained a steady low rate of GSRs indicating that externalization was necessary for producing a high rate of GSRs but not for inhibiting them. Ability to control GSRs did not correlate with responsiveness to external stimulation and yielded a significant correlation to only one of twenty-two personality scales—Lykken's Sociopathic Scale.

feedback
ideational
stimuli
voluntary
control
visual
signals

P 6   Stern, Robert M., and Lewis, Nancy L.: Ability of actors to control their GSRs and express emotions. *Psychophysiology,* 4:294, 1968.

Ability to control GSRs through the use of ideational stimulation was studied in twenty-six professional actors. During one 10-minute period, "Respond," Ss had to make as many GSRs as possible; during the other period, "Rest," Ss were instructed to inhibit their GSRs. All Ss received continuous visual feedback of their responses during both periods. No relationship was found between ability to control GSRs and emotional expression as measured by the ratings of directors. However, as predicted, method actors performed at a significantly higher level than nonmethod actors. An additional finding was that those actors who normally experience sweating as their primary response to stress performed at a higher level than nonsweaters.

feedback
ideational
stimuli
visual
signals
voluntary
control
emotions

P 7   Ton, William H., and Boulger, John R.: Voluntary inhibition of galvanic skin response. *Psychol Rep, 29:*603, 1971.

To assess the effectiveness of instructional set in voluntary inhibition of GSR forty-three male Ss were assigned to three treatment groups. All groups were shown four slides of female nudes once, were given a break or instructions, and were shown the slides again. Group 1 received instruction to try to inhibit their response. Group C_1 received instruction about the nature of the GSR measure. Group C_2 received no special instructions. Scores were changed in mean peak amplitude of skin conductance between presentations. Analysis of variance indicated no suppression had occurred. Inspection of the data led to the conclusion that the instructions were followed by higher skin conductance, probably from increased anxiety or skeletal artifact.

*voluntary
control
instruction-
al set
pictorial
stimuli
anxiety
EMG*

SECTION Q

LIE DETECTION

Q 1   Barland, G.H., and Raskin, D.C.: An experimental study of field techniques in "lie detection." *Psychophysiology, 9:*275, 1972.

The effectiveness of field polygraph techniques in detecting "guilt" and "innocence" was studied using a mock crime situation. Thirty-six Ss were "guilty" of having taken $10 according to instructions, and 36 Ss were "innocent." A field-type interview followed by a Backster Zone of Comparison control-question examination concerning the theft of $10 was administered. A field model Keeler Polygraph was used to record physiological responses, and field (semisubjective) and quantitative analyses of the charts were made. To prevent bias, the examiner and data scorers were not informed about the guilt or innocence of each S. On the basis of the field evaluations which include a category of inconclusive, 53 percent were correct, 12 percent were incorrect, and 35 percent were inconclusive. Excluding inconclusives, 81 percent were correct. Using quantitative scoring, significant discrimination between "guilty" and "innocent" was obtained with GSR, blood pressure (BP), and respiration cycle time and amplitude, with GSR and BP yielding the best results. Further analyses of the field evaluations showed discrimination with GSR, respiration and BP. This study demonstrates the effectiveness of field techniques and equipment in differentiating deceptive and truthful Ss, and, contrary to previous literature, shows significant discrimination for all three physiological measures employed in the field.

lie detection
field technique
recording channels
GSR
BP
respiration

Q 2   Cutrow, Robert J., Parks, Arthur, Lucas, Nelson, and Thomas, Kathryn: The objective use of multiple physiological indices in the detection of deception. *Psychophysiology, 9:*578, 1972.

Psychophysiological measures—breathing amplitude (BA), breathing cycle time (BCT), eyeblink rate (EBR), eyeblink latency (EBL), finger pulse volume (FPV), heart rate (HR), palmar galvanic skin response (GSR_p), volar-forearm galvanic skin response (GSR_v), and voice latency (VL)—were evaluated for effectiveness in detecting deception with sixty-three college students. A relevant-irrelevant stimulus presentation format was used with three treatment conditions: personal words, neutral words, and items involving money. All physiological variables were found significant indicators of deception, $p < .01$ or $p < .05$ through objective techniques. A combined effect index of six variables provided an advantage over any index taken separately. No significant treatment or sex differences were found between stimulus conditions except for the GSR_v measure.

deception
arousal
recording
  channels
motivation
verbal
  stimuli
GSR
finger pulse
  volume
respiration

Q 3   Gustafson, Lawrence A., and Orne, Martin T.: The effects of verbal responses on the laboratory detection of deception. *Psychophysiology, 2:*10, 1965.

Ss were given one of three different response tasks to perform in a detection of deception experiment using the galvanic skin response (GSR). The first group was told to say nothing as they heard each question, the second group to say "no" to each question, and the third group to make a word association to each question. Questions were presented in both a random order and a known sequential order. There were overall differences among the three groups for both conditions of question presentation. The second group was most frequently detected, the first group next, and the third group was detected least frequently. Differences between experimental procedures used in this study and other studies using word association do not permit comparison of the results of this study with other studies.

deception
performance
  tasks
attention
verbal
  behavior
stress
GSR

Q 4   Kugelmass, Sol, and Lieblich, Israel: Effects of realistic stress and procedural interference in experimental lie detection. *J Appl Psychol, 50:*211, 1966.

Two different samples of police trainees were used to investigate (1) the effect of realistic stress in experimental lie de-

lie detection
stress

tection, (2) the possible interference with the GSR channel resulting from the simultaneous recording of blood pressure. It was found that (1) GSR detection results under stress were essentially similar to those obtained in mild experimental situations, and far superior in detection efficiency to analysis of heart rate changes. (2) The introduction of a blood-pressure cuff inflated to 80 mm Hg for the ninety seconds of interrogation (similar to actual field measurement conditions) reduced the efficiency of detection of the GSR channel. (3) There is some suggestion that GSR reactivity may be related to ethnic origin.

recording channels
ethnic differences
HR
BP
GSR

Q 5   Kugelmass, S., Lieblich, I., and Bergman, Z.: The role of "lying" in psychophysiological detection. *Psychophysiology,* *3*:312, 1967.

An experiment was designed to examine the role of lying behavior, per se, as the basis for experimental psychophysiological detection of deception. In addition to the standard card-test procedure, a second procedure required the subject to say "yes" to every question posed relating to the card chosen. This variation involved telling the "truth" in respect to the critical card in contrast to the usual procedure in which he is required to "lie." With the use of the galvanic skin response (GSR) channel, significant detection rates were obtained for both procedures with no significant difference between them. Some theoretical issues related to the findings were explored.

deception
recording channels
GSR
response theory

Q 6   Kugelmass, Sol, and Lieblich, Israel: Relation between ethnic origin and GSR reactivity in psychophysiological detection. *J Appl Psychol, 52:*158, 1968.

Analyzed psychophysiological data of three Jewish and one Bedouin samples in connection with the detectability of a previously chosen card. Ss of Near Eastern origin tended to show lower pulse rate, higher basic skin conductance, and lower relevant GSR reactivity. It is proposed that psychocultural differences might explain the consistent differential GSR reactivity to the relevant stimuli.

lie detection
deception
GSR reactivity
ethnic differences

7 Lieblich, Israel: Manipulation of contrast between differential GSR responses through the use of ordered tasks of information detection. *Psychophysiology, 6:*70, 1969.

Three variables involved in the production of Short Term Physiological Activation (STPA) were identified: (1) frequency of usage of the stimulus by the organism, (2) relevance of the stimulus to the organism, and (3) whether or not a verbal response to the stimulus is required. Stimulus sequences for information detection were constructed by combining these variables, and physiological responsiveness was observed in the GSR. It was hypothesized that short-term physiological responsivity could be manipulated in an ordered fashion using combinations of the above-mentioned variables. Each one of 54 Ss was tested in six experimental sequences. It was found that it was possible to manipulate the contrast between the GSRs emitted by the S to the critical stimuli, and those produced to the alternative stimuli in information detection tasks in the predicted direction.

information detection
verbal behavior
spontaneous GSRs
elicited GSRs
behavioral arousal
orienting response

8 Lieblich, Israel, Kugelmass, Sol, and Ben-Shakhar, Gershon: Efficiency of GSR detection of information as a function of stimulus set size. *Psychophysiology, 6:*601, 1970.

The reported studies attempted to evaluate the influence of stimulus set size on the efficiency of detection of information through the analysis of GSR responses. Three stimulus set size variations of a standard card detection test were employed. No significant reduction in absolute detection scores was found as the number of cards was increased, and an analysis based on the Theory of Signal Detection also suggested better autonomic discrimination as the stimulus set size increased. The results suggest that the subject responds to the stimuli by dividing them into a single relevant stimulus and a reject category containing all others.

lie detection
stimilus information
signal detection

9 Orne, Martin T., and Thackray, Richard I.: Group GSR technique in the detection of deception. *Percept Mot Skills, 25:*809, 1967.

A technique to average GSR across Ss is proposed to facilitate

deception

detection of deception. Differential responsivity to "lie" versus "neutral" stimuli is augmented by averaging out idiosyncratic responses to neutral stimuli. Its feasibility was demonstrated by recording individual and group GSRs of Ss questioned in small groups. The probability of detecting shared information was greatly increased. Limitations and possible applications of the technique are discussed.

group registration technique

Q 10   Thackray, Richard I., and Orne, Martin T.: A comparison of physiological indices in detection of deception. *Psychophysiology, 4:*329, 1968.

Physiological measures—breathing amplitude (BA), breathing cycle time (BCT), galvanic skin response (GSR), skin potential response (SPR), systolic blood pressure (BP), oxygen saturation level (O₂S), finger volume (FV), and pulse volume (PV)—were compared with respect to their relative efficiency in discriminating deception in a lie detection experiment. Thirty Ss were tested. Stimuli consisted of personal words and neutral words made relevant in the context of a mock crime paradigm. Only GSR, SPR, and FV consistently discriminated better than chance, with GSR and SPR significantly superior to FV. BA and O₂S yielded some evidence of discrimination, but were inconsistent across stimulus material.

deception physiologic indices verbal behavior emotion stress

Q 11   Thackray, R.I., and Orne, M.T.: Effects of the type of stimulus employed and the level of subject awareness on the detection of deception. *J Appl Psychol, 52:*234, 1968.

An experiment was designed to compare detection of personal material with that of neutral material made relevant only in the experimental context. Each S acted the role of an espionage agent and attempted to conceal both his personal identity and certain code words he had learned. Personally relevant material was found to be significantly more detectable than the neutral material, although consequences of detection were the same for both types. In addition, the study attempted to provide exploratory data concerning physiological responsivity to lie-detection stimuli when Ss were unaware that responses were being monitored. While there was

lie detection deception emotional stimuli awareness

no evidence that detection was inferior under the nonaware condition, difficulties in achieving a completely convincing nonaware situation suggest caution in generalizing from these findings.

12 Worrall, Norman: Differential GSR conditioning of true and false decisions. *J Exp Psychol, 86:*13, 1970.

Used a series of questions to demonstrate differential conditioning of the GSR to decisions to give true or false answers to the questions. Following a mock theft, twenty personality inventory-type questions were asked, to any five of which undergraduate Ss were required to give a deliberate false answer. An experimental group (N = 60) had shock paired with each false answer, while control groups experienced either random shock (N = 60) or no shock (N = 60) at all. The GSR under examination appeared to have two components, one occurring several seconds before the overt answer and one approximately coinciding with the answer.

lie detection
differential conditioning
instructions
subjective judgments
response characteristics
anticipation
cognitive mediation

SECTION R

REVIEW,
THEORY, COMMENT

R 1   Crider, Andrew, Schwartz, Gary E., and Shnidman, Susan:
       On the criteria for instrumental autonomic conditioning: A
       reply to Katkin and Murray. *Psychol Bull, 71:*455, 1969.

In their recent review of instrumental conditioning of autonomic functions, Katkin and Murray criticized most of the
existing studies on the human level as artifactual on one or
more grounds. The criteria they employed for rejecting these
demonstrations are themselves open to criticism, however.
Specifically, it is argued that (1) peripheral or cognitive
mediation hypotheses are unlikely alternative explanations of
the obtained results; (2) an increase in response frequency
over a preconditioning operant level is not a necessary condition for demonstrating an increase in response probability
with contingent reinforcement; (3) yoked-control designs,
frequently used in this research, do not automatically invalidate experiments in which they are employed. It is concluded that the strongest hypothesis to account for the existing data remains the direct instrumental strengthening of
autonomic activity.

*operant con-
ditioning
criteria*

R 2   Dengerink, H.A., and Taylor, S.P.: Multiple responses with
       differential properties in delayed galvanic skin response con-
       ditioning: A review. *Psychophysiology, 8:*348, 1971.

Studies of delayed GSR conditioning have shown that when
an interstimulus interval (ISI) of sufficient duration is employed, multiple responses may occur within that interval.
The studies reviewed in this article indicate that GSRs which
occur early in the interval are present by the second conditioning trial. They tend to habituate, appear to be orienting
responses, and, under certain circumstances, they are condi-

*review
delayed con-
ditioning
orienting
response
defensive
response
adaptation*

174

tional. Those responses which occur during the later portion of the interval are minimal, if at all present, when conditioning is initiated but show a negatively accelerated growth curve across trials. These second responses are conditional and may be protective reflexes which prevent damage to the skin. It is concluded that in GSR conditioning the choice of an ISI and the specification of ISI responses may seriously affect the nature of the behavior observed and may have serious implications for other areas of psychological investigation.

3   Hagfors, Carl: The galvanic skin response and its application to the group registration of psychophysiological processes. *Jyvaskyla Studies in Education, Psychology & Social Research, 23*:128, 1970.

Describes a general model of the exosomatic GSR which permits the conceptualization of how the different components function. Also discussed is the group registration of psychophysiological processes by using mixed analogy signals. This suggests the possibility of a more general view of the patterning of autonomic reactivity and provides some practical application of the psychophysiological methods in communication research. Properties of the curves and specific sampling problems are considered, and models demonstrate that it is possible to obtain an error estimate on the group levels. An experiment to compare subjective push-button emotions with group GSR, using emotional reactivity of an audience of films, is included.

review
model
response
  components
group registration
theory
applications

4   Hume, W.I.: Electrodermal measures in behavioral research. *J Psychosom Res, 9*:383, 1966.

Reviews the methodology and theoretical understanding of the GSR. Since the measurement of resistance introduces too many artifacts and imponderables, where different Ss and different experiments are being compared with respect to absolute level values, the most valid measure is that of skin potential.

review
methodology
theory
measurement
indices

R 5 Karrer, R.: Autonomic nervous system functions and behavior: A review of experimental studies with mental defectives. *International Review of Research in Mental Retardation, 2:57*, 1966.

A review of the literature on ANS activity of mental defectives indicates that much basic information is needed. While
there have been a number of studies, they have generally
lacked the power to definitively determine ANS relations to
mental deficiency. There are trends in the available data
indicating that defectives (1) have a markedly lower than
normal basal skin resistance (with the possible exception of
Down's Syndrome); (2) exhibit fewer spontaneous fluctuations in GSR and acceleratory HR activity; (3) are less responsive than normal, at least to weak- and short-duration
stimuli; (4) have faster recovery from short-duration stimuli
and shorter GSR response latencies; (5) have a possible generalized patterning.

review
mental
defectives
response
character-
istics

R 6 Kimmel, H.D.: Instrumental conditioning of autonomically
mediated behavior. *Psychol Bull, 67:337*, 1967.

Recent evidence on the question of whether autonomically
mediated responses can be conditioned by instrumental
methods is summarized and interpreted to provide tentative
support for an affirmative answer. Studies have been done on
heart rate, vasomotor reflex, salivation, intestinal contractions,
and the GSR; and methods used have ranged from operant
reward training to instrumental avoidance training. Methodological problems due to confounding associated with the
yoked control design and mediation by somatically innervated responses are discussed and relevant evidence presented.

review
comment
theory

R 7 Kodman, Frank Jr.: Validity of GSR conditioning. *Psychol
Rep, 21:813*, 1967.

Discusses several theoretical issues related to the controversy
of sensitization or pseudoconditioning of the GSR coupled to
an auditory stimulus. Results of GSR audiometric studies
were cited to show that under controlled conditions, valid
auditory thresholds may be measured using the GSR method.

review
theory
mechanism

8   Lockhart, Russell A.: Comments regarding multiple response phenomena in long interstimulus interval conditioning. *Psychophysiology, 3:*108, 1966.

When the CS-US interval is longer than the latency of an autonomic response, multiple responses are obtained both during and after the CS-US interval on acquisition test or extinction trials. Certain terminologic, methodologic and conceptual problems concerning this multiple response phenomenon are outlined. A nontheoretical and, we hope, unambiguous terminology is presented. Methodologic problems concerning multiple-response measurement, between- and within-subject designs, trace and delay paradigms, intramodal and intermodal paradigms, and incompleteness of data presentation are discussed. It is felt that empirical analysis of the multiple response phenomenon will have important ramifications for our understanding of autonomic behavior in the classical conditioning situation.

comments
classical conditioning
conditioning procedures
review

9   Montagu, J.O.: Mechanism and measurement of the galvanic skin response. *Psychol Bull, 65:*261, 1966.

The measurement of the GSR is subject to error from many sources. Recent work has elucidated the peripheral mechanism of the response and has provided an appropriate electrical model. This review considers the measurement and analysis of the GSR in light of this recent work. The relative merits of constant current (resistance) and constant voltage (conductance) are discussed, the optimal electrode systems are defined, and DC and AC methods are compared. A brief survey of the organismic and environmental variables which influence the response is included.

review
peripheral mechanisms
measurement techniques

10   Neumann, Eva: The early history of electrodermal research. *Psychophysiology, 6:*453, 1970.

The historical origins and early development of electrodermal research are reviewed in the light of a substantial number of previously unexamined sources. Relevant literature in electrophysiology, neurology, electrodiagnosis and electrotherapy is examined with regard to the technology and

review
history

the context of ideas in science and medicine. The first reports of basal skin resistance (BSR) and stimulated skin resistance (GSR) change by Vigouroux and Fere, respectively, are related to their other research and that of other workers. Hermann's early work on the sudomotor system is seen as much more advanced than has been realized, providing a sound basis for theory which the French apparently never noticed. Several additional sources suggest that Tarchanoff's work was performed with awareness of Fere's and was probably not an independent discovery.

R 11   Stennett, R.G.: Alpha amplitude and arousal: A reply to Surwillo. *Psychophysiology,* 2:372, 1966.

Arguments are presented in answer to Surwillo's criticism of a statistical procedure used by Stennett (1957) to test the hypothesis of an inverted-U relationship between alpha amplitude and palmar conductance. Surwillo (1965), despite unwise methodology, produced data consistent with the hypothesis that alpha amplitude bears an inverted-U relationship to heart rate. In a recent paper, Surwillo claimed that Stennett (1957), in demonstrating an inverted-U relationship, between alpha amplitude and palmar conductance, "misused x^2 by violating the requirement that entries from which x^2 values are computed must be independent," and suggested further that Stennett's "positive finding is really an artifact of the method" (Surwillo, 1965, p. 250). In attempting to support this assertion, Surwillo states that "The method is clearly invalid, because data . . . were combined according to a rule which assumes that an inverted-U function relates the variables" (Surwillo, 1965, p. 251). He then refers to hypothetical data which are obviously arranged to "prove" his point (Surwillo, 1965, Fig. 2). The purposes of this paper are (1) to clarify the rationale of the statistical technique involved; (2) to illustrate the fallacy of the conclusion to which Surwillo is drawn by his hypothetical data; and (3) to point out certain methodological problems and pitfalls involved in studies along "the arousal continuum."

comment
arousal
EEG alpha
statistical
analyses

R 12   Tursky, Bernard, and O'Connell, Donald N.: Survey of practice in electrodermal measurement. *Psychophysiology,* 2:237, 1966.

This paper is a report on the results of a survey on electro-dermal recording procedures. A detailed questionnaire was sent to more than two hundred members of the Psycho-physiological Society. The results indicate a wide disagreement among investigators in most phases of the recording process. This indicates a lack of standardization in one of the most used of physiological measures.

review
measure-ment tech-niques
recording techniques

 13   Wilcott, R.C.: A reply to Surwillo on artificial skin potential basal level variation and skin potential response wave form. *Psychophysiology, 2:*377, 1966.

Surwillo had questioned Wilcott's evidence for a relation between skin potential basal level and response wave form. This report clarifies Wilcott's evidence.

comment
response
compon-ents
SP
BSP

Pre-1965 References

ELECTRODERMAL ACTIVITY

Aveling, F.: The conative indications of the psycho-galvanic phenomenon. *Proceedings of the Eighth International Congress of Psychology, 8:*227, 1926.

Ax, A.F.: The physiological differentiation between fear and anger in humans. *Psychosom Med, 15:*433, 1953.

Ayrapetyants, E. Sh., and Bykov, K.: Physiological experiments in the psychology of the subconscious. *J Philosophy Phenomenological Res, 5:*577, 1945.

Baitsch, H.: About sex and related differences in the level of GSR. *Confin Neurol, 14:*88, 1954.

Bartlett, R.J.: Does the psychogalvanic phenomenon indicate emotion? *Br J Psychol, 18:*30, 1927.

Bayley, N.: A study of fear by means of the psychogalvanic technique. *Psychol Rev Mon (Iowa Studies), 38:*1, 1928.

Becker, W.C., and Matheson, H.H.: GSR conditioning, anxiety, and extroversion. *J Abnorm Soc Psychol, 62:*427, 1961.

Berlyne, D.E., Graw, M.A., Salapatek, P.H., and Lewis, J.L.: Novelty, complexity, incongruity, extrinsic motivation and the GSR. *J Exp Psychol, 66:*560, 1963.

Berry, J.L., and Martin, B.: GSR reactivity as a function of anxiety, instructions and sex. *J Abnorm Soc Psychol, 54:*9, 1957.

Berry, R.N.: Skin conductance levels and verbal recall. *J Exp Psychol, 63:*275, 1962.

Bierbaum, W.B.: The temporal gradient in GSR conditioning. *J Gen Psychol, 59:*97, 1958.

Bitterman, M., and Holtzman, W.: Conditioning and extinction of the GSR as a function of anxiety. *J Abnorm Soc Psychol, 47:*615, 1952.

Bixenstine, E.V.: A case study of the use of palmar sweating as a measure of psychological tension. *J Abnorm Soc Psychol, 50:*138, 1955.

Bloch, V.: Nouveau aspects de la méthode psychogalvanique ou électrodermographique (E.D.G.), comme critere des tensions affectives. *Annee Psychol, 52:*329, 1952.

Botwinick, J., and Kornetsky, C.: Age differences in the acquisition and extinction of the GSR. *J Geront, 15:*83, 1960.

Brady, J.V.: Ulcers in "executive monkeys." *Sci Am, 199:*95, 1958.

Branca, A.A.: Sematic generalization at the level of the conditioning experiment. *Am J Psychol, 79:*541, 1957.

Bridger, W.H., and Mandel, I.J.: A comparison of GSR fear responses produced by threat and electric shock. *J Psychiatr Res, 2:*31, 1964.

Bronzaft, A., Hayes, R., Welch, L., and Kolutv, M.: Relationship between PGR and measures of extraversion, ascendance and neuroticism. *J Psychol, 50:*193, 1960.

Burch, N.R., and Greiner, T.H.: A bioelectric scale of human alertness: Concurrent recordings of the EEG and GSR. *Psychiatr Res Rep, 12:*183, 1960.

Cadoret, R.J.: Relationship between autonomic response patterns and conditioned learning. *Percept Mot Skills, 16:*67, 1963.

Calvin, A.D., McGuigan, F.J., Tyrrell, S., and Soyars, M.: Manifest anxiety and the palmar perspiration index. *J Consult Psychol, 20:*356, 1956.

Carmichael, E.A., Honeyman, W.M., Kolb, L.C., and Stewart, W.K.: A physiological study of the skin resistance response in man. *J Physiol, 99:*329, 1941.

Cattell, R.B., and Scheier, I.H.: The nature of anxiety; A review of thirteen multivariate analyses comprising 814 variables. *Psychol Rep, 4:*351, 1958.

Champion, R.A.: The calibration of the galvanic skin response as an indicant of a psychological dimension. *Aust J Psychol, 3:*99, 1951.

Champion, R.A., and Jones, J.E.: Forward, backward, and pseudoconditioning of the GSR. *J Exp Psychol, 62:*58, 1961.

Chatterjee, B.B., and Eriksen, C.W.: Conditioning and generalization of GSR as a function of awareness. *J Abnorm Soc Psychol, 60:*396, 1960.

Cohen, W., and Cadwallader, T.C.: Cessation of visual experience under prolonged uniform visual stimulation. *Am Psychol, 13:*410, 1958.

Collman, R.D.: The psychogalvanic reactions of exceptional and normal children. In *Contributions to Education.* New York, Tchrs Coll, 1931, p. 469.

Combs, C.: Adaptation of the galvanic response to auditory stimuli. *J Exp Psychol, 22:*224, 1938.

Conklin, J.I.: Three factors affecting general level of electrical skin resistance. *Am J Psychol, 64:*78, 1951.

Cook, S., and Harris, R.E.: The verbal conditioning of the galvanic skin reflex. *J Exp Psychol, 21:*202, 1937.

Darrow, C.W.: Differences in the physiological reactions to sensory and ideational stimuli. *Psychol Bull, 26:*185, 1929.

Darrow, C.W.: The equation of the galvanic skin reflex curve. I. The dynamics of reaction in relation to excitation "background." *J Gen Psychol, 16:*285, 1937.

Darrow, C.W.: The functional significance of the galvanic skin reflex and perspiration on the backs and palms of the hands. *Psychol Bull, 30:*712, 1933.

Darrow, C.W.: The galvanic skin reflex and finger volume changes. *Am J Physiol, 88:*219, 1929.

Darrow, C.W.: The galvanic skin reflex (sweating) and blood pressure as preparatory and facilitative functions. *Psychol Bull, 33:*73, 1936.

Darrow, C.W.: Neural mechanisms controlling the palmar galvanic skin reflex and sweating. A consideration of available literature. *Arch Neurol Psychiatry, 37*:641, 1937.

Darrow, C.W.: The rationale for treating the change in galvanic skin response as a change in conductance. *Psychophysiology, 1*:31, 1964.

Darrow, C.W.: Sensory, secretory and electrical changes in the skin following bodily excitation. *J Exp Psychol, 10*:197, 1927.

Darrow, C.W.: Simultaneous galvanic reactions in different skin areas. *Psychol Bull, 29*: 674, 1932.

Darrow, C.W., and Freeman, G.L.: Palmar skin resistance changes contrasted with non-palmar changes, and rate of insensible weight loss. *J Exp Psychol, 17*:739, 1934.

Darrow, C.W., Wilcott, R.C., Siegel, N., Wilson, J., Watanabe, K., and Vieth, R.: The mechanism of diphasic skin potential response. *Electroencephalogr Clin Neurophysiol, 9*:169, 1957.

Davis, R.C.: Modification of the galvanic skin reflex by daily repetition of a stimulus. *J Exp Psychol, 17*:504, 1934.

Davis, R.C., Buchwald, A.M., and Frankmann, R.W.: Autonomic and muscular responses, and their relation to simple stimuli. *Psychol Monogr, 69*:20, 1955.

Densham, H.B.A.R., and Wells, H.M.: The effect of the circulation on the skin-constrictor (Psychogalvanic) reflex. *Q J Exp Physiol, 18*:283, 1927.

Duffy, E., and Lacey, C.L.: Adaptation in energy mobilization in changes in general level of palmar skin conductance. *J Exp Psychol, 36*:437, 1946.

Duret-Cosyns, S. and Duret, R.L.: Contribution expérimentale á l'étude de l'électrodermogramme et du réflexe psychogalvanique chez l'homme. *Acta Neurol Belg, 56*: 312, 1956.

Durup, G., and Fessard, A.: Observations psycho-physiologiques relatives a l'action des stimuli visuels et auditos. *L Annee Psychol, 36*:1, 1935.

Dykman, R.A., Gantt, W.H., and Whitehorn, J.C.: Conditioning as emotional sensitization and differentiation. *Psychol Mongr, 70*:1, 1956.

Edelberg, R.: Effect of vasoconstriction on galvanic skin response amplitude. *J Appl Physiol, 19*:427, 1964.

Edelberg, R.: Electrophysiologic characteristics and interpretation of skin potentials. (Tech. Documentary Rep. No. SAM-tdr-63-95) Brooks Air Force Base, Texas: US Air Force School of Aerospace Medicine, 1963.

Edelberg, R.: The relationship between the galvanic skin response, vasoconstriction, and tactile sensitivity. *J Exp Psychol, 62*:187, 1961.

Edelberg, R., and Burch, N.R.: Skin resistance and galvanic skin response. Influence of surface variables and methodological implications. *Arch Gen Psychiatry, 7*:163, 1962.

Edelberg, R., Greiner, T., and Burch, N.R.: Some membrane properties of the effector in the galvanic skin response. *J Appl Physiol, 15*:691, 1960.

Edelberg, R., and Wright, D.J.: Two galvanic skin effector organs and their stimulus specificity. *Psychophysiology, 1*:39, 1964.

Ellsworth, R.A., and Clark, L.D.: Prediction of the response of chronic schizophrenics to drug therapy: A preliminary report on the relationship between palmar sweat and the behavioral effects of tranquilizing drugs. *J Clin Psychol, 13*:59, 1957.

Eysenck, S.B.G.: An experimental study of psychogalvanic reflex responses of normal, neurotic, and psychotic subjects. *J Psychosom Res, 1*:258, 1956.

Féré, C.: Note sur les modifications de la resistance électrique sous l'influence des excitations sensorielles et des émotions. *C R Soc Biol (Paris), 5*:217, 1888.

Féré, C.: Note sur les modifications de la tension électrique dans le corps humain. *C R Soc Biol (Paris)*, 5:210, 1888.

Fischer, S.: Body image and asymmetry of body reactivity. *J Abnorm Soc Psychol*, 57: 292, 1958.

Fjeld, S.P., Stern, J.A., and Zimny, G.H.: Effects of CS-UCS interval upon conditioning and extinction of GSR. *J Psychosom Res, 8:*45, 1964.

Forbes, T.W.: Problems in measurement of electrodermal phenomena — Choice of method and phenomena — potential, impedance, resistance. *Psychophysiology, 1:*26, 1964.

Forbes, T.W.: Skin potential and impedance response with repeated shock stimulation. *Am J Physiol, 2:*189, 1936.

Forbes, T.W., and Bolles, M.M.: Correlation of the response potentials of the skin with "exciting" and "non-exciting" stimuli. *J Psychol, 2:*273, 1936.

Fowler, R.L., and Kimmel, H.D.: Operant conditioning of the GSR. *J Exp Psychol, 63:* 563, 1962.

Fox, R., and Lippert, W.: Spontaneous GSR and anxiety level in sociopathic delinquents. *J Consult Psychol, 27:*368, 1963.

Freeman, G.L.: The galvanic phenomenon and conditioned responses. *J Gen Psychol, 3:*529, 1930.

Freeman, G.L., and Katzoff, E.T.: Methodological evaluation of the galvanic skin response, with special reference to the formula for R.Q. (recovery quotient). *J Exp Psychol, 31:*239, 1942.

Freeman, G.L., and Simpson, R.M.: The effect of the experimentally induced muscular tension upon palmar skin resistance. *J Gen Psychol, 18:*319, 1938.

Fujimori, B.: Studies on the galvanic skin response using the current and potential method. *Jap J Physiol, 5:*394, 1956.

Fujimori, B., and Yokota, T.: Central and peripheral mechanisms of galvanic skin reflex. *Acta Neuroveget, 24:*241, 1963.

Gendlin, E.T., and Berlin, J.I.: Galvanic skin response correlates of different modes of experiencing. *J Clin Psychol, 17:*73, 1961.

Gershuni, G.V.: Conditioned cutaneo-galvanic reactions and reactions of depression alpha rhythm following subthreshold and superthreshold sound stimulation in man. *Zh Vyssh Nerv Deiat, 5:*665, 1956. Also in: *The Central Nervous System and Human Behavior.* Trans. from the Russian Medical Literature. Bethesda, Russian Sci Tran Program, 1959, p. 587.

Gildemeister, M.: Der sogenannte psycho-galvanische reflex und seine physikalisch-chemische deutung. *Pfluegers Arch, 162:*489, 1915.

Goadby, K.W., and Goadby, H.K.: Simultaneous photographic records of the potential and resistance effects of the psychoemotive response. *J Physiol, 86:*11, 1936.

Graham, L.A., Cohen, S.I., and Shmavonian, B.M.: Physiologic determination and behavioral relationships in human instrumental conditioning. *Psychosom Med, 26:*321, 1964.

Grant, D.A., and Meyer, H.I.: The formation of generalized response sets during repeated electric shock stimulation. *J Genet Psychol, 24:*21, 1941.

Grant, D.A., and Schiller, J.J.: Generalization of the galvanic skin response to visual stimuli. *J Exp Psychol, 46:*309, 1953.

Greenfield, N.S., Alexander, A.A. and Roessler, R.: Ego strength and physiological responsivity. II. The relationship of the Barron ES scale to the temporal and recovery characteristics of skin resistance, finger blood volume, heart rate, and muscle potential responses to sound. *Arch Gen Psychiatry, 9:*129, 1963.

Greenfield, N.S., Katz, D., Alexander, A.A., and Roessler, R.: The relationship between physiological and psychological responsivity, depression and galvanic skin response. *J Nerv Ment Dis, 136:*535, 1963.

Greenwald, D.U.: Some individual differences in electrodermal response to continuous affective stimulation. *Psychol Monogr, 48:*1, 1936.

Gregor, A.: Beitrage zur Kenntniss des psychogalvanischen Phanomens. *Z Ges Neurol Psychiatr, 8:*393, 1912.

Grether, W.F.: Pseudo-conditioning without paired stimulation encountered in attempted backward conditioning. *J Comp Psychol, 25:*91, 1938.

Grings, W.W.: Methodological considerations underlying electrodermal measurement. *J Psychol, 35:*271, 1953.

Grings, W.W., and Lockhart, R.A.: Effects of "anxiety-lessening" instructions and differential set development on the extinction of the GSR. *J Exp Psychol, 66:*292, 1963.

Grings, W.W. et al.: Conditioning autonomic responses of mentally subnormal individuals. *Psychol Monogr, 558,* 1962-1963.

Gustafson, L.A., and Orne, M.T.: The effects of heightened motivation on detection of deception. *J Appl Psychol, 47:*408, 1963.

Gustafson, L.A., and Orne, M.T.: The effects of task and method of stimulus presentation on the detection of deception. *J Appl Psychol, 48:*383, 1964.

Haggard, E.A.: Experimental studies of affective processes: I. Some effects of cognitive structure and active participation on certain autonomic reactions during and following experimentally induced stress. *J Exp Psychol, 33:*257, 1943.

Haggard, E.A.: Experimental studies in affective processes: II. On the quantification and evaluation of "measured" changes in skin resistance. *J Exp Psychol, 35:*45, 1945.

Haggard, E.A.: On the application of analysis of variance to GSR data: I. The selection of an appropriate measure. *J Exp Psychol, 39:*378, 1949.

Haywood, H.C., and Shoemaker, D.J.: Measurement of palmar sweating: Effect of repeated measurement from the same area. *J Psychol, 55:*363, 1963.

Holmquest, D., and Edelberg, R.: Problems in the analysis of the endosomatic galvanic skin response. *Psychophysiology, 1:*48, 1964.

Hovland, C.I.: The generalization of conditioned responses: I. The sensory generalization of conditioned responses with varying frequencies of tone. *J Genet Psychol, 17:*125, 1937.

Howe, E.S.: GSR conditioning in anxiety states, normals and chronic functional schizophrenic subjects. *J Abnorm Soc Psychol, 56:*183, 1958.

Humphreys, L.G.: Generalization as a function of method of reinforcement. *J Exp Psychol, 25:*361, 1939.

Inman, V.T., Ralston, H.J., Saunders, J.B. de C.M., Feinstein, B., and Wright, E.W., Jr.: Relation of human electromyogram to muscular tension. *Electroencephalogr Clin Neurophysiol, 4:*187, 1952.

Ismat, F.: Galvanic skin responses from stimulation of limbic cortex. *J Neurophysiol, 24:*176, 1961.

Jeffress, L.A.: Galvanic phenomena of the skin. *J Exp Psychol, 11:*130, 1928.

Johnson, C.L., and Corah, N.L.: Racial difference in skin resistance. *Science, 139:*766, 1963.

Johnson, L.C.: Some attributes of spontaneous autonomic activity. *J Comp Physiol Psychol, 56:*415, 1963.

Jones, H.E.: Adolescent changes in electrodermal phenomena. *Am Psychol, 4:*390, 1949 (abstr).

Jost, H.: Some physiological changes during frustration. *Child Develop, 12:*9, 1941.

Jung, C.G.: On psychophysiological relations of the associative experiments. *J Abnorm Soc Psychol, 1:*247, 1907.

Kaplan, S.: Autonomic visual regulation. *Psychiatr Res Rep Am Psychiat Assoc, 12:*104, 1960.

Karrer, R., and Clausen, J.: A comparison of mentally deficient and normal individuals upon four dimensions of autonomic activity. *J Ment Defic Res, 8:*149, 1946.

Katsube, A., and Tadaki, E.: Studies on the psychogalvanic phenomenon in physical movements. V. The psychogalvanic phenomenon in response to Kendo play and Kyudo play in mind image pictures and viewed in motion pictures. *Res Phys Educ Kyushu Univ, 8:*7, 1964.

Kimmel, H.D.: Further analysis of GSR conditioning: A reply to Stewart, Stern, Winokur and Fredman. *Psychol Rev, 71:*160, 1964.

Kimmel, H.D., and Baxter, R.: Avoidance conditioning of the GSR. *J Exp Psychol, 68:* 482, 1964.

Kimmel, H.D., and Green, W.A.: Disinhibition in GSR conditioning as a function of the number of CS-UCS trials and the temporal location of the novel stimulus. *J Exp Psychol, 68:*567, 1964.

Kimmel, H.D., and Hill, F.A.: A comparison of two electrodermal measures of response to stress. *J Comp Physiol Psychol, 54:*395, 1961.

Kimmel, H.D., and Hill, F.A.: Operant conditioning of the GSR. *Psychol Rep, 7:*555, 1960.

Kimmel, E., and Kimmel, H.D.: A replication of operant conditioning of the GSR. *J Exp Psychol, 65:*212, 1963.

Konorski, J., and Miller, S.: On two types of conditioned reflex. *J Gen Psychol, 16:*264, 1937.

Lacey, J.I.: Individual differences in somatic response patterns. *J Comp Physiol Psychol, 43:*338, 1950.

Lacey, J.I., Bateman, D.E., and Van Lehn, R.: Autonomic response specificity: An experimental study. *Psychosom Med, 15:*8, 1953.

Lacey, J.I., and Lacey, B.C.: The relationship of resting autonomic activity to motor impulsivity. *Proc Assoc Res Nerv Ment Dis, 36:*144, 1958.

Lacey, J.I., and Lacey, B.C.: Verification and extension of the principle of autonomic response stereotype. *Am J Psychol, 71:*50, 1958.

Lacey, O.L.: An analysis of the appropriate unit for use in the measurement of level of galvanic skin resistance. *J Exp Psychol, 37:*449, 1947.

Lacey, O.L., and Siegel, P.S.: An analysis of the unit of measurement of the galvanic skin response. *J Exp Psychol, 39:*122, 1949.

Lader, M.H.: The effect of cyclobarbitone on the habituation of psychogalvanic reflex. *Brain, 87:*321, 1964.

Lader, M.H., and Montagu, J.D.: The psycho-galvanic reflex: A pharmacological study of the peripheral mechanism. *J Neurol Neurosurg Psychiatry, 25:*126, 1962.

Lader, M.H., and Wing, L.: Habituation of psychogalvanic reflex in patients with anxiety states and in normal subjects. *J Neurol Neurosurg Psychiatry, 27:*210, 1964.

Landis, C., and DeWick, H.N.: The electrical phenomena of the skin. *Psychol Bull, 26:* 64, 1929.

Landis, C.: Electrical phenomena of the skin. *Psychol Bull, 29:*693, 1932.

Laties, V.G.: Effects of meprobamate on fear and palmar sweating. *J Abnorm Soc Psychol, 59:*156, 1959.

Lazarus, R.S., and McCleary, R.A.: Autonomic discrimination without awareness: A study of subception. *Psychol Rev, 58:*113, 1951.

Lazarus, R.S., Speisman, J.C., Mordkoff, A.M., and Davison, L.A.: A laboratory study of psychological stress produced by a motion picture film. *Psychol Monogr, 76:*553, 1962.

Leiderman, P.H., and Shapiro, D.: Studies on the galvanic skin potential level: Some behavioral correlates. *J Psychosom Res, 7:*277, 1964.

Leonard, C., and Winokur, G.: Conditioning versus sensitization in the galvanic skin response. *J Comp Physiol Psychol, 56:*169, 1963.

Lindsley, D.B., and Sassaman, W.H.: Autonomic activation and brain potential associated with "voluntary" control of pilomotors. *J Neurophysiol, 1:*342, 1938.

Littman, R.A.: Conditioned generalization of the galvanic skin reaction to tones. *J Exp Psychol, 39:*868, 1949.

Lloyd, D.P.C.: Action potential and secretory potential of sweat glands. *Proc Natl Acad Sci, 47:*351, 1961.

Lockhart, R.A., and Grings, W.W.: Comments on "An analysis of GSR conditioning". *Psychol Rev, 70:*562, 1963.

Lockhart, R.A., and Grings, W.W.: Interstimulus interval effects in GSR discrimination conditioning. *J Exp Psychol, 67:*209, 1964.

Lovibond, S.H.: Positive and negative conditioning of the GSR. *Acta Psychol (Amst), 21:*100, 1963.

Luborsky, L., and Blinder, B.: Eye fixation and recall of pictures as a function of GSR responsivity. *Percept Mot Skills, 16:*469, 1963.

Lykken, D.T.: The GSR in the detection of guilt. *J Appl Psychol, 43:*385, 1959.

Lykken, D.T.: Properties of electrodes used in electrodermal measurement. *J Comp Physiol Psychol, 52:*629, 1959.

Lykken, D.T.: The validity of the guilty knowledge technique. *J Appl Psychol, 44:*258, 1960.

Lykken, D.T., and Roth, N.: Continuous direct measurement of apparent skin conductance. *Am J Psychol, 74:*293, 1961.

McCleary, R.A.: The nature of the galvanic skin response. *Psychol Bull, 47:*97, 1950.

McCowen, P.K.: The physico-psycho-galvanic reflex in neuroses and psychoses. *J Ment Sci, 72:*492, 1926.

McCurdy, H.G.: Consciousness and the galvanometer. *Psychol Rev, 57:*322, 1950.

Mandler, C., Mandler, J., and Uviller, E.: Autonomic feedback: The perception of autonomic activity. *J Abnorm Soc Psychol, 56:*376, 1958.

Mandler, G., Preven, D.W., and Kuhlman, C.K.: Effects of operant reinforcement of the GSR. *J Exp Anal Behav, 5:*317, 1962.

Martin, B.: Galvanic skin conductance as a function of successive interviews. *J Clin Psychol, 12:*91, 1956.

Martin, I.: Delayed GSR conditioning and the effect of electrode placement on measurement of skin resistance. *J Psychosom Res, 7:*15, 1963.

Martin, I.: A further attempt at delayed GSR conditioning. *Br J Psychol, 54:*359, 1963.

Martin, I.: GSR conditioning and pseudoconditioning. *Br J Psychol, 53:*365, 1962.

Martin, J.: Variations in skin resistance and their relationship to GSR conditioning. *J Ment Sci, 106:*281, 1960.

Maulsby, R.L., and Edelberg, R.: The interrelationship between the galvanic skin response, basal resistance, and temperature. *J Comp Physiol Psychol, 53:*475, 1960.

Moeller, G.: The CS-UCS interval in GSR conditioning. *J Exp Psychol, 48*:162, 1954.

Montagu, J.D.: Habituation of the psycho-galvanic reflex during serial tests. *J Psychosom Res, 7*:199, 1963.

Montagu, J.D.: The psycho-galvanic skin reflex: A comparison of the AC resistance and skin potential changes. *J Neurol Neurosurg Psychiat, 21*:119, 1958.

Montagu, J.D.: The psycho-galvanic reflex: A comparison of DC and AC. Methods of measurement. *J Psychosom Res, 8*:49, 1964.

Mordkoff, A.M.: The relationship between psychological and physiological response to stress. *Psychosom Med, 26*:135, 1964.

Mundy-Castle, A.C., and McKiever, B.C.: The psychophysiological significance of the galvanic skin response. *J Exp Psychol, 46*:15, 1953.

Noble, C.E.: Conditioned generalization of the galvanic skin response to a subvocal stimulus. *J Exp Psychol, 40*:14, 1950.

Obrist, P.A.: Skin resistance levels and galvanic skin response: Unilateral differences. *Science, 139*:227, 1963.

O'Connell, D.N., and Tursky, B.: Silver-silver chloride sponge electrodes for skin potential recording. *Am J Psychol, 73*:302, 1960.

O'Connell, D.N., Tursky, B., and Orne, M.T.: Electrodes for the recording of skin potential: An evaluation. *Arch Gen Psychiatry, 3*:252, 1960.

Orlansky, J.: An assessment of lie detection capability. Tech Rep 62-16, declassified version. Washington, D.C., Inst of Defense Anal, Res and Engin Sup Div., 1962.

Paintal, A.S.: A comparison of the galvanic skin response of normals and psychotics. *J Exp Psychol, 41*:425, 1951.

Perez-Reyes, M., Shands, H.C., and Johnson, G.: Galvanic skin reflex inhibition threshold: A new psychophysiologic technique. *Psychosom Med, 24*:274, 1962.

Peterson, F.: The galvanometer as a measurer of emotions. *Br Med J, 2*:804, 1907.

Peterson, F., and Jung, C.G.: Psychophysical investigations with the galvanometer and plethysmograph in normal and insane individuals. *Brain, 30*:153, 1907.

Peterson, F.: The galvanometer in psychology. *J Abnorm Psychol, 3*:43, 1908-09.

Prideaus, E.: The psychogalvanic reflex: A review. *Brain, 43*:50, 1920.

Prince, M., and Peterson, F.: Psycho-galvanic reactions from co-conscious ideas in a case of multiple personality. *J Abnorm Psychol, 3*:114, 1908.

Prokasy, W.F., Fawcett, J.T., and Hall, J.F.: Recruitment, latency, magnitude and amplitude of the GSR as a function of interstimulus interval. *J Exp Psychol, 64*:513, 1962.

Prokasy, W.F., Hall, J.F., and Fawcett, J.T.: Adaptation sensitization, forward and backward conditioning, and pseudoconditioning of the GSR. *Psychol Rep, 10*:103, 1962.

Rachman, S.: Galvanic skin response in identical twins. *Psychol Rep, 6*:298, 1960.

Radecki, W.: Recherches experimentales sur les phenomenes psychoelectrique. *Arch Psychol*, 209, 1911.

Rice, D.G.: Operant GSR conditioning and associated electromyogram responses. *Dissertation Abstracts, 25*:3693, 1964.

Richter, C.P.: The significance of the changes in the electrical resistance of the body during sleep. *Proc Natl Acad Sci USA, 12*:214, 1926.

Richter, C.P.: A study of the electrical skin resistance and the psychogalvanic reflex in a case of unilateral sweating. *Brain, 50*:216, 1927.

Richter, C.P.: The electrical skin resistance: Diurnal and daily variations in psychopathic and in normal persons. *Arch Neurol Psychiatry, 19*:488, 1928.

Richter, C.P., and Woodruff, B.G.: Facial patterns of electrical skin resistance. *Johns Hopkins Med J, 70:*442, 1942.

Richter, C.P., Woodruff, B.G., and Eaton, B.C.: Hand and foot patterns of low electrical skin resistance: Their anatomical and neurological significance. *J Neurophysiol, 6:*417, 1943.

Rickles, W.H.: Engineering considerations in GSR research. Brooks Air Force Base, Texas, US Air Force School of Aerospace Medicine, 1964.

Rieksher, C., and Jung, C.G.: Further investigations on the galvanic phenomenon and respiration in normal and insane individuals. *J Abnorm Psychol, 2:*189, 1908.

Ringness, T.A.: GSR during learning activities of children of low, average, and high intelligence. *Child Develop, 33:*879, 1962.

Rodnick, E.: Characteristics of delayed and trace conditioned response. *J Exp Psychol, 20:*409, 1937.

Roessler, R., Alexander, A.A., and Greenfield, N.S.: Ego strength and physiological responsivity. I. The relationship of the Barron ES scale to skin resistance, finger blood volume, heart rate and muscle potential responses to sound. *Arch Gen Psychiatry, 8:*142, 1963.

Ross, S., Dardano, J., and Hackman, R.C.: Conductance levels during vigilance task performance. *J Appl Psychol, 43:*65, 1959.

Schackel, B.: Skin-drilling: A method of diminishing galvanic skin potentials. *Am J Psychol, 52:*114, 1959.

Schlosberg, H., and Stanley, W.C.: A simple test of the normality of twenty-four distributions of electrical skin conductance. *Science, 117:*35, 1953.

Scripture, E.W.: Detection of the emotions by the galvanometer. *J Am Med Assoc, 50:* 1164, 1908.

Sears, R.: Psychogalvanic responses in arithmetical work: Effects of experimental changes in addition. *Arch Psychol, 24:*155, 1933.

Shapiro, D., Crider, A.B., and Tursky, B.: Differentiation of an autonomic reponse through operant reinforcement. *Psychon Sci, 1:*147, 1964.

Shapiro, D., and Leiderman, P.H.: Studies on the galvanic skin potential level: Some statistical properties. *J Psychosom Res, 7:*269, 1964.

Shaver, B.A., Jr., Brusilow, S.W., and Cooke, R.E.: Origin of the galvanic skin response. *Proc Soc Exp Biol Med, 110:*559, 1962.

Shock, N.W., and Combs, C.H.: Changes in skin resistance and affective tone. *Am J Psychol, 49:*611, 1937.

Sidis, B.: The nature and cause of the galvanic phenomenon. *J Abnorm Psychol, 5:*69, 1910.

Silverman, A.J., Cohen, S.I., and Shamavonian, B.M.: Investigation of psychophysiologic relationships with skin resistance measures. *J Psychosom Res, 4:*65, 1959.

Silverman, J.S., and Powell, V.E.: Studies on palmar sweating. *Psychosom Med, 6:*243, 1944.

Silverman, R.E.: Eliminating a conditioned GSR by the reduction of experimental anxiety. *J Exp Psychol, 59:*122, 1960.

Staats, A.W., Staats, C.K., and Crawford, H.L.: First-order conditioning of word meaning and the parallel conditioning of a GSR. *J Gen Psychol, 67:*159, 1962.

Staats, C.K., and Staats, A.W.: Meaning established by classical conditioning. *J Exp Psychol, 54:*74, 1957.

Starch, D.: Mental processes and concomitant galvanometric changes. *Psychol Rev, 17:* 19, 1910.

Sterling, K., and Miller, J.G.: Conditioning under anesthesia. *J Exp Psychol, 53*:92, 1940.

Stern, J.A., Edmonston, W., Ulett, G.A., and Levitsky, A.: Electrodermal measures in experimental amnesia. *J Abnorm Soc Psychol, 67*:397, 1963.

Stern, J.A., Stewart, M.A., and Winokur, G.: An investigation of some relationships between various measures of galvanic skin response. *J Psychosom Res, 5*:215, 1961.

Stern, J.A., Winokur, G., Stewart, M., and Leonard, C:. Electrodermal conditioning: Some further correlates. *J Nerv Ment Dis, 137*:479, 1963.

Stern, J.A., and Word, T.J.: Observations on the effect of electroconvulsive therapy and pharmacotherapy on the PGR. *J Neuropsychiat, 2*:149, 1961.

Sternbach, R.A.: The effects of instructional sets on autonomic responsivity. *Psychophysiology, 1*:67, 1964.

Stewart, M.A., Winokur, G., Stern, J.A., Guze, S.B., Pfeiffer, E., and Hornung, F.: Adaptation and conditioning of the galvanic skin response in psychiatric patients. *J Ment Sci, 105*:1102, 1959.

Stewart, M.A., Stern, J.A., Winokur, G., and Fredman, S.: An analysis of GSR conditioning. *Psychol Rev, 68*:60, 1961.

Switzer, St. C.A.: Disinhibition of the conditioned galvanic skin response. *J Gen Psychol, 9*:77, 1933.

Syz, H.C.: Psychogalvanic studies on sixty-four medical students. *Br J Psychol, 17*:54, 1926.

Takagi, K., and Nakayama, T.: Peripheral effector mechanism of galvanic skin response. *Jap J Physiol, 9*:1, 1959.

Tarchanoff, J.: Uber die galvanischen erscheinungen an der haut des menschen bei reizung der sinnesorgane unde bei verschiedenen formen der psychischen tatigkeit. *Pfluegers Arch, 46*:46, 1890.

Trehub, A., Tucker, I., and Cazavelan, J.: Epidermal b-waves and changes in basal potentials of the skin. *Am J Psychol, 75*:140, 1962.

Tschiriew, S., and Dewatteville, A.: On the electrical excitability of the skin. *Brain, 2*:161, 1880.

Venables, P.H.: The relationship between level of skin potential and fusion of paired light flashes in schizophrenic and normal subjects. *J Psychiatr Res, 1*:279, 1963.

Venables, P.H., and Sayer, E.: On the measurement of the level of skin potential. *Br J Psychol, 54*:251, 1963.

Veraguth, O.: Das psycho-galvanische reflex-phaenomen. *Mschr Psychiat Neurol, 21*:387, 1907.

Vigouroux, R.: Sur le role de la resistance electrique des tissues dans l'electro-diagnostic. *C R Soc Biol (Paris), 31*:336, 1879.

Vogel, M.D.: GSR conditioning and personality factors in alcoholics and normals. *J Abnorm Soc Psychol, 63*:417, 1961.

Wagner, H.N.: Objective testing of vision with the use of the galvanic skin response. *Arch Opthalmol, 43*:529, 1950.

Wang, G.H.: The galvanic skin reflex. A review of old and recent works from a physiologic point of view. Part I. Part II. *Am J Phys Med, 36*:295, 1957; *37*:35, 1958.

Wechsler, D.: The measurement of emotional reactions: Researches on the psychogalvanic reflex. *Arch Psychol, 76*:20, 1925.

White, C.T., and Schlosberg, H.: Degree of conditioning of the GSR as a function of the period of delay. *J Exp Psychol, 43*:357, 1952.

Wickens, D.D., Allen, C.K., and Hill, F.A.: Effect of instructions and UCS strength on extinction of the conditioned GSR. *J Exp Psychol, 66:*235, 1963.

Wickens, D.D., Schroder, H.M., and Snide, J.D.: Primary stimulus generalization of the GSR under two conditions. *J Exp Psychol, 47:*52, 1954.

Wiersma, E.D.: On the value of the simultaneous registration of the plethysmogram and the psychogalvanic reaction. *Kon Akad V Wet Amst, 7:*18, 1915.

Wilcott, R.C.: Correlation of skin resistance and potential. *J Comp Physiol Psychol, 51:* 691, 1958.

Wilcott, R.C.: Effects of high environmental temperature on sweating and skin resistance. *J Comp Physiol Psychol, 56:*778, 1963.

Wilcott, R.C.: Effects of local blood removal on the skin resistance and potential. *J Comp Physiol Psychol, 51:*295, 1958.

Wilcott, R.C.: Effects of partial puncture of the epidermis on skin resistance and skin potential. *Psychol Rep, 10:*27, 1962.

Wilcott, R.C.: On the role of the epidermis in the production of skin resistance and potential. *J Comp Physiol Psychol, 52:*642, 1959.

Wilcott, R.C.: Palmar skin sweating vs palmar skin resistance and skin potential. *J Comp Physiol Psychol, 55:*322, 1962.

Wilcott, R.C.: The partial independence of skin potential and skin resistance from sweating. *Psychophysiology, 1:*55, 1964.

Wilcott, R.C.: Silverman-Powell index of sweating vs skin conductance and a humidity index of surface moisture. *J Comp Physiol Psychol, 52:*33, 1959.

Wilcott, R.C.: Skin potential response variations as a function of skin potential base level and palmar location. *Psychophysiol Newsl, 7:*7, 1961.

Wilcott, R.C., Darrow, C.W., and Siegel, A.: Uniphasic and diphasic wave forms of the skin potential response. *J Comp Physiol Psychol, 50:*217, 1957.

Wilder, J.: The law of initial values in neurology and psychiatry: Facts and problems. *J Nerv Ment Dis, 125:*73, 1957.

Williams, J.A.: Novelty, GSR, and stimulus generalization. *Can J Psychol, 17:*62, 1963.

Winokur, G., Stewart, M., Stern, J. and Pfeiffer, E.: A dynamic equilibrium in GSR habituation: The effect of interstimulus interval. *J Psychosom Res, 6:*117, 1962.

Wishner, J.: Studies in efficiency: GSR conditioning as a function of degree of task centering. *J Abnorm Soc Psychol, 65:*170, 1962.

Wishner, J.: Neurosis and tension: An exploratory study of the relationship of physiological and Rorschach measures. *J Abnorm Soc Psychol, 48:*253, 1953.

Yokota, T., Takahashi, T., Kondo, M., and Fujimori, B.: Studies on the diphasic wave form of the galvanic skin reflex. *Electroencephalogr Clin Neurophysiol, 11:*687, 1959.

Zeaman, D., and Wegner, N.: The role of drive reduction in the classical conditioning of an autonomically mediated response. *J Exp Psychol, 48:*349, 1954.

Zimmern, A., and Logre, B.: Sur le reflexe galvanopsychique. *Rev Neurol, 24:*565, 1917.

DESCRIPTOR INDEX — ELECTRODERMAL ACTIVITY

PART II

HEART RATE

MEASUREMENTS

INSTRUMENTS

A 1 Hahn, W.W., and Flax, S.W.: An instrument for recording and printing heart rate data. *Psychophysiology, 3*:93, 1966.

An instrument has been designed which will print maximum, minimum and mean heart rate (HR) data for ten-second sample periods. The basic components are three detector circuits which sample and hold voltage levels proportional to the values measured, a digital voltmeter for "reading" these values, and a solenoid-operated adding machine to print out HR data in beats per minute. This apparatus greatly reduces the time required for transcribing cardiotachometer tracings into digital forms for statistical analysis.

instruments
data analysis

A 2 Krausman, David: Heart rate derived from blood pressure and other physiological signals. *Psychophysiology, 7*:503, 1970.

A device for providing a continuous on-line output of beat-by-beat HR in physiologic studies is described. The circuit eliminates the need for obtaining an EKG signal since it uses other vascular phenomena such as blood pressure, blood flow, or plethysmograph to produce an index of heart action to provide subsequent rate phenomena. Signal conditioning to produce the electrical analog of the vascular change is derived from either a pressure transducer, flow probe, plethysmograph, or other transducing device connected to the input of a Beckman-Offner, or Grass (Model 6) polygraph recorder. The output is in the form of a relay closure to provide initiating action to such devices as cardiotachometers, integrators, printers, counters, and many other instruments used in physiological studies.

instruments
recording
techniques
vascular
data

A 3   Pope, J.M., Deboo, G.J., and Smith, D.B.D.: A cardiotachometer with linear indication of beat-to-beat frequency.
*Psychophysiology, 4:*486, 1968.

The instrument described has a linear indication of beat-to-   *instrument*
beat heart rate with an overall accuracy of ±1 beat per mi-   *HR fre-*
nute. A linear output response over the range of thirty to   *quency*
270 beats per minute is achieved with a square law discharge
network. Input clipping and filter circuits permit reliable
operation with moderately active subjects. Details of the
circuit design and its performance are discussed.

A 4   Thorne, Philip R., Engel, Bernard T., and Quilter, Reginald
E. An instrument for predicting the occurrence of the P-R
interval of the normal human electrocardiogram. *Psychophysiology, 7:*138, 1970.

This report describes an instrument which will automatically   *instruments*
predict the occurrence of the P-R interval on a beat-to-beat   *prediction*
basis. Tests have demonstrated an almost perfect accuracy   *cardiac cycle*
in older subjects whose beat-to-beat variations are small. The *rate varia-*
average accuracy with a group of twenty-three men, nineteen   *tion*
of whom were twenty to thirty years old, was 95 percent
correct prediction. In young women with very large beat-to-
beat variations, the average accuracy achieved was 75 percent
correct prediction.

MEASUREMENT TECHNIQUES

A 5   Elliott, Rogers: Comment on the comparability of measures
of heart rate in cross-laboratory comparison. *J Exp Res Pers,
4:*156, 1970.

A sample of the literature on resting-level tonic heart rate is   *measure-*
surveyed to illustrate the fact that, with this measure, results   *ments*
from one laboratory can in some cases be compared with re-   *cross-labora-*
sults from another. Some implications are considered.   *tory com-*
                                                                  parisons

A 6   Fitzgerald, R.D., Vardario, R.M., and Taylor, T.J.: An on-
line method for measuring heart rate in conditioning experiments. *Psychophysiology, 4:*352, 1968.

An inexpensive system for analysis of heart rate data is described. It provides an accurate and highly reliable on-line printed record of the total number of heartbeats occurring in predetermined time intervals during successive conditioning trials.

*measure-
ments
data analysis
condition-
ing
digitizing
recording
techniques*

A 7   Galbrecht, Charles R., and Dykman, Roscoe A.: On the scoring of heart rate: Reply to criticisms. *Psychophysiology, 2:* 42, 1965.

Land and Hnatiow, who derived a measure of heart rate (HR) response different from that employed by Dykman, Reese, Galbrecht and Thomasson, reported better evidence of HR adaptation to serially presented tones than did Dykman, et al. The former authors found no habituation when Dykman's procedure for scoring HR responses was applied to their data. When Dykman's HR records were rescored by Lang's method, both measures yielded adaptation curves. McDonald, Johnson and Hord, who employed a measure of HR response similar to that of Lang and Hnatiow, noted that alert Ss adapted in HR while drowsy (by electroencephalogram [EEG] activity), Ss failed to adapt. They said that HR adaptation results of Dykman, et al. may have been influenced by inadequate control for arousal level of Ss. However, the most drowsy Ss (judged by behavioral notes) in Dykman's study provided good evidence of HR adaptation by both McDonald's and Dykman's measures. These discrepancies in results are believed to depend mainly upon differences in experimental procedures rather than upon methods of scoring or arousal level.

*scoring
stimulus
repetition
arousal
adaptation
EEG*

A 8   Graham, Frances K.: Analysis of heart rate response curves: A comment on pooled interaction error terms. *Psychophysiology, 7:*485, 1970.

Use of pooled interaction error terms in repeated measurement analyses of variance may lead to seriously erroneous conclusions. The danger is increased when designs contain both data sampled at short intervals of time, such as second-

*error vari-
ance
sampling
rate*

by-second heart rate (HR) responses, and data sampled at longer intervals, such as responses on different trials or stimulus presentations. Empirical examples illustrate the differing error variances typically found with such data.

trend analysis

A 9   Hayes, R.W., and Venables, P.H.: An accurate, direct reading, beat-by-beat, heart rate scale for measurement of the cardiac orientation reaction. *Psychophysiology, 9:*624, 1972.

An easily made, accurate, direct reading scale for obtaining beat-by-beat HR from paper chart EKG recordings is described for use where on-line computer analysis is not practicable, or where a check is wanted on the accuracy of the computer program.

measurements scoring EKG orienting response

A 10   Khachaturian, Z.S., Kerr, J., Kruger, R., and Schachter, J.: A methodological note: Comparison between period and rate data in studies of cardiac function. *Psychophysiology, 9:*539, 1972.

The purpose of the study was to compare two methods of analyzing EKG data, period (R-R intervals) and frequency (heart rate). Simulated data as well as EKGs recorded from newborn infants were utilized to show the effects of transforming cardiac periods into frequencies. The results showed that this transformation introduces errors which are reflected in the mean, variance, and the degree of skewness of the basic data. It is argued that the widely used convention of transforming period data into heart rate should not be used without valid justification.

measurement indices data transformation

A 11   Lykken, D.T.: Range correction applied to heart rate and to GSR data. *Psychophysiology, 9:*373, 1972.

The utility of the range correction, in which each individual autonomic level or response measure is expressed in terms of estimates of that S's maximum and minimum level or response amplitude, was evaluated in terms of the apparent reduction in error variance indicated by larger or more significant treatment effects. The data analyzed were from an experiment in which 48 Ss received twelve painful shocks in

range correction HR SCL

each of four conditions of shock predictability. A reduction in error variance resulted from correcting, for individual differences in tonic range, measures of tonic SC (a replication of previous findings) and measures of tonic HR (a new finding). A reduction in error variance also resulted from dividing each SCR to shock by that S's largest SCR, i.e. by correcting phasic SCR measures for individual differences in range of SCR. No marked improvement resulted from a similar correction of phasic HRR data.

A 12   Malmstrom, Edward J., Opton, Edward Jr., and Lazarus, Richard S.: Heart rate measurement and the correlation of indices of arousal. *Psychosom Med. 27*:546, 1965.

Twenty-two subjects watched a stressor motion picture film, *Subincision,* which was expected to stimulate autonomic arousal, and twenty-two control subjects saw a benign film, *The Corn Farmer.* Heart rate and skin conductance were recorded. When analyzed by previously used methods, skin conductance changes over time showed a close correspondence to film content, while heart rate did not. A new method of sampling heart rate records, the method of mean cyclic maxima gave results closely paralleling those of skin conductance. This method appears to be a major improvement over previous approaches to heart-rate measurement in that it produces greater correspondence to both skin conductance and to the known characteristics of the motion picture stimulus. Since an earlier study showed that phenomenological ratings of emotional reaction closely followed a similar curve of skin conductance, it is expected that future studies will show heart rate variation and phenomenological ratings also to be closely related.

measurement techniques
arousal
stress
emotional responses
SC

A 13   Malmstrom, Edward J.: Basal heart rate variations by day of week. *Psychophysiology, 10*:218, 1973.

Previous studies have shown large variations in basal heart rate (HR) in individuals over occasions. To examine long-term variability, one individual's HR was recorded daily for one year. Besides changes due to ambient temperature and periods of illness, obvious regular variations corresponded

variability
biological rhythms
cultural influences

to day of week. Weekends and Mondays differed from the other four weekdays: HR was high on Saturdays and Mondays and reached a nadir on Sundays. These fluctuations probably reflect the cultural pattern of activity over the week, rather than representing an intrinsic circaseptan rhythm.

A 14   Norman, A., and Melville, C.H.: Potential applications of telemetered heart rate to developmental psychology. *Develop Psychol, 5:*190, 1971.

It is possible to record heart rate changes with a small transmitter while a child engages in unrestrained activity. The use of split-screen videotape makes is possible to precisely relate overt behavioral changes to beat-by-beat heart rate changes. The recording of physiological data via biotelemetry is discussed in its potential application to developmental psychology and in specific regard to the activity to two subjects. It is anticipated that the study of developmental psychophysiology will now be extended to various groups, such as preschool children for whom limited data exists in the literature.

recording technique. telemetry children

A 15   Norman, Arthur, and Melville, Charles H.: The comparability of cross-laboratory resting heart rate: A reply to Elliott. *Psychophysiology, 9:*443, 1972.

Elliott's comments on the comparability of heart rate measures in cross-laboratory comparisons are discussed. The present paper attempts to show that the comparison of heart rate data across various laboratories in an attempt to infer motivational states may not be justified.

cross-laboratory comparisons motivation

A 16   Opton, Edward Jr., Rankin, Neil O., and Lazarus, Richard S.: A simplified method of heart rate measurement. *Psychophysiology, 2:*87, 1966.

Theoretical and practical considerations require a heart rate measurement method which produces substantial correspondence between heart rate and other autonomic and psychological measures of arousal, and which also is fast and inexpensive. A new heart rate measurement method, the peak

measurement techniques correlation activation

rate method, meets these criteria. The peak rate method
corresponds as closely to a skin conductance measure of reaction to a stressful movie as does the method of mean cyclic
maxima (Malmstrom, Opton and Lazarus, in press). The
peak rate method also yields heart rate curves which are
markedly elevated at the most psychologically stressful points
during the movie. The peak rate method does not involve
the laborious, expensive computations required by the method of mean cyclic maxima. Smoothing heart rate curves by a
method of moving averages is also shown to be desirable.

HR
SC

17   Varni, John G., Clark, R. Ernest, and Giddon, Donald B.:
Mean square and mean square successive difference components of heart rate fluctuation. *Psychophysiology, 5:*573,
1969.

The problem of measuring heart rate (HR) variability is
discussed with respect to error components. Traditionally,
"cardiac variability" has been described by the mean square
(MS) of deviations in the number of complete cardiac cycles
per unit time, following from the implication that variability
means nonlawfulness. Yet, variability denotes change, not
merely random change, and numerous biological processes
have already been shown to vary according to rather precise
rhythms (Soliberger, 1955). It was the purpose of the present
paper to examine the possibility that a portion of "cardiac
variability" can, and should, be regarded as nonrandom.
Specifically, the dynamics of von Neumann's time-series
statistic, called the mean squared successive differences
(MSSD), were compared to those of the simple MS. A subject
sample was desired possessing wide potential psychophysiological variability. Just such a sample are the anisocories (individuals with unequal pupil diameters) described earlier
this year by investigators of our laboratory. These and control subjects were subjected to cold pressor stimulation during which R-R intervals were continuously monitored. Cyclic
change in the MSSD measure of HR variability was observed
with a period of about forty seconds, individual MSSD
rhythms in HR appeared to become synchronous during the
experimental stress. In addition, the proportion of the MS
attributable to MSSDs was found to distinguish not only the
experimental periods, but the subject samples. Therefore, it

heart rate
fluctua-
tions
error com-
ponents
data analysis
cyclic
changes
stress

is suggested that future research estimate HR variability in other populations utilizing similar procedures designed to identify nonrandom components.

A 18   Varni, John G., Clark, R. Ernest, and Giddon, Donald B.: Analysis of cyclic heart rate variability. *Psychophysiology, 8:* 406, 1971.

The present paper contrasts the relative efficacies of the traditional mean square or variance and a time-series statistic, the mean square successive difference, as descriptors of cyclic heart rate variability. Estimates of fluctuation in the R-R interval during the prestimulus and cold pressor stimulus periods were obtained for two subject samples. The first sample was composed of individuals having bilateral differences in the diameter of their pupils, a condition known as anisocoria, while the pupils of the Ss in the second sample were of equal diameter. A group sinusoidal rhythm in the mean square successive difference of R-R interval variation was observed during the cold pressor stimulus for the anisocoric sample. However, the rhythm was obscured when the traditional mean square statistic was utilized to describe the same R-R interval variation. No rhythms were identified for the nonanisocoric sample. The mean square successive difference statistic would appear to provide a method for detecting cyclic autonomic variability patterns otherwise obscured by traditional analysis.

cardiac cycl *variability* *biological* *rhythms* *response* *analysis*

RESPONSE
CHARACTERISTICS

B 1   Berg, W. Keith, and Graham, Frances K.: Reproducible effect of stimulus intensity on heart rate response curves. *Psychophysiology, 7:653, 1970.*

> Graham and Clifton (1966) suggested that initial presentations of nonsignal auditory stimuli below 60-70 db re 0.0002 microbar should elicit monophasic HR deceleration and that, with increasing stimulus intensity, an accelerative component would be evident. The present paper used data from eight unpublished experiments to compare HR responsive curves following the first four presentations of 1000 Hz tones of 50 to 55 db (six experiments), 70 to 75 db (six experiments), and 90 to 95 db (five experiments). Rise time was controlled to prevent occurrence of a startle reflex.

*stimulus
intensity
response
patterns
reliability*

B 2   Campos, Joseph J., Langer, Alan, and Krowitz, Alice: Cardiac responses on the visual cliff in prelocomotor human infants. *Science, 170:196, 1970.* (Copyright 1970 by the American Association for the Advancement of Science.)

> Human infants younger than crawling age yielded reliable cardiac decelerations when placed directly atop the deep side of a visual cliff and generally nonsignificant changes when atop the shallow side. Distress was elicited less frequently on the deep side than on the shallow at these ages, in contrast to the behavior of older infants and other species. Prelocomotor infants thus can discriminate the two sides of the cliff, but not by means of distress at loss of optical support.

*infants
visual per-
ception
deceleration
develop-
ment
emotion
orienting
response*

B 3   Clifton, Rachel K., and Graham, Frances K.: Stability of individual differences in heart rate activity during the newborn period. *Psychophysiology, 5:37, 1968.*

Reliability of fourteen measures of newborn heart rate activity was estimated by intercorrelations among repeated daily testings and by the coefficient of concordance. Subjects were sixteen newborns tested for three days and a subsample of ten newborns tested for five days. Thirteen of the measures showed some significant stability although they differed in the size of correlations and in the degree of concordance. The two measures of temporal characteristics of response were among the least reliable, and measures taken at the point of minimal activity were among the most reliable. The only measure for which there was no evidence of significant reliability was the within-individual regression of poststimulus on prestimulus scores. This finding has obvious implications for the argument that individual regressions should be used instead of group regressions to adjust for prestimulus differences.

measurement indices
individual differences
reliability
newborn

B 4   Delfini, Leo F., and Campos, Joseph J.: Signal detection and the "cardiac arousal cycle." *Psychophysiology, 9:*484, 1972.

The hypothesis was tested that different phases of the cardiac cycle would be associated with differences in either sensory capacity or response bias, as estimated by signal detection analyses. Each of ten subjects was given 800 signal (SN) and 800 nonsignal (N) trials randomly distributed throughout the cardiac cycle. The signal was a 35 msec duration, 1000 Hz tone, which was preceded by a one second warning light. Electrocardiograph (EKG) cycles were subsequently divided into four phases, and the phase during which the SN or N trial fell was determined. Signal detection analyses performed on auditory sensitivity (d_s) and estimate of response bias (Criterion Location) showed no measurable effect of EKG phase on either parameter. Results are discussed in terms of recent neurophysiological findings of cardiac rhythmic input to the nucleus tractus solitarius (which can inhibit cortical arousal), but little cardiac rhythm in the observed output. These considerations imply that "cardiac cycle arousal effects" are likely to be minute or nonexistent.

phase of car diac cycle
signal detec tion
sensory sensitivity
response bias
central inhibition

B 5   Elliott, Rogers, and Graf, Virgil: Visual sensitivity as a function of phase of cardiac cycle. *Psychophysiology, 9:*357, 1972.

After preliminary threshold determination, each of 25 Ss was given 120 trials (twenty-four blank, ninety-six signal) in a visual signal detection task, with signal presentations being recorded with S's EKG. There was no relationship between hit rate and phase of cardiac cycle whether assessed over four measured phases, or as the difference in hit rate for signals presented either in the P-wave or the QRS complex. Implications for theory are discussed.

phase of cardiac cycle
signal detection
central inhibition

B 6   Elliott, Rogers, and Thysell, Richard: A note on smoking and heart rate. *Psychophysiology, 5:*280, 1968.

The effect of a cigarette on the heart rate (HR) of habitual smokers was assessed after brief abstinence and after regular smoking, with controls of sham smoking and deep breathing. Smoking, and only smoking, caused elevations in HR of about 20 bpm. The effect mimics habituation, and its dissipation, which may take about an hour, proceeds more slowly after continual smoking than after smoking a single cigarette after a few hours abstinence.

smoking

B 7   Engel, Bernard T., and Chism, Ray A.: Effect of increases and decreases in breathing rate on heart rate and finger pulse volume. *Psychophysiology, 4:*83, 1967.

Twenty percent changes in breathing rate (increases and decreases), sustained for ten minutes, do not change average heart rate; however, increases in breathing rate tend to decrease the standard deviation of heart rate and decreases in breathing rate tend to increase the standard deviation of heart rate. Neither increases nor decreases in breathing rate abolish sinus arrhythmia. Finger pulse volume is decreased by both increases and decreases in breathing rate. The standard deviation of finger pulse volume is decreased during slow-paced breathing and unchanged during fast-paced breathing. The decrease in finger pulse volume occurs within the first minute during slow-paced breathing; however, during fast-paced breathing the decrease does not occur until about four minutes after the onset of paced breathing.

paced respiration rate
HR change
variability
operant conditioning
finger blood flow

B 8   Hatton, H.M., Berg, W.K., and Graham, F.K.: Effects of acoustic rise time on heart rate response. *Psychosom Sci, 19:* 101, 1970.

Effects of acoustic rise time on heart rate (HR) response were tested in two experiments. With 50 and 75db tones, effects were not clear-cut, but at 90 db, fast onsets produced an initial deceleration and slow onsets an initial acceleration. Results were discussed in terms of orienting and startle responses.

*HR
response
auditory
stimuli
response
character-
istics
orienting
response*

B 9   Keefe, F. Barry, and Johnson, L.C.: Cardiovascular responses to auditory stimuli. *Psychon Sci, 19:*335, 1970.

Three cardiovascular responses to a moderate tone (about 70 dB) were studied in 25 Ss. Finger-pulse (FP) response was monophasic vasoconstriction. Head-pulse (HP) response was biphasic; vasoconstriction preceded vasodilation. Heart rate (HR) response usually consisted of an initial small deceleration followed by a more marked acceleration and a secondary deceleration. HP constriction and HR acceleration occurred almost simultaneously; their response magnitudes were highly positively correlated. FP and HP constriction responses were also positively correlated. All responses showed some effect of their prestimulus level.

*auditory
stimuli
HR
responses
finger pulse
volume
vasoconstric
tion
response
magnitude*

B 10   Malmstrom, E.J.: Heart rate synchronization to rhythmic auditory stimuli. *Psychophysiology, 6:*626, 1970.

When the subjects were played passages of recorded music under some conditions as yet unspecified, their heartbeats synchronized with the rhythmic beat of the music: each heartbeat tended to occur at each musical beat. This phenomenon was observed both with music having distinctly audible beats and with music of subtle, indistinct rhythm. Since heartbeats became more regular, cardiotachometer tracings showed flattening or decreased variability. No respiratory changes could be seen to account for this. The problem of objectively recording the phenomenon was partially solved by preparing a stereo tape recording having monaural music

*heart rate
synchrony
music
regularity*

on one channel and a recorded click on the other. The click was matched to the musical beat by tapping a microphone. The music channel was played to the subjects while the click channel was fed into a polygraph to provide a timing mark. Taped slow and fast classical music and slow and fast metronome beats were played to fourteen male subjects while heart rate (HR), EKG, respiration rate, and skin conductance were continuously recorded. Many instances of synchrony were observed, but problems of quantification remain, since a subject may fade in and out of synchronization during a long selection. Metronome beats generally did not produce the effect, possibly because of their rather noxious character. Best results were seen in pilot trials when popular rock music was played to college subjects who enjoyed it. The question is raised whether such results can be described in terms of orienting response patterns to isolated auditory stimuli, or whether different mechanisms must be assumed to induce such HR patterns under repetitive stimuli.

11 Meyers, William J., and Gullickson, Gary R.: The evoked heart rate response: The influence of auditory stimulus repetition, pattern reversal, and autonomic arousal level. *Psychophysiology, 4:*56, 1967.

A brief two-component auditory stimulus was repeatedly presented at ten-second intervals to forty-eight college students. Analysis of the pattern of second-by-second changes in heart rate (HR) revealed that the only reliable response to the first stimulus was HR deceleration. During the remainder of the first twenty trials, an acceleration was the predominant response in the HR curves. When the stimulus pattern was reversed on trial 21 to study "dishabituation," only a HR deceleration was again observed. A significant habituation effect appeared across trials employing an index based upon the difference between peak and trough values. Further analysis revealed that the two response components reflected in the peak and trough values of this index showed different rates of response decrement. The acceleratory component showed a rapid initial decrement and remained stable on subsequent trials, whereas the deceleratory component diminished more gradually. Level of autonomic arousal, as measured by skin conductance level, was unrelated to HR habituation.

*evoked HR
response
auditory
stimulus
repetition
acceleration
orienting
response
habituation
SC*

B 12   Meyers, W.J.: The influence of stimulus intensity and repetition on the mean evoked heart rate response. *Psychophysiology, 6:*310, 1969.

A second by second analysis was made of heart rate (HR) responses of children receiving an auditory stimulus pattern at either a moderate (70 db) or a loud (95 db) intensity. Only an initial deceleration to the first 70 db stimulus significantly departed from prestimulus level. The first 95 db pattern produced two components which statistically differed from prestimulus level: an initial deceleration and a sustained later deceleration. Differential habituation effects occurred at the two intensities with stimulus repetition. The only significant response to subsequent presentations of the 70 db tones was HR acceleration, and this response showed complete habituation, whereas significant HR deceleration occurred with repetition of the 95 db tones. The results are consistent with the hypothesis that a nonfamiliar stimulus will produce an orienting reaction (OR) and HR deceleration. Furthermore, the differential stimulus repetition effects indicate that loud tones may disrupt the process of HR habituation seen to moderate intensity tones, and produce a decelerative response which is resistant to habituation.

stimulus intensity
repeated stimuli
differential habituation
response analysis

B 13   Robinson, Brian F., Epstein, Stephen E., Beiser, G. David, and Braunwald, Eugene: Control of heart rate by the autonomic nervous system. Studies in man on the interrelation between baroreceptor mechanisms and exercise. *Circ Res, 19:* 400, 1966.

The control of heart rate by the autonomic nervous system was investigated in conscious human subjects by observing the effects of β-adrenergic blockade with propranolol, of parasympathetic blockade with atropine, and of combined sympathetic and parasympathetic blockade. The increase in heart rate with mild exercise in supine men was mediated predominantly by a decrease in parasympathetic activity; at higher levels of work, however, sympathetic stimulation also contributed to cardiac acceleration. When the response to 80° head-up tilt was compared with the response to exercise in the same subject supine, it appeared that the attainment

mechanisms
neural control
baroreceptors
exercise

of an equivalent heart rate was associated with a significantly greater degree of sympathetic activity during tilting than during exercise. Although heart rate was always higher at any given pressure during exercise than it had been at rest, the changes in heart rate that followed alterations in arterial pressure were found to be of similar magnitudes at rest and during exercise; it was therefore concluded that the sensitivity of the baroreceptor system was not altered during exercise. Investigation of the efferent pathways concerned in mediating the baroreceptor-induced changes in heart rate suggested that the relative roles of the sympathetic and parasympathetic systems were nearly equal in the resting state. During exercise, on the other hand, changes in sympathetic activity appeared to be the predominant mechanism by which speeding and slowing of the heart was achieved. It thus appears that baroreceptor-induced alterations in heart rate may be mediated by increased or decreased activity of either efferent system; the ultimate balance, however, is critically dependent on the preexisting level of background autonomic activity.

B 14   Roessler, Robert, Collins, Forrest, and Burch, Neil R.: Heart rate response to sound and light. *Psychophysiology, 5:*359, 1969.

The heart rate (HR) response to five intensities of sound was examined in eighteen subjects and to five intensities of light in twelve subjects. Each subject was tested on four occasions at monthly intervals. After covariance adjustment, significant acceleration to sound was found within the first five beats after stimulus onset but no significant deceleration occurred. There were no differences between testings. Individuals' HR acceleration was reliable over testings and differing experimental contexts. No habituation occurred and no consistent relationship between HR response and ego strength was found. There was no significant HR response to light stimulation. The results were discussed in relation to Graham and Clifton's (1966) hypotheses concerning the relationship of the HR response to the orienting reflex (OR).

stimulus intensity reliability habituation ego strength orienting response

B 15   Saxon, Samuel A.: Detection of near threshold signals during four phases of cardiac cycle. *Ala J Med Sci,* 7:427, 1970.

An attempt was made to explore the hypothesis that cardiac phasic activity is correlated with the ability to detect near threshold auditory signals. Tones of 1000 Hz were presented to four Ss randomly as EKG records were being taken on them. The analysis revealed that Ss heard significantly more than 50 percent of the tones occurring during the P phase of the cardiac cycle and significantly fewer than 50 percent of the tones occurring during the QRS phase of the cycle. The results are discussed in relation to previous findings relating cardiac activity and human performance and signal detection theory.

phase of cardiac cycle
signal detection
auditory acuity
individual differences
central inhibition hypothesis

B 16   Saxon, Samuel A., and Dahle, Arthur J.: Auditory threshold variations during periods of induced high and low heart rates. *Psychophysiology, 8:*23, 1971.

The study was designed to test Lacey's and Callaway's contention that individuals respond differently to sensory sensitivity tasks under conditions of high and low heart rates. A Bekesy audiometry threshold tracing was obtained from subjects after a period of inactivity and after a period of activity. The results indicated that the subjects' auditory thresholds for the 1000 Hz tone were significantly less acute under the condition of induced higher heart rates. Although the data collected is correlational in nature the possibility that the higher rate results in reduced sensory sensitivity from a causal point of view is suggested. Although Lacey's and Callaway's formulations are not synonymous with the traditional theories of activation, it is highly probable that their formulations may be merely delineating the mechanisms by which extreme arousal results in impaired performance.

induced HR changes
auditory thresholds
activation theory

B 17   Schulman, C., Kreiter, R., and Murray, J.: The relationship between heart rate change threshold and audiometric threshold in hearing-impaired children. *Psychophysiology, 9:*274, 1972.

The purpose of this study was to determine whether reliable audiometric curves can be obtained for children with known hearing losses by using averaged heart rate change to auditory stimuli. Two groups were studied: (1) neurologically

auditory thresholds
HR change threshold
children

normal Ss, four years old and older on whom conventional audiograms had been obtained; (2) Ss under four years old on whom behavioral observation audiograms had been obtained. A special purpose computer was used to average heart rate change to blocks of five stimuli at each frequency/intensity. The frequencies were 500, 1250, and 3150 Hz. The first block of trials at each frequency was presented at 10 dB ISO above the threshold indicated on the audiogram. The intensity of subsequent blocks was adjusted to 10 dB steps, depending upon whether or not a response was obtained to the first block. Results indicate that correspondence between audiometric threshold and heart rate change threshold are within 10 dB. Furthermore, the heart rate change audiograms had the same shape as conventional audiograms, indicating that profiles for sensorineural loss are clearly identifiable by the criterion of heart rate change.

B 18   Smith, D.B.D., and Strawbridge, P.J.: The heart rate response to a brief auditory and visual stimulus. *Psychophysiology, 6:* 317, 1969.

The adult heart rate (HR) response was studied in eighteen male subjects following a series of ten tones and ten light flashes. Both stimuli were of moderate intensity (54 db and 8.0 ml) and had rise times of thirty milliseconds. The tone evoked a predominantly acceleratory response and no decrement with repetition. Initially, the light flash evoked a predominantly deceleratory response which changed to one of acceleration as the stimulus was repeated. Analysis of respiration revealed that an increase in rate and amplitude followed both stimuli and that the magnitude of respiratory changes did not diminish with stimulus repetition. Viewed according to Sokolov's criteria for identifying orienting, defensive and adaptive responses the results support the conclusions that HR deceleration is a component of the orienting response and HR acceleration is neither an orienting, defensive nor adaptive response but is largely secondary to respiratory changes. On the basis of the evidence, a tentative model of the HR response to simple auditory and visual stimuli is offered.

stimulus discrimination
auditory signals
visual signals
respiration

B 19 Sroufe, L. Alan: Effects of depth and rate of breathing on heart rate and heart rate variability. *Psychophysiology, 8:* 648, 1971.

Effects of depth and rate of breathing on heart rate (HR) and HR variability were observed in two experiments. Respiration rate (RR) affected only cardiac stability, faster breathing producing more stable cardiac rate. Respiration depth (RD) affected both HR level and variability. Deep breathing produced faster, more variable HR, while shallow breathing had the opposite effects. A third experiment, in which Ss were trained to control HR using respiration, further illustrated the dramatic effects of respiration on cardiac rate. Implications of these results for experiments utilizing HR as a dependent variable and studies of autonomic control were discussed.

respiration
HR variability
HR level
controlled respiration

B 20 Stern, Robert M., and Anschel, Carol: Deep inspirations as stimuli for responses of the autonomic nervous system. *Psychophysiology, 5:*132, 1968.

The effects of four types of deep breaths on the latency, the magnitude, and the duration of finger volume pulse, heart rate and galvanic skin responses were studied in a quasi-learning situation. The respiratory stimuli were normal inspirations, three times deeper than normal, six times deeper and fast, and six times deeper and slow. Twenty Ss took each type of deep breath in random order six times in response to specific lights. Graphs and statistical tests are presented summarizing the above relationships and two unexpected findings are discussed.

controlled respiration
autonomic responses
HR
GSR
finger pulse volume

B 21 Stratton, Peter M.: The use of heart rate for the study of habituation in the neonate. *Psychophysiology, 7:*44, 1970.

The heart rate (HR), being readily affected by many forms of stimulation, is likely to be a particularly useful index of neonatal response. However measures of HR change have been applied without proper evaluation and without being tested against controls, with consequent loss of generality of findings. A procedure for choosing response measures, in-

infants (neonates)
habituation
measurement techniques

volving minimal assumptions about the experimental situation, is described. Applied to the habituation of neonates to medium intensity auditory stimuli, this procedure indicated an increase in HR as the most useful response characteristic. Habituation of the acceleratory response was found to take the form of a logarithmic (not exponential) function of trial number. Assumptions underlying the usual methods of correction for initial values are examined and most of them are shown to have been violated in the present data. Further, application of various corrections failed to improve the consistency of measures of habituation. Multiple regression analysis of fourteen measures of the acceleratory response showed that the increase in rate during the first six seconds following stimulus onset was the most consistent indicator of habituation. Addition of further measures did not contribute significantly to the relationship.

auditory stimuli
LIV
statistical assumptions

B 22   Thompson, Larry W., and Botwinick, Jack: Stimulation in different phases of the cardiac cycle and reaction time. *Psychophysiology, 7:57*, 1970.

Several studies have suggested that reaction time (RT) may be related to variations in blood pressure which occur with each heartbeat. This was tested in a series of four studies in which possible effects of the preparatory interval (PI) were controlled. Stimuli were presented at 0, 200, 400, and 600 msec following the R wave, and during the ascending slope of the R, T, and P waves of the cardiac cycle. No relationship was found in any of the four studies between RT and the phase within the cardiac cycle when the stimulus occurred.

phase of cardiac cycle
preparatory interval
reaction time

B 23   Williams, Thomas A., Schachter, Joseph, and Tobin, Michael: Spontaneous variation in heart rate: Relationship to the average evoked heart rate response to auditory stimuli in the neonate. *Psychophysiology, 4:104*, 1967.

The relationship of spontaneous variation in heart rate during the prestimulus period to average evoked heart rate response to repetitive auditory stimuli was investigated in the neonate. Spontaneous variation was measured as the slope from horizontal from the peak or trough, preceding the

neonate
HR variability
auditory stimuli

stimulus on the cardiotachometer record to the time of   *measure-*
stimulus presentation. The data suggest that the stimulus   *ment*
evoked heart rate response varies significantly as a function of   *indices*
the spontaneous variation in the prestimulus heart rate slope,
independent, in part, of the prestimulus heart rate level.

ORIENTING RESPONSE

C 1 Chase, William G., and Graham, Frances K.: Heart rate response to nonsignal tones. *Psychon Sci, 42:*244, 1967.

The heart rate response to onset of eighteen-second nonsignal tones heard over 71 db white noise was solely decelerative and habituated rapidly; the response to tone offset was similar to the onset response. It is suggested that cardiac deceleration is a component of the orienting reflex.

non-signal stimuli (tones) orienting response habituation

C 2 Graham, Frances K., and Slaby, Diana Arrezzo: Differential heart rate changes to equally intense white noise and tone. *Psychophysiology, 10:*347, 1973.

The psychophysiological literature has often ignored possible differences in the effects of white noise and tone stimulation. Twelve undergraduate Ss presented with ten white noise and 12 Ss presented with ten tone stimuli of five-second duration, uncontrolled, fast rise time, and equal SPL (85 dB re 0.0002 microbars) showed large differences in heart rate (HR) response. Noise elicited a diphasic response of marked acceleration followed by deceleration and tone a triphasic response of deceleration-acceleration-deceleration. The short-latency acceleration following noise habituated rapidly although some acceleration persisted throughout the ten trials. With stimulus repetition, the response to tone showed lessened deceleration and an insignificant increase in long latency acceleration. It was suggested that stimulus onset characteristics determine the short-latency HR response and steady-state characteristics the longer-latency phases. The relationship to fast and slow components of startle was discussed, as well as possible mechanisms that may account for the differing effects of noise and tone.

orienting response noise auditory stimuli startle habituation

C 3 Hare, Robert D.: Cardiovascular components of orienting and defensive responses. *Psychophysiology, 9:*606, 1972.

Data from an earlier study of physiological responses to affective visual stimulation were reanalyzed in an attempt to delineate the cardiovascular components of the OR and the DR. A HR response profile to unpleasant stimulation was obtained for each of 49 Ss by computing his average beat-by-beat HR response to slides of homicide victims. A hierarchical grouping procedure was then used to group these profiles in terms of similarity. An optimum grouping of three distinct groups of profiles emerged. Group A consisted of 9 Ss whose HR responses were accelerative in nature, Group D of 12 Ss who gave marked decelerative responses, and Group MD of 28 Ss who gave moderate decelerative responses. The cephalic vasomotor response given by Group A to the homicide slides was vasoconstriction, while the response of Groups D and MD was vasodilation. The results provide some support for the suggestion that the OR consists of HR deceleration and cephalic vasodilation, while the DR consists of HR acceleration and cephalic vasoconstriction. However, it is possible that these "classic" patterns of cardiovascular activity occur in only some Ss and only under certain conditions, and that they may be obscured by the use of undifferentiated group data.

orienting response
defensive responses
affective stimuli
individual differences
GSR

C 4   Raskin, David C., Kotses, Harry, and Bever, James: Cephalic vasomotor and heart rate measures of orienting and defensive reflexes. *Psychophysiology, 6:*149, 1969.

The problem of differentiating orienting (OR) and defensive reflexes (DR) was investigated by measurements of forehead-skin pulse amplitude (PA), forehead-skin blood content (BC), and heart rate (HR). Thirty male college students received thirty stimulations of .5 sec white noise at either 80 db or 120 db. Beat-by-beat analyses of the physiological measures indicated that both intensities of stimulation produced decreases in PA. Forehead BC showed larger increases to 120 db than to 80 db, and successive stimulations produced a change to overall decreases in BC at both intensities. HR acceleration occurred to both stimuli, and a short-latency deceleration occurred to 80 db. The results were interpreted as showing that cephalic vasoconstriction is the dominant response to auditory stimulation, and cephalic vasomotor responses do not differentiate between ORs and

orienting response
defensive response
habituation
subjective judgments
BP
SC

DRs. The short-latency HR deceleration and smaller HR acceleration differentiated the OR from the DR.

C 5   Uno, Tadao, and Grings, William W.: Autonomic components of orienting behavior. *Psychophysiology, 1:*311, 1965.

Changes in skin conductance (GSR), skin potential (SP), heart rate (HR), finger blood volume (BV), and pulse volume (PV) were recorded in response to two-second bursts of white noise. Five intensity levels of sound (60, 70, 80, 90, and 100 db) were presented over five repetitions. Results showed that (1) response magnitudes and latencies were directly related to stimulus intensity and inversely related to number of repetitions; (2) for BV, SP and GSR the effect of repetition varied with stimulus intensity; (3) HR changes were primarily monophasic; and (4) BV and PV were more sensitive to stimulus intensity differences than were the electrodermal responses.

orienting response
stimulus intensity
stimulus repetition
GSR
vasomotor responses

C 6   Zimny, George H., and Miller, Frank L.: Orienting and adaptive cardiovascular responses to heat and cold. *Psychophysiology, 3:*81, 1966.

The purpose of the study was to test nine hypotheses derived from the theory of E.N. Sokolov. The hypotheses tested dealt with the habituation and return of the orienting response and with the relationship between the orienting and adaptive responses. Three presentations of an auditory stimulus were interpolated among a series of twenty-eight presentations of a cold stimulus administered to one group of thirteen human subjects and among twenty-eight presentations of a hot stimulus administered to another group of thirteen subjects. Heart rate and amplitude and latency of vasomotor response to all stimuli were measured using a finger photoplethysmograph. When vasoconstrictive orienting responses to hot and to cold habituated out, vasoconstrictive adaptive responses to cold and vasodilatory adaptive responses to heat appeared. Eight of the nine hypotheses were confirmed, thereby providing strong support for Sokolov's theory, upon which the hypotheses were based.

orienting response
stress
habituation
adaptation

RESPONSES TO EMOTIONAL STIMULI

D 1   Bowers, Kenneth S.: The effects of UCS temporal uncertainty on heart rate and pain. *Psychophysiology, 8:*382, 1971.

> Every one of the 8 Ss in this experiment showed lower heart rate in anticipation of a temporally uncertain UCS than he did during anticipation of a temporally certain one. Vigilance for uncertainty removing cues during UCS uncertain trials was offered as an explanation for the reduced heart rate of this condition. Previous investigations showing acceleration in heart rate under conditions of UCS temporal uncertainty were criticized, particularly with respect to the adequacy of the cardiac baseline employed. One unexpected and unexplained finding of this study was that 7 out of 8 Ss rated shocks as more painful when the UCS was certain than when it was uncertain.

uncertainty
anticipation
vigilance
deceleration
pain

D 2   Buckhout, Robert, and Terrence, Grace: The effect of food deprivation and expectancy on heart rate. *Psychon Sci, 6:* 153, 1966.

> Ss fasted for twenty-four hours after being on a controlled diet. Group A expected to fast for twenty-four hours and had heart rate measured with food cues present. Group B expected to fast for thirty-six hours and were tested without food cues. At the twenty-four hour mark, Group A showed significantly higher heart rate. It was concluded that significant heart rate arousal occurs in deprived human beings anticipating immediate satiation.

food deprivation
expectancy
acceleration
arousal

D 3   Collen, A., and Libby, W.L.: Effects of hunger upon the cardiac deceleratory response to food pictures. *Psychophysiology, 9:*280, 1972.

When people observe a series of different pictures, the greater the interest-value of a picture, the greater the attendant cardiac deceleration. It was therefore reasoned that, when the same picture (or one of equal interest-value) is observed on two occasions, once when the observer is highly motivated to find the picture interesting and once when he is not, greater deceleration should occur when interest in the picture has been heightened. The forty male undergraduate Ss observed two series of chromatic slides, matched for interest value. Each series included twelve appetizing pictures of food and twelve nonfood pictures. Ss observed one series when hungry, the other when satiated, while heart (HR) was recorded, then rated the interest value and pleasantness of the slides in that series. The greater the pre-experimental interest-value of a picture, the more deceleration it produced (p < .025). Moreover, hungry Ss' ratings indicated that they perceived the food slides, taken separately or in contrast to nonfood slides, as far more interesting and pleasant than satiated Ss (p < .001). Nevertheless no corresponding differences in HR even approached significance. Results are related to writings of Berlyne, the Laceys, and Elliott.

hunger
pictorial
stimuli
interest
value
deceleration
motivation
subjective
reports

D 4   Elliott, Roger: Effects of uncertainty about the nature and advent of a noxious stimulus (shock) upon heart rate. *J Pers Soc Psychol, 3*:353, 1966.

Heart rate (HR) and ratings of tension were obtained from six groups of ten randomly selected male undergraduates while they awaited a shock. A group knew or did not know when the shock would arrive, and knew that the shock would be mild, that it would be strong, or knew nothing about it. The only significant effect on both the HR acceleration scores and the tension ratings was associated with whether or not S knew anything about the nature of the shock to come.

uncertainty
tension
HR acceler-
ation

D 5   Elliott, Rogers: Tonic heart rate: Experiments on the effects of collative variables lead to an hypothesis about its motivational significance. *J Pers Soc Psychol, 12*:211, 1969.

Five experiments assessed the effects of conflict and uncertainty on tonic heart rate (HR) in a variety of situations, in-

uncertainty
conflict

cluding comparisons of having versus not having control over an escape response from shock, making easy versus hard tone discriminations, naming colors or reading names of colors versus naming the hue of an incompatible color-word (Stroop test) , and performing in a reaction-time task with predictable versus unpredictable preparatory intervals. These collative variables either had no effect on tonic HR or they had an effect (deceleratory) opposite to expectations; but response factors and incentive factors had strong accelerating effects. A hypothesis is stated to the effect that under the usual boundary conditions of the psychological experiment, the critical features controlling tonic HR acceleration are the instigation, anticipation and initiation of responses, and the presence of incentives. Studies are reviewed in which "emotionality" was present but in which no rise in tonic HR occurred unless either of the two features was present. Other studies are reviewed in which both HR and palmar conductance (PC) were used, and a hypothesis about the difference in their motivational significance is suggested.

reaction time performance visual discrimination tasks avoidance HR change theory

D 6   Epstein, S., and Fenz, W.D.: Steepness of approach and avoidance gradients in humans as a function of experience: Theory and experiment. *J Exp Psychol, 70:1, 1965.*

Thirty-three experienced and thirty-three nonexperienced parachutists rated approach and avoidance feelings at different points in time preceding and following a parachute jump. It was concluded that with experience the point of greatest anxiety is displaced backwards in time. The theory presented assumed that with continued exposure to threat, a heightening of the gradient of anxiety and development of the gradient of inhibition to anxiety developed.

parachutists subjective responses threat anxiety inhibition

D 7   Fenz, Walter D., and Jones, G. Brian: The effect of uncertainty on mastery of stress: A case study. *Psychophysiology, 9:615, 1972.*

A highly experienced sport parachutist was tested under conditions of uncertainty as well as under normal jumping conditions; the dependent measures recorded during the sequence of events leading up to a jump were heart rate and

parachutists uncertainty anticipatory responses

respiration rate. Uncertainty produced a disruption of the *HR change* orderly pattern of anticipatory physiological responding; this *respiration* disruption was more pronounced for heart rate than for respiration rate.

> 8   Frazier, Thomas W., Weil-Malherbe, Hans, and Lipscomb, Harry S.: Psychophysiology of conditioned emotional disturbances in humans. *Psychophysiology, 5:*478, 1969.

A discriminative avoidance conditioning technique was used   *conditioned* to study urinary excretion of selected adrenal hormones in   *emotional* response to a stimulus which had acquired conditioned   *responses* noxious properties through association with availability of   *avoidance* punishment. A four-day test procedure was employed: (1) to   *discrimina-* habituate subjects to the test environment, (2) obtain con-   *tion* trol data, (3) condition subjects, and (4) test reactions to the   *catechola-* conditioned noxious stimulus. Urine samples were taken at   *mine* two-hour intervals preceding and following each of the four   *excretion* trials and were analyzed for epinephrine, norepinephrine,   *corticoste-* total 17-hydroxycorticosteroids, and other urinary constitu-   *roid excre-* ents. These results were correlated with results obtained from   *tion* monitoring of heart rate, skin resistance, blood pressure, and   *vigilance* three measures of panel monitoring performance. Data an-   *habituation* alyses revealed significant changes from control levels during   *stress* the test period for each of the principal measures described above and some specification of life systems interrelationships through correlation and factor analyses. Factors were identified which related to behavioral efficiency, psychological effort, fluid transport regulation, cardiovascular-adrenal, and specific epinephrine and norepinephrine factors.

D 9   Hare, R.D., Wood, K., Britain, S., and Frazelle, J.: Autonomic responses to affective visual stimulation: Sex differences. *J Exp Res Pers, 5:*14, 1971.

Physical responses of twenty-five male and twenty-five female   *emotional* subjects who viewed in random order slides on homicide,   *stimuli* nude females, and ordinary objects were taken. Female sub-   *HR change* jects had higher tonic heart rates but lower levels of electro-   *sex differ-* dermal than males. There were no significant sex differences   *ences* in overall magnitude of cardiac deceleration and vasomotor   *GSR* responses elicited. Males gave larger initial electrodermal responses than females. In males the largest cardiac responses were elicited by homicide and the largest electrodermal and vasomotor response elicited by nudes. The opposite was true of females.

D 10   Hare, Robert D.: Response requirements and directional fractionation of autonomic responses. *Psychophysiology, 9:* 419, 1972.

Physiological responses were monitored while twenty-seven male Ss were shown a series of forty-five colored slides of homicide victims. Nine of the Ss were required to simply look at each slide (Nonraters), nine were required to push one of seven buttons after each trial to indicate how disturbing they found the slide to be (Raters). Evidence for directional fractionation of autonomic responses to the slides was obtained for only the Nonraters. Their responses included cardiac deceleration, an increase in skin conductance, digital vasoconstriction, and cephalic vasodilation. The Raters responded with cardiac acceleration, an increase in skin conductance, and both digital and cephalic vasoconstriction. The Raters also showed a larger increase in tonic skin conductance over trials than did the Nonraters. To determine whether the physiological responses of the Raters were influenced by the requirement to make a motor response, nine other Ss pressed a button after each slide. The physiological responses of these latter Ss were almost identical with those of the Nonraters. The results are consistent with the hypothesis that the requirement to rate the stimuli was associated with appraisal and cognitive elaboration. They also indicate that response requirements can have a profound effect upon autonomic responsivity.

affective stimuli
directional fraction-ation
response re-quirement
cognitive elaboration
vasomotor activity
GSR

D 11   Higgins, J.D.: Set and uncertainty as factors influencing anticipatory cardiovascular responding in humans. *J Comp Physiol Psychol, 74:*272, 1971.

Human heart rate and vasomotor activity were monitored while the subjects' expectancies concerning which of two stimuli would occur were manipulated. One stimulus de-

expectancy
uncertainty

manded a button press response while the other required the
subject not to respond. In one group this response served
merely to detect the respond stimulus, while in a second
group it was given the added dimension of being a reaction
time response. In both groups cardiovascular activity leading
up to stimulus onset was observed to be a function of stimulus uncertainty rather than a simple function of the respond
stimulus' expectancy. It was concluded that anticipatory cardiovascular responding reflected the attentional requirements
of the task rather than simple motor preparation.

*task require-
ments*

*motor
prepara-
tion*

*vasomotor
activity*

D 12 Libby, W.L.: Awareness of own cardiac and pupillary response to pictures. *Psychophysiology, 9:*273, 1972 (Abstr.) .

According to several studies people are able to report changes
in heart rate occurring upon presentation of stimuli which
vary in acceleratory effect. The present fifty-four male undergraduate Ss, using seven-point scales, reported changes in
both heart rate and pupil size in response to pictorial stimuli
which vary in known deceleratory effect upon the heart and
dilatant effect upon the pupil. The stimuli consisted of black
and white pictures selected primarily upon the basis of their
rated attention-value from photography magazines and other
sources. Results indicated that (1) accuracy in reporting
dilations approached, but did not reach significance, (2) the
greater the actual average cardiac deceleration produced by a
picture, the greater the acceleration reported by Ss (p < .01).
Pictures for which greater accelerations were reported were
rated by Ss as more exciting and attention-getting. Evidently
Ss' reports were based upon picture content rather than upon
awareness of their own autonomic responses. Implications for
learning self-control of autonomic responses are drawn.

awareness

HR change

*affective
stimuli*

*response
fractiona-
tion*

*stimulus
effect*

D 13 Lykken, D.T., Macindoe, I., and Tellegen, A.: Perception
Autonomic response to shock as a function of predictability
in time and locus. *Psychophysiology, 9:*318, 1972.

Signals were used to manipulate S's ability to predict when
and where (i.e. on which limb) he would receive each of
forty-eight painful shocks. Two groups of 24 Ss received
twelve shocks in each of four predictability conditions. Heart

*prediction
(precep-
tion)*

*electric
shock*

rate and palmar SC were monitored throughout. Both HR and SC responses to shock were consistently reduced when shock was preceded by a warning signal; predictability of locus had no effect on HRR and a weak effect on SCR. More anxious Ss showed greater postshock HR acceleration under all conditions; less anxious Ss showed greater anticipatory HR acceleration. In a separate experiment, 9 Ss in whom the later components of the vertex AER increased systematically with shock intensity showed a decrease in these same components when shock was made predictable in time.

anxiety
post-shock responses
anticipatory responses
auditory evoked responses
SC

D 14   Malcuit, Gerard: Cardiac responses in aversive situation with and without avoidance possibility. *Psychophysiology, 10:295,* 1973.

This experiment is concerned with evaluating the cardiac responses of human Ss in an aversive situation. Two main conditions were investigated: control of shock occurrence (Avoidance) and Passivity, that is, Ss were instructed to passively receive the shocks. Sixty Ss were used. The Avoidance condition was further divided into three specific groups. One group of Ss had to avoid the aversive stimulus by a proper task (depressing keys) without any certainty about the result of their action until the habitual moment of shock occurrence. Ss in a second group were provided immediate feedback from their action via a light bulb. A third group of Ss kept receiving shocks whatever they tried. After completion of thirty trials the conditions for each S were reversed by appropriate instructions and run for another twenty trials. A decelerative cardiac response was found in anticipation of shock for Ss in the Passivity condition. In the Avoidance condition, such a deceleration was found for trials during which Ss had had a feedback of their failure to avoid (second group) and were expecting an oncoming shock. Furthermore, only the Ss in Avoidance condition displayed HR acceleration after the signal onset of the ISI. Specific variations were found in the second phase of the experiment for the third group of Avoidance condition.

aversive stimuli
avoidance
passivity
feedback
anticipation

D 15   Rice, David G., and Greenfield, N.S.: Psychophysiological correlates of La Belle Indifference. *Arch Gen Psychiatry, 20:* 239, 1969.

The degree to which psychologic defense patterns inhibit physiologic arousal was studied in nine patients with conversion reaction and with La Belle Indifference. Controls were patients with organic disease processes of lesions and with matching appropriate symptoms. Few differences between experimental and control patients were found in heart rates, GSRs or frontal EEGs while the patients were at rest, during interview, word associating, or during visual and auditory stimulation. The results suggested that psychologic defense processes do not prevent arousal of covert physiologic emotional correlates.

conversion reaction
defense patterns
arousal
word association
auditory stimuli
GSR

) 16 Valins, Stuart: Emotionality and autonomic reactivity. *J Exp Res Pers,* 2:41, 1967.

Several recent experiments have found that in emotion-arousing situations, chronically unemotional individuals are more autonomically reactive than more emotional ones. The present experiment attempted to determine whether similar differences are manifested when Ss are anticipating and receiving varying intensities of neutral as well as noxious stimuli. Ss who were psychometrically classified as unemotional were found to consistently increase in heart rate when anticipating noxious electric shock whereas the heart rates of more emotional Ss decreased. Contrary to expectations, the cardiac reactions of unemotional types were not relatively indiscriminate. No group differences in heart rate were observed in anticipation of neutral tone stimuli or in reaction to tone or shock.

emotionality
autonomic reactivity
electric shock
discriminative responses
anticipation

CORRELATES OF BEHAVIORAL STATES

E 1   Berg, Kathleen M., Berg, W. Kieth, and Graham, Frances K.:
Infant heart rate response as a function of stimulus and state.
*Psychophysiology, 8:*30, 1971.

Heart rate (HR) response to simple stimuli apparently
changes from an accelerative to decelerative response in the
first few months of life. The present study of four-month-old
infants showed that response depends on state and on the intensity and rise time of stimuli. The response was solely decelerative in alert infants but in less alert states of increasing
agitation or increasing somnolence, deceleration lessened and
acceleration appeared. Rapid rise time had an acceleratory
effect which was more pronounced during sleep than during
the waking state. Results were compared with those obtained
to the same stimuli in parallel studies of newborns and
adults. It appears that the decelerative response in awake Ss,
presumably an orienting response, has a curvilinear relationship to age which cannot be ascribed to differences in initial
HR level, state, stimulus intensity, or stimulus rise time.

*stimulus
character-
istics
behavioral
state
infants
orienting
response*

E 2   Fenz, Walter D., and Epstein, Seymour: Gradients of physiological arousal in parachutists as a function of an approaching jump. *Psychosom Med, 29:*33, 1967.

Continuous recordings of skin conductance, heart rate, and
respiration rate were obtained from experienced and novice
parachutists during a sequence of events leading up to and
following a jump. While novice jumpers showed a sharp rise
in physiological activity up to final altitude, experienced
jumpers produced an inverted V-shaped curve, i.e. an initial
rise was followed by a decline. It was concluded that with
repeated exposure to threat, expanding gradients of activa-

*parachutists
experience
response
patterns
threat
activation
inhibition*

tion and of inhibition develop, the latter with steeper slope. The early rise in activation provides an automatic signal of danger, while the inhibitory reaction prevents the arousal from becoming excessive, thus providing a highly adaptive mechanism for the mastery of threat.

E 3   Fenz, Walter D., and Jones, G. Brian: Individual differences in physiologic arousal and performance in sport parachutists. *Psychosom Med, 34*:1, 1972.

The study illustrates the relationship between autonomic arousal and performance in sport parachutists. The most adaptive autonomic response pattern, the one related to the best performance, is shown to be that of an increase in arousal early during the jump sequence, followed by a sharp decrease in arousal which extends to the time when the subject exits from the aircraft. The study supports earlier findings that fear of a stressful event does not simply dissipate, but rather is inhibited or controlled. Individual differences, in the extent to which a person has learned to cope with his fear, do arise. The study shows that while repeated exposure to a stressor is an important variable, there are also other variables not related to experience which are responsible for differences between subjects in their ability to deal effectively with stress.

stress
autonomic arousal

E 4   Hepps, Robert B., and Brady, John Paul: Hypnotically induced tachycardia: An experiment with simulating controls. *J Nerv Ment Dis, 145*:131, 1967. (Copyright 1967 by the Williams & Wilkins Co.)

The present experiment would seem to bear out the general point that simulated control subjects behave very much like hypnotized Reals in terms of general appearance and physiological variables. However, in a group of twenty-five subjects the use of a potent anxiety stimulus did demonstrate differences between Reals and Simulators. The hypnotized subjects showed a greater average heart rate during the anxiety stimulus and during the postanxiety rest period. Perhaps the most startling finding is that Reals showed positive correlations between susceptibility to hypnosis and heart rate during

hypnosis
simulators
anxiety
hypnotic suscepti- bility
acceleration

these two periods. In contrast, the Simulators showed negative correlations between susceptibility to hypnosis and heart rate during the anxiety stimulus and the postanxiety period.

E 5   Johnson, Laverne C., and Karpan, Wayne E.: Autonomic correlates of the spontaneous K-complex. *Psychophysiology,* *4:*444, 1968.

Spontaneous K-complexes during stage 2 sleep were scored on nine subjects to study (1) rate of occurrence and (2) autonomic correlates: specifically the heart rate response, number of finger vasoconstrictions, number of galvanic skin responses, and number of skin potential responses. Records for two nights of sleep were available for five subjects. Spontaneous K-complexes occur with considerable regularity at a rate of 1.21 per minute with a range over subjects from .75 to 1.93 per minute. There was no significant change in this rate over six hours of sleep nor was there a significant difference over two nights of sleep. When compared with control portions of the record, spontaneous K-complexes were significantly associated on both nights one and two with an increase in heart rate, increased frequency of vasoconstrictions, an increase in number of GSRs, and an increase in number of skin potential responses. There were no autonomic changes associated with isolated sleep spindles.

sleep
K-complex
HR acceler-
  ation
vasomotor
  activity
GSR

E 6   Lewis, Michael, Kagan, Jerome, Campbell, Helen, and Kalafat, John: The cardiac response as a correlate of attention in infants. *Child Develop, 37:*63, 1966.

Sixty-four 24-week-old infants were employed to demonstrate that cardiac deceleration accompanies attention, as well as to demonstrate that the length of time the infant fixates on the array is directly related to the degree of deceleration. Each infant received a thirty-second stimulus period consisting of a flashing-light pattern, followed by thirty seconds of rest until twelve stimulus trials were accrued. Total fixation time and cardiac rate were recorded for Ss and reveal that a monophasic response of deceleration typically accompanied orientation. The degree of deceleration was directly related to the amount of time S fixated on the visual array.

infants
attention
deceleration

7   Lewis, M., Bartels, B., and Goldberg, S.: State as a determinant of infants' heart rate response to stimulation. *Science,* *155:*486, 1967. (Copyright 1967 by the American Association for the Advancement of Science.)

With each infant serving as his own control, the data indicate that waking or sleeping states, independent of the prestimulation heart rate, can significantly affect the heart rate response to tactile stimulation.

infants
waking
sleep
tactile
 stimuli
HR
 response

SECTION F

CORRELATES OF
TASK PERFORMANCE

F 1   Andreassi, J.L., Rapisardi, S.C., and Whalen, P.M.: Autonomic responsivity and reaction time under fixed and variable signal schedules. *Psychophysiology, 6*:58, 1969.

Heart rate (HR), palmar skin conductance (PSC), galvanic skin responses (GSRs), and reaction time (RT) were measured while Ss detected critical signals which occurred at either fixed or variable intervals. Ss were required to make responses in order to detect the signals. The results showed that (1) RT was significantly faster with a fixed signal schedule; (2) HR was significantly higher with a variable interval (VI) schedule than with the fixed interval (FI); (3) PSC and GSRs were significantly higher with FI than with VI. It was suggested that the term "improved expectancies" (Adams and Boulter, 1964) be adopted to explain the reason for superior RT performance with FI patterning. The findings concerning HR were interpreted within the framework of the Lacey, et al. concept (Lacey, Kagan, Lacey, and Moss, 1963) that acceleration of HR occurs in tasks involving cognitive activities, while deceleration is observed in situations involving primarily perceptual functioning. It was suggested that PSC and GSRs represent physiological correlates of expectance and that their elevated level may reflect readiness to respond when critical signals occur at regular intervals.

stimulus schedules reaction time performance HR GSR PSC expectancy differential fractionation

F 2   Bull, Kenneth, and Lang, Peter J.: Intensity judgments and physiological response amplitude. *Psychophysiology, 9*:428, 1972.

Heart rate and cortical evoked responses to five sound intensities were examined in seven subjects, who were in-

stimulus intensity

structed to judge the intensity rank of each stimulus. The
cortical potential exhibited a predominantly linear relationship to intensity, with larger responses evoked by the louder
tones. However, heart rate showed both a significant linear
and a significant quadratic relationship. The latter tendency,
for larger responses to occur for high and low tones, increased
progressively over trial series. These results were paralleled
by a quadratic relationship between stimulus intensity and
judgment errors and between intensity and reaction time to
stimulus offset (fewer errors and shorter latencies for high
and low "anchor" tones). These findings show that both
physical intensity and the subject's ability to discriminate
stimuli modulate the amplitude of some physiological responses, and the latter factor increases in influence as the
subject becomes more familiar with the stimulus set.

*discrimina-
tion task
reaction
time
evoked
cortical
potential*

F 3   Chase, William G., Graham, Frances K., and Graham, David
T.: Components of HR response in anticipation of reaction
time and exercise tasks. *J Exp Psychol, 76:*642, 1968.

Examined cardiac rate changes during the four-second foreperiod of an RT task involving either exercise or the traditional button push response. Three components of the heart
rate response were identified: (1) an initial deceleration to
the ready signal, (2) an intermediate component which
stabilized below prestimulus level in anticipation of a button
push but accelerated in anticipation of exercise, and (3) a
deceleration immediately preceding the go signal. The initial
stimuli modulate the amplitude of some physiological reflex to the ready signal and the deceleration preceding the go
signal, a conditional attention response. It is suggested that
energy and stimulus reception requirements determined
cardiac responses.

*reaction
time task
foreperiod
anticipation
orienting
response
conditioned
attentional
response*

F 4   Edwards, David C., and Alsip, Jonathan E.: Stimulus detection during periods of high and low heart rate. *Psychophysiology, 5:*431, 1969.

The study was designed to test Lacey's suggestion that elevated heart rate and blood pressure could lead to decreased
sensory sensitivity and that a reduction in heart rate and

*signal
detection
HR change*

blood pressure may facilitate sensory sensitivity. A tone of five intensities encompassing the subject's intensity threshold was presented randomly twenty-five times under high and twenty-five times under low transient heart rate. The results indicated no differences in the number of correct detections under high and low heart rate and no interaction between heart rate level and tone intensity. It was concluded that low heart rate may well be a necessary condition for increased sensory sensitivity, but that it is not a sufficient condition. Discussion was directed to the range of possible HR changes and the possible requirements of the sensitivity mechanism.

intake-rejection hypothesis

F 5   Granger, L.: Variations of cardiac rate in different types of situations of visual attention. *Can J Psychol, 24:*370, 1970.

The heart rate of human subjects is recorded in three different experimental situations. In the first situation subjects must simply look at certain visual stimulations. In the second one they must press a lever when a specific stimulation is presented. In the third one they must also press a lever when a specific stimulus is presented, but they are told that they will receive an electric shock on the left arm if they do not do it at a certain speed. The results suggest that the explanation of increase in heart rate proposed by Lacey in terms of rejection of the environment by the organism is limited to certain types of situations.

reaction time performance visual attention threat information rejection

F 6   Jennings, J. Richard, Averill, James R., Opton, Edward M., and Lazarus, Richard S.: Some parameters of heart rate change: Perceptual versus motor task requirements, noxiousness, and uncertainty. *Psychophysiology, 7:*194, 1971.

Sensory-motor integration and physiological patterns were investigated in a modified reaction time task. Following a *ready* signal, one of two *discriminative* signals indicated that a right or left reaction was to be made to a *go* signal. For one group, the *discriminative* and *go* signals occurred simultaneously; for another group, the *go* signal was delayed ten seconds. In different sessions, shock occurred with the *discriminative* signal on 0 percent, 33 percent, or 100 percent of the trials. The basic pattern of heart rate response was the same

task requirements perceptual tasks motor tasks noxiousness uncertainty attention HR change

in all conditions, namely, acceleration followed by deceleration immediately prior to the *discriminative* and *go* signals. All experimental manipulations appeared to contribute to cardiac deceleration; for example, the greatest decrease occurred prior to the simultaneous *discriminative-go* signal with 33 percent shock probability. The least deceleration (and fastest reaction times) occurred to the delayed *go* signal. Anticipation of a motor response and/or shock also accentuated the accelerative limb of the heart rate curve, as well as producing increased skin conductance. Muscle action potentials from the chin showed an equivocal relationship to cardiac acceleration (or less deceleration) and to faster reaction times. Results are discussed in terms of an attentional hypothesis, and their relevance to speculations by Lacey and Obrist is examined.

7 Meyers, William J.: Heart rate fluctuations and fixed foreperiod reaction time. *Psychophysiology, 3:*40, 1966.

Visual reaction times were recorded in a fixed foreperiod situation to study the relation between sensorimotor performance and heart rate measures. With forty-two male college students as Ss, both resting and performance levels of heart rate and heart rate fluctuations were obtained. Reaction time data were collected from blocks of trials at given foreperiods which ranged from one to nine seconds. Three groups of subjects, formed on the basis of high, medium and low levels of peak-trough differences in heart rate during the reaction-time trials, showed different foreperiod functions. The hypothesis that fluctuations in heart rate are related to fixed foreperiod reaction time performance was supported.

visual performance tasks reaction time foreperiod HR fluctuations

8 Morris, Joanna D., and Thompson, Larry W.: Heart rate changes in a reaction time experiment with young and aged subjects. *J Gerontol, 24:*269, 1969.

Recent work by Lacey and Lacey has shown consistent beat-by-beat heart rate deceleration in young subjects during a four-second preparatory interval (PI) in a reaction time task. The present experiment attempted to repeat the investigations using a healthy aged population as well as a young

reaction time performance age foreperiod respiration

group and employed greater range of PIs. Twenty-four young males were given an auditory reaction time task consisting of blocks of forty trials each of a four-, nine-, and fourteen-second PI in either ascending or descending order. Heart rate and respiration were monitored continuously. Both the young and aged groups showed significant deceleration from beginning to end of the PI in all three intervals. Amount of acceleration was approximately equal for all with the aged showing consistently less deceleration than the young. Deceleration during the three heart beats before stimulus-to-response was greater for the shorter intervals, indicating more gradual deceleration in the longer PIs. In the three beats following the stimulus to respond, there was a consistent, highly significant heart rate acceleration in all conditions which was greater for the young than the aged. Heart rate change showed no uniform pattern during the early part of the interval for either aged or young, with some subjects accelerating and some decelerating. Respiration phase was not significantly related to amount of deceleration. Neither aged nor young showed a relationship between heart rate level and reaction time. However, low negative correlations were found between reaction time and amount of deceleration in young Ss for all PIs. The older group showed a more indirect relationship between deceleration and reaction time. The results are considered within the framework of Lacey's theory of decelerative facilitation of environmental intake and performance.

F 9   Nowlin, John B., Thompson, Larry W., and Eisdorfer, Carl: Cardiovascular response to reaction time performance. *Psychophysiology, 5:*568, 1969 (Abstr.) .

Heart rate (HR) and arterial blood pressure response to reaction time (RT) performance was evaluated in sixteen healthy young subjects. Two sets of visual RT trials were employed: one set with a four-second preparatory interval (PI) , the other with a nine-second PI. During the four-second PI, heart rate decelerated beat-by-beat with a poststimulus acceleration to baseline levels. Systolic pressure remained unchanged during the four second PI, then decreased during the post response-stimulus period. Diastolic pressure parallel-

reaction time performance
HR response
BP

ed closely the direction and degree of heart rate change during and following the reaction time PI. In response to the nine-second PI, HR decelerated; systolic pressure was initially unchanged, then declined as the PI progressed. The trend of diastolic pressure response corresponded to that of HR. Following the nine-second PI, there was a marked overshoot of all three cardiovascular measures. Magnitude of HR change over the four-second PI correlated negatively and significantly with RT performance, while changes in systolic and diastolic pressure did not show such a significant relationship. Degree of cardiovascular measure change over the nine-second PI did not correlate significantly with response speed. RT trials with faster response speed, irrespective of PI duration, were associated with lower pressure levels when compared to trials with slower response speed. Overall, these data imply that both HR and blood pressure response during the reaction time PI are important determinants of response speed.

10 Obrist, P.A., Howard, J.L., Sutterer, J.R., Hennis, H.S., and Murrell, D.J.: Cardiac-somatic changes during a simple reaction time task: A developmental study. *Psychophysiology,* *6:*649, 1969.

This study used the developing organism to evaluate further the hypothesis that the cardiac deceleration and cessation of ongoing somatic events, found in adults to be coincident with and directly related to performance on a simple reaction time (RT) task, are different aspects of the same biological mechanism associated with attentional processes. For this purpose, approximately 35 Ss in each of three experimental age groups, i.e. five, eight, and twenty years, were evaluated on heart rate and four somatic measures while they executed a simple RT task consisting of sixty trials with a four-second preparatory interval. The results supported the experimental hypothesis by demonstrating parallel developmental trends with regard to both cardiac and somatic events as well as performance. These were as follows: (1) All age groups demonstrated a reliable deceleration of heart rate and decrease in somatic events coincident with executing the RT task. (2) The extent to which somatic activities decreased

reaction time task
age
development
somatic responses

was directly related to age with five-year-olds showing the least decrease and adults the most. (3) Although the magnitude of the cardiac deceleration did not reliably differentiate adults from children, base levels of heart rate appreciably decreased with age, which precluded any meaningful overall comparison of magnitude. Despite base level differences, however, the magnitude of the deceleration was larger in eight- than five-year-olds. Also, within the five-year-old group, Ss with the greatest decrease of somatic activities decelerated heart rate more. (4) Performance time paralleled in particular the somatic effects in that it reliably decreased with age.

F 11   Obrist, Paul A., Webb, Roger A., Sutterer, James R., and Howard, James L.: Cardiac deceleration and reaction time: An evaluation of two hypotheses. *Psychophysiology, 6:695,* 1970.

The purpose of this experiment was to evaluate two hypotheses concerning the basis of the association between performance on a simple reaction time (RT) task and the deceleration of heart rate found as the S responds. The RT task consisted of ninety-six trials in which the foreperiod was randomly varied between two, four, eight and sixteen seconds. Two groups of 31 Ss each were used, with the cardiac response blocked pharmacologically in one group in order to determine if the occurrence of the cardiac response facilitated performance through an afferent feedback mechanism. Two aspects of somatic activity, EMG bursts from chin muscles and eye movements and blinks, were also assessed in order to determine if the cardiac response and the associated behavioral facilitative effects were linked to a common mediating process involving cardiac deceleration and the inhibition of ongoing, task-irrelevant somatic activities. The latter hypothesis was consistently supported. Blocking the cardiac response did not significantly influence performance. However, a within-S analysis revealed a pronounced direct relationship between RT and the magnitude of the inhibition of somatic effects and the magnitude of the cardiac deceleration when the latter was not blocked pharmacologically. These data, along with several other lines of evidence, are considered to

*reaction
  time per-
  formance
foreperiod
  schedule
deceleration
cholinergic
  blockage
EMG
somatic
  activity
mechanisms*

indicate that heart rate deceleration may not be significantly involved in an afferent mechanism but rather can be best understood as a peripheral manifestation of central processes.

F 12   Pearson, David W., and Thackray, Richard I.: Consistency of performance change and autonomic response as a function of expressed attitude toward a specific stress situation. *Psychophysiology, 6:*561, 1970.

A persistent problem in stress research has been that some individuals may show impairment, while others show improvement or no change in performance under stress. Attempts to relate this variance in performance to general anxiety or other personality variables have generally not been too successful. Based upon responses to a fear of shock item in an attitude questionnaire, Ss were classified as "high fear of shock" or "low fear of shock" types. Half of the Ss in each group were assigned a preceptual-motor task; the others were assigned a cognitive-interference task. After training, all Ss were informed that they would be required to maintain their training performance levels in a situation in which they would be shocked if performance declined. Performance and heart rate measures taken during training were compared with the same measures taken under the threat-of-shock conditions. Results indicate significant differences between groups in both performance and physiological activity with "high fear of shock" Ss exhibiting relatively greater performance impairment and increased heart rate.

performance variability
perceptual-motor tasks
cognitive-interference tasks
fear
stress
anxiety
attitudes

F 13   Schwartz, Gary E., and Higgins, J. David: Response imperativeness and the cardiac waveform during the preparation of a motor and "mental" reaction response. *Psychophysiology, 8:*244, 1971.

Given the intimate relationship of cardiovascular activity to the energy requirements of the skeletal musculature, several investigators have suggested that preparatory cardiac changes may be similarly explained as reflecting adaptive, but anticipatory, changes in somatic mobilization. One experiment specifically varied the energy requirements of an impending task and found concomitant changes in the preparatory

motor performance tasks
mental tasks
preparatory responses

cardiac wave form. The present experiment extended the above approach to its logical limit by measuring the time course of human cardiac rate changes during the preparation of a response characterized by the total absence of any required muscle involvement, i.e. a purely mental response. Seventeen Ss received forty reaction time trials, half a traditional motor response (button press), the other half a mental response (silently thinking the word "stop"). The design also varied task imperativeness for each response type via the use of two five-second warning stimuli (lights labeled "fast" and "slow"). Computer averaging of heart rate yielded nearly identical foreperiod waveforms regardless of whether the response was motor or mental. While the amplitude of the initial acceleration and subsequent deceleration was unaffected by response type of speed, time to peak deceleration was closely related to response speed. This phasing effect occurred in both the motor and mental mode. The data indicate that the shape of the cardiac waveform in a conventional reaction time situation is not simply a function of making a specific motor response per se. Rather, factors such as directed attentional requirements and/or general response readiness must also be involved.

F 14   Surwillo, Walter W.: Human reaction time and endogenous heart rate changes in normal subjects. *Psychophysiology, 8:* 680, 1971.

The present findings are clearly in agreement with those of Nowlin, et al. (1970). RT performance appears to be relatively independent of endogenous as well as exogenous changes in HR. Taken together, the evidence from both studies argues strongly in favor of the conclusion that background HR level is not an important determinant of RT. Finally, it is worth noting that this conclusion applies equally well to differences between subjects. Thus, the r between mean RT and mean HR for the group of 100 Ss tested was equal to −.16, which was not significantly different from zero.

reaction time spontaneous HR changes response distribution

F 15   Webb, Roger A., and Obrist, Paul A.: The physiological concomitants of reaction time performance as a function of preparatory interval and preparatory interval series. *Psychophysiology, 6:389, 1970.*

The cardiac deceleration which occurs during the preparatory interval (PI) of a reaction time (RT) task was examined with reference to a facilitatory feedback model in contrast with a model which viewed the response as part of a somatic inhibitory response. Sixty-three male Ss were run in three independent groups in an RT study. Two groups received ninety-six trials (divided into blocks of twenty-four) with PIs of two, four, eight, and sixteen seconds presented in a regular series counterbalanced for order. The third group received the same number of trials of each PI in a restricted random order. Heart rate (HR), chin electromyograph (EMG), eye blinks, and eye movements were recorded as dependent variables. Results indicated an orderly, time-locked decline in EMG, eye blinks and movements, which was closely concomitant with a deceleration in HR during the PI. With some exceptions, the various measures demonstrated similar functional relationships with Group and PI variables. The results failed to differentiate between the feedback and somatic inhibitory models because the only combination of variables which eliminated HR deceleration also eliminated the inhibition of the somatic measures. This fact is consistent with the somatic inhibitory model, but is neutral with respect to the feedback model. Different statistical methods for examining the cardiac-somatic concomitance were discussed.

reaction time performance
preparatory interval
feedback model
sensory inhibitory model
orienting response
EMG
eye movements

F 16   Wilkinson, Robert T., El-Beheri, Sami, and Gieseking, Charles C.: Performance and arousal as a function of incentive, information load, and task novelty. *Psychophysiology,* 9:589, 1972.

Pulse and respiration rate, pulse volume, skin conductance level, and muscle tension were recorded from 12 Ss while they carried out a forty-minute test of choice serial reaction in which incentive level, task difficulty (number of choices), and task novelty (or practice) were varied. (1) Little unanimity was observed among the physiological measures in responding to these task variables. Incentive was reflected in pulse rate, respiration rate, and skin conductance level; task difficulty in pulse volume; and novelty in respiration rate and muscle tension. (2) Only when the effects of information load and practice could be held constant was there any sign

task performance
task difficulty
task novelty
reaction time
arousal
incentive
information load
practice

of an inverted-U relationship between performance and physiological level. (3) Although both choice and incentive had significant effects on performance, the two did not interact.

CORRELATES OF
COGNITIVE ACTIVITY

G 1 Blaylock, Barbara: Some antecedents of directional fractionation: Effects of "intake-rejection," verbalization requirements, and threat of shock on heart rate and skin conductance. *Psychophysiology, 9*:40, 1972.

Following recent contradictory claims in the literature regarding the phenomenon of directional fractionation, the
present study was designed to investigate variables related to
this differential patterning of autonomic response. Heart rate
(HR) and skin conductance (SC) were recorded from eighty-
nine male students who either attended to flashing lights
or worked a subtraction problem under threat-of-shock or
no-shock conditions. Effects of instructions to verbalize later
were also investigated. While significant task differences were
demonstrated which were consistent with the directional
fractionation hypothesis, instructions to verbalize later affected neither HR nor SC. Threat of shock significantly elevated
HR during the task only for Ss attending to flashing lights.
However, threat of shock significantly raised HR and SC
levels immediately after instructions (and preceding the
task) when combined with instructions for subtraction. Results were contrary to arousal theory, supportive of Lacey's
theory of an "intake-rejection" dimension, and contrary to
Campos and Johnson's verbalization findings.

*directional
fractiona-
tion
intake-rejec-
tion
verbaliza-
tion re-
quirements
threat
performance
tasks
attention*

G 2 Bowers, K.S., and Keeling, K.R.: Heart rate variability in
creative functioning. *Psychol Rep, 29*:160, 1971.

Measured the heart rate variability of 20 Ss (chosen by their
scores on the Harvard Group Scale of Hypnotic Susceptibility) during an inkblot test. Average creativity scores for
each S correlated .49 with heart rate variability. It is sug-

*HR vari-
ability
creativity
imagery*

247

gested that cardiac variability may be greater in more creative Ss because they shift more from realistic to imaginal modes of thinking than do relatively less creative Ss.

G 3   Campos, Joseph J., and Johnson, Harold J.: The effects of verbalization instructions and visual attention on heart rate and skin conductance. *Psychophysiology, 2:*305, 1966.

This study investigated the effects of verbalization instructions and amount of visual attention on direction of change of heart rate (HR) and skin conductance (SC). Little evidence for directional fractionation of SC and HR was found with the conditions used. The variable of verbalization instructions produced a highly significant effect on HR and SC, and conditions of no-verbalization produced a consistent but nonsignificant decrement in HR. Other degrees of verbalization produced increments in HR. A visual attention variable produced no significant effect on either HR or SC, although means were arranged in order of increasing activation with increase in visual attention (stimulus complexity). Results were interpreted as being opposed to an intake-rejection hypothesis such as has been proposed by Lacey to account for directional fractionation of response and for HR decrements. Instead, the authors suggest that the requirement to verbalize can produce important changes in degree and direction of autonomic activation.

directional fractionation
verbalization instructions
visual attention
autonomic activation

G 4   Campos, Joseph J., and Johnson, Harold J.: Affect, verbalization, and directional fractionation of autonomic responses. *Psychophysiology, 3:*285, 1967.

An experiment was designed to evaluate the effects of pleasantness and unpleasantness and instructions to verbalize on directional fractionation of autonomic response. Degrees of pleasant and unpleasant stimulation were presented to Ss under two verbalization instruction conditions. Something like directional fractionation was found for the very unpleasant no-verbalization condition only, but the pattern disappeared upon the addition of a later-verbalization requirement. More generally, it was found without exception that conditions of no verbalization are accompanied by cardiac

directional fractionation
affect
verbalization instructions
environment attention
SC

deceleration, regardless of degree or of quality of effect, while later verbalization conditions produce cardiac acceleration, again regardless of degree or quality of effect. The authors conclude that verbalization instructions are important for determining the degree and direction of cardiac activation.

3 5   Costello, C.G., and Hall, Maria: Heart rates during perform-
       ance of a mental task under noise conditions. *Psychon Sci,*
       *8:*405, 1967.

Gibson and Hall (1966) reported that performance of men-   *mental tasks*
tal tasks under noise conditions resulted in significantly great-   *noise*
er heart rate acceleration than performance under no-noise   *anxiety*
conditions. Three experiments are reported here. One is an
exact replication of the Gibson and Hall experiment with
essentially the same results. In a second experiment, it was
found that noise alone did not result in heart rate acceleration. A third experiment found that extreme scorers on a
scale of anxiety did not show heart rate acceleration under
the Gibson and Hall conditions.

3 6   Crow, L.T., Godfrey, C.C., and Parent, R.J.: Repeated heart
       rate acceleration with a pre-verbalization stimulus complex.
       *Psychophysiology, 9:*277, 1972.

Changes in heart rate of seventeen female college students   *performance*
were observed in response to the presentation of a series of   *tasks*
ten consecutive stimuli requiring verbalization of a complex   *verbaliza-*
judgment made prior to the experimental sessions. Measures   *tion*
of distances between EKG R-wave components (R-R interval)   *demands*
three seconds preceding and following each stimulus presen-   *orienting*
tation yielded a significant heart rate acceleration effect of   *response*
the stimulus which was associated with neither a Trials effect   *cardiac-*
nor a Heart Rate x Trials interaction. Data are interpreted   *somatic re-*
as support for formulations of a cardiac-somatic relationship   *lationships*
which differs from, or adds dimensions to, the basic orienting
response. If the orienting response of heart rate is an acceleration, and if orienting responses occur to the stimuli of the
present study, then verbalization, and perhaps other somatic
demands of a stimulus may alter the rate of habituation.

G 7   Dahl, Hartvig, and Spence, Donald P.: Mean heart rate pre-
      dicted by task demand characteristics. *Psychophysiology, 7:*
      369, 1970.

Mean HRs recorded during sequences of perceptual-motor
and cognitive tasks were predicted from ratings of task
characteristics such as complexity and frequency of stimuli,
transformations and responses. In three separate groups of
Ss and tasks the correlations between mean HRs and task demand rating were ≥ .91.

task demand characteristics
perceptual-motor task
cognitive tasks
information processing
attention

G 8   Edwards, D.C., and Alsip, J.E.: Intake rejection, verbaliza-
      tion and affect: Effects on heart rate and skin conductance.
      *Psychophysiology, 6:*6, 1969.

Visual tasks judged to require stimulus intake or stimulus
rejection were accompanied by instruction to verbalize or
not to verbalize as they were presented to male students.
Heart rate and skin conductance measures indicated that
Lacey's directional fractionation occurred to intake stimuli
which were rated pleasant and to those rated unpleasant; an
instruction to verbalize following the task increased heart
rate within the limits of a supposed ceiling effect, removing
evidence of directional fractionation; and there was no direct
relationship between the measures and rated affect. The conclusions of other researchers were examined in relation to
these findings.

intake rejection
visual discrimination tasks
verbalization instructions
directional fractionation
SC

G 9   Eisdorfer, Carl, Nowlin, John, and Wilkie, Frances: Im-
      provement of learning in the aged by modification of auto-
      nomic nervous system activity. *Science, 170:*1327, 1970.
      (Copyright 1970 by the American Association for the Ad-
      vancement of Science.)

Partial blockade of beta-adrenergic end-organ response to the
autonomic nervous system was effected in a group of older
men by administration of propranolol. The result was improved performance in a learning task. The data support the

learning
performance
verbal learning

hypothesis that the learning decrement found among older men is not simply a manifestation of structural change in the central nervous system but is, at least in part, associated with the heightened arousal of the autonomic nervous system that accompanies the learning task.

free fatty acids

GSR

G 10   Gibson, Davis, and Hall, Maria K.: Cardiovascular change and mental task gradient. *Psychon Sci, 6:*245, 1966.

Twenty-four Ss in two groups engaged in three intensity dimensions and two duration dimensions of problem solving for a Lacey type "silent elaboration" task. One group performed under a white-noise environment and the other under a silent environment. The results indicate that contrary to general expectation, difficult mental tasks are associated with less heart rate acceleration than easy mental tasks. These findings obtain under the white-noise condition only. The results are considered in relation to the Lacey formulation and arousal theory.

problem solving

HR correlates

task difficulty

directional fractionation

arousal

G 11   Israel, Nancy Rule: Leveling-sharpening and anticipatory cardiac response. *Psychosom Med, 31:*499, 1969.

This study demonstrated that the anticipatory cardiac response to visual stimuli reflects the interaction between the cognitive "style" of the subject and his attitude toward the future stimulus. During periods of anticipation, cardiac deceleration was particularly characteristic of sharpeners, whose style is one of paying attention to all aspects of stimuli, whether interesting, dull, or emotionally-arousing. In contrast, levelers, whose style is one of withdrawing attention from both uninteresting and arousing stimuli, showed an anticipatory cardiac response that was closely tied to their attitude toward the coming stimulus. For them, cardiac acceleration may have reflected a defensive reaction analogous to the environmental rejection pattern which the Laceys have heuristically proposed. The findings add validity to the Laceys' concept of directional fractionation and their theory of the functional significance of cardiovascular change.

anticipatory response

visual stimuli

cognitive style

attitude

defensive reaction

directional fractionation

G 12   Jennings, J. Richard: Cardiac reactions and different developmental levels of cognitive functioning. *Psychophysiology, 8:*433, 1971.

Beat-by-beat heart rate was observed during perceptual and *children*
cognitive performance in seventy-eight kindergarten to third *perceptual*
grade boys. Children at different Piagetian levels of per- *develop-*
ceptual and cognitive functioning were compared to see if *ment*
changes in cardiac reactions mirrored different developmental levels of functioning. The cardiac reactions appeared
to be a joint function of attention and cognitive operations.
Perceptual tasks produced deceleration in all subjects. In
contrast, all cognitive tasks produced cardiac deceleration
followed by acceleration. Larger amounts of cardiac acceleration were observed with higher levels of cognitive performance in conservation of length and in a verbal form of class
inclusion, but not in class inclusion administered with pictures. Lower amounts of deceleration occurred with higher
cognitive levels of performance only in conservation. Skin
conductance reactions and rated motoric and motivational
involvement were not related to cognitive level of performance.

G 13   Johnson, Harold J., and Campos, Joseph J.: The effect of
cognitive tasks and verbalization instructions on heart rate
and skin conductance. *Psychophysiology, 4:*143, 1967.

This study investigated the effects of cognitive tasks and *cognitive*
verbalization instructions on heart period (HP) and skin *tasks*
conductance (SC). Two tasks (imagining common scenes *verbaliza-*
and solving mental arithmetic puzzles) were used to test the *tion in-*
hypothesis that conditions requiring attention to internal *structions*
processes (rejection of the environment) are accompanied by *activation*
cardiac acceleration and SC increases. Each type of task was *attention*
administered under three instruction conditions: no verbal- *verbaliza-*
ization, later verbalization and concurrent verbalization. It *tion*
was found that the imagination task was associated with no *GSR (SC)*
significant changes in HP or SC unless the S was preparing
to talk or actually talking. Mental arithmetic resulted in
cardiac acceleration and SC increase even when no verbalization was required; however, this result is perhaps due to the
covert verbalization inherent in the process of solving mental
arithmetic problems. Both later and concurrent verbalization
also produced significant increases in physiological activation
during the arithmetic task. The findings of this study do not
support the notion that conditions requiring rejection of the

environment are associated with specific physiological changes. Rather the changes are generally attributable to the verbalization requirement. The effects of instructions requiring S to verbalize later are interpreted as due to either a motor set phenomenon or fear of being evaluated while talking.

G 14 Kahneman, Daniel: Pupillary, heart rate, and skin resistance changes during a mental task. *J Exp Psychol, 79:*164, 1969.

The Ss performed a paced mental task at three levels of difficulty, while time-locked recordings of pupil diameter, heart rate, and skin resistance were made. A similar pattern of sympathetic-like increase was found in the three autonomic functions during information intake and processing, followed by a decrease during the report phase. The peak response in each measure was ordered as a function of task difficulty.

*paced mental tasks
task difficulty
autonomic response patterns
GSR
pupillary responses*

G 15 Kaplan, Burt E.: Psychophysiological and cognitive development in children: The relationship of skin conductance and heart rate to word associations and task requirements. *Psychophysiology, 7:*18, 1970.

Heart rate and skin resistance were recorded from male and female children five to seven years of age during the following conditions: low arousal (rest), high arousal (auditory and visual stimulation), and administration of a Word Association Test (WAT) and the Peabody Picture Vocabulary Test (PPVT). Children who gave a mature response pattern (paradigmatic) on the WAT tended to have lower conductance levels than immature responders. Heart rate decreased during environmental intake (high arousal), increased during environmental rejection (WAT), and was unchanged during a combined intake and rejection situation (PPVT). The skin conductance data were interpreted as being consistent with recent theories concerning the development of mature cognitive behaviors in children and the psychophysiological correlates of complex and simple behaviors.

*task requirements
word associations
child development
cognitive activity
arousal
environmental rejection
intake rejection*

G 16 Kaplan, Burt E., Corby, James C., and Leiderman, P. Herbert: Attention and verbalization: Differential responsivity of cardiovascular and electrodermal systems. *J Psychosom Res, 15*:323, 1971.

A recent study showed (1) that changes in heart rate (HR) were indicators of a subject's attention: acceleratory HR corresponding to environmental rejection (thinking) and deceleratory HR to environmental intake; and (2) that skin conductance (SC) increased in both rejection and intake situations. These results were challenged by several authors who failed to find differential GSR and HR responding and who found some evidence to suggest that HR acceleration was an artifact of verbalization. In order to clarify these contradictory findings the present study used constant stimuli for intake rejection and verbalization conditions since the previous designs were confounded by the use of different stimuli for the various manipulations. GSR and HR were recorded from forty-eight male Ss who observed slides under four conditions: (1) looking at (INV: intake-no verbalization), (2) reading aloud (IV: intake-verbalization), (3) adding silently (RNV: rejection-no verbalization), and (4) adding aloud (RV: rejection-verbalization). Each slide was presented for fifteen seconds and consisted of thirteen numbers arranged to elicit interest. The 48 Ss were divided into four groups of twelve with a Latin Square design utilized for presenting the four conditions (four slides per condition) in four different orders. The analysis of the data showed that for both the SC and HR variables, responsivity differed among the four conditions. For the HR data, (1) the RV and IV conditions resulted in acceleratory changes with the RV change being greater, (2) the RNV condition resulted in virtually no change, and (3) the INV heart rate was deceleratory. The means for the amount of SC change and base HR paralleled those of the HR change with the RV condition demonstrating the greatest amount of change in SC and highest base HR, and the INV condition the smallest change in SC and the lowest base HR. Correlations among the HR change scores across conditions showed that the changes for the INV conditions were independent of the changes for the other three conditions which were related to each other. Results of the study suggested (1) that HR

visual stimuli information intake verbalization instructions attention arousal changes are a function of an interaction between verbalization and attention, (2) that a modified concept of general arousal theory which posits separate arousal continuums for either situations resulting in HR acceleration or situations resulting in HR deceleration may explain previous contradictory findings, and (3) that it may be profitable to classify Ss into categories of HR accelerators and HR decelerators.

G 17   Lewis, Michael, and Wilson, Cornelia Dodd: The cardiac response to a perceptual cognitive task in the young child. *Psychophysiology, 6:*411, 1970.

It has been argued that an important determinant of the cardiac response is the subject's intended transaction with his environment. The present study was designed to investigate whether cardiac deceleration would accompany the solution of a perceptual discrimination problem, whether the degree of cardiac deceleration would be related to the accuracy of the response, and the relationship between general intellectual ability and the cardiac response to the problem. Fifty-one subjects, forty-four months of age, were each given twenty trials of a matching figures task. This task required that S match a figure (called standard) to one of four variations (one of which was identical to the standard). EKG was continuously recorded along with the latency and the accuracy of the response. If the first response was incorrect, S was asked to choose again. The results indicated (1) There was a significant cardiac deceleration from the time S received the standard until he made his first choice. If the first response was correct, the cardiac rate, within one to three beats, returned to resting level; however, if S were told to guess again, the cardiac rate remained decelerated. (2) While accuracy of response was found to be related to the cardiac response, the effect was eliminated when response speed was controlled. (3) The degree of cardiac deceleration was correlated with general intellectual function as measured by a standard IQ test; however, it was significant only for girls.

children
perceptual
discrimination task
intelligence
cognitive activity
deceleration

G 18   Libby, William L. Jr., Lacey, Beatrice C., and Lacey, John I.: Pupillary and cardiac activity during visual attention. *Psychophysiology, 10:*270, 1973.

Thirty pictures, rated on twenty-two scales, were shown to thirty-four males, while pupillary diameters and heart rates were recorded to test the prediction that attention to the environment leads to sympathetic-like dilation and parasympathetic-like cardiac slowing, and to study the relationships of the responses to stimulus-attributed. The prediction was satisfied, demonstrating directional fractionation and situational stereotypy. Tonic levels changed significantly during the experiment and also showed directional fractionation. A few individuals and stimuli, however, yielded reliable pupillary constriction, demonstrating intrastressor stereotypy. Four factors characterized the ratings, two of which were associated with the autonomic responses. Pupillary dilation and cardiac slowing increased as the Attention-Interest value increased. Pupillary dilation was greatest to pictures midway on the Pleasantness-Evaluation factor and greater to unpleasant than to pleasant stimuli. Cardiac slowing was linearly related to pleasantness, with unpleasant stimuli provoking the greatest slowing. The two responses were correlated less than measurement reliability would have allowed, demonstrating quantitative dissociation. When base-corrected scores were used the correlations again were low and highly variable among subjects and stimuli, even in direction.

attention
stimulus characteristics
directional fractionation
situational stereotypy
stimulus pleasantness
LIV

G 19 McNulty, John A., and Noseworthy, William J.: Physiological response specificity, arousal, and task performance. *Percept Mot Skills, 23*:987, 1966.

Two groups of 25 Ss were given three different tasks to perform (1) a verbal paired-associate learning task, (2) a pursuit rotor task, and (3) a finger dexterity task. One group performed the tasks under high arousal (electric shock) and the other under low arousal (no shock). A number of physiological measures, including muscle tension, heart rate, skin resistance, and blood pressure, were also recorded. On the basis of these physiological measures, each S was classified according to the physiological function in which he showed the greatest relative activity over the three tasks. This was done in order to determine whether S's most active physiological index was related in any systematic way to his task performance. Results showed that neither arousal condition

cognitive task
motor tasks
arousal level
measurement indices
HR
EMG
GSR

nor most active index was related to performance on the verbal learning task. On the two motor tasks, however, performance was, in general, better under high arousal than under low arousal, and, in addition, varied with S's most active physiological index. It appears, therefore, that S's typical mode of channelling activation may influence his performance on certain tasks.

G 20   Niemela, P.: Heart rate response during anticipation of an electric shock of variable probability. *Scand J Psychol, 10:* 232, 1969.

Tested Lacey, Kagan, Lacey and Moss's model associating heart-rate deceleration with attention and acceleration with mental activity. Thirty undergraduates concentrated on a figure indicating probability of receiving an electric shock after twenty seconds. Deceleration was predicted when shock positively would or would not come. Acceleration followed by deceleration was predicted for Ss anticipating .50 probability of shock since the beginning of anticipation would demand assessment of the situation. The hypotheses were supported by the data excluding the last trials. Electrodermal reactivity was linearly related to shock probability.

electric shock
mental activity
anticipatory responses
GSR

G 21   Sadler, Timothy G., Mefferd, Roy B. Jr., Wieland, Betty A., Benton, Richard G., and McDaniel, C. Douglas: Physiological effects of combinations of painful and cognitive stimuli. *Psychophysiology, 5:*370, 1969.

Sympathetic activity (SA) was reduced when a cognitive task was imposed during an ongoing response to cold pressor. However, this reduction effect was not obtained when CP was imposed forty seconds after the onset of a cognitive task. Rather, the response level appeared to be about that which would have been obtained from cold pressor alone. These results suggest that the reduction found in the former situation is not the result of distraction due to cognitive activity per se, as we had previously proposed, but it is the initial SA resulting from presentation of the cognitive task that causes the interaction. This suggests that the competition occurs at a level below that of cognition.

cognitive tasks
painful stimuli
distraction
variability
respiration
GSR

G 22 Schwartz, Gary E., and Higgins, J. David: Cardiac activity preparatory to overt and covert behavior. *Science, 173:*1144, 1971. (Copyright 1971 by the American Association for the Advancement of Science.)

The heart rates of seventeen women subjects were recorded as they prepared to make both overt (key press) and covert (silently thinking the word "stop") responses. A very reliable preparatory cardiac response was obtained regardless of whether the overt or covert response mode was employed. The temporal development of this cardiac response faithfully reflected the speed with which the subjects were asked to respond, suggesting that in the covert condition, heart rate could be used to detect the time at which a mental event was being generated.

discrete thoughts performance tasks mental events response rates

G 23 Schwartz, Gary E.: Cardiac responses to self-induced thoughts. *Psychophysiology, 8:*462, 1971.

A psychophysiological procedure is described for obtaining time-locked autonomic responses to specific internal (thought) stimuli in the absence of different external (environmental) stimuli. The procedure is illustrated by a heart rate experiment in which 10 Ss silently generated numbers followed by letters or affect-laden words, all in synchrony with externally paced tones. The shape of the cardiac response was found to be a function of the specific thought sequence. The data are interpreted as demonstrating that specific thoughts can act as potential stimuli of autonomic responses. General implications of the finding and the procedure are considered.

internal stimuli paced thoughts HR response

G 24 Spence, D.P., Lugo, M., and Youdin, R.: Cardiac changes as a function of attention to and awareness of continuous verbal text. *Science, 176:*1344, 1972. (Copyright 1972 by the American Association for the Advancement of Science.)

Played a seventeen-minute tape passage taken from a patient's talking in a psychoanalytic interview to forty trained therapists, therapists in training, and inexperienced undergraduates. Ss were alerted to the organizing theme (termination of the patient's treatment) and asked to attend to direct

attention awareness cognition HR change

or indirect references to this theme. Tonic heart rate, averaged over thirty-second periods, was lower when clues were present on the tape than during control periods when clues were not present. Profiles of phasic heart rate were drawn for eleven-second periods that overlapped the end of each clue and control passage. Profiles associated with clues were significantly lower than profiles for control passages; profiles for recalled and recognized clues showed a wave form distinct from that of profiles associated with unrecognized clues.

G 25   Steele, William G., and Lewis, Michael: A longitudinal study of the cardiac response during a problem-solving task and its relationship to general cognitive function. *Psychon Sci, 11*:275, 1968.

It has been hypothesized that cardiac responsivity should vary as a function of the S's intended transaction with his environment. A developmental inquiry was instigated to determine the cardiac response of 150 six to twenty-seven-year-old Ss to a mental arithmetic problem. Across age levels, Ss showed cardiac acceleration during problem solution. While there was no developmental pattern in the amount of acceleration, the results did indicate that the amount of cardiac acceleration was positively related to Ss' IQ.

problem solving cognitive function cardiac (HR) responsivity

G 26   Thackray, Richard I., and Pearson, David W.: Effects of cognitive appraisal of stress on heart rate and task performance. *Percept Mot Skills, 27*:651, 1968.

The effects of threat of shock on heart rate and motor performance were studied on Ss differing in previously expressed fear of shock. Twenty-four high fear-of-shock (HFS) and an equal number of low fear-of-shock (LFS) were given fifteen training trials on a conventional pursuit rotor. Following training one third of the Ss were informed that during subsequent trials shock would be administered if performance fell below training levels, one-third were told that shock would be randomly administered, and the remaining third served as control. No shocks were actually administered. HFS Ss revealed significantly greater heart rate acceleration and performance impairment, but only under the condition in which

cognitive activity stress task performance acceleration

Ss were told that receipt of shock would be contingent on poor performance level.

G 27   Tursky, Bernard, Schwartz, Gary E., and Crider, Andrew: Differential patterns of heart rate and skin resistance during a digit-transformation task. *J Exp Psychol, 83:*451, 1970.

Fifteen Ss performed a paced digit-transformation task at two levels of difficulty under an overt or covert response requirement. Time-locked recordings of heart rate and skin resistance showed heart-rate deceleration during the information-intake phase of the task and acceleration during cognitive processing. Skin resistance showed a generalized arousal pattern during both information intake and processing. Response magnitudes in both measures were generally enhanced in the more difficult condition and under the requirement to make an overt response indicating task fulfillment. The results support Lacey's hypothesis of directional fractionation of autonomic response as a function of the internal-external attention demands of imposed tasks.

paced cognitive task
task difficulty
information intake
cognitive processing
directional fractionation
GSR

SECTION H

ANXIETY

H 1 Deane, George E.: Human heart-rate responses during experimentally induced anxiety: Effects of instructions on acquisition. *J Exp Psychol, 71:*772, 1966.

Base-level measurements of cardiac activity were made while 12 Ss watched the sequence of No. 1-12 appear on a memory drum. Each S was then told that he would sometimes receive a shock during one of the numbers. Each S received ten shocks on No. 10 during the fifteen shock-anticipation trials. An acceleration in rate during No. 1-8 appeared on the first trial and gradually decreased in amplitude over trials, whereas a deceleration in rate during No. 10 appeared only near the end of the trials.

experimental anxiety
instructions
anticipation

H 2 Deane, George E.: Cardiac activity during experimentally induced anxiety. *Psychophysiology, 6:*17, 1969.

Three studies are reported in which subjects (Ss) were instructed to watch a sequence of numbers appear on a memory drum and, after base-level determinations of cardiac and respiratory activity, were told to expect an aversive stimulus at a specific point in the number of sequence. Subjects typically showed an acceleration in cardiac rate early in the number series and a deceleration just prior to and during the expected locus of shock. The acceleration was found to be greater for Ss told to expect strong shock than for those told to expect weak shock, greater for those receiving strong shock than those receiving weak shock, and under all conditions the acceleration decreased as a function of the number of shocks received. The deceleration, however, remained essentially constant across both trials and conditions and also occurred in groups told merely to expect a weak tone or a faint click. It appears that the acceleration may be a component of an anxiety response but the deceleration appears

experimental anxiety
stimulus discrimination
fear
expectancy (anticipation)
paced respiration

261

to occur under the present conditions in anticipation of any stimulation.

H 3   Epstein, Seymour, and Clarke, Samuel: Heart rate and skin conductance during experimentally induced anxiety: Effects of anticipated intensity of noxious stimulation and experience. *J Exp Psychol, 84*:105, 1970.

Divided thirty undergraduates into three groups according to instructions designed to produce an overestimate, an underestimate, or a correct estimate of the intensity of an unavoidable, noxious sound stimulus delivered on the tenth count of a twenty-point count-up presented six times. Results show that (1) physiological arousal during the anticipatory period was directly related to anticipated intensity of noxious stimulation; (2) since the high-threat group showed the greatest reaction to impact but later rated the stimulus as least intense, it is concluded that immediate impact varies directly with expectancy, while reappraisal is influenced by the contrast between the real and the expected stimulus; (3) over trials, there was a reduction in reactivity and the groups became more alike; (4) for heart rate, an increase in deceleration immediately before impact served to reduce heart rate immediately following impact.

experimental anxiety
noxious stimuli
anticipation
threat
arousal
HR change

H 4   Epstein, Seymour: Heart rate, skin conductance, and intensity ratings during experimentally induced anxiety: Habituation within and among days. *Psychophysiology, 8*:319, 1971.

Twenty Ss were divided into two groups according to whether they received as a noxious stimulus in a count-up a mild shock or a punishing sound. Trials were varied over as well as within days. Among the findings: (1) There was considerable evidence of response fractionation among and within measures of heart rate, skin conductance, and rated stimulus intensity. (2) Trials over days exhibited an incubation effect for shock in the skin conductance data, a displacement of maximum heart rate reactivity toward the beginning of the time dimension, and a greater degree of habituation of the rated intensity of the shock stimulus than of the sound stimulus. It was concluded that habituation and incubation

experimental anxiety
aversive stimuli
response fractionation
incubation
habituation
GSR
cognitive elaboration

reflect cognitive processes, that the forward displacement of heart rate is the result of a centrally mediated inhibitory process, and that the gradient of such inhibition is steeper than the gradient of anxiety.

H 5   Harleston, Bernard W., Smith, M. Glenn, and Arey, Donald: Test-anxiety level, heart rate, and anagram problem solving. *J Pers Soc Psychol, 1:*551, 1965.

This experiment is concerned with the identification of physiological correlative evidence of test anxiety in a problem-solving situation. While low-anxious, medium-anxious, and high-anxious Ss attempted to solve anagrams, pulse-monitored heart-rate recordings were taken. The principal findings were that high-anxious Ss produced significantly larger increases in heart rate with the onset of the problem-solving task than low-anxious Ss. Also, large increases in heart rate were consistently associated with poorer anagram problem solving. It was concluded that the physiological correlative index was sensitive to both anxiety level and the task situation.

anxiety problem solving HR correlates

H 6   Hodges, W.F., and Spielberger, C.D.: The effects of threat of shock on heart rate for subjects who differ in manifest anxiety and fear of shock. *Psychophysiology, 2:*287, 1966.

Although there is growing consensus that psychophysiological response to stress is in part a function of the Ss' definition of the situation, many investigators continue to ignore individual differences in Ss' interpretation of stressor situations. In this study, high (HA) and low (LA) anxiety Ss were run in Threat of Shock and No Threat Conditions. The Threat Condition produced a significant mean increase in heart rate (HR) as compared to the No Threat Condition, but there was no difference in the HR response of HA and LA Ss to threat of shock. However, Ss who reported moderate to extreme fear of shock two months prior to the experiment responded with greater HR acceleration than Ss who reported little or no fear. These findings were discussed in terms of a conceptualization of "anxiety" which distinguishes between anxiety as a transitory state of the organism

anxiety fear threat HR response personality

and as a relatively permanent personality trait. It was concluded that Ss' "cognitive appraisal" of an experimental situation was an important determinant of psychophysiological response of stress.

H 7   Smith, David B.D., and Wenger, Marion A.: Changes in autonomic balance during phasic anxiety. *Psychophysiology, 1:*267, 1965.

Measurements of autonomic nervous system function were made for eleven graduate students of psychology on two occasions: (1) in the hours shortly before they were to take the preliminary oral examination for the Ph.D. degree; and (2) at the same time of day approximately one month later or earlier. Scores of autonomic balance were derived from standardized weighted data in order to test the hypothesis that such scores would significantly decrease during the phasic anxiety experienced by students just before oral examinations. The hypothesis was supported. All students showed markedly lower values in the preexamination tests. The results thus indicate an apparent dominance of sympathetic nervous system activity in such phasic anxiety states. Moreover, significant differences in the predicted direction were obtained for six of eight variables. On the day of the oral examination subjects had less salivary output, higher sublingual temperature, shorter heart period, greater systolic and diastolic arterial pressures, and less change in log palmar skin conductance.

anxiety
autonomic balance
HR
BP
SC

PSYCHOPATHOLOGY

I 1   Boissonneault, D.R., Dorosh, M.E., and Tong, J.E.: The effect of induced heart rate change and neuroticism on the resolution of temporally paired flashes. *Psychophysiology, 7:* 465, 1970.

> Normal high extraversion male subjects with high scores on a neuroticism scale were compared with similar subjects with low neuroticism scores, as to changes in the discrimination of paired flashes, brought about by activation-induced heart rate increase. A threshold for fusion indicated slightly improved resolution for the low neuroticism group under increased heart rate, but a marked deterioration for the high neuroticism group. Two signal detection analyses indicated that the differential effects could not be attributed to response criteria and one analysis indicated group differences in sensitivity under activation.

induced heart rate change neuroticism visual discrimination

I 2   Dykman, R.A., Reese, W.G., Galbrecht, C.R., Ackerman, P.T., and Sunderman, R.H.: Autonomic responses in psychiatric patients. *Ann NY Acad Sci, 147:*239, 1968.

> The cardiac, respiratory, skin resistance, and muscle potential reactions of forty-five young male psychiatric patients to sets of tones and questions, were contrasted with those of medical students of the same sex and age range. The patient group included fifteen diagnosed as schizophrenic, twelve with personality disorders, eleven neurotics, and seven with organic or suspected organic impairment. Findings are summarized in terms of general psychophysiology (those common to students and patients) and implications for pathology (those not shared by the two groups).

psychopathology sensory stimuli emotional stimuli psychiatric diagnosis

I 3   Levene, H.I., Engel, B.T., and Schulkin, F.R.: Patterns of autonomic responsivity in identical schizophrenic twins. *Psychophysiology, 3:*363, 1967.

Autonomic functions (blood pressure, heart rate, breathing rate, skin conductance, finger temperature, and face temperature) were studied in a set of identical schizophrenic twins who showed marked behavioral differences. The resting data confirmed previous reports that Ss who are more anxious and behaviorally disorganized have greater sympathetic activity. Stimulation data showed subject-specific response patterns (i.e. individual response specificity). Inasmuch as there is evidence that autonomic functioning in identical twins is quite similar, i.e. genetically controlled, it would appear that these pattern differences are related to behavioral differences.

schizo-phrenia twins individual differences anxiety stress

I 4   Levine, Fredric M., and Grinspoon, Lester: Telemetered heart rate and skin potential of a chronic schizophrenic patient especially during periods of hallucinations and periods of talking. *J Consult Clin Psychol, 37:*345, 1971.

Telemetric recordings of a chronic schizophrenic patient's heart rate and skin potential were taken while the patient was on the ward. During periods of hallucinations, the patient's skin potential increased significantly, while there were no changes in heart rate. Neither heart rate nor skin potential increased during periods of the patient's talking. In addition, when the patient became very angry, his heart rate showed a substantial deceleration followed by a large increase. There was no change in skin potential during the period of anger.

schizo-phrenia hallucina-tions emotion GSR (SP)

I 5   Marks, I.: Physiological accompaniments of neural and phobic imagery. *Psychol Med, 1:*299, 1971.

Used a treatment method of flooding and desensitization in a balanced cross-over design with sixteen phobic patients. Changes were measured by a polygraph during which S fantasized for sixty seconds and the therapist remained silent. This was immediately followed by the therapist's description of neutral and phobic scenes. Physiological assessment of heart rate, skin conductance, and subjective anxiety differed significantly between neutral and phobic imagery. Increase in autonomic activity was relative to the intensity and hier-

imagery phobia anxiety desensitiza-tion subjective reports SC

archy of the phobic images. Autonomic changes in imagery in silence or stimulated by commentary did not differ significantly. During the brief periods of imagery, heart rate, skin conductance, and subjective anxiety did not intercorrelate significantly.

6   Miller, W.H., and Bernal, M.E.: Measurement of the cardiac response in schizophrenic and normal children. *Psychophysiology, 8:*533, 1971.

In a previous study (Bernal and Miller, 1970), striking differences were found between schizophrenic and normal children in the magnitude of their galvanic skin responses (GSRs) to simple sensory stimuli. However, the Lang and Hnatiow (1962) measure of cardiac response failed to demonstrate these GSR group differences. The present paper is a follow-up of the Bernal and Miller study and its purpose was to evaluate the use of various measures of heart rate (HR) in discriminating between clinical and normal groups of children. The cardiac data were converted to measures that were (1) independent of and dependent upon prestimulus HR level, and (2) based upon individually and group derived decelerative trough in HR. The main results of the analyses of variance for repeated measurements were (1) no single HR measure was found to delineate the cardiac response reliably across stimulus conditions or between groups of Ss; and (2) individually determined HR deceleration, especially when corrected via covariance analysis for prestimulus level, was superior to a group-determined decelerative HR measure in demonstrating both habituation and group effects.

*schizo-
phrenia
children
HR
responses
GSR
deceleration
orienting
response
habituation*

7   Reese, William G., Sundermann, Richard H., Galbrecht, Charles R., and Dykman, Roscoe A.: Physiological concomitants of affect during psychiatric interviews. *J Psychosom Res, 13:*347, 1969.

Lexically derived affects were related to skin resistance, heart rate, and muscle potentials in nine psychiatric patients during three recording sessions over a three-month span. For these particular subjects we found that by group analysis SR

*affect
verbaliza-
tion be-
havior*

and HR were directly proportional to the degree of psycho- *anxiety*
pathology; total affect was negatively related to SR in the *attention*
first interview and positively related to HR and MP in the *direction*
second, and these small but statistically significant relationships were enhanced by increasing the size of the verbal
sample; few subjects showed multiple system synchrony; and
HR and MP increased more often with anxiety or anger-in
than with overt anger-out, and SR increased more often with
anger-out than with anxiety or anger-in. We confirmed our
previous observations that physiological measures are singly
considerably consistent for individuals; physiological patterns and psychophysiological patterns are considerably variable within and between individuals. Although we found
some specificity of physiological patterns for anxiety, anger-
out and anger-in, we proposed that these were secondary relationships, with both affect and pattern primarily related to
a hypothetical degree of central integration. We proposed a
hypothesis that peripheral physiological patterns, to the extent that they are subject to psychological influence, are related to the degree of involvement with an object and the
position of that object in psychological space.

I 8   Wallace, R.M., and Fehr, F.S.: Heart rate, skin resistance,
       and reaction time of mongoloid and normal children under
       baseline and distraction conditions. *Psychophysiology, 6:*722,
       1970.

Reaction time, body movement, heart rate, and skin resist- *mongoloid*
ance of Mongoloid and "normal" control children were *children*
evaluated under baseline and distraction conditions. Relative *distraction*
to controls, Mongoloids demonstrated (1) slower reaction *HR fluctua-*
time under both conditions, (2) a reduced skin resistance *tion*
response and fewer heart rate fluctuations during the base- *reaction*
line period, and (3) fewer skin resistance fluctuations dur- *time*
ing the distraction condition. Furthermore, skin resistance *GSR*
fluctuations were negatively correlated with reaction time,
and heart rate fluctuations, although not significant, were in
the same direction. These findings offer some support for
the theoretical assertions of Lacey and Lacey (1958) that
spontaneous activity is related to motor impulsivity, cortical

activity, and general skeletal-motor functions. Body movement was negatively related to these measures of spontaneous activity and thus cannot be invoked as an explanation for the findings.

CLASSICAL
CONDITIONING

J 1   Clifton, Rachel: Heart rate conditioning in the newborn infant. *Psychophysiology, 9*:272, 1972.

Classical conditioning has been difficult to demonstrate in the human neonate. The present study used an autonomic response, HR, rather than the motor responses that have been predominately used in the past. Fourteen newborns were given either paired (Conditioning Group) or random (Control Group) presentations of tone (CS) and glucose via nipple (UCS). The procedure for the Conditioning Group was nine base trials of either tone or nipple alone, thirty training trials consisted of an eight-second tone, six-second CS-UCS interval, and a ten-second glucose presentation that overlapped with tone for two seconds. The Controls had tone and glucose randomly presented during training. Groups did not differ in their response to tone, but the Conditioning Group showed a HR deceleration of twenty beats on the first extinction trial when the UCS did not appear at the usual time. This result was interpreted as an OR to the absence of a stimulus that had normally appeared at a signaled time. In light of previous failures to elicit an OR in the newborn to nonsignal stimuli, this finding is of particular interest.

classical conditioning
infants
orienting response
non-signal response
auditory signals
gustatory signals

J 2   Craig, Kenneth D., and Lowery, H. Jane: Heart-rate components of conditioned vicarious autonomic responses. *J Pers Soc Psychol, 11*:381, 1969.

Examined heart-rate and skin-resistance responses within a paradigm for the classical conditioning of vicariously instigated autonomic responses using electric shock to a model as the UCS. Fifty-six undergraduate Ss were assigned to one

vicarious conditioning
empathy
anticipation

of four groups in which Ss either (1) anticipated going *movement* through the model's task, (2) were assured that such would *GSR* not be the case, (3) simply observed the model move, rather than be shocked, or (4) did not see the model move or be shocked. Results indicated that both GSR and heart rate could be conditioned. Observing the model being shocked, or simply moving, produced heart-rate deceleration of varying degrees of magnitude.

3   Dronsejko, Krystyna: Effects of CS duration and instructional set on cardiac anticipatory responses to stress in field dependent and independent subjects. *Psychophysiology, 9:1,* 1972.

The study showed that within a modified delayed condition- *delayed con-* ing paradigm the shape of the anticipatory cardiac response *ditioning* to shock can be modified by changing the CS duration. When *anticipatory* the tone (CS) duration was only four seconds, there was a *responses* significant HR acceleration. When the CS duration increased *response* stepwise, from four to twelve seconds, the anticipatory cardiac *compon-* response to the UCS became biphasic. The acceleratory com- *ents* ponent of this response was bound to the CS and time locked, *instruction-* and, on the average, reached its peak within five seconds after *al set* the onset of the CS. The deceleratory component was direct- *field de-* ly related to the length of the time interval between the on- *pendence* set of the CS and the UCS: there was no anticipatory deceleration when the tone duration was four, five, or six seconds; the most pronounced deceleration was observed during the ten-second interval. Instructional sets did not significantly affect cardiac activity by themselves, but did influence responses in interaction with the individual difference variable of field dependence; this was found to be the case only on the first trial. Field dependence was also a meaningful variable and accounted for some of the differences in the patterns of HR responding in anticipation of shock.

J 4   Hastings, Shirley E., and Obrist, Paul A.: Heart rate during conditioning in humans: Effect of varying the interstimulus (CS-UCS) interval. *J Exp Psychol, 74:431,* 1967.

The interstimulus interval (ISI) was varied, using .8, 7, and *conditioned* 13 seconds, in a test of whether the monophasic deceleration *responses* found during heart rate conditioning of humans is a CR developed through CS-US pairings, an orienting response, or a previously conditioned response mediated by anticipation. The deceleration was small and early with an .8-second ISI and progressively larger and later with longer ones, favoring the last hypothesis. Analysis indicates that respiration did not cause the deceleration. A conditioned GSR was larger with the .8-second interval than with either of the others, suggesting that the sympathetic acceleration found previously under atropine may also be augmented by the short interval.

HR change
orienting
response
respiration
GSR

J 5   Headrick, Mary W., and Graham, Frances K.: Multiple-component heart rate responses conditioned under paced respiration. *J Exp Psychol, 79:*486, 1969.

Three groups of human Ss were given differential conditioning trials with respiration uncontrolled, controlled at normal rates, or controlled at rapid rates. Significant differential heart rate responding occurred in all groups and, except in the rapid breathing group, improved across trials. Respiration did not affect the form of the conditioned response. There were three significant components: deceleration immediately following CS onset, subsequent brief acceleration, and marked deceleration just prior to UCS onset. Analysis indicated that the triphasic response was neither a homeostatic adjustment nor an unconditioned orienting response (OR). Discrepant findings in earlier studies may be largely explained by experimental conditions that differentially affect the three components.

differential
condition-
ing
paced
respiration
response
compon-
ents

J 6   Hein, P.L., Cohen, Sanford I., and Shmavonian, B.M.: Perceptual mode and cardiac conditioning. *Psychophysiology, 3:* 101, 1966.

Conditional heart rate responses were measured for field-dependent and field-independent subjects. The conditional stimulus (CS) was a colored light, and the unconditional stimulus (US) was an electric shock delivered to the finger. The CS-US interval was ten seconds. The field-independent subjects demonstrated an initial cardiac acceleration followed

classical con-
ditioning
field de-
pendency
response
patterns
GSR

by a cardiac deceleration, whereas the field-dependent subjects showed only the cardiac deceleration. When these data
are compared with the previously reported galvanic skin
response (GSR) data, a model of sympathetic-parasympathe-
tic reactivity is evolved wherein the field-independent group
shows both conditioned sympathetic and parasympathetic
autonomic activity, while the field-dependent group shows
only parasympathetic activity.

autonomic responsivity

7   Jones, G. Brian, and Fenz, Walter D.: Relationships between
     cardiac conditionability in the laboratory and autonomic
     control in real life stress. *Psychophysiology, 9:*267, 1972.

Experienced parachutists, when tested during a jump sequence, have shown a reliable early increase in HR, followed
by a steady decline; the more pronounced and orderly pattern was related to better overall performance. The conditioned cardiac response, in an aversive conditioning situation,
is one of cardiac acceleration, followed by deceleration during the CS-UCS interval. A similar pattern is also found
when the UCS is substituted by a signal to respond in a RT
task. There is a clear analogy between the observations from
real life and the laboratory; is there a relationship between
the two? Continuous HR recordings of thirty experienced
sport parachutists were obtained throughout thirty trials in
a RT situation, which included an incentive to respond
quickly; termination of an eight-second tone served as the
cue to respond. The same Ss were also tested throughout a
jump sequence, and their performance was evaluated by independent raters. There was a clear relationship between
laboratory and real life in (1) cardiac conditionability during the eight-second anticipatory interval, an orderliness in
the invested V-shaped HR pattern during the jump sequence,
and (2) the magnitude of the deceleratory component of the
cardiac response averaged over trials, and the amount of continuous decline in HR before the jump. Both measures were
directly related to performance. The discussion explores the
analogies between laboratory and real life conditioning.

*classical con-
ditioning
stress
anticipation
experience*

8   Malcuit, Gerard: Cardiac responses in aversive situation with
     and without avoidance possibility. *Psychophysiology, 10:*295,
     1973.

This experiment is concerned with evaluating the cardiac *avoidance*
responses of human Ss in an aversive situation. Two main *aversive*
conditions were investigated: Control of shock occurrence *stimuli*
(Avoidance) and Passivity—that is, Ss were instructed to *feedback*
passively receive the shocks. Sixty Ss were used. The Avoid- *anticipator*
ance condition was further divided into three specific groups. *responses*
One group of Ss had to avoid the aversive stimulus by a
proper task (depressing keys) without any certainty about
the result of their action until the habitual moment of shock
occurrence. Ss in a second group were provided immediate
feedback from their action via a light bulb. A third group of
Ss kept receiving shocks whenever they tried. After completion of thirty trials the conditions for each S were reversed
by appropriate instructions and run for another twenty trials.
A decelerative cardiac response was found in anticipation of
shock for Ss in the Passivity condition. In the Avoidance
condition, such a deceleration was found for trials during
which Ss had had a feedback of their failure to avoid (second
group) and were expecting an oncoming shock. Furthermore,
only the Ss in Avoidance condition displayed HR acceleration after the signal onset of the ISI. Specific variations were
found in the second phase of the experiment for the third
group of Avoidance condition.

J 9   Obrist, Paul A., Wood, Donald M., and Perez-Reyes, Mario:
Heart rate during conditioning in humans: Effects of UCS
intensity, vagal blockade and adrenergic block of vasomotor
activity. *J Exp Psychol, 70*:32, 1965.

Two experiments concerned with the influence of the vagal *classical con*
and sympathetic innervations of the heart and of peripheral *ditioning*
reflex mechanisms are reported on the deceleration of heart *deceleratior*
rate observed on test trials during classical conditioning in *cholinergic*
human Ss. An increase in vagal restraint was observed to be *blockade*
the basis of the deceleratory response, which in turn masks *mechanisms*
the manifestation of sympathetic acceleratory effects. The latter were only observed when the vagus was pharmacologically
blocked and when a very intense UCS was used. When the
conditioned pressor responses were blocked pharmacologically, as evaluated by direct recordings of arterial blood pressure, the deceleratory response was not changed, indicating

that the peripheral homeostatic reflex mechanisms are not the basis for this response and that it is likely a conditioned response.

10 Obrist, Paul A.: Heart rate and somatic-motor coupling during classical aversive conditioning in humans. *J Exp Psychol,* 77:180, 1968.

Provides evidence that anticipatory cardiac changes in nineteen male students during classical aversive conditioning are coincident with the modification of somatic-motor activity. With a seven-second interstimulus interval (ISI), both cardiac activity and bursts of EMG activity measured from three muscle groups are attenuated at about the time the UCS is expected. When respiratory activity is not controlled under these conditions, both the frequency and the magnitude of respiration are similarly attenuated. When the ISI is shortened to one second, the acceleration of heart rate, observed on test trials to follow a small deceleratory response, is associated with an increase in EMG and respiratory activity. Data are considered to be consistent with a hypothesis which views cardiac and somatic-motor events as different aspects of the same response process. Implications of this position for behavioral processes are discussed.

aversive conditioning
anticipatory response
somatic-motor activity
acceleration
EMG
respiration

11 Obrist, Paul A., Webb, Roger A., and Sutterer, James R.: Heart rate and somatic changes during aversive conditioning and a simple reaction time task. *Psychophysiology,* 5:696, 1969.

Four experiments are reported, all of which are concerned with evaluating in human Ss the relationship between the deceleration of heart rate (observed to anticipate both aversive and nonaversive stimuli) and several aspects of somatic-motor activity. In a simple reaction time task, a decrease in spontaneous bursts of EMG activity and both respiration amplitude and frequency were found to be concomitant with the deceleration of heart rate during the foreperiod and to be directly correlated with reaction time. The decrease in anticipatory somatic activity to an aversive stimulus was found in a second experiment to extend to spontaneous eye

aversive conditioning
reaction time performance
foreperiod
deceleration
anticipatory responses
somatic-motor activity

movements and blinks which also had a marked concomit- *EMG*
ance with the anticipatory deceleration of heart rate. How- *respiration*
ever, experimentally imposed somatic activity, i.e. continuous finger tapping, increased in intensity around the time the
UCS was expected. A third experiment provided additional
evidence that the anticipatory cardiac deceleration to aversive
stimuli was not mediated significantly by respiratory maneuvers. Finally, evidence was provided that the basis for the
spontaneous EMG bursts may be related to somatic responses
elsewhere in the body, such as postural adjustments.

J 12   Riege, Walter H., and Peacock, L.J.: Conditioned heart rate
deceleration under different dimensions of respiratory control. *Psychophysiology, 5*:269, 1968.

Both accelerative and decelerative cardiac responses have *classical con*
been observed in studies on human heart rate conditioning. *ditioning*
An interpretation of the contradictory responses regarded as *signal detec-*
conditioned seems to remain equivocal. Experiments general- *tion*
ly have used shock or loud sound as the US, so that effects of *controlled*
respiratory and pressor reflexes on heart rate appeared to be *respiration*
implicated in the conditioning process. In the present ex- *deceleration*
periment, the period following a simple nonaversive signal-
detection task established a heart rate deceleration as the UR.
During this period, subjects of three experimental groups
controlled part of their respiratory cycle for twenty seconds.
Respiratory control was either sustained inhalation, sustained
exhalation, or maintained shallow resting cycle, while control
subjects exercised no respiratory restraint. The nonaversive
stimulation excluded excessive heart rate acceleration and
permitted a CS to coincide with onset of relaxation in the
postdecision period. Only in experimental subjects was a
significant conditional deceleration of heart rate found. Conditional deceleration occurred in addition to a gradual drop
in heart rate level during the experiment. When respiratory
activity was not controlled, a biphasic response of heart rate
was observed.

J 13   Smith, Robert W.: Discriminative heart rate conditioning
with sustained inspiration as respiratory control. *J Comp
Physiol Psychol, 61*:221, 1966.

In a classical discrimination paradigm with instructions to expect shock at certain temporal loci used to obtain anticipatory heart rate CRs, Ss expected shock on a specific flash in five red sequences (CS + trials), but not in five white sequences (CS–). Two groups were compared with their pre-conditioning controls with the same respiration. The Normal Respiration group showed acceleration-deceleration on CS+, but no reliable form on CS–. The Sustained Inspiration group showed strong acceleration on CS+ and weak acceleration on CS–. Respiratory mediation of deceleration, often observed in HR conditioning, is strongly suggested. Stimulus substitution theory is lent support, given accelerative CR and UR.

classical conditioning
stimulis discrimination
anticipatory responses
respiration

J 14   Van Egeren, Lawrence F., Headrick, Mary W., and Hein, Peter L.: Individual differences in autonomic responses: Illustration of a possible solution. *Psychophysiology, 9*:626, 1972.

A factor analysis methodology for the study of individual differences in response functions developed by Tucker (1958, 1966) was illustrated by analysis of conditional cardiac responses. Three cardiac (factor) responses were found—one acceleratory-deceleratory, a second monophasic, and a third deceleratory-acceleratory—over the CS-UCS interval. Individual conditional responses were composed of the acceleratory-deceleratory component plus either positive or negative parts of the second and third components. Individual differences in conditional cardiac response forms were substantial. The factor model provided a better fit of observed responses than the average response model provided. The advantages of determining psychophysiological functions (laws) having explicit parameters for individuals were discussed.

classical conditioning
factor analysis model
individual differences

15   Wilson, Ronald S., and Duerfeldt, Pryse H.: Cardiac responsiveness and differential conditioning. *J Comp Physiol Psychol, 63*:87, 1967.

Discrimination difficulty was systematically varied in two experiments involving a visual discrimination problem. During sixty trials of differential conditioning with a shock US, beat-to-beat pulse-rate changes, measured for selected trials,

classical conditioning
differential conditioning

showed a characteristic biphasic pattern on nonshock trials— initial deceleration followed by acceleration. Shock-produced changes were similar, although acceleration was more prominent. Magnitude of change was related to discrimination difficulty and did not depend on training procedure (converging discriminable stimuli versus maintaining fixed level of difficulty throughout). Results replicate a previous study and generally conform to Liddell's analysis of differential conditioning. Vigilance is proposed as the intermediary process linking discrimination difficulty to magnitude of pulse-rate change.

visual discrimination task response patterns vigilance

J 16 Wilson, Ronald S.: Cardiac response: Determinants of conditioning. *J Comp Physiol Psychol, 68:*1, 1969.

Five variables were manipulated in a pulse-rate conditioning study: CS duration, trace versus delay procedures, order of presentation of CS, US, and CS-US trials, blocked versus randomly mixed trials, and shock versus noise US. One hundred ninety-two Ss were distributed across twelve conditions. The form of the cardiac response during extinction was a composite of the spontaneous response to the tone CS plus the conditional deceleration established by training. Conditioning efficiency was maximized by giving the training trials first, and by using a five-second CS-US interval. An outline of the factors influencing cardiac conditioning is presented, and this outline is congruent with the theoretical analysis of classical conditioning proposed by Dykman and Grings.

classical conditioning stimulus schedules conditioning efficiency

J 17 Wood, Donald M., and Obrist, Paul A.: Effects of controlled and uncontrolled respiration of the conditioned heart rate response in humans. *J Exp Psychol, 68:*221, 1964.

In order to determine whether respiration amplitude increases during the conditioning of the heart rate and then whether such increases influence the biphasic heart rate response, twenty-one human male Ss were conditioned using differential procedures, first without respiration control, then with respiration control. The latter method involved maintaining S's normal frequency and depth of respiration. The biphasic acceleration-deceleration of heart rate was observed

controlled respiration differential conditioning biphasic response when respiration was not controlled. Respiration amplitude was significantly increased during the acceleratory period, and the amplitude of the respiratory change was directly correlated with the amount of heart rate acceleration. When respiration was controlled, the acceleratory component was no longer found while the deceleratory component of the response was unchanged.

18   Wood, Donald M., and Obrist, Paul A.: Minimal and maximal sensory intake and exercise as unconditioned stimuli in human heart-rate conditioning. *J Exp Psychol, 76:254,* 1968.

The anticipatory human heart rate responses resulting from the use of three classes of unconditioned stimuli were evaluated. These stimulus classes were derived from a proposal that high stimulus intake results in a deceleratory heart rate UCR, that rejection of environmental intake results in an acceleratory cardiac UCR, and that physical exercise results in cardiac acceleration. It was expected that the typical conditioning process would produce CRs comparable in direction of the UCRs. With the respiratory pattern controlled, the cardiac changes to each stimulus class were essentially as expected. However, the anticipatory response was deceleratory in each case. It appears that the cardiac change in anticipation of stimulation of any type is deceleratory and the result of an atypical conditioning process.

classical conditioning
stimulus intake
controlled respiration

OPERANT CONDITIONING AND HEART RATE CONTROL

K 1   Cohen, Michael J.: The relation between heart rate and electromyographic activity in a discriminated escape-avoidance paradigm. *Psychophysiology, 10:*8, 1973.

Experiment I attempted to train both increases and decreases in heart rate using a discriminated escape-avoidance paradigm. Noncontingent control Ss were yoked to both experimental groups. Subjects were given sixty-four training trials and sixteen extinction trials. Experiment II employed essentially the same design except that the contingent response was a specific amount of muscular tension (either forty to sixty microvolts, or ninety to 110 microvolts) from the chin area. Seven Ss were run in each group. Heart rate, chin electromyogram (EMG), and respiration were continuously monitored during each study. The results of Experiment I indicated that the response contingencies produced significant heart rate increases and decreases in the appropriate experimental groups. Neither yoked control group showed a significant heart rate change. No group exhibited any significant EMG activity. Respiration amplitude increased significantly only in the heart rate increase group. Both experimental groups in Experiment II learned to emit the correct EMG response. However, only the group in the forty to sixty microvolt range showed a relationship between heart rate and EMG changes.

stimulus di. crimination

escape/ avoidance

muscle tension

somatic coupling

K 2   Engel, Bernard T., and Hansen, Stephen P.: Operant conditioning of heart rate slowing. *Psychophysiology, 3:*176, 1966.

The purpose of this study was to see if heart rate (HR) slowing could be operantly conditioned. Ten experimental Ss and five yoked-control Ss were studied. Experimental Ss

heart rate control

operant con ditioning

were positively reinforced for slowing their HR on a beat-by-beat basis, whereas yoked-control Ss were reinforced in a pattern based on the performance of paired experimental Ss. The data showed that some Ss can be taught to slow their HR by means of an operant conditioning procedure; Ss appear to learn better when they do not infer correctly what the response is that they are controlling; the conditioned HR response is apparently not mediated by changes in breathing; and reinforcement, per se, is not adequate to lower HR.

awareness subjective reports respiration

K 3   Engel, Bernard T., and Chism, Ray A.: Operant conditioning of heart rate speeding. *Psychophysiology, 3:418,* 1967.

The purpose of this study was to see if heart rate (HR) speeding could be operantly conditioned. Five experimental Ss and five yoked-control Ss were studied. Experimental Ss were positively reinforced for speeding their HR on a beat-by-beat basis, whereas yoked-control Ss were reinforced in a pattern based on the performance of paired experimental Ss. The data showed that all Ss learned to speed their HR; some yoked-controls responded with a pattern of response that included increased HR; and the techniques which Ss used to regulate their HR varied widely from one S to another.

operant conditioning heart rate control subjective reports

K 4   Engel, Bernard T.: Operant conditioning of cardiac function: A status report. *Psychophysiology, 9:161,* 1972.

The mechanisms of operant conditioning of cardiac function can be analyzed in terms of cardiodynamics, hemodynamics, neural regulations, and psychological regulations. These separate analyses help to suggest a number of experimental hypotheses. Analyses of data from early and late phases of conditioning show that performance at these two stages of training is different: Analyses of acquisition mechanisms must come from the early phase of training; however, analyses of control mechanisms should probably be derived from chronic studies.

operant conditioning heart rate learning feedback review response specificity motor learning arrhythmias blood pressure

K 5   Frazier, Thomas W.: Avoidance conditioning of heart rate in humans. *Psychophysiology, 3:188,* 1966.

An avoidance conditioning technique was employed to obtain external control over heart rate. A contingency was set
up between heart rate maintenance and punishment avoidance. During periods of time signified by a visual stimulus,
punishments were dispensed when the total number of beats
per minute decreased from the previous minute's total. Subjects (Ss) performed an instrument-panel-monitoring task
without awareness of the biological avoidance contingency,
but they were correctly informed that shocks were available
only when the visual stimulus was present. After punishments had been dispensed on the basis of the contingency
for several periods, punishment was discontinued and the
visual stimulus was used alone as a conditioned aversive
stimulus, in order to shape predetermined response patterns.
Results included clear evidence of heart rate control over all
Ss after training periods, maintenance of heart rate control
over continuous forty-minute periods through continuous
presentation of the visual stimulus, and shaping and replication of three prespecified response patterns. These findings
demonstrate that punishment avoidance contingencies can
be used to impose effective control over cardiovascular functioning.

*operant con-
ditioning
avoidance
contingent
punish-
ment
heart rate
control*

K 6   Levene, H.I., Engel, B.T., and Pearson, J.A.: Differential
operant conditioning of heart rate. *Psychosom Med, 30:*837,
1968.

Reports the results of a differential operant conditioning
study in which five normal female Ss were taught to increase
and decrease cyclically their heart rate from resting rates.
"Discrimination between slowing and speeding was easily
demonstrated; however, the ability significantly to increase
and decrease heart rate relative to resting rate was less apparent. Although each S could do this on at least one occasion,
only two Ss did so with consistency. Breathing or musculo-
skeletal responses did not seem to mediate the learned responses."

*stimulus dis-
crimina-
tion
heart rate
control
cyclic
responses
muscle
responses
arrhythmias*

K 7   Makey, M.S., Jr., and Kotses, H.: Heart rate as an independent variable in a reaction time task. *Psychophysiology, 9:*278,
1971.

The hypothesis proposed by Lacey, Kagan, Lacey and Moss (1963) that heart rate (HR) is causally related to variations in sensory motor integration was tested. Unlike previous investigations, HR was manipulated as a true independent variable in an unsignaled reaction time (RT) task. Volunteer female Ss were used. Heart rates of eight experimental Ss were instrumentally conditioned to a rate at least 10 percent higher than base levels, using Frazier's (1966) avoidance procedure. A 115 dB white noise burst of one second duration was used as the aversive stimulus. Heart rates of eight control Ss were similarly maintained at base levels. Unsignaled RT performance was scored during a baseline period and during subsequent periods of high and normal HR activity. A 2 × 3 × 12 mixed ANOVA of RT measures as a function of groups, HR periods, and trials revealed no predictable differences in RTs as a function of HR. However, increases in RTs were observed across measurement periods for all Ss.

operant conditioning
reaction time task
aversive stimuli
sensory motor integration

K 8   Murray, E. Neil, and Katkin, E.S.: Comment on two recent reports of operant heart rate conditioning. *Psychophysiology,* 5:192, 1968.

This paper examined two reports of operant heart rate (HR) conditioning, one of which reported apparently successful cardiac slowing, and the other apparently successful cardiac speeding. Although the authors of these two studies concluded that they had demonstrated instrumental modification of HR independent of somatic mediators, this review of their results indicated that voluntary activity was a crucial mediator of the obtained effects. New statistical analyses were presented to support the notion that Ss' cognitive and somatic activities influenced HR change more than the reinforcement contingencies utilized.

operant conditioning
heart rate control
voluntariness
comment
voluntary control
review

K 9   Obrist, P.A., LeGuyader, D.D., Howard, J.L., Lawler, J.E., and Galosy, R.A.: Operant conditioning of heart rate: Somatic correlates. *Psychophysiology,* 9:270, 1972 (abstr).

The operant modification of heart rate was attempted using shock avoidance as reinforcement in five groups of either

operant conditioning

twelve or fifteen human Ss each. The groups varied with regard to the extent of experimental control of somatic activity. Effective discriminative control of heart rate was achieved only where (1) either no control or minimal control of somatic activity was attempted, and (2) when only heart rate increases were reinforced. Discriminative control of heart rate was either minimal or absent when (1) maximum control of somatic activity was used, both for reinforcement of increases and decreases of heart rate, and (2) where no control of somatic activity was attempted and heart rate was reinforced for decreasing. Consistent with these heart rate results was the observation that three of the parameters of somatic activity assessed on each S (general activity, chin EMG, and respiration) showed similar influences of the operant contingency. There was observed, however, a modification of heart rate which was independent of both somatic indices as well as the reinforcement contingencies.

stimulus discrimination

heart rate control

somatic correlates

K 10 Shapiro, David, Tursky, Bernard, and Schwartz, Gary E.: Differentiation of heart rate and systolic blood pressure in man by operant conditioning. *Psychophysiol, 6*:637, 1970.

Recent research in our laboratory has shown that human systolic blood pressure (BP) can be increased or decreased through operant conditioning without concomitant changes in heart rate (HR). In the present study, the effects of feedback and reinforcement on the control of HR were examined, while systolic BP was simultaneously monitored. Ten subjects were reinforced for increasing (up) HR and ten for decreasing (down) HR. Automatic equipment was used to detect whether each heartbeat was above or below a median rate. Each S received twenty-five conditioning trials, each trial lasting fifty heart cycles. Information about each heartbeat was fed back to S by equipment which produced a flash of light for each success. Twenty successes produced a three-second reinforcement, a slide from *Playboy* magazine. Although both groups tended to show a decrease in HR, the down group evidenced significantly greater HR decrease over time than the up group (p < .01). An analysis of variance yielded no significant BP effects, indicating HR-BP differentiation. The extent of HR-BP decoupling was tested by

operant conditioning

feedback

response (C-V) differentiation

HR

BP

comparing the five best HR-up with the five best HR-down conditioners. By the end of conditioning, the HR difference was almost fourteen beats/minute while BP showed the same pattern for both groups. A comparable analysis was made of the study in which BP was reinforced and HR monitored. Using the five best BP conditioners in each direction, an 8 mm difference in BP was obtained by the end of conditioning, whereas HR changes were the same in both groups. The present data offer strong evidence for operant autonomic conditioning in man by demonstrating that one autonomic function can be changed without an overall change in autonomic arousal, even within one system.

K 11   Shapiro, David, Tursky, Bernard, and Schwartz, Gary E.: Differentiation of heart rate and systolic blood pressure in man by operant conditioning. *Psychosom Med, 32:*417, 1970.

Human heart rate-systolic blood pressure decoupling was tested by operant conditioning procedures. Twenty normal male subjects were given feedback of their heart rate, half operantly reinforced for increasing and half for decreasing their heart rate, while systolic blood pressure was continuously monitored. Significant heart rate conditioning was obtained in a single session without concomitant effects on blood pressure. Further analyses of the best conditioners in the present study and those in a previous blood pressure conditioning study indicate the strength of operant heart rate-blood pressure decoupling and demonstrate that intrumental fractionation of closely related visceral behavior is possible in man.

operant conditioning
response differentiation
HR
BP

K 12   Weiss, Theodore, and Engel, Bernard T.: Operant conditioning of heart rate in patients with cardiac arrhythmias. *Psychophysiology, 6:*636, 1970.

One patient was a fifty-two-year-old woman with a history of several myocardial infarctions. She had 10 PVCs per minute initially. During nine speeding sessions her resting heart rate increased from 62 to 74. In association with this, PVC frequency increased to 24/min. During the next six sessions, she successfully learned to slow her heart, decreasing it to 64

operant conditioning
arrhythmias

bpm. Concurrently her PVCs diminished to about 3/min. During subsequent conditioning sessions, her PVC frequency fell further to about one every five minutes. The low PVC frequency has persisted during sixteen months of follow-up evaluation. Studies with autonomically active drugs strongly suggest that she had learned to decrease the level of sympathetic input to her heart. The second patient was a sixty-two-year-old man with a history of one myocardial infarction and essential hypertension and PVCs. He learned both to speed and to slow his heart rate. Over several sessions, he also was able alternately to speed and slow his heart during each of eight consecutive two-minute periods. PVCs were rare during the speeding periods and frequent during slowing periods. The results in these patients suggest that clinically significant, sustained changes in heart rhythm can be produced by operant conditioning techniques.

K 13   Weiss, Theodore, and Engel, Bernard T.: Operant conditioning of heart rate in patients with premature ventricular contractions. *Psychosom Med, 33*:301, 1971.

Operant conditioning of heart rate (HR) was carried out in eight patients with premature ventricular contractions (PVCs). All of the patients showed some degree of HR control. Five of these patients showed a decrease in PVCs in association with the learning of HR control. Four patients have shown persistence of a low PVC frequency after study, the longest follow-up being twenty-one months. Pharmacologic studies suggested that decreased PVC frequency was mediated by diminished sympathetic tone in one patient and increased vagal tone in another. These findings suggest that some aspects of cardiac ventricular function can be brought under voluntary control. Once such control has been acquired, it can mediate clinically significant changes in cardiac function.

operant conditioning
PVCs
learned control

K 14   Wilett, J.R., and Tepas, D.I.: Human heart rate change during performance of an operant task. *Psychophysiology, 9*:273, 1972.

In a series of three experiments human heart rate changes were investigated in relation to performance in a free operant

free operant task

situation. A total of 52 Ss were tested either individually or in pairs. In the first experiment (EI) Ss were reinforced on an FI = 1 sec schedule by a flashing red light contingent upon their pressing a push button. In the second and third experiments (EII and EIII) they were similarly reinforced on an FI = 5 sec schedule. A series of nine trials was employed, each trial consisting of a two-minute free operant period and a two-minute nonoperant period. HR for each S was monitored throughout all trials. Ss who responded on the FI schedule according to the predetermined criterion were considered learners (L). Ss who did not were considered nonlearners (NL). L had a greater HR during the nonoperant (rest) period than during the operant (work) period. The reverse was true for NL. These results were significant at the .001 level for both individual and paired Ss in EII. In EIII Ss were preselected as L or NL and the results were replicated. In addition, a statistically significant effect of decreasing HR across trials for all Ss was found. There were no significant differences in the HR of individual or paired Ss. These results are discussed in the light of current theories concerning the relationship between HR and learning.

reinforce-
ment
schedule

learning
ability

SECTION L

FEEDBACK AND
VOLUNTARY CONTROL

L 1   Bergman, Joel S., and Johnson, Harold J.: The effects of
instructional set and autonomic perception on cardiac control. *Psychophysiology, 8:*180, 1971.

Fifty-four Ss were divided into three instructional groups.
One group was instructed to increase their heart rate (HR)
every time a signal was presented; a second group was told
to decrease their HR; and a control group was not instructed
to change their HR in any direction. Results indicate that
Ss can increase or decrease their HR in the absence of ex-
ternalized feedback. These HR changes do not appear to be
mediated by respiration or skin resistance variations. In
addition, Ss were divided into groups on the basis of their
APQ scores. The group with middle APQ scores displayed
more HR control in both directions than Ss with high or
low APQ scores. The study was replicated with 42 Ss and results support the HR increase, but not the HR decrease
findings.

*feedback
instruction-
al set
absence of
feedback
autonomic
perception
subjective
reports
respiration
GSR*

I. 2   Bergman, Joel S., and Johnson, Harold J.: Sources of information which affect training and raising of heart rate. *Psychophysiology, 9:*30, 1972.

This study was concerned with the effects of cardiac information and reinforcement on raising heart rate (HR). The
experiment consisted of a 3 × 2 design with three types of
cardiac information and two reinforcement conditions. The
cardiac information given to Ss consisted of instructions to
control an internal response (no specific HR information),
instructions to increase HR (specific HR information), or
instructions to increase HR while hearing heartbeats through
earphones (augmented HR information). External reinforce-

*feedback
HR control
instruction-
al set
operant con
ditioning
criterion
awareness*

ment was given to one half of these Ss, while the remaining Ss received no external reinforcement. Sixty female undergraduates were randomly assigned to one of these six experimental groups. Analyses of these data indicate that Ss in both the augmented and specific HR information groups were able to increase their HR. The no-specific HR information groups showed no increases in HR, suggesting that awareness of the criterion response plays an important role in raising HR. No differences were found between the reinforcement conditions.

L 3   Blanchard, Edward B., Young, Larry D., and McLeod, Philip: Awareness of heart activity and self-control of heart rate. *Psychophysiology, 9:*63, 1972.

Ss, high and low in awareness of heart functioning as determined by scores on the heart functioning items of the Autonomic Perception Questionnaire (APQ), were given ten trials each on which they were to raise or lower their heart rate (HR) using continuous proportional visual feedback. Low aware Ss successfully raised and lowered their HRs on command whereas high aware Ss were not able to make significant alterations in their HRs.

feedback
heart rate
control
awareness
autonomic
perception
question-
naire

L 4   Blanchard, E.B., and Young, L.D.: Relative efficacy of visual and auditory feedback in the self-control of heart rate. *J Gen Psychol, 87:*195, 1972.

The relative efficacy of continuous proportional feedback, delivered in either a visual or auditory mode, for the self-control of HR was determined by comparing groups of ten Ss who received either: (1) auditory-auditory; (2) first auditory, then visual; (3) visual-visual; (4) visual, then auditory; or no feedback of HR at two different sessions. Ss were given eight trials of each direction on which they were to raise or lower their HR at each session. Sensory feedback of either variety aided Ss in raising HR more than did no feedback, but did not yield an advantage in lowering it. Although neither auditory nor visual feedback yielded any differential advantage in self-control of HR when tested by between S comparisons, there was some advantage in visual feedback in lowering HR as shown by within S comparisons. The de-

feedback
signal effici-
ency
auditory
signals
visual
signals
learned
control

cision as to which type of feedback to use in long-term studies must thus rest on factors other than relative efficacy of the two sensory modes of feedback.

L 5   Botto, Ronald W., and Stern, Robert M.: False heart rate feedback: The relationship of choice behavior to true EKG and GSR. *Psychophysiology, 5:*582, 1969.

What seems to be indicated from these studies is that, contrary to Valins' findings, there are distinct physiological differences between the increased heartbeat and the increased extraneous sound conditions which may account for some of the behavioral results obtained. Furthermore, these behavioral and physiological differences are closely associated with the degree of attention paid the stimulus. One may conclude from these experiments, therefore, that what Valins ascribes to as merely the belief that physiological reactions were occurring may have, in fact, been due to actual physiological changes precipitated by a general attention factor.

false feedback
choice behavior
belief
attention

L 6   Brener, Jasper: Heart rate as an avoidance response. *Psychol Rec, 16:*329, 1966.

Two experiments are described in which predefined heart rate changes served to escape or avoid an aversive stimulus complex in Experiment I, low heart rates within S's repertoire were effective in avoiding the aversive stimuli and in Experiment II high heart rates were the effective response. All Ss received visual feedback of criterion and noncriterion heart rate responses. Comparison of the performances of experimental and yoked-control Ss supports a conclusion that heart rate may be subject to the law of effect.

feedback
aversive stimuli
operant conditioning

L 7   Brener, Jasper, and Hothersall, David: Heart rate control under conditions of augmented sensory feedback. *Psychophysiology, 3:*23, 1966.

Five human Ss were presented with a high frequency tone on the emission of each short interheartbeat interval and a low frequency tone on the emission of each long interheartbeat interval. Under these conditions, all Ss learned within a short

augmented feedback
voluntary control

period of time to produce significantly lower heart rates in the presence of one visual stimulus than in the presence of another. On the basis of this finding, it is suggested that an important determinant of where a given response falls on the voluntary/involuntary continuum is the availability of specific feedback from the response in question.

stimulus discrimination

L 8   Brener, Jasper, and Hothersall, David: Paced respiration and heart rate control. *Psychophysiology, 4:*1, 1967.

Five human subjects were presented with a high frequency tone on each short interheartbeat interval (IBI) and a low frequency tone on each long IBI. They were instructed to produce high tones in the presence of one visual stimulus and low tones in the presence of another under conditions of paced and unpaced respiration. The results indicated that control of heart rate is not dependent upon respiratory mediation.

feedback
HR control
paced
* respiration*

L 9   Brener, Jasper, Kleinman, Roger A., and Goesling, Wendell J.: The effects of different exposures to augmented sensory feedback on the control of heart rate. *Psychophysiology, 5:* 510, 1969.

The aim of this experiment was to determine the effect of different exposures to augmented sensory feedback of heart rate performance on the development of voluntary control of heart rate. Three groups of five Ss each received augmented sensory feedback on 100 percent, 50 percent, or 0 percent of training trials respectively. The amount of heart rate control exhibited by Ss was observed to be a direct function of the percentage of training trials on which feedback was given. Respiration rate changes were not systematically influenced by this variable although higher respiration rates were consistently associated with high heart rates and lower respiration rates with low heart rates.

augmented
* feedback*
metered
* feedback*
respiration

L 10   Donelson, F.E.: Discrimination and control of human heart rate. *Dissertation Abstracts, 27:*4571B, 1967.

It was concluded that the heart rate can be discriminated and the perception of heart rate manipulated; also heart rate may

feedback
heart rate
* control*

be controlled specifically, without a change in respiration rate or general activation. The importance of feedback was shown most conclusively in Experiment I and only very tentatively in Experiment II. It is suggested for both discrimination and control that internal feedback is of primary importance and that the role of external information is to enhance it. The importance of conditioning, emotional behavior, and therapy is discussed. Attention is drawn to the importance of the individual's interpretation of autonomic activity for the discrimination of behavior.

autonomic perception

L 11   Fenz, Walter D., and Plapp, Jon M.: Voluntary control of heart rate in a practitioner of yoga: Negative findings. *Percept Mot Skills, 30:*493, 1970.

Recordings of heart rate were obtained from a yogi in a reaction time task without and with instructions to decelerate during the anticipatory interval, as well as under a condition of augmented feedback. We found no evidence that S was able voluntarily to control his heart rate.

yoga voluntary control reaction time task instructions

L 12   Headrick, M.W., Feather, B.W., and Wells, D.T.: Voluntary changes from baseline heart rate with augmented sensory feedback. *Psychophysiology, 6:*636, 1970.

Two studies employing augmented sensory feedback were conducted to (1) determine whether reliable heart rate (HR) increases and decreases from baseline can be produced on discrete trials, and (2) increase the magnitude of HR change with extended practice. In the first study two groups of twelve Ss were required either to raise or lower HR relative to pretrial level by altering a tone which changed frequency with HR. Ss were given ten one-min training trials in which they were instructed either to raise or lower tone frequency. Ss were told that EEG rather than HR was the relevant response. Results indicated a highly reliable elevation in HR from baseline in the Increase group, averaging 8.5 beats per minute (bpm). In contrast to previous reports, the Decrease group failed to decrease, but rather showed a small, nonsignificant increase in HR. No significant differential changes

feedback voluntary control HR change direction HR change magnitude

in breathing were detected in either group. The second study was an attempt to increase the magnitude of HR change with one highly motivated, randomly selected S who was given extended practice under feedback conditions similar to those above. After 64 one-minute increase trials over six sessions, sustained HR increases of 15 to 35 bpm were observed. The responses were characterized by short onset and offset latencies, reduced sinus arrhythmia, and verbal reports of an anxiety-like state during maximal elevation. After 100 one-minute decrease trials over eight sessions, nonsignificant HR decreases averaging 5 bpm occurred.

L 13   Headrick, Mary W., Feather, Ben W., and Wells, David T.: Unidirectional and large magnitude heart rate changes with augmented sensory feedback. *Psychophysiology, 8:*132, 1971.

In the first of two studies, subjects (Ss) were required to either raise or lower heart rate (HR) relative to pretrial baseline by altering a tone which changed frequency with HR. Reliable increases but no decreases in HR were found. In a second study extended training of a single S with visual feedback resulted in consistent sustained HR increases of fifteen to thirty-five beats per minute (bpm), but only slight decreases. Sustained elevated rate was accompanied by anxiety. No reliable changes in breathing occurred in either study.

feedback
sensory
signals
response dis-crimina-tion
subjective responses
respiration

L 14   Hnatiow, Michael, and Lang, Peter J.: Learned stabilization of cardiac rate. *Psychophysiology, 1:*330, 1965.

Human subjects learned to reduce cardiac-rate variability when a visual display provided synchronous feedback of their own heart rate. The increased stability was unaccompanied by significant changes in average heart rate and was relatively unrelated to respiration changes.

feedback
learned
control
HR stabil-ization

L 15   Hnatiow, M.: Learned control of heart rate and blood pressure. *Percept Mot Skills, 33:*219, 1971.

Cardiac rate variability control and an initial demonstration of systolic blood pressure variability control using visual feed-

feedback

back of physiological information were examined. Continuous measurements of respiration, heart rate, ERG waveform analysis, and systolic blood pressure were obtained for both experimental groups and for yoked controls who saw the same visual display as the experimental Ss. Ss successful at reducing heart rate variability showed clear changes in the P-R wave relationships of the EKG, indicating possible direct attempts to manipulate heart rate so as to reduce the variability. Ss controlling blood pressure variability who had high heart rates were more successful in reducing variability than those with low rates, possibly because of differential feedback to Ss with high and low heart rates. In addition, apparently as a reaction to E's adjustment of the visual target range, experimental Ss showed decreases in mean blood pressure levels.

HR variability
BP variability
respiration

L 16 Lang, Peter J., Sroufe, Alan, and Hastings, James E.: Effects of feedback and instructional set on the control of cardiac rate variability. *J Exp Psychol, 75:*425, 1967.

This experiment with sixty male college students assesses their ability to control cardiac rate when they are provided with a continuous feedback display, and also when a comparable display is presented, not controlled by S's own heart rate. It also evaluates changes in cardiac rate variability induced by a simple tracking task, using the same display apparatus. All Ss viewed the display in a 5-min-on-5-min-off format. The results provide a clear demonstration that Ss learn to significantly reduce heart rate variability when appropriately instructed and provided with heart rate feedback. Neither tracking task Ss, nor those misinformed about the feedback, showed a significant reduction in variability.

heart rate control
heart rate variability
instructional set
false information

L 17 Levenson, Robert W., and Strupp, Hans H.: Simultaneous feedback and control of heart rate and respiration rate. *Psychophysiology, 10:*200, 1973.

Thirty subjects were asked to either increase or decrease their heart rate (HR), relative to a pretrial baseline period, while keeping their respiration rate (RR) at its baseline level. Subjects were provided with external feedback of their HR and RR independently via a digital display device which presented numerical representations of their current HR and

feedback
heart rate control
respiration
computer analysis

RR relative to baseline rates. The amount of feedback was varied on different trials to consist of either no feedback, HR feedback, or HR and RR feedback. HR and RR data were quantified on-line by a digital computer and were analyzed in terms of (1) HR inter-beat-interval (IBI) changes; (2) RR inter-cycle-interval (ICI) changes; (3) the number of heartbeat intervals which were in the instructed (i.e. increase or decrease) direction; and (4) the number of heartbeat intervals in the instructed direction and accompanied by respiration intervals at the baseline rate. Data analysis revealed that subjects were reliably able to produce HR changes regardless of the amount of feedback available, but that parallel changes in RR accompanied these HR changes. These RR changes occurred in spite of specific instructions not to use breathing changes to effect HR change and regardless of whether feedback of RR was available. On the basis of the combined measure of HR and RR intervals which met the instructed criteria, it was concluded that subjects were unable to produce HR change without accompanying RR changes. Implications of this finding for the general question of mediation in autonomic control research and for future studies using human subjects were discussed.

L 18   Ray, W.J., and Strupp, H.H.: Locus of control and the voluntary control of heart rate. *Psychophysiology, 9:*270, 1972.

Twenty internal locus of control and twenty external locus of control Ss were instructed to increase heart rate on the initial part of the trial and to decrease heart rate on the second part of the trial pair for eight trial pairs. This order was counterbalanced. During the first four trial pairs, no feedback concerning heart rate was given. During the second four trial pairs, the Ss received analog feedback via a light panel of sixteen lights concerning the IBI interval. Across groups there was a significant increase in the magnitude of heart rate changes on the feedback trials as compared to those without. Across all trials, the internal locus of control Ss were better able to increase their heart rate as compared with externals, and the external locus of control Ss were better able to decrease heart rate as compared with internals. Self-report measures concerned with the strategies utilized for control-

feedback
voluntary
 control
locus of
 control
personality
subjective
 reports
response
 strategies

ling heart rate demonstrated locus of control differences· in each group's approach to the task. These strategy differences relate to previous heart rate studies not involving the direct control of heart rate.

L 19   Schwartz, Gary E., Shapiro, David, and Tursky, Bernard: Learned control of cardiovascular integration in man through operant conditioning. *Psychosom Med, 33*:57, 1971.

In previous research, it has been shown that subjects can learn to increase or decrease their systolic blood pressure without corresponding changes in heart rate, or they can learn to increase or decrease their heart rate without corresponding changes in blood pressure. The present paper outlines a method for directly conditioning a combination of two autonomic responses. A system was developed which, at each heart cycle, determines on line whether heart rate and blood pressure are integrated (both increasing or both decreasing) or differentiated (one increasing and one decreasing). To test this method, five subjects received a brief light and tone feedback only when their heart rate and blood pressure were simultaneously increasing, and five subjects received the feedback only when their heart rate and blood pressure were simultaneously decreasing. Subjects earned rewards consisting of slides and monetary bonuses each time they produced twelve correct heart rate-blood pressure combinations. Significant cardiovascular integration was obtained in a single session. Subjects rewarded for simultaneous increases in heart rate and blood pressure showed small, comparable increases in both, while subjects rewarded for simultaneous decreases showed sizable decreases in both. Applications of the method in research and treatment are discussed.

feedback
operant conditioning
learned control
response integration
HR
BP

L 20   Schwartz, Gary E.: Voluntary control of human cardiovascular integration and differentiation through feedback and reward. *Science, 175*:90, 1972. (Copyright 1972 by the American Association for the Advancement of Science.)

Human subjects can learn to control the relation between their systolic blood pressure and heart rate when they are given feedback and reward for the desired pattern of blood

feedback
reward
voluntary control

pressure and heart rate. They can learn to integrate these functions (increase or decrease both jointly), or to a lesser degree, differentiate them (raise one and simultaneously lower the other). The extent of this learning is predicted by a behavioral and biological model that explains specificity of learning in the autonomic nervous system.

cardiovascular integration
cardiovascular differentiation
BP

21 Schwartz, G.E., Shaw, G., and Shapiro, D.: Specificity of alpha and heart rate control through feedback. *Psychophysiology, 9*:269, 1972.

To explore the effects of repeated alpha wave training on cardiovascular functioning, twelve Ss were pre- and posttested in the laboratory on their ability to control their alpha and heart rate after four daily one-hour sessions of feedback training to increase and decrease alpha. All Ss received full instructions concerning the nature of the feedback and the desired responses controlled with the following pre- and post-within S design: 3 min base period, 5 min increase alpha with feedback (100 msec tone per criterion alpha burst), 5 min decrease alpha with feedback; a second 3 min base period, 5 min decrease heart rate with feedback (100 msec tone per heart beat), 5 min increase heart rate with feedback. The pretest data indicated that Ss were initially unable to differentially increase or decrease alpha, but they were able to produce 5 bpm differences in heart rate which were unaccompanied by alpha changes. However, after the four sessions of alpha training, Ss evidenced significant alpha control unaccompanied by heart rate changes, while their ability to control their heart rate was unaffected (identical to the pretest). Analysis of the subjective report data supports the notion that the mechanisms of alpha and heart rate control are different. Implications for the direct feedback control of patterns of alpha and heart rate are discussed.

feedback
response discrimination
instructions
EEG alpha

22 Sroufe, L. Alan: Learned stabilization of cardiac rate with respiration experimentally controlled. *J Exp Psychol, 81:* 391, 1969.

Within a previously used cardiac rate stabilization task, respiration was experimentally controlled by having thirty of

feedback
HR control

forty male Ss breathe in synchrony with a respiration simula-
tor either at 14, 16, or 18 cpm. One half of the Ss received
visual feedback of their own heart rate changes; one-half
viewed the rate changes of a yoked control. Results showed
that even with restricted respiration, Ss viewing their own
heart rate achieved greater heart rate control during feedback
than nonfeedback periods. Also, as compared to control Ss,
feedback Ss showed both better control of heart rate level
and a greater reduction of heart period variability across the
session. Assigned respiration rate did not affect task success.

*HR stabil-
ization
respiration*

L 23   Stephens, Joseph H.: Large magnitude heart rate changes in
       subjects instructed to change their heart rates and given
       exteroceptive feedback. *Psychophysiology, 9:283, 1972.*

Four subjects who were given exteroceptive, auditory and
visual feedback and were asked to raise and to lower their
heart rate on signal, were able to produce large magnitude
changes in both directions. The fact that some of these
changes occurred immediately suggests that feedback may not
be as important as some authors have suggested. Respiratory
changes and changes in muscle tension did not appear to be
mediators.

*feedback
HR control
instructions
cognitive
  mediation
respiration
muscle
  tension*

L 24   Stern, Robert M., and Tyler, Robert W.: Augmented heart
       rate feedback: Differential effects during rest and stress.
       *Annual Meeting of the Soicety for Psychophysiological Re-
       search, Washington, D.C., 1968.*

The purpose of this study was to determine the effects of
providing subjects with continuous auditory feedback of
their heartbeat during periods of rest and periods of stress.
The initial hypothesis of this experiment, that heart rate feedback would effect Ss during a stress period but not a rest
period was supported by the heart rate data but not the GSR
data. This study, the first in a series, is thought to be a good
laboratory analog with which to manipulate the degree to
which S awareness of specific ANS changes contributed to behavioral and physiological responses to stress situations.

*augmented
feedback
HR control
rest
stress*

L 25   Stern, Robert M., Botto, Ronald W., and Herrick, Christine
       D.: Behavioral and physiological effects of false heart rate

feedback: A replication and extension. *Psychophysiology, 9:* 21, 1972.

Three experiments were conducted to study the behavioral and physiological effects of false heart rate feedback. These experiments were based on a paradigm advanced by Valins (1966) who stressed that the mere belief that one's heartbeat is changing, regardless of actual physiological changes, is sufficient to affect behavior. The three experiments involved (1) a replication of Valins' original study with a closer examination of actual physiological responses, (2) examination of the role which subject attention plays, and (3) a substitution of unpleasant stimuli for the pictures of nude females used in the earlier studies. It was concluded that what Valins ascribed to is merely the belief that physiological actions were occurring may have, in fact, been due to actual physiological changes precipitated by a general attention factor.

*false feed-
back
belief
attention
emotional
stimuli*

L 26   Valins, Stuart: Cognitive effects of false heart rate feedback. *J Pers Soc Psychol, 4:*400, 1966.

This experiment was concerned with some of the cognitive effects of internal events. The objective was to ascertain whether the labeling of emotional stimuli would be affected by information concerning internal reactions. Ss viewed ten slides of seminude females while hearing sounds that were allegedly their heartbeats. One group of Ss heard their "heart rates" increase markedly to five of the slides and not change to the other five; a second group of Ss heard a marked decrease in the bogus heart rate to five of the slides and no change to the other five. In comparison with the slides to which Ss did not hear a change in the bogus rate, the slides to which they heard a marked change, whether increased or decreased, were (1) rated significantly more attractive during the experiment proper and during a disguised interview conducted four to five weeks later, and (2) chosen significantly more as remuneration for experimental participation.

*false feed-
back
HR
responses
autonomic
cognition
pictorial
stimuli*

L 27   Wells, D.T.: Large magnitude voluntary heart rate changes under conditions of high motivation and extended practice. *Psychophysiology, 6:*636, 1970.

A study was conducted to maximize the magnitude of heart rate (HR) changes voluntarily produced by human subjects. The experiment was designed to demonstrate the effects of the experimental procedures rather than to test specific hypotheses. Three factors were considered to be the primary determinants of response magnitude: motivation, practice, and quality of feedback. Nine subjects were selected from a larger group of volunteers on the basis of their interest in and enthusiasm for the experiment. They were fully informed about the purposes of and the procedures used in the experiment. Each subject attempted to increase and decrease HR for ten trials each in each of eleven sessions. Each trial was a ninety second meter display of a Grass Model 7 tachograph output, adjusted automatically so that the subjects' baseline rate read center scale on the meter. Results showed increases of fifteen to forty beats per minute (BPM) over baseline in five subjects. These increases were specific to trial periods, had short onset and offset latencies, and were accompanied by a marked reduction in sinus arrhythmia. Control sessions showed that deliberate deep breathing failed to produce increases comparable to those observed during the trials. Deliberate muscle tensing could, in some subjects, produce increases equal to or exceeding those on their trials, but only with maximum effort that resulted in general body rigidity. Reliable decreases from baseline in the range of two or three bpm were observed in six subjects. The subjects were generally unable to verbalize their methods for producing large increases. However, they consistently reported anxiety-like experiences during periods of sustained elevated HR.

HR control feedback quality maximizing motivation subjective reports

L 28   Wells, David T.: Large magnitude voluntary heart rate changes. *Psychophysiology, 10*:260, 1973.

An experiment was performed to demonstrate methods for enabling subjects (Ss) to produce large magnitude heart rate (HR) changes under conditions which include adequate controls for basal HR changes and elicitation of the HR response by breathing changes. The methods used were an attempt to optimize motivational feedback and practice variables. Of nine Ss, six displayed mean HR increases ranging from 16.7 bpm to 35.2 bpm. The greatest mean HR decrease for

voluntary control controls respiration feedback operant conditioning

any S was 3.1 bpm. Control procedures indicated that breathing changes accompanying large increases in HR were not sufficient to account for the magnitude of HR change.

L 29   Young, Larry D., and Blanchard, Edward B.: Sex differences in the ability to control heart rate. *Psychophysiology, 9:*667, 1972.

Despite the lack of physiological explanation for the phenomenon, there appear to be several implications of the results that deserve mention. First, the results provide partial explanation for the difficulty (i.e. several training trials were necessary before data were collected) experienced by Levene, Engel and Pearson (1968) in obtaining alternating changes in HR: all of their Ss were female. Secondly, the results of a much cited study by Brener, Kleinman and Goesling (1969), which reported that Ss presented feedback exhibit superior control to that shown by Ss in a no feedback condition, are called somewhat into question since the sex of the Ss was not specified. A larger proportion of males in the augmented sensory feedback condition relative to the no feedback condition could help account for the reported difference, especially since (1) the no feedback Ss did show some degree of self-control, and (2) trials were given for HR changes in both directions. Finally, it should be emphasized that investigators in the area of biofeedback and operant conditioning of HR should be aware of this sex-related differential ability and, if using Ss of both sexes, should be careful to distribute them equally across conditions.

HR control
feedback
mental
control
sex differences

SECTION M

REVIEW

M 1   Crider, Andrew, Schwartz, Gary E., and Shnidman, Susan: On the criteria for instrumental autonomic conditioning: A reply to Katkin and Murray. *Psychol Bull, 71:455*, 1969.

In their recent review of instrumental conditioning of autonomic functions, Katkin and Murray criticized most of the existing studies on the human level as artifactual on one or more grounds. The criteria they employed for rejecting these demonstrations are themselves open to criticism, however. Specifically, it is argued that (1) peripheral or cognitive mediation hypotheses are unlikely alternative explanations of the obtained results; (2) an increase in response frequency over a preconditioning operant level is not a necessary condition for demonstrating an increase in response probability with contingent reinforcement; (3) yoked-control designs, frequently used in this research, do not automatically invalidate experiments in which they are employed. It is concluded that the strongest hypothesis to account for the existing data remains the direct instrumental strengthening of autonomic activity.

review
operant conditioning
autonomic conditioning criteria
hypotheses
critique

M 2   Elliott, Rogers: Further comment on the significance of heart rate in cross-laboratory comparison. *Psychophysiology, 9:450*, 1972.

Norman and Melville appear to feel that differences from laboratory to laboratory are so pervasive and effective that no useful cross-laboratory interpretations of differences in HR can be made. Elliott argues that the differences, and the absolute levels as well, are useful clues to motivational states, in rough proportion to the size of the samples involved, given certain boundary conditions about what we are willing to call "rest"; and that many of the dimensions of difference said by Norman and Melville to be fundamental are probably

review
comment
critique
definitions
variability
HR
responses

302

irrelevant. A variety of misrepresentations of Elliott's case made by Norman and Melville are discussed.

M 3 Gantt, W. Horsley: The meaning of the cardiac conditional reflex. *Cond Reflex, 1:*139, 1966.

Cardiac conditional reflex is defined as (1) response to a specific stimulus such as food, or (2) a supporting generalized function such as emotional excitement, tachycardia, or muscular tension. Because heart rate can only be altered by an increase or decrease, there is no easy method for determining the factors that do change heart rate, and there is no absolute criterion for doing so. Several previous studies of this problem are reviewed with special emphasis on the work of Pavlov and the later work at the Pavlovian Laboratory; much more experimentation toward solving this problem is called for.

review cardiac conditional reflex

M 4 Graham, Frances K., and Clifton, Rachel Keen: Heart rate change as a component of the orienting response. *Psychol Bull, 65:*305, 1966.

Both Sokolov and the Laceys have proposed that autonomic feedback to central neural structures amplifies or reduces the effects of stimulation. Lacey and Lacey distinguished between the effects of feedback from the cardiovascular system and from other autonomic systems and suggested, specifically, that heart rate (HR) acceleration should be associated with stimulus "rejection" and HR deceleration with stimulus enhancement. This appeared to be contradicted by evidence that HR increased with the orienting reflex whose function, according to Sokolov, is the enhancement of stimulus reception. However, when studies using simple "nonsignal" stimuli were reviewed, it was found that the criteria identifying an orienting reflex were satisfied by responses of HR deceleration and that instances of HR acceleration probably reflected a "defense," "startle," or "acoustic-cardiac" response.

review response components orienting response

M 5 Katkin, Edward S., and Murray, E. Neil: Instrumental conditioning of autonomically mediated behavior: Theoretical and methodological issues. *Psychol Bull, 70:*52, 1968.

Research on instrumental conditioning of electrodermal responses, peripheral vascular activity, and heart rate is reviewed. Major problems with research in the area are described, emphasizing such methodological shortcomings as inappropriate controls and systematic biasing effects, and focusing on alternative explanations of positive findings. A distinction is drawn between "conditioning" and "controlling" autonomic activity.

review
operant conditioning
autonomic control
methodology

M 6   Lykken, David T.: Valins' "Emotionality and autonomic reactivity": An appraisal. *J Exp Res Pers, 2:*49, 1967.

Research on Schachter's theory of emotionality is reviewed with special attention to work reported by S. Valins (see *41: 8*). The argument that emotionality is strongly affected by S's cognitive interpretation of his visceral reactions seems well-taken. The hypothesis that autonomic hyperreactivity can, through habituation, lead like hyporeactivity to emotional flatness has not found experimental support. Valins' method of measuring "emotionality" is criticized as is the tendency of the Schachter group to rely on heart rate as their sole indicant of autonomic arousal. A different interpretation of Valins' findings is offered, based on a speculation by J. Lacey, which suggests that the cardio-acceleration shown by "high emotional" Ss in anticipation of noxious unavoidable stimuli may be part of an adaptive defense reflex of reticular inhibitory and afferent "detuning."

review
theory
emotionality
cognitive activity

M 7   Obrist, Paul A., Webb, Roger A., Sutterer, James R., and Howard, James L.: The cardiac-somatic relationship: Some reformulations. *Psychophysiology, 6:*569, 1970.

The purpose of this paper is to propose a scheme as to how the activities of the heart might be viewed in psychophysiological endeavors and theory. It is proposed that a necessary starting point is the metabolically relevant relationship between cardiac and somatic processes. This relationship is relevant to both an understanding of basic behavioral processes as well as psychopathological states of cardiac functioning. For these purposes, a strategy is outlined which, among other things, involves the evaluation of the influence of the

review
research strategy
cardiac-somatic relationships
mechanisms
operant conditioning

cardiac innervations. Here it is proposed that heart rate most unequivocally reflects vagal activity, while the contractile properties of the heart manifest most unequivocally sympathetic effects. The implications of these arguments are discussed with regard to current studies involving the operant modification of heart rate. It is suggested that the significance of current operant studies to both issues of learning theory and psychopathology of cardiac function is questionable.

Pre-1965 References

HEART RATE

Belanger, D., and Feldman, S.M.: Effects of water deprivation upon heart rate and instrumental activity in the rat. *J Comp Physiol Psychol, 55*:220, 1962.

Bersh, P.J., Schoenfeld, W.N., and Notterman, J.M.: The effect upon heart rate conditioning of randomly varying the interval between conditioned and unconditioned stimuli. *Proc Natl Acad Sci USA, 39*:563, 1953.

Birren, J.E., Cardon, P.V., and Phillips, S.L.: Reaction time as a function of the cardiac cycle in young adults. *Science, 140*:195, 1963.

Black, R.W.: Heart rate response to auditory stimuli of varying duration. *Psychon Sci, 1*:171, 1964.

Blatt, S.J.: Patterns of cardiac arousal during complex mental activity. *J Abnorm Soc Psychol, 63*:272, 1961.

Blatz, W.E.: The cardiac respiratory, and electrical phenomena involved in the emotion of fear. *J Exp Psychol, 8*:109, 1925.

Bloch-Rojas, S., Toro, A., and Pinto-Hamy, T.: Cardiac versus somatomotor conditioned responses in neodecorticate rats. *J Comp Physiol Psychol, 58*:233, 1964.

Bond, D.D.: Sympathetic and vagal interaction in emotional responses of the heart rate. *Am J Physiol, 138*:468, 1943.

Bowerman, W.G., and Brett, J.H.: Pulse rates. *Q Rev Biol, 16*:90, 1941.

Brown, C.C., and Thorne, P.R.: An instrument for signaling heart rate to unrestrained human subjects. *Psychophysiology, 1*:192, 1964.

Chatterjee, B.B., and Eriksen, C.W.: Cognitive factors in heart rate conditioning. *J Exp Psychol, 64*:272, 1962.

Deane, G.E.: Human heart rate responses during experimentally induced anxiety. *J Exp Psychol, 61*:489, 1961.

Deane, G.E.: Human heart rate responses during experimentally induced anxiety: A follow-up with controlled respiration. *J Exp Psychol, 67*:193, 1964.

Deane, G.E., and Zeaman, D.: Human heart rate during anxiety. *Percept Mot Skills, 8*:103, 1958.

Diven, K.: Certain determinants in the conditioning of anxiety reactions. *J Psychol, 3*:291, 1937.

Docter, R.F., Kaswan, J.W., and Nakamura, C.Y.: Spontaneous heart rate and GSR changes as related to motor performance. *Psychophysiology, 1*:73, 1964.

Dykman, R.A., and Gantt, W.H.: The parasympathetic component of unlearned and acquired cardiac responses. *J Comp Physiol Psychol, 52*:163, 1959.

Fleck, S.: The cardiac component of orienting behavior.: Response to stimuli of varying intensity. *J Gen Psychol, 48:*163, 1953.

Fuhrer, M.J.: Differential verbal conditioning of heart rate with minimization of changes in respiratory rate. *J Comp Physiol Psychol, 58:*283, 1964.

Gantt, W.H.: Cardiovascular component of the conditional reflex to pain, food and other stimuli. *Physiol Rev, 40* (Suppl 4):266, 1960.

Geer, J.H.: Measurement of the conditioned cardiac response. *J Comp Physiol Psychol, 57:*426, 1964.

Glickstein, M., Chevalier, J.A., Korchin, S.J., Basowitz, H., Sabshin, M., Hamburg, D.A., and Grinker, R.R.: Temporal heart rate patterns in anxious patients. *Arch Neurol Psychiatry, 78:*101, 1957.

Harwood, C.W.: Operant heart rate conditioning. *Psychol Rec, 12:*279, 1962.

Jenks, R.S., and Deane, G.E.: Human heart rate responses during experimentally induced anxiety: A follow-up. *J Exp Psychol, 65:*109, 1963.

Kagan, J., and Rosman, B.L.: Cardiac and respiratory correlates of attention and an analytic attitude. *J Exp Child Psychol, 1:*50, 1964.

Kanfer, F.H.: Effect of a warning signal preceding a noxious stimulus on verbal rate and heart rate. *J Exp Psychol, 55:*73, 1958.

Kotliarevsky, L.I.: Cardio-vascular conditioned reflexes to direct and to verbal stimuli. *Fiziol Zh SSSR, 20:*228, 1936.

Kozenko, T.M.: Cardiovascular reflexes conditioned to interoceptive and exteroceptive stimuli by means of auditory reinforcement. *Sechenov Physiol, 44:*384, 1958.

Lang, P.J., and Hnatiow, M.: Stimulus repetition and the heart rate response. *J Comp Physiol Psychol, 55:*781, 1962.

Lazarus, R.S., Speisman, J.C., and Mordkoff, A.M.: The relationship between autonomic indicators of psychological stress: Heart rate and skin conductance. *Psychosom Med, 25:*19, 1963.

McDonald, D.A., Stern, J.A., and Hahn, W.H.: Classical heart rate conditioning in the rat. *J Psychosom Res, 7:*97, 1963.

Meyers, W.J., Valenstein, E.S., and Lacey, J.I.: Heart rate changes after reinforcing brain stimulation in rats. *Science, 140:*1233, 1963.

Notterman, J.M., Schoenfield, W.N., and Bersh, P.J.: A comparison of three extinction procedures following heart rate conditioning. *J Abnorm Soc Psychol, 47:*674, 1952.

Notterman, J.M., Schoenfeld, W.N., and Bersh, P.J.: Conditioned heart rate response in human beings during experimental anxiety. *J Comp Physiol Psychol, 45:*1, 1952.

Notterman, J.M., Schoenfeld, W.N., and Bersh, P.J.: Partial reinforcement and conditioned heart rate response in human subjects. *Science, 115:*77, 1952.

Obrist, P.A.: Cardiovascular differentiation of sensory stimuli. *Psychosom Med, 25:*450, 1963.

Oswald, I.: The human alpha rhythm and visual alertness. *Electroenceph Clin Neurophysiol., 11:*601, 1959.

Reese, W.G., and Dykman, R.A.: Conditional cardio-vascular reflexes in dogs and men. *Physiol Rev, 40:*250, 1960.

Requin, J., and Brouchon, M.: Mise en evidence chez l'homme d'une fluctuation des seuils perceptifs visuels dans la periode cardiaque. *C R Soc Biol (Paris), 158:*1891, 1964.

Rushmer, R.F., and Smith, O.A., Jr.: Cardiac control. *Psychol Rev, 39:*41, 1959.

Rushmer, R.F., Smith, O.A., Jr., and Lasher, E.P.: Neural mechanisms of cardiac control during exertion. *Psychol Rev,* (Suppl 4):27, 1960.

Samaan, A.: The antagonistic cardiac nerves and heart rate. *J Physiol, 83:*332, 1934-35.

Shapiro, D., Crider, A., and Tursky, B.: Differentiation of an autonomic response through operant reinforcement. *Psychon Sci, 1:*147, 1964.

Shearn, D.: Does the heart learn? *Psychol Bull, 55:*452, 1961.

Shearn, D.W.: Operant conditioning of heart rate. *Science, 137:*530, 1962.

Shock, N.W., and Schlatter, M.J.: Pulse rate response of adolescents to auditory stimuli. *J Exp Psychol, 30:*414, 1942.

Skaggs, E.B.: Changes in pulse, breathing, and steadiness under conditions of startledness and excited expectancy. *J Comp Physiol Psychol, 6:*303, 1926.

Venables, P.H.: Amplitude of the electrocardiogram and level of skin potential. *Percept Mot Skills, 17:*54, 1963.

Welford, N.T., Lacey, B., and Peckham, C.: Computer identification and measurement of cardiac activity. *Psychophysiology, 1:*111, 1964.

Wenger, M.A., and Bagchi, B.K.: Studies of autonomic functions in practitioners of Yoga in India. *Behav Sci, 6:*312, 1961.

Wenger, M.A., Bagchi, B.K., and Anand, B.K.: Experiments in India on "voluntary" control of the heart and pulse. *Circulation, 24:*1319, 1961.

Wenzel, B.M.: Changes in heart rate associated with responses based on positive and negative reinforcement. *J Comp Physiol Psychol, 54:*638, 1961.

Westcott, M.R., and Huttenlocher, J.: Cardiac conditioning: The effects and implications of controlled and uncontrolled respiration. *J Exp Psychol, 61:*353, 1961.

Wieland, W.F., Stein, M., and Hamilton, C.L.: Intensity of the unconditional stimulus as a factor in conditioning out of awareness. *Psychosom Med, 25:*124, 1963.

Wood, D.M., and Obrist, P.A.: Effects of controlled and uncontrolled respiration on the conditioned heart rate response in humans. *J Exp Psychol, 68:*221, 1964.

Zeaman, D., Deane, G., and Wegner, N.: Amplitude and latency characteristics of the conditioned heart response. *J Psychol, 38:*235, 1954.

Zeaman, D., and Wegner, N.A.: A further test of the role of drive reduction in human cardiac conditioning. *J Psychol, 43:*125, 1957.

DESCRIPTOR INDEX — HEART RATE

PART III

BLOOD PRESSURE

MEASUREMENTS

A 1   Horwitz, J., and Averill, J.: An inexpensive transducer for remote determination of arterial blood pressure. *Psychophysiology, 2:*168, 1965.

> A low-cost transducer for monitoring arterial blood pressure by remote auscultation is described. It employs a miniature earphone attached to the diaphragm of a conventional stethoscope. The Korotkov sounds picked up by the diaphragm are converted to electrical signals by the earphone. These are amplified and monitored over a loudspeaker or headphones.

transducer
remote
  recording

A 2   Krausman, David: Automatic, on line printout of peak systolic and diastolic blood pressures. *Psychophysiology, 5:*337, 1968.

> A system for on line printout of beat-by-beat systolic and diastolic blood pressures is described. The system incorporates both commercial and laboratory constructed components. The blood pressure signal is derived from a cannulated pressure transducer, the output of which is peak sampled, V to F converted, and printed in digital form at the occurrence of each R-wave. The printer output is a continuous column of figures representing the values for beat-by-beat peak systolic and diastolic blood pressures displayed to the nearest ±2 mm Hg when compared with those recorded on the polygraph tracing. This system greatly reduces the manual operation of reading peak blood pressures from polygraph records which in the past were tedious, somewhat inaccurate, and a time-consuming process.

BP recording
digital
  printing

A 3   Wieland, Betty A., and Mefferd, Roy B. Jr.: Identification of periodic components in physiological measurements. *Psychophysiology, 6:*160, 1969.

Baseline diastolic blood pressure measurements made on a *diastolic BP*
single subject for 120 consecutive days were utilized to *periodic*
demonstrate the use of autocorrelation techniques for the *components*
identification of cycles of one or more periods present in the
data. Provided only a single period is present, averaging *reliability*
techniques using this period as the base may be used to *autocorrelation*
smooth the data. However, few physiological variables cycle
so simply. Smoothing not only may introduce spurious cycles, *crosscor-
relation*
but it also eliminates much nonrandom (and, therefore,
meaningful) variance.

A 4   Wieland, Betty A., and Mefferd, Roy B. Jr.: Systematic
       changes in levels of physiological activity during a four-
       month period. *Psychophysiology, 6:*669, 1970.

Intraindividual differences over a four-month period in a *variability*
number of physiological variables for three subjects are *reliability*
examined. Autocorrelation techniques revealed the presence *individual
differences*
of systematic changes (cycles and trends). It is concluded
that intraindividual differences in these variables may be *biological
cycles*
nearly as large as interindividual differences and that they
cannot be explained merely as errors of measurement. Possi- *stress*
ble sources of variability are discussed.

PSYCHOSOCIAL FACTORS
AND BLOOD PRESSURE

B 1 Bohm, M., Trlica, J., and Veljacikova, N.: The Czechoslovak EEG Commission: The EEG in different phases of essential vascular hypertension. *Electroencephalogr Clin Neurophysiol, 22*:286, 1967.

Hypertensive patients without neurological signs or symptoms were divided into two groups: Group A—forty-three 15 to 25-year-old Ss with hypertension not exceeding five-year duration, all of them belonging to Stage I; Group B—thirty-one 26 to 72-year-old Ss having essential hypertension, in 39 percent of less than five-year and in 61 percent of more than five-year duration. In Group B it appeared that there was a prevalence of EEG abnormalities as compared with Group A. This finding was in direct relation with the stage and duration of the illness. In Group B focal slow waves were three times more frequent than in Group A. Background alpha rhythm at 10 to 13 cps prevailed in Group A, while in Group B an alpha frequency below 10 cps occurred three times more often. In both groups episodic discharges were recorded in 20 percent without clinical seizures, and there was no difference between Groups A and B in voltage or in the occurrence of fast activity. EEG abnormalities were not specific in essential vascular hypertension, and their incidence was different from various anomalies seen in normal senescence and among normal young adults.

age
EEG alpha
EEG abnormalities

B 2 Davies, Martin: Blood pressure and personality. *J Psychosom Res, 14*:89, 1970.

Six pairs of resting blood pressure readings were obtained by an independent observer in 128 middle-aged male factory workers employed in a single workshop. The subjects were divided into three groups of high, average and low blood

personality
high BP
constitutional factors

319

pressure. A significant positive correlation was confirmed between the level of blood pressure and body weight, arm
circumference, a square body build, and a family history of
cardiovascular disease. A significant negative relationship
of the blood pressure level, independent of these factors, was
found with a history of neurotic traits in childhood, current
neurotic symptoms, and the neuroticism scale of the Eysenck
Personality Inventory. These findings were regarded as supporting the hypothesis that there is a psychosomatic component in the aetiology of high blood pressure.

B 3   Ettema, J.H.: Blood pressure changes during mental load
       experiments in man. *Psychother Psychosom, 17:*191, 1969.

Several experiments are discussed showing an increase in   *increased*
systolic and diastolic blood pressure as a function of the   *BP*
amount of information handling per time unit. In short-   *mental stres.*
term experiments, this rise in blood pressure was not very   *HR change*
impressive and remained within the normal physiological   *information*
range. There were some indications, however, that pro-   *processing*
longed severe mental stress induces a more important increase in blood pressure. An increase in blood pressure, together with changes in other physiological phenomena such
as heart rate and sinus arrhythmia, indicate that mental
stress may alter the level of activity of the autonomic nervous
system. In the experiments, an auditory binary choice task
(high or low tone in random sequence and of differing frequency to be answered by pressing a right, then a left pedal)
was used to evoke mental load.

B 4   Forrest, M., and Kroth, J.A.: Psychometric and physiological
       indices of anxiety. *J Clin Psychol, 27:*40, 1971.

Three groups of 105 Ss each, selected on the basis of high,   *anxiety*
medium and low scores on psychometric indices of anxiety,   *avoidance*
were subjected to a continuous matching task upon which   *diastolic BP*
was superimposed a shock avoidance contingency. Ss with
high state anxiety scores exhibited higher systolic blood
pressure readings then did the other two groups, and the
findings were consistent with the state-trait theory of anxiety
and the emotional reactivity hypothesis. A significant rela-

tionship was found between the Trait Anxiety Index and diastolic blood pressure and between the MA scale and diastolic blood pressure.

B 5   Gentry, William D.: Sex differences in the effects of frustration and attack on emotion and vascular processes. *Psychol Rep, 27*:383, 1970.

The effects of frustration (test-failure) and attack (insult) on mood, aggression, and vascular arousal were explored in thirty male and female Ss. Systolic and diastolic blood pressure were recorded prior to and immediately following provocation and Ss were asked to rate their feelings on a post-experimental mood questionnaire. The results indicated that both types of provocation led to increased vascular activity. Males evidenced a greater rise in systolic pressure than did females; whereas, no sex differences were noted for diastolic changes. No differences were found between frustration and attack regarding their effect on vascular arousal. On the mood ratings, female Ss tended to rate themselves as being weaker than males, regardless of the treatment. Females also reported more felt depression after being frustrated or attacked than did control females, a pattern of emotional response not shown by male Ss. No differential effects were observed for aggression.

frustration increased BP vascular arousal emotional responses sex differences

B 6   Heine, Bernard: Psychogenesis of hypertension. *Proc R Soc Med, 63*:1267, 1970.

The writer concludes from the present observations that repeated spells of depressive illness, when characterized by marked anxiety and agitation, are accompanied by repeated exposure to stimuli that increase blood pressure may well lead to a maintained increase.

chronic emotional illness anxiety-agitation depression

B 7   Henry, J.P., and Cassel, J.C.: Psychosocial factors in essential hypertension. Recent epidemiologic and animal experimental evidence. *Am J Epidemiol, 90*:171, 1969.

Recent developments in the epidemiology of essential hypertension permit more emphasis to be placed on the etiologic role of psychosocial stimulation and early experience. Evidence is presented suggesting that obesity and dietary

psychosocial factors epidemiology

factors such as salt or fat intake may not be as significant in explaining variations in blood pressure levels in different populations as is the organism's perception of events in the social environment. Animal and human studies are cited which indicate that repeated arousal of the defense alarm response may be one important mechanism involved. In man such arousal follows when previously socially sanctioned patterns of behavior, especially those to which the organism has become adapted during critical early learning periods, can no longer be used to express normal behavioral urges. Difficulties of adaptation, as where there is status ambiguity, may result in years of repeated arousals of vascular, autonomic and hormonal function due to the organism's perception of certain events as threatening. These, in turn, can lead to progressive and eventually irreversible disturbances such as renal hypertension, heart failure, or cerebrovascular disease.

B 8   Kasl, Stanislav V., and Cobb, Sidney: Blood pressure changes in men undergoing job loss: A preliminary report. *Psychosom Med, 32*:19, 1970.

It is the purpose of this paper to describe the blood pressure changes in men who go through a social stress situation very much like the one described by Ostfeld and Shekelle (1967): job loss because of a permanent plant shutdown. The men are followed as they go through the stages of employment on the old job, loss of job, unemployment (for some), probationary reemployment, and stable employment on a new job. The subjects are fifty-six married men in the age range of thirty-five to sixty years, employed in a single company. The control group consists of forty-six subjects continuously employed in comparable jobs. Preliminary information on some sixty men from another company are also considered.

psychosocial factors
social stress
BP levels

B 9   Lee, S.G., Carstairs, G.M., and Pickersgill, Mary J.: Essential hypertension and the recall of motives. *J Psychosom Res, 15*: 95, 1971.

Aims: This study was designed to test the hypotheses (1) that repressed aggression was implicated in cases of essential hy-

essential hypertension

pertension, (2) that, in a group of hypertensive patients, those with relatively high systolic blood pressure would tend to forget a "fear" stimulus; those with relatively high diastolic pressure would tend to forget an "aggression" stimulus, (3) that significant differences in recall orders for pictures of motives would occur between groups of essential hypertensives, renal hypertensives, "mixed-bag" hospitalized controls, and "normals." *Procedure:* Four groups, each of forty subjects, selected for the categories in (3) above and matched for age, sex, and social class, were asked to recall ten pictures of "needs" (Forrest and Lee) which were randomized with ten dummy (nonmotive) pictures. *Results:* No evidence for late recall of aggression by essential hypertensives was found, but narcism was recalled significantly early, rejection significantly late by this group. Nurturance differentiated between the sexes, being remembered earlier by women, and essential hypertensive females recalled nurturance significantly early. Within the essential hypertensive group, exclusively, patients with relatively high systolic BP tended to forget, statistically significantly, the harmavoidance (fear) stimulus. Those with relatively high diastolic BP tended to forget aggression. It would appear that the findings of Ax and Schachter which showed differential rises in systolic and diastolic pressures to fear and anger, respectively, have their counterparts in human forgetting. It seems probable that, in essential hypertension, habitual overreaction to fear stimuli (in terms of a rise in systolic pressure) is accompanied by a tendency to forget an abstract representation of a fear situation.

repressed aggression

recall of motives

B 10   Mitschke, H.: The EEG in arterial hypertension. I. The question of a central nervous system etiopathogenesis of essential hypertension. EEG findings in patients with juvenile essential hypertension. *Dtsch Gesundheitsw, 23*:481, 1968.

The EEG findings in thirty cases of juvenile essential hypertension, in the early stage without complications or attendant diseases, were compared with those of fifty intact persons of the same age group. On the one hand, a regular, well-marked, medium high alpha rhythm was found much more rarely in the patients than in the intact controls (23% as

juvenile essential hypertension

EEG activity

EEG alpha

compared to 56%). On the other hand, the hypertensives manifested increased hyperventilation reactions much more frequently than the controls (42% as compared to 6%). Altogether—allowing for significant variations—60 percent of the findings obtained from the hypertensives proved to be pathological, as compared to only 14 percent in the control group. These pathological findings were characterized by nonspecific, nonuniform and nonfocal changes. The potential importance of these findings in the etiopathogenesis of essential hypertension is discussed.

*EEG abnor-
malities*

B 11   Mitschke, H., and Enderlein, J.: The EEG in arterial hypertension. III. Side localization of focal findings in the EEG of hypertensive patients. *Dtsch Gesundheitsw, 24:*1585, 1969.

From a study of 3,782 EEG records taken from 806 hypertensive patients, 326 cases with unilateral localization were found. They were analyzed according to type, age distribution and side of localization. As expected, the abnormalities increased with age and in each age group were found to predominate in the left hemisphere. This was particularly marked in patients over fifty years and was mainly caused by an increased number of clinically latent left-sided focal disturbances. The significance of these findings is discussed.

*EEG
activity
left hemi-
sphere
age
focal dis-
turbances*

B 12   Nestel, P.J.: Blood pressure and catecholamine excretion after mental stress in labile hypertension. *Lancet, 1:*692, 1969.

The effect of mild mental stress on blood pressure and excretion of free adrenaline and noradrenaline in the urine was studied in seventeen controls and twenty patients with mild labile hypertension. The mean ages of the two groups were 31.4 and 35.2 years and the mean resting prestress pressures were 117/75 and 147/95 mm Hg, respectively. The mean basal excretion rates of the catecholamines were not significantly different. The stress, which was of forty-minute duration and required the solution of visual puzzles, led to changes in systolic and diastolic pressures which were significantly greater in the hypertensive patients. The output of adrenalin rose in all subjects and was significantly greater

*labile hyper-
tension
mental stress
catechola-
mine
excretion*

among the hypertensive. The output of noradrenalin rose in seventeen hypertensives, but in only nine controls; and the mean poststress value and the mean change in excretion were significantly higher in the hypertensive patients. The changes in blood pressure were significantly correlated with the changes in catecholamine output in the thirty-seven subjects studied. Labile hypertensive patients show on the average a heightened sympathetic response to mental stress.

B 13   Richter, Heinrich E., and Sprung, H.: Psychophysiological studies in the initial stage of essential hypertension. *Z Gesamte Inn Med, 24:*17, 1969.

essential hypertension arousal level GSR reactivity conditioning

A group of thirty essential hypertensives of grade I severity, twenty-five of grade II severity, and twenty normotensives aged twenty to forty years were submitted to the following psychophysiological tests: registration of autonomic functions (systolic and diastolic blood pressure, heart rate, skin potentials) at rest and under emotional stress; application of a backward conditioned galvanic skin reflex; testing of absolute acoustic thresholds; and adaptation to an acoustic stimulus (Feldmann). The essential hypertensives, compared to the normotensives, showed in the first test a generally heightened level of arousal. Only in the group I hypertensives did the diastolic blood pressure show any significant difference from that of the normals, nor did the galvanic skin reactivity differ in the two given special stress situations. Both hypertensive groups differed significantly only in respect to their blood pressure levels. Moreover, the hypertensives, contrary to the normotensives, showed significantly more frequent predominance of excitation in conditioned reflex experiments, further on lower acoustic thresholds as well as significantly less adaptation to an acoustic stimulus. The different reaction patterns of normotensives and hypertensives were interpreted as due to increased sympathetic activity of the hypertensives possibly determined by psychophysical dysregulation.

B 14   Sapira, Joseph D., Scheib, Eileen T., Moriarty, Richard, and Shapiro, Alvin P.: Differences in perception between hypertensive and normotensive populations. *Psychosom Med, 33:* 239, 1971.

A group of hypertensive patients (N = 19) and a control group of normotensive patients (N = 15) were shown two movies depicting two types of doctor-patient interaction. In the first movie, the doctor was rude and disinterested in the patient (the bad doctor). In the second movie, the doctor was relaxed and warm (the good doctor). After viewing the two movies, all patients were interviewed as to their impressions of the two scenes. During the viewing, blood pressure and pulse rate responses in the hypertensive group were small but significantly greater than those in the normotensive group; during the interview, the significantly greater response in the hypertensives was physiologically meaningful. The urinary catecholamine and cortisol excretion rates were no different between the two groups. Most striking was the finding that the hypertensive group tended to deny seeing any differences between the doctors depicted in the two movies, while the normotensive group could clearly identify differences in the behavior of the good doctor versus that of the bad doctor. In a second experiment, the same movies were shown to a hypertensive group and to three normotensive groups. The patients were asked to fill out a questionnaire derived from auditing the tape recordings in the first experiment. This questionnaire made it possible to differentiate significantly between the hypertensive and normotensive groups. These data are compatible with the hypothesis that the hypertensive patient may perceptually screen out potentially noxious stimuli as a behavioral response to his hyper-reactive pressor system.

psychologic factors
perception
emotional responses
emotional blocking
catecholamine excretion

B 15   Shatalov, N.N., and Murov, M.A.: The influence of intense noise and neuropsychic tension on the level of the arterial pressure and the incidence of hypertensive vascular disease (Russian). *Klin Med (Mosk), 48:*70, 1970.

The studies convened testify to the unfavorable effect of intensive noise and neuropsychic tension on the state of the arterial pressure. In persons working under the influence of such factors the level of the arterial pressure and the incidence of hypertensive disease rise. The incidence of hypertensive vascular disease in workers of the so-called noisy oc-

psychologic factors
noise
BP levels
hypertension

cupations, as well as scientists of similar age groups, are very similar. In the combined effect of the referred to two factors, noise and neuropsychic tension, there occurs a greater increase in the number of pressor reactions, in connection with which the incidence of hypertensive vascular disease significantly augments.

3 16   Silverstone, Stanley, and Kissin, Benjamin: Field dependence in essential hypertension and peptic ulcer. *J Psychosom Res, 12:*157, 1968.

The data presented tend to support the hypotheses suggested in the introduction to this report in that the hypertensive subjects were significantly more field independent than were the peptic ulcer patients. Our finding that patients with essential hypertension tend to be field independent is of interest, since to the best of our knowledge no other report of a tendency to field independence in psychosomatic patients has been made. Our study suggests that if, ultimately, aberrations in field dependence are found to be related to psychosomatic disease, the possibilities of both increased and decreased field dependence will have to be considered.

essential hyperten-sion psychopath-ology peptic ulcer

B 17   Torgersen, Svenn, and Kringlen, Einar: Blood pressure and personality. A study of the relationship between intrapair differences in systolic blood pressure and personality in monozygotic twins. *J Psychsom Res, 15:*183, 1971.

The aim of this investigation was to study the relationship between personality and blood pressure. A relatively unselected sample of forty-eight monozygotic twin pairs, twenty-four female and twenty-four male, within the general population were investigated. It was found that the twin who was the more submissive as a child and who was the more quiet, withdrawn, obedient, and insecure had the higher systolic blood pressure. In adult life the twin who was the more depressive and shy had the higher blood pressure. The relationship was a relatively weak one, manifesting itself mainly in a supine position. Some explanations have been suggested in the discussion.

personality systolic BP monozygotic twins

B 18 Williams, Donald H., and Cartwright, Rosalind D.: Blood pressure changes during EEG-monitored sleep. *Arch Gen Psychiatry, 20:*307, 1969.

The blood pressures of five normotensive and five hypertensive Negro women were recorded during two nights of EEG-monitored sleep. Analysis of the mean blood pressures showed that there was significantly greater variability of the blood pressure during REM stage sleep of the normotensive group compared to their NREM sleep. There was no significant difference in the variability of blood pressure of the hypertensive group between the two sleep stages. In addition, the variability of the hypertensive Ss' blood pressures in both phases was significantly greater than the variability during NREM sleep of the normotensive Ss' blood pressure and equal to the variability found during the REM stage of the normotensive Ss' sleep. These findings indicate a high level of neurophysiological activity during all stages of sleep in these hypertensive women.

sleep
BP variability
EEG activity
REM sleep

OPERANT CONDITIONING —
LEARNED CONTROL OF BLOOD PRESSURE

C 1 Benson, H., Shapiro, D., Tursky, B., and Schwartz, G.E.: Decreased systolic blood pressure through operant conditioning techniques in patients with essential hypertension. *Science, 173:*740, 1971. (Copyright 1971 by the American Association for the Advancement of Science.)

Operant conditioning-feedback techniques were employed to lower systolic blood pressure in seven patients with essential hypertension. In five of the patients, meaningful decreases of systolic blood pressure were obtained in the laboratory, ranging from sixteen to thirty-four millimeters of mercury. The therapeutic value of such techniques remains to be established.

operant conditioning
essential hypertension
applications

C 2 Miller, Neal E., DiCara, Leo V., Solomon, Henry, Weiss, Jay M., and Dworkin, Barry: Psychological aspects of hypertension. Learned modifications of autonomic functions: A review and some new data. *Suppl 1 to Circulation Research, 26 & 27:*I-3, 1970.

The experiments from my laboratory which prove that the ancient strong prejudice against the autonomic nervous system is wrong have recently been summarized elsewhere and also published in the relevant journals. Therefore, this paper will primarily state the conclusions to be derived from this extensive series of experiments and their implications for cardiovascular function; a few new unpublished results will be included. Topics covered are: Typical Experiment on Heart Rate; Variety of Responses Learned; Similarities of Visceral to Skeletal Learning; Specificity of Various Responses Learned; Slower Visceral Learning by Noncurarized People; Improved Indirect Measure of Blood Pressure; and Possibilities for Improving Human Visceral Learning.

instrumental conditioning
curare
visceral learning
HR recording techniques
review
applications

329

C 3 Patel, C.H.: Yoga and biofeedback in the management of hypertension. *Lancet, 2:*1053, 1973.

Yogic relaxation and biofeedback techniques were used in the treatment of twenty patients with hypertension. As a result, antihypertensive therapy was stopped altogether in five patients, and reduced by 33 to 60 percent in a further seven patients. Blood pressure control was better in four other patients, while four patients did not respond to therapy. Of these four patients, at least one had derived indirect benefit by the relief of migraine and depression. The results of this study promise a useful new approach to the treatment of hypertension.

hyper-tension
bio-feedback
yogic relaxation

C 4 Schwartz, Gary E.: Operant conditioning of human cardiovascular integration and differentiation. *Psychophysiology, 8:*245, 1971.

Many studies have demonstrated specificity of learning in operant autonomic conditioning. For example, research in our laboratories on two closely related responses in man has shown that reinforcing increases or decreases in systolic blood pressure (BP) leads to BP learning without corresponding changes in heart rate (HR), while reinforcing increases or decreases in HR leads to HR learning without corresponding changes in BP. In view of these data, a behavioral-physiological (ID) model for explaining and predicting learned autonomic Integration and Differentiation was developed. Based on the ID model, a system was constructed for measuring on line the integration and differentiation of two or more responses. Using this system, an experiment was then performed to teach individuals to directly integrate or differentiate their BP and HR. Ten male Ss received a brief light and tone (feedback) only when their BP and HR were simultaneously increasing; ten Ss received the feedback only when their BP and HR were both decreasing; ten Ss received the feedback only when their BP was increasing and their HR was simultaneously decreasing; and ten Ss received the feedback only when their BP was decreasing and their HR was increasing. Ss earned rewards consisting of slides of landscapes, nude females, and monetary bonuses each time

operant conditioning
feedback
cardio-vascular integration
cardio-vascular differentiation
HR
BP

they produced twelve correct BP-HR combinations. All Ss received five resting, five random reinforcement, and thirty-five conditioning trials, each trial fifty beats in length. Significant BP-HR integration and differentiation was obtained in a single session (p < .0001). The results confirmed the predictions of the ID model that BP-HR integration is more easily learned than BP-HR differentiation, and that decreasing BP-increasing HR is more readily learned than increasing BP-decreasing HR.

C 5 Schwartz, G.E., Shapiro, D., and Tursky, B.: Learned control of cardiovascular integration in man through operant conditioning. *Psychosom Med, 33*:57, 1971.

In previous research, it has been shown that subjects can learn to increase or decrease their systolic blood pressure without corresponding changes in heart rate, or they can learn to increase or decrease their heart rate without corresponding changes in blood pressure. The present paper outlines a method for directly conditioning a combination of two autonomic responses. A system was developed which, at each heart cycle, determines on line whether heart rate and blood pressure are integrated (both increasing or both decreasing) or differentiated (one increasing and one decreasing). To test this method, five subjects received a brief light and tone feedback only when their heart rate and blood pressure were simultaneously increasing, and five subjects received the feedback only when their heart rate and blood pressure were simultaneously decreasing. Subjects earned rewards consisting of slides and monetary bonuses.

operant conditioning
cardiovascular integration
feedback
HR
BP

C 6 Shapiro, David, Tursky, Bernard, Gershon, Elliot, and Stern, Melvin: Effects of feedback and reinforcement on the control of human systolic blood pressure. *Science, 163*:588, 1969. (Copyright 1969 by the American Association for the Advancement of Science.)

An automatic procedure providing information about human systolic blood pressure at each successive heartbeat under routine laboratory conditions is described. Twenty normal male subjects were given feedback of their own

feedback
reinforcement
systolic BP

systolic pressure, half operantly reinforced for increasing and half reinforced for decreasing their pressure. Significant differences in pressure were obtained in a single session. The apparatus and results suggest a possible approach to the treatment of essential hypertension.

HR applications

C 7   Shapiro, David, Tursky, Bernard, and Schwartz, Gary E.: Differentiation of heart rate and systolic blood pressure in man by operant conditioning. *Psychosom Med, 32:*417, 1970.

Human heart rate-systolic blood pressure decoupling was tested by operant conditioning procedures. Twenty normal male subjects were given feedback of their heart rate, half operantly reinforced for increasing and half for decreasing their heart rate, while systolic blood pressure was continuously monitored. Significant heart rate conditioning was obtained in a single session without concomitant effects on blood pressure. Further analyses of the best conditioners in the present study and those in a previous blood pressure conditioning study indicate the strength of operant heart rate-blood pressure decoupling and demonstrate that instrumental fractionation of closely related visceral behavior is possible in man.

operant conditioning feedback response differentiation HR BP

C 8   Shapiro, David, Tursky, Bernard, and Schwartz, Gary E.: Control of blood pressure in man by operant conditioning. *Suppl I to Circ Res, 26 & 27:*I-27, 1970.

The aim of this research was directed toward one basic question. With all other variables held constant, if you reward increases in systolic blood pressure in one group of human subjects and decreases in another, will pressure levels become differentiated? An affirmative answer was given by the results of this study, replicating the previous finding. The differences, although relatively small, are of significance when considering the tightly controlled experimental conditions, the use of minimal instructions, and the relatively short period of training (about thirty minutes). The data on the specificity of conditioning suggest that at least, on the average, a function such as blood pressure can be treated or modified without in turn having any corresponding effect on

operant conditioning feedback affective stimuli response differentiation

heart rate. It appears that conditioned blood pressure changes are not dependent on changes in heart rate. The data on practice and transfer effects, although preliminary in nature, support the view that specific prior training has an effect on subsequent conditioning within a given autonomic function.

C 9   Shapiro, David, Schwartz, Gary E., and Tursky, Bernard: Control of diastolic blood pressure in man by feedback and reinforcement. *Psychophysiology, 9:*296, 1972.

When provided with external feedback of their diastolic blood pressure and incentives to respond appropriately, normal male Ss learned to raise or lower their diastolic pressure in a thirty-five-minute training session. The difference between increase and decrease groups at the end of conditioning was 7.0 mm Hg or 10 percent of baseline. This difference was augmented to 10.4 mm Hg or 15 percent of baseline during extinction when half the Ss were asked to maintain continuing "voluntary control" even though feedback and incentives were withdrawn. Heart rate was also influenced when diastolic blood pressure was reinforced, although less markedly. Further analysis indicated that when diastolic pressure is reinforced, heart rate is partially reinforced in the same direction, accounting for the coincidental conditioning of the related cardiovascular measure. No consistent changes in respiration or postsession verbal reports were obtained. These results lend support to the possibility of therapeutic application of the techniques in patients with essential hypertension.

feedback
reinforcement
diastolic BP
HR
response integration
response differentiation

ANIMAL STUDIES

D 1   Benson, Herbert, Herd, J. Alan, Morse, W.H., and Kelleher, Roger T.: Behavioral induction of arterial hypertension and its reversal. *Am J Physiol, 217:30,* 1969.

Mean arterial blood pressure was measured in three squirrel monkeys through chronically implanted aortic catheters. The monkeys were trained to press a key which turned off a light thereby preventing the delivery of noxious stimuli. As training progressed and each animal pressed the key rapidly, mean arterial blood pressure consistently rose in association with the key pressing. Following this training period, the key was removed from the apparatus and the schedule was altered so that increases in blood pressure per se turned off the light, preventing the delivery of noxious stimuli. Mean arterial blood pressure rose to hypertensive levels during each session. Finally, the schedule was changed so that only decreases in mean arterial blood pressure prevented the delivery of noxious stimuli. Mean blood pressure consistently returned toward control values. Thus, mean arterial blood pressure was made to rise and fall predictably when environmental stimuli were scheduled according to variations in blood pressure.

monkey
mean arterial BP
operant conditioning
experimental hypertension
reinforcement schedules

D 2   DiCara, Leo V., and Miller, Neal E.: Instrumental learning of systolic blood pressure responses by curarized rats: Dissociation of cardiac and vascular changes. *Psychosom Med, 30:*489, 1968.

Rats with skeletal muscles paralyzed by curare to rule out the effect of muscular activity were given artificial respiration and were rewarded by escape and/or avoidance of mild electric shock for either increasing or decreasing their systolic blood pressure. A chronic catheter was implanted within the abdominal aorta for measurement of same. Each

rats
curare
operant conditioning
stimulus discrimination

334

trial was signaled by the onset of a light and tone; each ex- *electric* perimental rat was yoked to a control rat. The yoked con- *shock* trol received exactly the same treatment as the experimental *implications* S, except that it could do nothing to avoid being shocked, and was shocked whenever the experimental S was shocked. Overall group increases and decreases of 22.3 percent and 19.2 percent, respectively, were obtained for the experimental groups and were significantly different from the changes in the control groups. All experimental Ss without exception changed their blood pressure in the rewarded direction. Analyses of heart rate and temperature did not reveal any significant changes either between experimental groups at the beginning, at the end of training, or within experimental groups during training. Implications for learning theory, psychosomatic pathology, and treatment are discussed.

D 3   Forsyth, Ralph P.: Influence of blood pressure on patterns of voluntary behavior. *Psychophysiology,* 2:98, 1966.

The relation between cardiac activity and motor activity was *monkey* investigated in a monkey with normal blood pressure work- *avoidance* ing on a ten-second Sidman avoidance schedule. The mon- *condition-* key's lever-pressing activity and his blood pressure, mea- *ing* sured from an arterial catheter, were simultaneously re- *BP influ-* corded on a dynograph. A total of 2536 lever presses were *ence* recorded in three test periods, and each response was related *voluntary* to the phase of the blood pressure wave in which it occurred. *behavior* A Spearman rank correlation coefficient of −0.63 was found *reticular* between the time of onset of the response and the height of *activity* the pressure wave when the data were grouped into 10 percent periods and adjusted for a 119-msec delay. These results were interpreted as additional support for the idea that the autonomic afferent fibers maintaining homeostatic circulatory adjustment can also modulate midbrain reticular activity and thus influence the expression of voluntary behavior.

D 4   Gruner, M., and Nitschkoff, S.: The possibilities of producing an experimental neurotic hypertension in dogs. *Acta Biol Med Ger,* 24:593, 1970.

Dogs were either exposed daily to strong exogenous stimuli *experimen-*
for twenty-three months (subsequent and additive spectacle *tal neuro-*
stimulation, sound, noise, stroboscope and electrical stimula- *tic hyper-*
tion of the rear extremities) or neurotized after developing *tension*
a conditioned nutritional stereotype by irregular coincidence *stress con-*
of nutritive and aversive stimuli. Daily measurements of the *ditioning*
blood pressure prior to and following the experiment, as
well as in the resting state, showed that in the first group
the systolic blood pressure rose only transiently (as long as
the stimulus was new), subsiding within the period of stimulation. In the second group, the systolic pressure rose during
neurotization by 55 to 65 mm Hg and remained on a significantly higher level for two months. It is concluded that the
adaptability of the body to constant extreme environmental
conditions can prevent the formation of a pathological focus,
and conversely that excessive CNS stress by exposure to continuously varying biological factors can reduce adaptability
and cause a major upset of blood pressure regulation.

D 5   Harris, Alan H., Gilliam, Willie J., Findley, Jack D., and
      Brady, Joseph V.: Instrumental conditioning of large-magni-
      tude, daily, 12-hour blood pressure elevations in the baboon.
      *Science, 182:*175, 1973. (Copyright 1973 by the American
      Association for the Advancement of Science.)

Blood pressure and heart rate were monitored continuously *animal*
in four baboons during extended exposure to a daily twelve- *baboon*
hour conditioning procedure providing food and shock- *condition-*
avoidance as contingent consequences of prespecified in- *ing*
creases in diastolic blood pressure. Sustained and significant *hyper-*
increases (30 to 40 mm Hg) in both systolic and diastolic *tension*
blood pressure were maintained throughout the daily twelve-
hour conditioning sessions, accompanied by elevated heart
rates.

D 6   Plumlee, Lawrence A.: Operant conditioning of increases in
      blood pressure. *Psychophysiology, 6:*238, 1969.

Four monkeys were presented with ten-second tones which *monkey*
terminated with shocks. The tones were immediately termi- *operant con-*
nated without shock if the animal's diastolic blood pressure *ditioning*
                                                              avoidance

rose above a criterion level and remained high for one second. Termination of the tone was followed by a five-second time-out. Trials began whenever the pressure dropped below the criterion level. All subjects learned the avoidance task, showing diastolic elevations of up to 60 mm of mercury in response to the tones. A linear relationship was seen between the minimum pressure required for avoidance and the pressure achieved. No change in blood pressure accompanied a second stimulus which was never paired with shock. A fifth control monkey was yoked to one of the experimental monkeys and simultaneously received all shocks and tones as determined by the blood pressure of the experimental animal. The yoked control showed no pressure changes to the tones, but normal pressure elevations to shock.

diastolic BP
increased
BP

7 Williams, R.B., and Eichelman, B.: Social setting: Influence on the physiological response to electric shock in the rat. *Science, 174:*613, 1971. (Copyright 1971 by the American Association for the Advancement of Science.)

A significant fall in tail blood pressure occurs in paired rats after shock-induced aggression. Pressure returns to baseline levels within four hours after fighting. Conversely, single rats subjected to jump threshold measurements or to shocks identical to those used in the aggression paradigm show significant elevations in tail blood pressure. The size of the pressure increase in rats shocked alone appears dependent on the intensity of the shocks, while the pressure fall in rats shocked in pairs occurs over a broad range of shock intensities.

social factors
aggression
electric
shock

Pre-1965 References

BLOOD PRESSURE

Acker, C.W.: An investigation of the variability in repeated psychophysiological measurements in tranquilized mental patients. *Psychophysiology, 1:*119, 1964.

Binger, C.N.W., Cohn, A.E., Schroeder, H.A., and Steele, J.H.: Personality in arterial hypertension. *Psychosom Med Monogr (NY),* April 1951.

Brod, J., Fenel, V., Hejl, Z., and Jirka, J.: Circulatory changes underlying blood pressure elevation during acute emotional stress (mental arithmetic) in normotensive and hypertensive subjects. *Clin Sci, 18:*269, 1959.

Engel, B.T., and Bickford, A.F.: Response specificity: Stimulus-response and individual response specificity in essential hypertensives. *Arch Gen Psychiat, 5:*479, 1961.

Hines, E.A., and Brown, G.E.: Standard test for measuring variability of blood pressure: Its significance as index of prehypertensive state. *Ann Intern Med, 7*:209, 1933.

Hokanson, J.E., Burgess, M., and Cohen, M.F.: Effects of displaced aggression on systolic blood pressure. *J Abnorm Soc Psychol, 67*:214, 1963.

Kotliarevsky, L.I.: Cardio-vascular conditioned reflexes to direct and to verbal stimuli. *Fiziol Zh SSSR, 20*:228, 1936.

Landis, C., and Wiley, L.E.: Changes of blood pressure and respiration during deception. *J Comp Psychol, 6*:1, 1926.

Miller, N.E., and DiCara, L.V. *et al:* Learned modification of autonomic functions: A review and some new data. *Circ Res,* Suppl I, July 1970.

Moos, R.H., and Engel, B.T.: Psychophysiological reactions in hypertensive and arthritic patients. *J Psychosom Res, 6*:227, 1962.

Snyder, F., Hobson, J.A., Morrison, D.J., and Goldfrank, F.: Changes in respiration, heart rate, and systolic blood pressure in human sleep. *J Appl Psychol, 19*:417, 1964.

DESCRIPTOR INDEX — BLOOD PRESSURE

PART IV

MUSCLE SYSTEM

MEASUREMENTS

INSTRUMENTS

A 1   Budzynski, Thomas H., and Stoyva, Johann M.: An instrument for producing deep muscle relaxation by means of analog information feedback. *J Appl Behav Anal, 2:*231, 1969. (Copyright 1969 by the Society for the Experimental Analysis of Behavior.)

An instrument that assists subjects in attaining deep muscle relaxation by means of analog information feedback is described. Subjects hear a tone with a pitch proportional to the electromyographic activity in a given muscle group. Results showed that subjects receiving this type of analog feedback reached deeper levels of muscle relaxation than those receiving either no feedback or irrelevant feedback. The basic method employed—electronic detection, immediate information feedback, and systematic shaping of responses— would seem potentially applicable to a variety of physiological events, and might be useful both in behavior therapy and in certain psychosomatic disorders.

EMG feedback
relaxation
auditory signals
applications

A 2   Kowing, B.E., and Ginzel, K.H.: A new device for electromyographic integration and its application to the evaluation of muscle relaxant activity. *Proc West Pharmacol Soc, 13:* 25, 1970.

A new circuit for a self-contained analog EMG integrator based on the principle of continuous averaging has been developed. Unlike the direct EMG, the integrator permits the faithful display and resolution of electrical activity from a large sample of motor units and the accurate determination of onset of drug effect. A time constant of one second was chosen to emphasize the recording of tonic rather than phasic events. With this method a good correlation between electrical and mechanical muscle activity was observed.

EMG integration

RECORDING TECHNIQUES

A 3   Harding, R.H., and Sen, R.N.: Evaluation of total muscular activity by quantification of electromyograms through a summing amplifier. *Med Biol Eng, 8*:343, 1970.

In the present investigation a method of quantifying electromyograms (EMG's) from different muscle groups of the body to evaluate total muscular activity is described. A unipolar pickup, i.e. one standard silver cup surface electrode over each active muscle, was used because the EMG outputs with this electrode configuration during the same muscular activity were found to be greater than those with a bipolar pickup, i.e. two electrodes over each muscle. It was observed that for the purpose of quantification the root mean square (r.m.s.) value of a "steady" level or the average r.m.s. value of a varying level of EMG is related in a linear fashion to the absolute mean value of the wave obtained by integrating the EMG for a specified time interval after making the waveform unidirectional. A similar relationship was observed with different voltage levels from a noise generator which was used for calibration purposes. EMG's from different muscle groups during isometric as well as isotonic voluntary contractions were found to summate together outside the body in a manner similar to noise voltages, i.e. the r.m.s. value of the combined voltages is equal to the square root of the sum of the mean square values of the individual waves. A method of passing EMG's through a summing amplifier and then quantifying the output for the evaluation of total muscular activity was developed, which greatly reduces the system components normally necessary for such studies. The results obtained from a series of experiments are discussed in detail.

analysis techniques
recording techniques
total muscular activity

A 4   Kahn, David, Bloodworth, Donald S., and Woods, Robert: Comparative advantages of bipolar abraded skin surface electrodes over bipolar intramuscular electrodes for single motor unit recording in psychophysiological research. *Psychophysiology, 8*:635, 1971.

Dual recordings of single motor unit (SMU) biopotentials were made utilizing abraded skin surface and intramuscular

motor units

(IM) bipolar electrode placements. Time relationships and waveform isomorphy between the recorded potentials suggest that, within limits, surface electrode recording is a useful technique for registering certain muscle action potentials when intramuscular placements are not desirable. Pen records of good resolution were obtained to supplement oscilloscope photographs when the physiological signal was initially recorded on magnetic tape at high speed and then played back at low speed through a standard electroencephalograph-electromyograph oscillograph.

recording
techniques
electro-
myography
electrodes
feedback
covert
operants
unconscious
cognition

5 Kahn, S.D., Swint, E.B., and Bowne, G.W.: A film demonstration of biofeedback technology in which covert operants control the visual environment. Psychophysiology Program, 1972.

This film illustrates a basic methodology for linking covert operants to the perceptual field, while quantifying the relevant data by computer. The system is illustrated by showing a closed-loop biofeedback system in which single motor units are allowed to control a figure-ground projector system, with the option of giving the subject auditory feedback as well. The use of a small, dedicated, real time computer (PDP-12A) to analyze the physiological data on line is also shown. The experimental paradigm selected to illustrate the system demonstrates the acquisition of voluntary control over the discharge of a single motor unit, and the simultaneous suppression of surrounding motor units. The subject achieves this task utilizing the information obtained by visual and auditory feedback. Since the discharge of a single motor unit cannot ordinarily be discriminated by interoceptive feedback, this paradigm may also be used to study certain unconscious cognitive processes. For example, when the subject is unaware that he is determining the figure-ground relationships of his perceptual field, his motor unit "behavior" may reveal stimulus preferences that are uncontaminated by those social factors and demand characteristics of the experiment which would ordinarily affect conscious choice.

film
biofeedback
techniques
motor units
computer
analysis

6 Prentke, E.M., and Beard, J.E.: A surface electrode design for myoelectric control. *Orthot Prosth, 23*:63, 1969.

The surface electrode described in this article has been used *techniques* on six C4 and C5 quadriplegics with flexor hinge splints. It *electrodes* is used with a myoelectric control which has rechargeable batteries and a flexible cable. The electrode consists of three stainless buttons each 8 mm in diameter and 6 mm high with small tips for soldering to the wires. The buttons are set 20 mm apart and are encapsulated with Dow Corning Silastic 588.® It may be taped to the shoulder for upper trapezius pick up or attached to a specially designed collar for platysma pick up.

CORRELATES OF
MUSCLE TENSION

B 1 Berg, Kristina, Kadefors, Roland, and Petersen, Ingemar:
Effect of muscular exhaustion on myoelectric functions in
adolescents with athetosis and/or dystonia. *Scand J Rehabil
Med, 1*:143, 1969.

EMG studies of ten dystonic and/or, athetoid subjects before
and after severe physical exercise revealed their EMG response to be unaffected by fatigue. Their EMG spectrum
during isometric contraction was similar to that in normal
subjects. Fatigue, however, significantly increased their
voluntary muscular control as studied in a man/machine
system.

*measure-
ments
fatigue
muscle
control*

B 2 Berger, Seymour M., Irwin, Deborah Smith, and Fromme,
Gabriel, P.: Electromyographic activity during observational
learning. *Am J Psychol, 83*:86, 1970.

A previous study used the learning of hand signals to show
that observers practice the model's responses during the exposure period. Since only overt practice was measured, it was
felt that more sensitive techniques were needed to measure
possible covert practice. In this study, electromyogram
(EMG) recordings were made while observers learned hand
signals and word-number pairs, either in the presence of the
experimenter or alone. Observers showed greater EMG activity while learning hand signals than while learning word-
number pairs regardless of whether the experimenter was
present or not. However, more overt practice of the hand
signals (hence larger EMGs) occurred when the experimenter was absent. The results are interpreted as additional
evidence for the elicitive function of the model's behavior
during observational learning.

*motor
learning
observation-
al learning
covert
practice
EMG
activity*

B 3   Boman, Kurt: Effect of emotional stress on spasticity and
       rigidity. *J Psychosom Res, 15:*107, 1971.

Eighteen patients with long-standing muscular hypertonia   *muscle*
due to various chronic neurological diseases were investi-   *activity*
gated in order to evaluate the effect of emotional stress on   *muscle*
the pathophysiological muscle reflexes which occur in these   *reflexes*
diseases. Quadriceps reflexes were elicited under identical   *emotional*
circumstances and the reflex movements of the free-swinging   *stress*
leg were recorded with an electric goniometer. Emotional   *hypertonia*
stress invariably resulted in an increase of the jerk ampli-   *muscle tone*
tude in the spastic patients, while the jerk amplitude and   *regulation*
the swinging time of the leg decreased in Parkinsonian rigidity without evidence of spasticity. Thus, both spasticity and
rigidity increased during the period of emotional stress. In
hemiplegic patients the effect of emotional stress on the
muscle reflex pattern was variable. These observations show
that psychic factors have an important influence on the regulation of muscle tonus in spasticity and rigidity.

B 4   Butler, K.N.: The effect of physical conditioning and exer-
       tion on the performance of a simple mental task. *J Sport
       Med Phys Fitness, (Torino), 9:*236, 1969.

The purpose of this study was to determine the effect of a   *muscle*
ten-week physical conditioning program and a three-item   *activity*
physical fitness test on the performance of a simple mental   *physical*
task of symbol substitution. Ninety-three male college sub-   *fitness*
jects were selected within the confines of a stratified random   *mental per-*
sample. The strata were divided by the lower 27 percent,   *formance*
middle 46 percent and upper 27 percent scores of the subjects on the American College Testing Program. The subjects were further divided into a control and an experimental
group. The control group took part in the physical conditioning program but was not involved with exertion prior to
the simple mental task. The experimental group received
both the physical conditioning program and was administered a three-item fitness test prior to taking the simple
mental task test. Analysis of the data revealed no significant
difference between the control group and the experimental
group, nor was there a difference among the stratified groups

on the criterion measurement of a simple mental task. A significant difference was observed between the pretest and posttest scores in both the experimental and the control group. A significant difference was also indicated among the stratified groups in the control group's pretest and posttest scores.

B 5   Goldstein, Iris Balshan: The relationship of muscle tension and autonomic activity to psychiatric disorders. *Psychosom Med, 27*:39, 1965.

Physiologic recordings of palmar resistance, respiration rate, heart rate, blood pressure, and muscle action potentials in seven different skeletal muscles were recorded among psychiatric patients and normal persons during a resting state and in response to a white noise. Results showed that these patients, all in the early stages of illness, responded at physiologic levels which were at least as high as those of the normals. Psychotic and depressive disorders were two types of maladjustment characterized by exaggerated physiologic responses. This was particularly true for the skeletal muscles in response to the auditory stimulus.

psychopathology
muscle
psychoses
depression
tension

B 6   Griffin, C.J., and Munro, R.R.: Electromyography of the masseter and anterior temporalis muscles in patients with temporomandibular dysfunction. *Arch Oral Biol, 16*:929, 1971.

The electromyograms of the masseter and anterior temporalis muscles of thirty-one patients with clinically definite temporomandibular joint dysfunction have been examined, both in the open-close-clench cycle and by elicitation of the jaw jerk. The results have been compared both metrically and nonmetrically with the normal series previously reported (Griffin and Munro, 1969; Munro and Griffin, 1969 and 1971). The incidence of malocclusion was much higher than in the normal series, and centric slides were demonstrated in twenty-four of the thirty-one patients. The duration of muscle contraction before initial tooth contact (d.m.c.) was found to be significantly longer than in the normal series; and in contrast to the normal series, no positive correlation

muscle
activity
masseter
muscle

between the d.m.c. and the duration of the inhibitory period could be demonstrated. The latency in the masseter muscle was significantly shorter than in the normal series, although the difference was not significant for the anterior temporalis muscle. In fourteen of the thirty-one patients the inhibitory reflex response was either absent or incomplete in one or more cycles; seventeen patients showed increased activity of the masseter and/or the anterior temporalis muscle during the open phase of the cycle as compared with the normal series. Eleven patients showed both absent or incomplete inhibitory phases and also hyperactivity of the mandibular elevators investigated. When the inhibitory response was present in these patients, its duration was within normal limits. In most patients the jaw jerk responses were similar to those previously reported (Munro and Griffin, 1971). However, on four occasions the normal monosynaptic response from the masseter muscle was followed by a polysynaptic type of response similar to that normally found in the anterior temporalis muscle. It is suggested that the abnormalities demonstrated in the inhibitory reflex in patients with temporomandibular dysfunction are due either to inadequate stimulation of dental pressoreceptors (due to premature contact or gross tooth loss) or to hyperactivity of the reticular formation associated with malalignment of the temporomandibular joint.

B 7   Heath, H.A., Oken, D., and Shipman, W.G.: Muscle tension and personality: A serious second look. *Arch Gen Psychiatry,* *16:*720, 1967.

This paper reports a study designed specifically to confirm an earlier finding which indicated a relation between certain personality characteristics and muscle tension in a group of depressed patients. Subjects were chosen from applicants at our outpatient psychiatric clinic; they were selected to represent the high and low extremes on six criteria which were believed to be related to muscle tension. Twenty men and twenty-four women, ranging in age from eighteen to forty-nine years, participated in the research. Muscle tension scores were obtained under five experimental conditions; rest, white noise, recovery, psychological stress, and a second

psychopath-
ology
personality
muscle
tension
depression

recovery. All results failed to confirm the hypotheses which were derived from the earlier study. Attempts were made to explain these negative findings on the bases of possible artifacts either in the earlier study or in the present study, and/or on the bases of a different patient population. The chief conclusion was that relations between muscle tension and personality factors vary as a function of the type of individuals being studied, and that findings concerning depressives do not necessarily apply to other patient groups.

B 8   Hundal, P.S., and Surishtha, Gill: A comparative study of the effects of electrical and psychological stimulation on muscular fatigue. *Psychophysiology, 9:*368, 1972.

An experiment was designed to study the effects of local electrical stimulation (LES) and verbal psychological stimulation (VPS) on the output of the fatigued muscles. The task was to operate Palmer's finger ergograph with the middle finger of the preferred hand. The LES was given by passing alternate square pulses through the operating muscles of the hand. The VPS was provided by applauding the performance of the S while he was still at work. Ten Ss provided the data under five experimental conditions. The results suggest that (1) Both LES and VPS tend to increase the output as measured by the ergograph. (2) LES is superior to VPS in the initial stages of the work period, but the situation is reversed at a later stage. (3) Neither the LES nor the VPS delay or enhance the onset of fatigue, but they tend to increase the duration of work period when applied in the after-decline period. (4) Continuous application of LES leads to rapid adaptation to its effect in comparison with VPS.

muscle fatigue electric stimuli verbal stimuli encouragement adaptation

B 9   Hutton, Robert S.: Kinesthetic aftereffect, a measure of kinesthetic awareness. *Percept Mot Skills, 23:*1165, 1966.

It was hypothesized that scores on similar tests for kinesthetic awareness (KA) and kinesthetic aftereffects (KAE) should correlate negatively. Fifty-seven male university students were administered tasks designed to measure KA and KAE. Low inter-test Pearsonian correlation coefficients indicated negligible relationships between the two tasks. Further in-

kinesthetic awareness kinesthetic after effect

vestigation is suggested since the correlation values fell in
the posited direction.

B 10   Inouye, Tsuyoshi, and Shimizu, Akira: The electromyo-   *muscle*
graphic study of verbal hallucination. *J Nerv Ment Dis, 151:*   *activity*
415, 1970. (Copyright 1970 by the Williams and Wilkens   *auditory*
Co., Baltimore.)   *hallucina-*
   tions

Investigated the hypothesis that auditory hallucinations are
expressions of "inner speech." All Ss experienced frequent
auditory hallucinations. Bipolar electrodes were used to obtain EMG recordings of change in potential for five muscles.
Ss were instructed to depress a switch whenever experiencing
an auditory hallucination. Switch-pressing and EMG changes
are associated 47.6 percent. EMG change also is strongly associated with experienced "loudness" of the hallucination
$(p < .005)$.

B 11   Lader, M.H., and Mathews, A.M.: Electromyographic studies
of tension. *J Psychosom Res, 15:*479, 1971.

Surface electromyography is a relatively simple technique,   *muscle*
and EMG levels bear a close relationship to muscle tension   *tension*
under conditions of isometric contraction. In normal sub-   *physiologic*
jects the EMG level has been found to correlate with be-   *analysis*
havioral performance and level of motivation. A clear dis-   *subjective*
tinction must be maintained between muscular tension and   *reports*
subjective reports of "tension," since in EMG studies of emotional states the relationship between the two may be weak
or even absent. Psychiatric patients in general have raised
EMG levels reflecting their heightened affective state rather
than any more specific features. In some conditions, e.g.
writers' cramp, the primary pathological state appears to be
that of excessive uncontrolled muscle activity, so ways of
lessening or controlling such activity might prove of direct
therapeutic benefit. These techniques include hypnosis, relaxation and feedback, and the most promising use of the
EMG is in assessing the effect of such treatment.

B 12   Levin, Irwin Paul: Induced muscle tension and response
shift in paired-associate learning. *J Exp Psychol, 73:*422,
1967.

The present study shows the empirical relationships between induced muscle tension and performance in a paired-associates task in which the response originally correct for a given stimulus item is switched after an initial criterion is reached. By alternating training and test trials and by assigning some Ss to tension-during-training groups and others to tension-during-test groups, the effects of tension during training and the effects of tension during testing are separated and compared. For tension-during-test group measures of correct response probability and proportion of errors due to competition from previously correct responses reached their maxima at an intermediate level of muscle tension and then decreased at a higher level. For tension-during-training group error scores grew progressively larger as tension level was increased.

muscle tension training association task learning

B 13   Noble, P.J., and Lader, M.H.: An electromyographic study of depressed patients. *J Psychosom Res, 15:*233, 1971.

Thirty-four depressed patients were assessed before and two weeks subsequent to a course of ECT. Psychometric measures were taken and recordings were made of the forearm extensor EMG under basal conditions and during a stressful mental arithmetic procedure. On retesting there was a marked improvement in depressive symptomatology but little change in anxiety levels. Subsequent to ECT basal EMG levels decreased significantly and EMG reactivity to stress increased significantly as compared to pre-ECT values. Prior to ECT, high basal EMG levels and diminished reactivity were correlated with the severity of the depression and with high scores for anxiety, gastrointestinal somatic symptoms, loss of libido, and weight loss. It is suggested that depressive illness, and in particular symptomatology of a biological type, is associated with raised forearm extensor EMG activity. The correlation between the basal EMG and anxiety was too low for this measure to be useful as an index of anxiety or arousal in these depressed patients. However, the stress of mental arithmetic produced a marked and significant increase in both anxiety and in mean EMG levels.

depressive illness stress responses anxiety ECT

B 14   Okaichi, Hiroshige: The effects of induced muscular tension and original muscular tension in verbal learning. *Jap J Psychol, 41:*20, 1970.

Eighty-eight undergraduates in two experiments learned a list of nonsense syllables or paired verbs. Time intervals between list presentation and recall were 0, 100, 200, and 360 seconds for nonsense syllables, and 0, 60, 120, and 180 seconds for paired verbs. Ss were divided into four groups by whether they were given induced muscular tension (MT) during learning and recall, and then further divided into subgroups of high and low MT. Results indicate that recall was facilitated under induced MT and was better in high MT groups than in low. The after effect of inducted MT was shown up to 120 seconds after acquisition.

*muscle
tension
verbal
learning
recall*

B 15   Pallas, Janet Ruth Laur: Mental and motor efficiency as a function of induced muscle tension, relaxation and level of manifest anxiety. *Diss Abst, 31:4343*, 1971.

The present experiment was designed to study the effects of induced muscle tension, relaxation, and manifest anxiety on mental and motor efficiency. On the basis of a review of the literature, it was concluded that activation or tension can be expected to produce increased performance on a simple task. Relaxation or deactivation should produce decreased performance. Since a review of the literature indicated an interaction between activation and anxiety, the present study proposed to investigate this relationship. The study was designed to use groups of subjects in a classroom setting. The following conditions were utilized: (1) Tension-Control, (2) Relaxation-Control, and (3) Control-Control. The mental task was an anagram task which required subjects to make up words from a group of seven letters. For the motor task, subjects were required to mark X's in rows or squares. The general procedure required all subjects in each of the three groups to perform both the mental and motor tasks. Each subject also performed under both a Treatment Set (Tension, Relaxation, or Control) and a No Treatment Set (Control) thereby serving as his own control. The experiment consisted of twenty-four trials: twelve on the mental task and twelve on the motor task. The various combinations of mental and motor tasks and Treatment and No Treatment Sets were presented in randomized order to control for the effects of practice, fatigue and boredom. Tension was induced by

*muscle
(EMG)
tension
relaxation
mental task
motor tasks*

having the subject make a fist half as hard as he could. Relaxation was induced by the method of deep muscle relaxation. Groups were equated for sex, intellectual ability, and level of manifest anxiety. The results of the experiment showed that the Mark Making Task and the Word Making Task were affected quite differently by the conditions of tension and relaxation. For the motor task, the effects were in the predicted direction with tension producing the highest performance level and relaxation producing the lowest. However, even though the order of effects was as predicted, the tension conditions did not produce performance significantly above that of the Control condition. The Relaxation condition produced significantly poorer performance on the Mark Making Task. The mental task, on the other hand, produced results contrary to those expected. In this task, the best performance was elicited in the Control group, and the tension condition was significantly below the Control level of performance. Relaxation produced somewhat lower performance than the Control group and higher performance than the Tension group, but neither difference was significant. The effect of set was not significant for either task. Based on the results of the study, it was concluded that the mental task used in the present experiment was considerably more complex than suspected. It was suggested that the dimension of complexity is more important in determining the effects of relaxation or tension on performance than the mental-motor dimension. The results of the experiment supported the conclusion that even low levels of tension can interfere with the performance of a more complex task. The results provided little support for the predicted interaction between tension and anxiety.

B 16   Rimon, R., Stenback, A., and Huhmar, E.: Electromyographic finding in depressive patients. *Psychosom Res, 10:* 159, 1966.

Resting levels of muscle tension in the frontalis, masseter, right forearm, and right leg were determined by means of surface electrodes over a series of fifty-three unselected, depressed psychiatric patients. The degree of depression, measured by Beck's Depression Inventory, was correlated with

muscle tension depression anxiety

the muscle tension in frontalis, masseter and forearm. The changes in anxiety (Taylor MA scale) were not consistently correlated with the muscle tension. The milder the depression, the greater the masseter muscle tension. Patients who improved during one month of treatment showed an increase in muscle tension.

B 17   Smith, Robert P. Jr.: Frontalis muscle tension and personality. *Psychophysiology, 10:*311, 1973.

Balshan (1962) found no significant correlation between resting muscle tension and personality traits. Shipman, et al. (1970a, 1970b) , in a broad study of muscle potential involving fifteen personality test variables, noted only a chance number (2) of significant relationships with the frontalis muscle at rest. The positive results obtained in this study may be due to the more sensitive measuring techniques now available, or they may reflect a qualitative difference in the sample used. In any case, the observation of a positive relationship between frontalis EMG level at rest and the personality traits of anxiety, neuroticism, and external control may be of significance in the understanding and treatment of tension-related psychosomatic disorders, such as tension headaches and insomnias.

muscle tension frontalis muscle personality

B 18   Vaughn, Avery O., and McDaniel, James W.: Electromyographic gradients during complex visual discrimination learning. *Psychon Sci, 16:*203, 1969.

Muscle activity levels recorded during cognitive and motor performances from various electrode placements have been shown to follow monotonically rising gradients throughout the experimental task. A complex match-to-sample visual discrimination task demonstrated a tonic neuromuscular adjustment during performance, as well as the occurrence of phasic shifts in activity corresponding to orienting reactions. These phasic responses tend to habituate rapidly with repetitive performance and are rarely identified in overlearned Ss.

cognitive performance motor performance muscle tension

B 19   Whatmore, George B.: Some neurophysiologic differences between schizophrenia and depression. *Am J Psychiatry, 123:* 712, 1966.

Fatigue of neurons after a prolonged hyperponesis (measurable electromyographically) may be one factor in the production of depressive states. On the other hand, in acute schizophrenic episodes a disorganization of activity in neuronal networks may take place before fatigue of neurons has time to develop—occurring shortly after the onset of hyperponesis.

psychopathology
schizophrenia
depression
muscle tension
neuronal fatigue

B 20 Williams, James G.L., and Williams, Barbara: The effect of meprobamate on the somatic responses of anxious patients and normal controls. *Psychophysiology, 3:*403, 1967.

The skeletal muscle activity and digital volume pulse of anxious psychiatric patients and normal controls were used as measures to confirm the hypothesis that meprobamate would reduce the level of muscle activity and autonomic responsivity of the patients to that of the controls when both groups experienced a mild "stress"—delayed auditory feedback (DAF).

muscle (EMG) tension
digital pulse volume
stress
delayed auditory feedback
meprobamate

B 21 Yemm, R.: Variations in the electrical activity of the human masseter muscle occurring in association with emotional stress. *Arch Oral Biol, 14:*873, 1969.

Human subjects were asked to perform a task while recordings were made of the electrical activity of the right masseter muscle. The task apparatus consisted of a series of lamps illuminated in random order, and a button panel. The subjects were asked to press the buttons to correspond with the lamps illuminated. Recordings made from the muscle during this task showed an increase in electrical activity. The magnitude of this increase was related to the number of errors made by the subject. Muscle activity with similar characteristics has been shown by earlier workers to occur elsewhere in the body. It is suggested that such psychogenic activity in the masticatory muscles could affect mandibular posture, and the findings reported are discussed in relation to the current hypothesis of the control of mandibular posture.

muscle tension
masseter muscle
motor tasks

MUSCLE RELAXATION

RELAXATION TECHNIQUES

C 1   Grim, P.F.: Psychotherapy by somatic alteration. *Ment Hyg,* *53:*451, 1969.

Thoughts and feelings are determined by physiologic as well as by psychologic factors. Psychotherapy, however, tends to emphasize psychodynamic methods to the neglect of somatic methods which alter reactivity or cortical-subcortical balance. Autogenic training is a representative somatic method, yet despite its therapeutic potential and wide clinical and experimental development outside the United States, it is almost unknown here. In this method patients are taught a series of hypnotic conditioning exercises which automatically relax their muscles and vascular systems under stress. Once these are learned, neurotic and psychosomatic disorders improve spontaneously. Should depth therapy still be required, the autogenic state can be sustained until a meditative state is reached in which unconscious material is hallucinated in visual form. This experience may be of an existential nature, with consequent reorganization of values and philosophy, or may disclose symbolic material for later discussion. It would appear that input stimulation—gross environmental activity on residual tension in the muscles—is the mechanism through which unconscious feelings are repressed or crowded out of consciousness. Thus, in stimulus-deprived environments or states of prolonged, deep relaxation (reduced proprioceptive stimulation), unconscious thoughts and feelings spring into awareness or even project outward. But feelings are always dependent on a motor set or bodily reaction. The sequence is as follows: event, evaluation, bodily reaction, feeling. Traditional systems of therapy alter the evaluation, whereas somatic systems alter the reaction. Both approaches probably achieve equivalent results,

psycho-
therapy
autogenic
training
comment

so that the "uncovering" versus "symptom removal" controversy may be irrelevant, although both methods would be more efficient in combination.

C 2   Kahn, M., Baker, B.L., and Weiss, J.M.: Treatment of insomnia by relaxation training. *J Abnorm Psychol, 73:*556, 1968.

Sixteen students with chronic insomnia were given two weeks Autogenic Training in an attempt to determine whether this would help the insomnia. The study was based on the hypothesis that tension in large skeletal muscles is the necessary and sufficient condition for insomnia, whatever its origin. Thirteen subjects were available for the post-treatment interview. Of these, eleven reported improvement. Two follow-ups, covering a period of almost one year, showed approximately the same results. With one exception, no symptom substitution could be found.

*relaxation
training
insomnia
subjective
reports*

C 3   Lader, M.H., and Mathews, A.M.: Comparison of methods of relaxation using physiological measures. *Behav Res Ther, 8:*331, 1970.

The effects of a single injection of methohexitone sodium or saline were monitored in eighteen anxious patients using forearm blood flow, heart rate, skin conductance, and frontalis electromyogram. The physiological changes were compared to those when the patients listened to tape-recorded instructions to relax or listened to a tape of neutral content. No differences were found between the treatments except for an increase in skin conductance fluctuations following the injection. A marked dose-dependent tachycardia was induced by methohexitone sodium.

*EMG
frontalis
frontalis
muscle
SC
HR
blood flow*

C 4   Paul, Gordon L.: Inhibition of physiological response to stressful imagery by relaxation training and hypnotically suggested relaxation. *Behav Res Ther, 7:*249, 1969.

In summary, the results of the present study add further support to the growing body of evidence in favor of response suppression or modified counter-conditioning as the major

*anxiety
desensitization*

mode of operation in systematic desensitization therapy, in addition to nonspecific factors present in most therapeutic encounters (see Paul, 1966). Such data regarding the modifiability of response to the imaginal representation of anxiety-eliciting stimuli is crucial, even if *in vivo* desensitization procedures (e.g. Bandura, 1968) should be found to be as effective as systematic desensitization, since, excluding a few phobic reactions to concrete objects, the broad range of anxiety-eliciting configurations presented for treatment cannot be therapeutically manipulated in real life.

stress responses hypnotic suggestion

C 5   Paul, Gordon L.: Extraversion, emotionality, and physiological response to relaxation training and hypnotic suggestion. *Int J Clin Exp Hypn, 17:*89, 1969.

The possible predictive relationship of extra-version and emotionality, singly and combined into Eysenck's (1961) four-fold classification, was examined for differential cognitive and physiological responsiveness to relaxation training, hypnotic suggestion, and a self-relaxation control procedure, and to the degree of inhibition of the physiological response to stressful imagery resulting from the treatment procedures. A total of sixty unselected female Ss, covering the full range on both personality scales, participated in two experimental sessions, one week apart. Nonsignificant relationships were found between the personality characteristics and the previously reported individual or combined response to treatment procedures.

personality stress responses hypnotic suggestion

C 6   Paul, Gordon L.: Psychological effects of relaxation training and hypnotic suggestion. *J Abnorm Psychol, 74:*425, 1969.

Evaluated the comparative effects of hypnotic suggestion and brief relaxation training with regard to reduction of subjective tension and distress (anxiety differential) and physiological arousal (heart rate, respiratory rate, tonic muscle tension, skin conductance). Three groups (N = 20 each) of undergraduate females participated individually for two sessions, one week apart, receiving (1) abbreviated progressive relaxation training as used in systematic desensitization therapy; (2) a hypnotic induction emphasizing direct sug-

relaxation training hypnotic suggestion muscle tension subjective tension physiologic arousal

gestions of relaxation, heaviness, warmth, drowsiness and sleep; or (3) a self-relaxation control procedure, included to evaluate the effects of merely resting quietly for an equal period of time with instructions to relax. Both relaxation training and hypnotic suggestion produced significantly greater effects than controls, and relaxation training resulted in significantly greater effects than hypnotic suggestion. The superiority of relaxation training was most pronounced in response systems not under direct voluntary control.

7 Spoerri, Th.: Autogenic training and psychosomatic disorders. *Psychother Psychosom, 17*:354, 1969.

The reason for the frequent use of autogenic training (AT) and the combination of AT with other methods of treatment are discussed. The clinical effect (which is difficult to verify scientifically) lies, as well as the motoric-affective-vegetative simultaneous effect, in the particular therapist-patient relationship made possible by AT. In the group of psychophysiological disorders, the indication is not according to the genesis (limits, however, are set by the capability to learn) but according to the actual possibility to influence the primary or secondary emotional vegetative disturbance. Treatment until now only fulfills the scientific demands conditionally. Amelioration, (seldom cure) is, especially by subacute complaints, described. Success by cardiovascular disorders are most frequent. Observations on the practice of AT, on the complications by different disorders and on diverse variations, e.g. pre- or parahypnotic AT, are made.

autogenic training psycho-somatic disorders discussion comment

8 Wickramasekera, I.: Effects of EMG feedback training on susceptibility to hypnosis: Preliminary observations. *Proceedings, 79th Annual Convention, Am Psychol Assoc, 6*: 783, 1971.

The purpose of this study was to determine if taped verbal relaxation instructions and response-contingent EMG feedback training will increase suggestibility or hypnotic susceptibility over that obtained with instructions and false or noncontingent feedback. The specific hypothesis tested was that six sessions of relaxation practice with response-con-

relaxation hypnotic suscep-tibility

tingent EMG feedback will result in greater increase in hypnotic susceptibility as measured by the Stanford scales than will relaxation and noncontingent feedback. Not all experimental Ss reached the preestablished criterion of relaxation training, but all approximated it at the end of the sixth session of training. None of the control Ss even approximated the criterion for forehead muscle relaxation.

C 9   Wilson, Alan, and Wilson, Arthur S.: Psychophysiological and learning correlates of anxiety and induced muscle relaxation. *Psychophysiology, 6:*740, 1970.

Recently, extensive use has been made of voluntary muscle relaxation as a response which presumably inhibits anxiety in "systematic desensitization" psychotherapies. This study attempted to test the hypothesis that muscle relaxation would reciprocally inhibit anxiety during a paired-associate learning task. Subjects (Ss) were divided into high, medium and low anxiety levels and muscle tension, muscle relaxation, and normal tension groups. Paired-associate learning efficiency, as well as heart rate, skin conductance, integrated electromyogram, respiration rate, and finger temperature during learning were measured. Partial substantiation for the hypothesis was obtained for high anxiety Ss, but data for other groups was inconsistent with the hypothesis. An alternative explanation was suggested. Heart rate was the physiological variable which best discriminated the groups.

anxiety
muscle
* tension*
relaxation
learning
* tasks*
HR
SC
respiration
finger temperature

DESENSITIZATION

C 10   Agras, S.W., Leitenberg, H., Barlow, D.H., Curtis, N., Edwards, J., and Wright, D.: Relaxation in systematic desensitization. *Arch Gen Psychiatry, 25:*511, 1971.

The contribution of muscular relaxation to systematic desensitization therapy was studied in four phobic patients. Removal of relaxation during a control phase of therapy made no difference to the patients' improving ability to perform in their phobic situation. In two subjects, progress through the hierarchy and therapeutic progress, as measured by self-rating, slowed on removal of relaxation. However, the

phobias
desensitiza-
* tion*
muscle
* relaxation*
visualization
self-rating

overall effects were small. This suggests that variables other than relaxation are in large part responsible for the therapeutic effects of desensitization. Relaxation paired with visualization of feared scenes helps some patients to approach their feared object or situation in imagination and may motivate them to approach it in reality.

C 11 Badri, Malik B.: A new technique for the systematic desensitization of pervasive anxiety and phobic reactions. *J Psychol, 65:*201, 1967.

This paper describes a modification of Wolpe's treatment of neurotic behavior by imaginative systematic desensitization. The modification consists of shifting the main responsibility of emitting verbal behavior from the therapist to the patient. To achieve this, a more flexible approach to systematic desensitization was suggested, and the technique applied to a case of pervasive anxiety, phobic reactions, and reactive depression.

desensitization
progressive relaxation
anxiety
phobias
verbalization

C 12 Kondas, O.: Reduction of examination anxiety and "stage fright" by group desensitization and relaxation. *Behav Res Ther, 5:*275, 1967.

The results of the experiment in group desensitization, relaxation and imagination of exam situations in groups of children (n = 23) and students (n = 13) show that systematic desensitization is an efficient method for reducing stage fright. Some transient positive effects were also achieved with a modification of the Schultz method of relaxation. Interviews, a Fear Survey Schedule, and a test of palmar perspiration were used in the assessment of effects. The main conclusions are concordant with previous studies in desensitization (e.g. Land and Lazovik, 1963; Rachman, 1965, 1966 a and b; Lazarus, 1961; Paul and Shannon, 1966) and the present results provide interesting comparisons.

group desensitization
relaxation
imagery
anxiety

C 13 Lader, M.H., and Mathews, A.M.: A physiological model of phobic anxiety and desensitization. *Behav Res Ther, 6:*411, 1968.

The relationship between arousal and phobic anxiety is
discussed with regard to recent psychophysiological studies
of habituation in normal subjects and in groups of anxious
and phobic patients. A physiological model of the mechanisms underlying generalized and phobic anxiety is postulated. Some criticisms of Wolpe's conception of systematic
desensitization are offered, and an alternative explanation
consistent with the above postulate is put forward. This
alternative states that the underlying mechanism of systematic desensitization is identical with that of habituation pro-
ceeding under optimal conditions (the "maximal habituation" hypothesis). The two accounts of desensitization are
compared and contrasted.

*phobic
anxiety
arousal
desensitiza-
tion
habituation
relaxation
training*

C 14   Lehrer, Paul: A laboratory analog of "systematic desensitization": Psychophysiological effects of relaxation. *Psychophysiology, 6:634,* 1969.

The effect of muscular relaxation on habituation of the skin
potential response elicited by electric shock was studied as
an experimental analog of Wolpe's procedure of "systematic
desensitization." A group instructed to relax was compared
to groups who were instructed to increase their muscle tension, instructed to sustain a moderate level of muscular tension, and a group receiving no instructions. Each group, consisting of ten subjects, received three shock sessions. A session
was comprised of forty shocks of gradually increasing intensity. As in systematic desensitization the intensity of the
shock was increased only when the skin potential response
had habituated to shock of a lower level of intensity. The
muscle instructions were presented concurrently with the
shocks, but began five minutes before the first shock. DC
skin potential, breathing rate, EMG from the submental
area, and gross skeletal activity were also monitored. The
relaxation group habituated to shock significantly more
quickly than either the increased tension or sustained tension groups. There was no difference, however, between the
group receiving relaxation instructions and the group receiving no instructions. Other physiological measures clearly
differentiated the increased muscular tension group from the
other three groups. The high tension group manifested more

*relaxation
desensitiza-
tion
muscle
tension
electric
shock
GSR
habituation*

EMG activity and gross skeletal activity, higher heart rate, and more frequent spontaneous skin potential responses than any of the other three groups.

15   Lomont, James F., and Edwards, James E.: The role of relaxation in systematic desensitization. *Behav Res Ther, 5:* 11, 1967.

Two experimental questions were investigated: (1) Is the efficacy of systematic desensitization due at all to the contiguity of muscular relaxation with anxiety stimulus visualization? (2) Can the efficacy of the technique be more satisfactorily explained in terms of reciprocal inhibition than on the basis of extinction? Two groups of female, snake phobic, college students (N = 11 in each group) were administered two different treatment procedures for reducing fear. One group received systematic desensitization with relaxation. The other group underwent a procedure that was intended to be as similar as possible to the desensitization procedure except for the omission of relaxation. The latter procedure was intended to be the extinction procedure involved in systematic desensitization. On three out of five measures of snake fear change, systematic desensitization produced significantly greater, or very nearly significantly greater, fear reduction than the extinction procedure. Extinction appeared totally ineffective. These results are taken to indicate affirmative answers to the two experimental questions.

desensitization
relaxation
visualization
phobias

16   McGlynn, F. Dudley, Reynolds, E. Joyce, and Linder, Lowell H.: Systematic desensitization with pretreatment and intratreatment therapeutic instructions. *Behav Res Ther, 9:*57, 1971.

Three groups of ten Ss each received tape-recorded desensitization along a snake approach hierarchy. One group (SD++) received therapeutic instructions before each desensitization session. A second group (SD+) was presented with therapeutic instructions before only the initial desensitization session. The third group (SD) received no therapeutic instructions. As compared with ten untreated and ten "pseudo-desensitized" Ss, the Ss in the SD++ and SD+ conditions

desensitization
relaxation

displayed significant behavioral improvements, while those in the SD group did not. Improvements for Ss in the SD++, SD+ and SD conditions did not differ.

C 17 Mathews, A.M., and Gelder, M.G.: Psychophysiologic investigations of brief relaxation training. *J Psychosom Res, 13:*1, 1969.

In an experiment to investigate effects of brief relaxation training as used in systematic desensitization treatment of phobias and psychosomatic disorders, five phobic patients were trained using Jacobson's technique, and their ability to voluntarily reduce muscular and autonomic activity before and after training was compared with a control group of the same size. No significant differences emerged, although both groups showed a significant decline in skin conductance activity over time. A second experiment using fourteen patients in a cross-over design showed that both frontalis electromyogram (EMG) and skin conductance activity declined significantly during relaxation training sessions as compared with control sessions in the same patients, while no differences were found in heart and respiration rates. Subjective reports of relative success in achieving required state of relaxation were obtained and correlated with each physiologic variable in turn. Significant correlations were obtained with all autonomic measures (although not with EMG changes), and these were generally found to be highest in skin conductance activity. It may be concluded that emphasis on muscular control in brief relaxation training as used in desensitization simply induces a state of calm and reduced physiologic arousal. Conditions conducive to such a state are incorporated in relaxation training procedures (e.g. reduction of irrelevant afferent stimulation, use of familiar monotonous instructions, and reduction of attention to internal stimuli). Finding of significant changes in both subjective relaxation and autonomic activity during training sessions suggests that relaxation may reduce autonomic response to stressful stimuli during desensitization or may lead the patient to reinterpret these stressful stimuli in light of a changed subjective state.

progressive relaxation
phobias
desensitization
subjective reports

18 Phillips, Robert E., Johnson, Gordon D., and Geyer, Anne: Case histories and shorter communications: Self-administered systematic desensitization. *Behav Res Ther, 10:*93, 1972.

One of the more promising aspects of systematic desensitization is the possibility of increasing the therapist's efficiency over that possible with the traditional one-to-one relationship. Although Wolpe (Wolpe and Lazarus, 1966) has primarily used a one-to-one technique, systematic desensitization has been effective with groups (Robinson and Suinn, 1969), when automated (Donner, 1970), and on a partially self-administered basis (Kahn and Baker, 1968). Kahn and Baker (1968) compared the effectiveness of the traditional therapist-administered desensitization with a technique that involved minimal therapist contact. The self-administered group received one interview devoted to hierarchy construction and then were contacted once a week by phone. They also received a manual explaining the procedure of systematic desensitization and a record containing relaxation instructions which also gave nineteen minutes of visualization and relaxation commands at appropriate intervals for desensitization. The results indicated that the self-administered was as effective as the traditional procedure. However, as the authors themselves indicated ". . . the home group was not run under pure do-it-yourself conditions (p. 199)."

desensitization
home training

19 Rachman, S.: Studies in desensitization—I: The separate effects of relaxation and desensitization. *Behav Res Ther, 3:* 245, 1965.

The purpose of the study was to investigate the separate effects of desensitization and relaxation in Wolpe's technique of "systematic desensitization." Four small groups of spider-phobic, normal subjects were allocated to the following treatments: desensitization with relaxation, desensitization without relaxation, relaxation only, no-treatment controls. The effects of treatment were assessed by subjective reports, avoidance tests and fear estimates. Marked reductions in fear were obtained only in the desensitization-with-relaxation group, and it was concluded that the combined effects of re-

desensitization
relaxation
phobias

laxation and desensitization are greater than their separate effects.

C 20 Rachman, S.: The role of muscular relaxation in desensitization therapy. *Behav Res Ther, 6:*159, 1968.

The role of muscular relaxation is considered, and it is argued that although training in progressive relaxation facilitates treatment it is not a necessary element in therapy.

muscle relaxation desensitization

MUSCLE TENSION FEEDBACK

1   Aarons, Louis: Diurnal variations of muscle action potentials and word associations related to psychological orientation. *Psychophysiology, 5:*77, 1968.

Theoretical analysis has suggested that the feedback of neuromuscular activity affects quantitative but not qualitative aspects of responses, i.e. arousal provides energy but not direction for behavior. This study was carried out to determine whether or not qualitative aspects of ideation vary with the normal diurnal fluctuations of neuromuscular activity. Word association tests revealed qualitative differences among responses before sleep, upon awakening and at noon. Some differences were related to psychological test variables of kinesthetic orientation, need for change, and anxiety; other differences were independent of psychological test scores but related to the time of the word tests and intensity of muscle action potential (EMG). Subjects with low and high scores on the psychological tests were similar in both body temperature variation and amount of time spent in different EEG sleep stages. EMG levels during sleep were highly correlated with EEG sleep stages for both groups, but low psychological test scorers exhibited more EMG activity than high scorers. Neuromuscular arousal was accompanied by qualitative changes in verbal responses that were related to psychological orientations.

feedback
EMG levels
diurnal
* variation*
ideation
word associ-
* ation tests*
sleep

2   Aarons, Louis: Subvocalization: Aural and EMG feedback in reading. *Percept Mot Skills, 33:*271, 1971.

Explored functional relations of variables in reading for arithmetic problem-solving for six 21 to 25-year-old male medical students who showed much high subvocalization (HVs) compared with six Ss who showed little low subvocalization (LVs) speech-muscle activity during silent reading.

reading
subvocaliza-
* tion*
speech
* muscle*
* feedback*

Higher relative sound intensities were used by LVs in normal reading aloud. EMG feedback training was effective in reducing speech-muscle activity in both groups. Delayed auditory feedback (DAF) eliminated the difference in relative sound intensities. Latency to correct answer in silent problem-solving was shorter for LVs before but not after feedback training. Variations in heart rate, eye-movement rate, regressive eye movements, reading speed, rate of integrated speech peaks, syllable rate, eye-voice span, eye movements/syllable, and correct answers were related to experimental conditions but were not different for HVs and LVs. The correlation of eye-voice span with speech-muscle activity was related to levels of subvocalization in normal reading aloud but modified by DAF and feedback training. The measurement of speech-muscle activity, feedback training, general and developmental differences in the use of auditory versus kinesthetic cues by HVs and LVs and implications of subvocalization for speech, memory, thought and reading are discussed.

delayed auditory feedback
HR
eye movements
theory

D 3   Block, James D.: Operant conditioning with augmented feedback: New perspectives in motor rehabilitation of the brain damaged. *NY Acad Med,* 1969.

Discusses the applicability of the feedback-operant conditioning method to the alleviation of spasticity.

operant conditioning
augmented feedback
learned control
applications
motor rehabilitation
brain damage

D 4   Booker, Harold E., Rubow, Rick T., and Coleman, Patrick J.: Simplified feedback in neuromuscular retraining: An automated approach using electromyographic signals. *Arch Phys Med, 50:*621, 1969.

Since rehabilitation encompasses many features of the learning process, simplification of feedback could be used to in-

feedback techniques

crease learning potential. In the present example, one-dimensional visual feedback was substituted for feedback of total facial appearance, and an automated system was used to facilitate this process. The electromyogram (EMG) signal from the affected muscle served as the feedback source. Excellent cosmetic and functional results were obtained, and it is suggested the method has wider application in the field of neuromuscular rehabilitation.

EMG activity facial muscles rehabilitation

) 5   Budzynski, Thomas, Stoyva, Johann, and Adler, Charles: Feedback-induced muscle relaxation: Application to tension headache. *J Behav Ther Exp Psychiatry, 1:*205, 1970.

This paper describes a technique for producing deep muscle relaxation by means of an information feedback technique —the subject hears a tone with a frequency proportional to the EMG level of the muscle being monitored. The new technique was applied to several tension headache patients —the first five individuals available for the study. With this "bio-feedback" training in relaxation, the patients not only learned to produce low frontalis EMG levels but showed subsequent reductions in headache activity.

EMG feedback learned control tension headache

) 6   Budzynski, Thomas, and Stoyva, Johann: An electromyographic feedback technique for teaching voluntary relaxation of the masseter muscle. *J Dent Res, 52:*116, 1973.

A muscle relaxation training technique that provides a person with immediate auditory or visual feedback of his electromyographic activity was developed. The forty subjects who received feedback reduced their masseter electromyographic activity significantly more than the forty subjects who did not receive feedback.

feedback voluntary relaxation masseter muscle

) 7   Green, E.E., Walters, E.D., Green, A.M., and Murphy, G.: Feedback technique for deep relaxation. *Psychophysiology, 6:*371, 1969.

Zero firing or single motor unit firing in large forearm muscle bundles was achieved in less than twenty minutes, in seven out of twenty-one subjects, through the use of a feed-

BF techniques relaxation

back meter which showed the subject his own electromyographic tension level. Five of these seven subjects reported body image illusions. The behavior of single motor units under these conditions indicates the existence of a reflex type neural oscillator in the striate neuromuscular domain, whose operation is gated or controlled from the central nervous system. The electronic system needed to operate the feedback meter can be assembled from standard amplifiers but standard EMG Integrator (rectifier) couplers usually must be modified in order to detect single motor unit firing.

motor unit training instruments altered consciousness subjective reports

D 8   Green, Elmer E., Green, Alyce M., and Walters, E. Dale: Self-regulation of internal states. Progress of Cybernetics: Proceedings of the International Congress of Cybernetics, London, 1969.

This paper is concerned with the development and use of tools and techniques for investigating states of internal awareness, psychological and physiological, which until recently have been considered unapproachable by scientific means. Experimental subjects have been trained by physiological feedback methods in the voluntary control of normally unconscious physiological functions which represent three major neuroanatomical regions: craniospinal, autonomic and central. Subjects who have been most successful have demonstrated control by volitional relaxation of striate muscle tension down to the "zero" region, by volitional increase of temperature in the hands as much as 5°C in two minutes, and by volitional increase in percentage of alpha rhythm up to 100 percent alpha over ten second epochs, while speaking, with eyes open. The purpose of this physiological training is to enhance and make possible the study of those psychological states which appear as functional concomitants of a passive peripheral nervous system and an "alpha-activated" central nervous system. This ongoing project has significant implications for psychology, psychosomatic medicine, psychiatry, education, and research in creativity.

relaxation learned voluntary control internal awareness EEG alpha skin temperature

D 9   Green, E., Green, A., and Walters, D.: Voluntary control of internal states: Psychological and physiological. *J Transpersonal Psychol, 11*:1, 1970.

A need to shorten the learning time of autogenic training techniques and to adapt the system to states of consciousness research have spawned the methodology used in this report. That is, a combination of the conscious self-regulation aspects of yoga, the psychological method of autogenic training, and the instrumental technique of physiological feedback is used. Preliminary experiments showed that seven of twenty-one subjects could reduce muscle activity to zero levels through muscle feedback in twenty minutes with associated body image changes such as the arm feeling like a bag of cement. A larger project used triple feedback to train simultaneous reduction of muscle tension in the right forearm, increase in temperature in the right hand (autogenic relaxation), and increase in percentage of alpha activity. Projected research into imagery, etc. includes percentage-of-alpha, frequency-of-alpha, and percentage-of-theta training using visual and auditory feedback. Home training is described along with an arm balancing technique (subliminal dredging) to prevent drowsiness and aid in recognition and recall of imagery. In conclusion the possible significance of the voluntary control of internal states research is presented. Areas of important application would include education, creativity, psychology, psychotherapy, and psychosomatic medicine (i.e. chronic headache, etc.). A dramatic application involves starvation and absorption of cancerous growths through blood flow control.

EEG
alpha
autogenic training
biofeedback
subjective states
voluntary control

10   Jacobs, Alfred, and Felton, Gary S.: Visual feedback of myoelectric output to facilitate muscle relaxation in normal persons and patients with neck injuries. *Arch Phys Med, 50:* 34, 1969.

Two groups of ten subjects each, one group consisting of physically normal subjects and the other of patients with diagnosed injury of the upper trapezius, were asked to relax first under the condition where the monitoring of the relaxation consisted only of the proprioceptive-kinesthetic cues available to the subject and subsequently under a condition where the extent and amount of myoelectric activity was transformed into a visually presented feedback signal. Subjects were given two series of ten 15-second trials for both

EMG
feedback
neck injury
relaxation
visual signals

conditions. Four additional subjects in each of the above groups served as controls for practice and order effects by receiving only visual oscilloscopic trials. The ability of the visual feedback to facilitate relaxation was significantly supported for all subjects. Although originally there was a significantly greater difficulty in relaxation observed in the injured group, the visual signal enabled these patients to reduce muscle activity to a level indistinguishable from that of the normal persons. Subjects were able to approach or match their basal level of muscular performance after only one brief demonstration trial of exposure to the visual monitoring signal.

D 11 Kohlenberg, R.J.: Operant-conditioning of human anal sphincter pressure. *J Appl Behav Anal, 6:*201, 1973. (Copyright 1973 by the Society for the Experimental Analysis of Behavior.)

Anal sphincter pressure in a thirteen-year-old encopretic boy was modified by reinforcing increases in pressure exerted on a fluid-filled balloon inserted into the rectum. It was found that pressure changes were a function of the reinforcement schedule and that baseline levels (resting pressure) during extinction conditions tended to increase throughout the experiment.

operant con ditioning anal sphinc ter

D 12 Raskin, M., Johnson, George, and Rondestvedt, Joanne W.: Chronic anxiety treated by feedback-induced muscle relaxation. *Arch Gen Psychiatry, 28:*263, 1973.

The effects of daily deep muscle relaxation, achieved through electromyographic feedback training, on the symptoms of ten chronically anxious patients were assessed. All ten successfully learned to sustain twenty-five minutes of profound relaxation of the frontalis muscle with or without feedback. The most striking results occurred when a patient learned to use relaxation techniques at critical times. Three patients learned to use partial relaxation to control previously intolerable situational anxiety, and four patients learned to abort tension headaches in the same manner. However, a limited period of relaxation gives insufficient relief from

anxiety feedback relaxation frontalis muscle

symptoms which endure in time. Only one patient had a marked lessening of his pervasive anxiety and although patients with insomnia learned to put themselves to sleep by relaxing, most experienced frequent awakenings.

D 13 Rubow, Rick T., and Smith, Karl U.: Feedback parameters of electromyographic learning. *Am J Phys Med, 50:*115, 1971. (Copyright 1971 by the Williams & Wilkins Co., Baltimore.)

This study determined the optimal modes and conditions of integrating EMG signals for prosthetic control and training procedures for individuals with disturbed muscle control. Integration of EMG signals for patient muscle control introduces feedback delays between muscular contraction and the observed sensory effects of such contraction. A moving-average and an intermittent-average mode of integration were compared in regard to their effectiveness in producing electromyographic learning under two conditions of integration-produced feedback delays of 0.25 and 0.75 seconds. Results indicated that the continuous moving, average technique of integration was superior to the intermittent-average technique. The variation in integration delays had different effects with the two modes of average action-current signals. The findings indicate that feedback timing is a critical factor in determining learning with artificial electromyographic muscle control and training techniques.

muscle learning techniques muscle contraction feedback electromyographic tracking integrated EMG signals applications disturbed muscle control prosthetic control

D 14 Wagman, Irving H., Pierce, Donald S., and Burger, Ray E.: Proprioceptive influence in volitional control of individual motor units. *Nature (Lond), 207:*957, 1965.

It appears from our observations that, without training, volitional activation of descending pathways does not result in invariable responses of specific motor cells. Otherwise, the response of particular motor units would not be dependent on maintenance of certain positions of the limb or reproduction of a certain pattern of muscle contraction. During minimal or moderate contractions, the action of the descending pathways is modified, and perhaps controlled, probably in the anterior horn of the spinal cord, by peripheral input

motor units learned control proprioceptive influences audio/visual feedback

—proprioception, muscle contraction, or cutaneous stimuli. Appropriate sensory information, therefore, must be present for volitional activation of specific motor units. However, after an intensive period of training, precise conscious control over motor units can be established with a lessened influence of peripheral stimuli.

D 15   Whatmore, G.B., and Kohli, Daniel R.: Dysponesis: A neurophysiologic factor in functional disorders. *Behav Sci,* *13:*102, 1968.

This paper discusses a physiopathologic state that is a hidden etiologic factor in a number of common clinical syndromes and can give rise to a variety of functional disturbances within the organism. It is basically a reversible physiopathologic state composed of errors in energy expenditure that interfere with nervous system function and thus with control of organ function. Its detrimental influence is exerted by means of excitatory and inhibitory patterns of signal input at widespread points within the complex networks of the nervous system, resulting in reduction in the organism's productivity and disturbance of its emotional reactivity, ideation, and central regulation of various organs of the body. Most of this energy expenditure, covert in nature, goes unnoticed by both the person expending it and those who observe him. Diagnosis is based upon history, physical examination, and laboratory and psychological tests. Electromyometric studies are a necessary part of each patient workup whenever dysponesis is suspected. Treatment is a form of neurophysiologic engineering wherein basic principles of neurophysiology are used to carry on a retraining within the nervous system. Specific instances to which the patient overreacts are identified so that he can be "desensitized" to them through application of the principles of effort management. The patient is trained to observe at least some of the covert efforts that he makes unknowingly. Electromyometry, electromyophony, electromyoscopy, and other procedures are used for teaching purposes to delineate and objectify these efforts and bring them into the realm of observable phenomena, and much electronically monitored instruction and practice are necessary. The patient is then trained to

EMG feedback motor energy applications (psycho-somatic)

take these energy expenditures into account with a minimum of fuss and attention as he goes about his daily activities. The quality of therapeutic result is directly proportional to the proficiency attained by the patient.

16 Wickramasekera, Ian: Instructions and EMG feedback in systematic desensitization: A case report. *Behav Ther, 3:* 460, 1972.

This case study describes the apparently successful treatment of an "examination phobia" with systematic desensitization. Videotape and verbal instructions were used as "advanced organizers" to prepare the patient for systematic desensitization. The patient was trained to relax with verbal instructions and electromyographic feedback training.

relaxation
desensitization
phobias

17 Wickramasekera, Ian: The application of verbal instructions and EMG feedback training to the management of tension headache—preliminary observations. *Headache, 13:*74, 1973.

Inspection of the records of all patients appeared to suggest a decline in the frequency and intensity of headache activity after the baseline period. The decline in the frequency and intensity of headache activity seems even more dramatic for four of the five patients and after the EMG feedback period. The small size of the sample and the confounding of the effects of verbal instructions and EMG feedback training made it difficult to draw conclusions and generalize from this data. Nevertheless, clinical impression and the more dramatic decline in frontalis EMG associated with the feedback training procedure appears to suggest that the addition of response-contingent EMG feedback training results in a more specific and powerful procedure for the clinical management of tension headache. Further factorial studies should separate out the effects of verbal instructions and EMG feedback training on tension headache and also study the interaction effects of the procedures. In order to control for "placebo effects" and experimenter bias, this should be repeated with noncontingent but nonfrustrative EMG feedback and a "blind experimenter."

tension
headaches
biofeedback
relaxation
verbal instructions

REVIEW-THEORY-COMMENT

E 1   Davison, G.C.: Anxiety under total curarization: Implications for the role of muscular relaxation in the desensitization of neurotic fears. *J Nerv Ment Dis, 143:*443, 1966.

The Jacobson-Wolpe position on the use of deep muscular relaxation as an anxiety inhibitor assumes that considerable reduction in proprioceptive feedback from muscles which are in a relaxed state is incompatible with a state of anxiety. Various studies have used paralytic drugs, primarily d-sub-curarine chloride, to show the acquisition of fear responses under complete striate muscle paralysis: the fact that these animals are able to acquire classically conditioned fear responses under drugs which act peripherally at the neuromuscular junction was taken as evidence inconsistent with the views of Jacobson and Wolpe inasmuch as little, if any, feedback is possible from a muscle which cannot be innervated by efferents. Several studies were then reviewed which purport to furnish evidence for Jacobson's peripheralistic position: these studies show considerable central depression during curare paralysis. These investigations were reinterpreted, however, in light of the overriding importance of exteroceptive stimulation: the animals in the curare conditioning experiments were likewise deprived of proprioceptive feedback and yet were hardly nonanxious, the important difference being that the animals in the conditioning experiments were stimulated frequently from the environment while curarized, this stimulation maintaining an alert, often anxious state. Finally two hypotheses were put forward as to why training in muscle relaxation does, in fact, inhibit anxiety. The one suggested that relaxing ones own muscles generates strong positive affect states, which, in turn, inhibit anxiety; the other hypothesis called attention to the fact that the states of muscular relaxation under curare differ from self-induced relaxation in the important respect that

proprioception
curare
anxiety
theory

only with self-induced relaxation must there be a reduction in efferent messages from the cortex—perhaps this alteration in efferents, rather than afferants, inhibits anxiety.

2   DeLong, Mahlon: Central control of movement: Central patterning of movement. *Neurosci Res Program Bull, 9:*10, 1971.

Reviews the interaction between central patterning and peripheral feedback in the production of coordinated motor input in certain basic movements. "While the contribution of central patterning is enormous in almost every instance, it is striking how varied is the role of proprioceptive feedback —in some instances exerting only a nonspecific tonic effect (wing-beat frequency control in the locust flight system), in other cases providing phasic reinforcement of discrete phases of the movement (lobster swimmeret), and elsewhere providing timing cues for the overall patterning (dogfish swimming)."

mechanisms
motor movements
motor control
central control

3   Evarts, Edward V., and Thach, W. Thomas: Central control of movement: Strategies and tactics in research on central control of movement. *Neurosci Res Program Bull, 9:*113, 1971.

Reviews summaries of contributions to a work session by K. Frank on the use of neural signals to control external devices, J.M. Brookhart on a technique for investigating central control of posture, E. Henneman on "size principle" of motoneuron recruitment, M. Ito on the special role of the cerebellum in movement control, and C.G. Phillips on corticomotoneural and corticofusimotor projections in movement control.

motor movements
central control

4   Evarts, Edward V.: Central control of movement: Feedback and corollary discharge: A merging of the concepts. *Neurosci Res Program Bull, 9:*86, 1971.

Reviews that part of a work session concerned with three types of feedback in the control of movements: (1) internal

motor movement

feedback, i.e. feedback arising from within the nervous system (e.g. Sperry's "corollary discharge," von Holst and Mittelstaedt's "efference copy," and Mackay's "feedforward control"); (2) response feedback, i.e. afferent feedback; and (3) knowledge of results, i.e. feedback arising from the external environment as an indirect consequence of movement. Included is a contribution by O. Oscarsson on "recent developments on internal feedback" with regard to "flexor reflex afferents."

*central
control
neurophysi-
ologic
theory*

E 5   Huxley, H.E.: The mechanism of muscular contraction. *Science, 164*:1356, 1969. (Copyright 1969 by the American Association for the Advancement of Science.)

A review of recent structural studies suggesting a revealing model for cross-bridge action at variable filament spacing.

*muscle
control
review
theory*

E 6   Keele, Steven W.: Movement control in skilled motor performance. *Psychol Bull, 70*:387, 1968.

The speed and accuracy of single movements depend on several factors, such as direction of movement, distance to the target, and accompaniment by simultaneous movements. The relation between speed, accuracy and distance appears to be determined by the time required to process feedback and to make corrective alterations in the movement. For a repetitive series of movements, there is some evidence suggesting that control is shifted from feedback to a motor program. This view receives further support from demonstrations that the reproduction of single movements may be under programmed control. How the study of movements may be relevant to understanding perceptual and memory skills, as well as motor skills, is briefly mentioned.

*motor
control
theory*

E 7   MacNeilage, Peter F.: Motor control of serial ordering of speech. *Psychol Rev, 77*:182, 1970.

Many have assumed that speech sound sequences result primarily from rule-governed permutations of a finite set of invariant unit commands, usually phonemes. The absence,

*motor
control
speech*

at the periphery, of invariant consequences of these commands is often attributed to mechanical and neuromuscular limitations of the production apparatus and temporal overlap in commands. This model neither solves the problem of motor equivalence in speech (achievement of relatively invariant motor goals from varying origins) nor takes into account recent neurophysiological findings indicating extensive closed-loop possibilities for motor control. Motor equivalence may be achieved by an internalized space coordinate system which specifies invariant "targets" which control the generation of necessarily context-dependent movement patterns, with the aid of closed-loop control, at least in the initiation of utterances.

model theory

E 8   Marsden, C.D., Merton, P.A., and Morton, H.B.: Servo action in human voluntary movement. *Nature (Lond), 238:*140, 1972.

Muscular movements are under the control of a servo similar in many ways to those used in engineering control systems but with a subtlety of design not found in man-made servo mechanisms, including an automatic gain compensation for altered load which must be useful, for example, for adjusting to reduced g on the moon.

muscle control theory

E 9   Ross, Leonard E., and Nelson, Michael N.: The role of awareness in differential conditioning. *Psychophysiology, 10:* 91, 1973.

A view of the processes involved in single cue and differential skeletal conditioning is presented, and the implications for studies investigating the effects of awareness on autonomic conditioning are discussed. Skeletal conditioning studies are described which indicate that masking tasks can greatly reduce and in some cases largely eliminate differential responding, but not response acquisition per se. These effects occur even when Ss report the conditioning contingencies. The data thus suggest that Ss given masking tasks may be "functionally unaware" during conditioning with an attendant decrease in differential conditioning performance, even though they have knowledge of the conditioning contingencies as demonstrated by post experimental report.

autonomic conditioning
skeletal conditioning
contingency awareness
awareness masking
comment

E 10   Schmidt, Richard A.: Proprioception and the timing of motor responses. *Psychol Bull,* 76:383, 1971.

Two hypotheses that relate motor response timing to proprioceptive feedback are presented, along with specific predictions. The input hypothesis states that the subject uses the inflow of proprioceptive feedback from an earlier portion of a movement sequence to cue the timing of a later portion, and considerable evidence was found to support this point of view. The Adams and Creamer decay hypothesis states that the subject uses the decay of proprioceptive feedback in short-term memory to cue the timing of a latter movement, and only recently has clear support for this view been provided. Finally, there was the possibility that feedback is not used at all, with the timing of the various sequences being programmed.

proprioception
feedback
timing
mechanisms

E 11   Smith, Karl U., and Ansell, S.D.: Closed-loop digital computer system for study of sensory feedback effects of brain rhythms. *Am J Phys Med,* 44:125, 1965. (Copyright 1965 by the Williams & Wilkins Co., Baltimore.)

This research has developed a closed-loop digital computer system for sensory-feedback research on behavioral and physiologic mechanisms of significance in physical medicine. The computer is arranged with appropriate physical transducers to record activity in different types of physiologic and response mechanisms and to control many different patterns of sensory and excitatory feedback in relation to such recording. The concept of design is based on use of the computer to produce different modes of delay, space-displacement, kinetic modulation, and other forms of sensory-feedback perturbation. In a series of experiments the effects of brain-wave-generated stimulus feedback patterns on perception and on the frequency pattern of the electroencephalogram were investigated. No effects of these stimuli were found. Similarly, delay of these feedback stimuli relative to their generating source had no effect on perception or on the brain-wave pattern. Furthermore, subjects were unable to judge the magnitude of the delay of cyclic auditory stimuli produced by the electroencephalogram. In contrast, computer-delayed auditory-feedback effects of speech had the

computer
systems
delayed,
displaced
feedback
pattern
feedback
applications
perception
EEG
patterns

effects of slowing, slurring, and producing repetitive defects in reading. The results of the experiments clarify problems of dynamic correlation between perception and the brain wave pattern and, at the same time, substantiate the concepts of design of the computer feedback control system. The methods developed hold promise of defining new techniques of real-time dynamic simulation of physiologic and behavioral disorder in the normal individual.

E 12   Smith, K.U., and Henry, J.P.: Cybernetic foundations for rehabilitation. *Am J Phys Med, 46:*379, 1967. (Copyright 1967 by the Williams & Wilkins Co., Baltimore.)

Defines a feedback concept of human motion, physiological regulation, and learning, particularly as it applies to therapeutic training and exercise. A cybernetic theory of behavior and physiological control interprets activity and learning as self-regulated processes. Feedback mechanisms as self-regulatory, closed-loop processes that control patterned, organized behavior are described for internal and external behavior. Cybernetic interpretation ascribes learning to changes in self-regulatory, feedback-control patterns by means of which the organism governs itself and modifies the environment. Feedback training of organic systems is described.

feedback theory motion learning feedback

MOTOR UNITS

TECHNIQUES

F 1   Basmajian, John V., and Cross, G. Lee III: Duration of motor unit potentials from fine-wire electrodes. *Am J Phys Med, 50:*144, 1971. (Copyright 1971 by the Williams & Wilkins Co., Baltimore.)

> The mean duration of motor unit potentials recorded from bipolar fine-wire electrodes is considerably shorter than that of potentials recorded from needle electrodes (5 versus 9 msec.). There are many short duration potentials in spite of the greater polyphasic nature of these potentials compared to those obtained with needle-electrodes. Comparison of four different muscles (biceps brachii, first dorsal interosseus of the hand, quadriceps femoris, and tibialis anterior) reveals no marked differences, although there is a somewhat longer mean duration in the hand muscle, which is statistically significant.

recording techniques response character- istics

F 2   Basmajian, J.V., Forrest, W.J., and Shine, G.: A simple connector for fine-wire EMG electrodes. *J Appl Physiol, 21:* 1680, 1966.

> To connect very fine (0.025 mm) intramuscular electrode wires to the input cables of electromyograph apparatus, a simple, brass spring connector has been devised. It can be snapped on the free end of the hair-thin wires in moments and makes excellent electrical connection.

measure- ments recording techniques

F 3   Gassel, M. Michael, and Ott, Kenneth H.: Motoneuron excitability in man: A novel method of evaluation by modulation of tonic muscle activity. *Electroencephalogr Clin Neurophysiol, 29:*190, 1970.

The excitability of a population of motoneurons in humans has been investigated classically by the recovery curve of the monosynaptic reflex following a conditioning stimulus. The classical technique is applicable only to a few large muscles with prominent stretch reflexes. The inherent variability of the monosynaptic reflex makes this method both arduous and time-consuming. An alternative means of excitability testing is described. The technique is based upon the observation that during tonic activity, motor unit discharge increased with facilitation of the reflex and decreased with inhibition of the reflex. A system was developed for graphic recording of the modulation of electromyographic activity following a conditioning stimulus. The electromyogram is passed through an absolute-value rectifier circuit and then summed by computer whose sweeps are triggered by the conditioning stimulus. An X-Y plot is then made of the summed potentials ("modulation curve") representing the graph of activity changes following the conditioning stimulus. The modulation curve resembled, but did not reflect precisely, changes in central excitability recorded by the classical recovery curve. The modulation curve is rapidly and easily performed. It can be elicited from any muscle, flexor or extensor, and is not restricted to the few large muscles with prominent stretch reflexes as is true in the classical technique. The method is especially adapted to the study of the response characteristics of spontaneous activity in clinical electromyography.

techniques
conditioning stimuli
spontaneous EMG

MECHANISMS

F 4   Basmajian, John V.: Electromyography comes of age. *Science, 176*:603, 1972. (Copyright 1972 by the American Association for the Advancement of Science.)

A review documenting evidence that the conscious control of individual motor units in man may be used to improve his physical performance.

motor units
conscious control
physical performance
theory

F 5   Fjeld, Stanton P.: Motor response and muscle action po-
       tential in the measurement of sensory threshold. *Psycho-
       physiology, 1:*277, 1965.

There was a significant improvement in the accuracy of de-   *subliminal*
tection of visual stimuli at or below Ss' thresholds when de-   *perception*
tection was measured overtly by gross muscle movement re-   *stimulus*
sponses and covertly by muscle action potential (MAP re-   *detection*
sponses, as opposed to overt responses alone). In addition to   *EMG*
yielding a lower threshold value for the series of light   *motor*
stimuli, the MAP measures became more useful as an in-   *action*
dicator of accuracy at the weaker rather than the brighter   *potential*
light values, whereas the overt response measures became   *covert*
relatively less useful. These results suggest that events of   *responses*
which the S is "unaware" (covert responses) can convey information about performance to an experimenter, provided
suitable methods of measurement can be devised.

F 6   Houk, James C.: On the significance of various command
       signals during voluntary control. *Brain Res, 40:*49, 1972.

The author suggests a tentative interpretation of the signifi-   *proprio-*
cance of the various command signals that are involved in   *ceptive*
voluntary control. Somewhere in the nervous system there   *feedback*
must be a signal which is concerned only with desired posi-   *voluntary*
tions. The central command which is postulated is one step   *motor*
down from this—it also has a component which can speed up   *control*
movements. The pyramidal command represents everything   *mechanisms*
contained in the central command plus a component pro-   *review*
viding compensation for steady-state errors in position. The   *theory*
latter correlates well with the magnitude and direction of
disturbance forces. The peripheral command represents
everything contained in the pyramidal feedback pathways.
The latter are related to the length, velocity and force in the
muscles involved in carrying out the movement.

F 7   Kimm, Joseph: On the specification of control in single
       motor units. *Diss Abst, 30:*869, 1969. (Order No. 69-12, 558.)

The purpose of this research was to objectively and quantita-   *motor units*
tively assess control capabilities in the single motor unit. The   *voluntary*
                                                                      control

specific objectives were structured into three general areas of investigation. The first concerns the effects of rehearsal on simple reaction time performance of the single motor unit. The second compared median reaction time latencies for producing a single spike discharge for inhibiting the repetitive discharge activity of a single motor unit following a stimulus presentation. The third area compared single motor unit reaction time performance of two muscles, the abductor pollicis brevis and the abductor pollicis. Indwelling wire electrodes were placed either in the abductor pollicis brevis or abductor pollicis. Measurements were made of reaction time latency, variability and number of criterion responses per experimental session for the session for the specific units studied. In the study of effects of rehearsal versus no rehearsal on single motor unit reaction time performance, it was found that rehearsal preceding the onset of the stimulus decreased both the reaction time latency and variability. A typical median latency for rehearsal trials was 253 msec with an interquartile of 217 msec in a sample of approximately 200 trials. Corresponding no-rehearsal trials for the same motor units produced a median reaction time latency of 382 msec with an interquartile range of 232 msec. Comparison between rehearsal and no-rehearsal trials were statistically significant beyond the .001 level. The number of trials failing to reach response criteria was not statistically significantly different between rehearsal and no-rehearsal treatments. In the study comparing median reaction time latencies for inhibition with the median reaction time latency for the production of a single spike discharge, inhibition median reaction times were briefer and usually less variable than for excitation. The median reaction time latency for a typical unit studied was 178 msec for inhibition and 383 for excitation. Statistical significance beyond the .001 level was achieved in comparisons of these median reaction time latencies. In addition, analysis of poststimulus responses in the inhibition phase of this research suggested that a short latency effect (within 75 msec following the stimulus) did occur. This was demonstrated by an observed increase in variability of the first poststimulus response. Statistical comparisons of measures obtained from units in the two different muscles did not reveal any differences.

practice reaction time performance inhibition

F 8   Lieblish, Israel: Note on Thysell's "Reaction time of single
        motor units." *Percep Mot Skills, 30:*152, 1970.

Suggests that the lower mode reported in a study by R.V.   *motor unit*
Thysell (see PA, Vol. *44:*3235) may represent the orienting   *activity*
response manifested by the single motor units to the onset of   *comment*
the reaction light. Internal data analysis is suggested to clari- *orienting*
fy whether the lower mode of the RT distributions was   *response*
generated by responses, some of which have the character of
the orienting response.

F 9   Scott, C.H.: An electromyographic investigation of bilateral-
        ly recorded action potentials from the orbicularis oris muscle
        in stutterers and nonstutterers. *Arch Phys Med, 53:*589, 1972.

To define further certain neurophysiological behavior in a   *stuttering*
stuttering population, electromyography was used to record   *EMG*
absolute temporal differences in milliseconds in the onset of   *analysis*
clustered motor unit action potentials between the right and
left orbicularis oris muscle commissures and latency from
visual stimulus presentation to the production of five speech
phonemes (sounds). Twenty male adult stutterers and
twenty normal male adults were used as subjects. Implanted
hooked-wire electrodes on each side of the commissures were
used to record EMG activity. A tachistoscope was electronically synchronized with the EMG. Stimulus presentations
were made during a white noise auditory masking and a
quiet condition. Dissynchronous neuromuscular behavior
was observed in all subjects under both conditions. A significantly longer latency period was observed in the stuttering
group. EMG has made it possible to quantify dynamic behavior in stuttering individuals.

VOLUNTARY CONTROL
OF MOTOR UNITS

G 1   Antonelli, Daniel J., and Waring, Worden: Circuit for a
one degree of freedom myoelectric control. *Med Res Eng,*
Fourth Quarter 1967, 35-38.

The object of this design effort was the development of a *instruments*
circuit to process myoelectric signals from persons with *myoelectric*
paralysis and to use this processed signal to control the *signals*
actuator of an orthotic device. The imposed constraints were *orthotic*
(1) The system must be portable by a handicapped person, *devices*
and (2) the available power is a center-tapped twelve-volt *applications*
battery. An impaired muscle has myoelectric signals available with a much lower signal strength than the normal
muscle, and therefore the circuit and electrodes must be of
an efficient and "quiet" design. The circuit consists of two
channels, each of six sections: a different amplifier, a voltage
amplifier, a high pass filter, a rectifier, a Schmitt trigger, and
a relay. Signals applied to one channel cause the orthotic device and its associated limb to move in one direction, and
signals to the other channel cause the device and limb to
move in the opposite direction. The Schmitt trigger has
been modified to obtain a low hysteresis. This allows a lower
overall gain to be utilized in distinguishing between activity
and rest and increases the noise immunity of the circuit.

G 2   Baginsky, R.G.: Voluntary control of motor unit activity by
visual and aural feedback. *Electroencephalogr Clin Neurophysiol,* 27:724, 1969 (Abstr).

Most clinical electromyographers have been employing *motor unit*
audiovisual feedback empirically. Only very recently a few *activity*
investigators have been conducting research using such a *feedback*
feedback mechanism on an experimental basis. Our in- *voluntary*
control

389

vestigation involved twenty right-handed informed volunteers of both sexes, twenty-one to twenty-five years of age,
students or graduates of paramedical professions. A dual-
channel electromyograph, providing visual and audio monitoring of muscle signals, and bipolar coaxial needle electrodes were employed as follows. Audiovisual feedback or
visual feedback and aural feedback, alone, were employed.
Fastest results were obtained with audiovisual feedback. The
mechanism of individual motor unit control will be discussed.

*aural/visual
signals*

G 3   Basmajian, J.V., and Simard, T.G.: Effects of distracting
movements on the control of trained motor units. *Am J
Phys Med, 46:*1427, 1967. (Copyright 1967 by the Williams
& Wilkins Co., Baltimore.)

Ss can be trained to maintain the activity of and to change
the frequency of discharge in a single motor unit while the
remainder of the body is relaxed. Fine control can also be
retained under distracting influences.

*learned
control
audio/visual
feedback
distraction
ipsilateral
limb move-
ments
contralater-
al limb
movements*

G 4   Basmajian, J.V., Baeza, M., and Fabrigar, C.: Conscious control and training of individual spinal motor neurons in
normal human subjects. *J New Drugs, 5:*78, 1965.

Several fundamental considerations and a host of lesser questions arise from these findings. Most important is our clear
demonstration of a very fine conscious control of pathways to
single spinal motor neurons. Not only can human subjects
fire single neurons with no overflow (or with an active suppression of neighbors), but they can also produce deliberate
changes in the rate of firing. Most persons can do this if they
are provided with aural (and visual) cues from their muscles.
Although the skills learned in the experiments initially depend on artificial feedbacks, they are learned so quickly and

*motor units
voluntary
control*

are so exquisite in some persons that they are retained after the feedbacks are eliminated. We do not know the reason because the subjects cannot explain their success or failure, being quite oblivious of any special feeling. They state that they "think" about the previous tests with the cues. This aspect of these studies deserves large-scale investigations, for it appears to be of fundamental significance in motor learning. A number of problems were raised but not solved by our attempts to relate the skill of subjects with their obvious general ability, personality and other variables. We did not see any clear trend and were surprised to find that some persons who "should" perform well do not do so. This also is of fundamental interest, but a much longer series of cases is needed before any conclusions can be reached. The extremely fine ability to adjust the rate of firing of individual motor neurons in isolation presents a novel concept. Also the demonstration of a characteristic threshold of the rate of firing for each neuron, above which neighbors are invariably recruited, deserves attention: rarely does this exceed sixteen per second. However, one must not infer that motor units are restricted to these rates. Indeed, the upper limit of fifty per second generally accepted for human muscle is probably correct.

G 5   Basmajian, John V.: Control of individual motor units. *Am J Phys Med, 46*:480, 1967. (Copyright 1967 by the Williams & Wilkins Co., Baltimore.)

These novel experiments and findings suggest that pathways from the cerebral cortex can be made to stimulate single motoneurons while neighboring ones remain dormant or more likely are actively suppressed. Although the skills learned by our subjects at first depend on aural and visual "feedbacks" from muscles, the controls are learned so quickly, are so exquisite, and are so well retained after artificial feedbacks are eliminated that one cannot help believing that fundamental processes are involved. Equally gratifying to me and my associates is the recent successful use by bioengineering groups of single, trained motor units in the control of myoelectric prostheses and orthoses. A host of other applications also have been suggested, e.g. pharmacological

learned control
visual feedback
performance variables

testing, training of disabled persons (patients with cerebral palsy, etc.) to improve motor controls, neurophysiological studies of cortical delays and conduction times in the various parts of the pyramidal pathway, and psychological testing. All of these and many more possibilities await investigation on a broader front than any one of two groups can handle. Fortunately, enthusiasms have been kindled and many investigators are now engaged in preliminary studies employing the training of individual motor units and spinal motoneurons in both basic and applied research.

G 6   Fruhling, M., Basmajian, J.V., and Simard, T.G.: A note on the conscious controls of motor units by children under six. *J Mot Behav, 1:*65, 1969.

A simple form of training the conscious control of motor units in skeletal muscle has been demonstrated in a series of children under age six. Easy boredom is the chief deterrent in the very young. So long as a child understands and cooperates, he can learn to isolate single units in a period of about thirty minutes.

learned voluntary control children

G 7   Gray, Edwin R.: Conscious control of motor units in a tonic muscle. The effect of motor unit training. *Am J Phys Med, 50:*34, 1971. (Copyright 1971 by the Williams & Wilkins Co., Baltimore.)

This research deals with the training of motor units in a tonic muscle, the external anal sphincter. The effect of training of motor units on the control of tonic motor units under reflex control was tested in nine healthy subjects. The training of six large independent motor units influenced the control of other tonic motor units normally under reflex control. Before training of the larger and more independent units, the tonic units could not be suppressed; thus these units could not be trained. The observations suggest that, once the independent large units are trained to become active or remain suppressed, they exert their influence over the tonic motor units.

tonic muscle learned control subjective reports

G 8   Harrison, Ann, and Connolly, Kevin: The conscious control of fine levels of neuromuscular firing in spastic and normal subjects. *Develop Med Child Neurol, 13:762,* 1971.

An experiment was designed to investigate the ability of normal and spastic subjects to learn to recognize, isolate and produce on command fine degrees of neuromuscular activity. Surface electromyographic techniques were used to record activity from the front flexor muscle-groups of the arm, and simultaneous visual feedback was presented to the subjects in the form of an oscilloscope display of the muscle activity. No significant difference was found between the two groups in the degree of control finally achieved, though the spastic subjects took appreciably longer to attain such control. The results are discussed in terms of the nature of the motor control deficit displayed by spastic patients, and the use of augmented feedback in controlling muscle activity is considered.

learned control visual feedback spastic subjects

G 9   Leibrecht, Bruce C., Lloyd, Andree J., and Pounder, Sadie: Auditory feedback and conditioning of the single motor unit. *Psychophysiology, 10:*1, 1973.

The effects of direct auditory feedback of the electromyogram (EMG) on learning to control a single motor unit (SMU) were investigated. Seventeen human subjects were injected with bipolar fine-wire electrodes into the tibialis anterior muscle. A trial light indicated the onset of a trial. If the subject activated an SMU, a correct light appeared. A non-SMU response was followed by an incorrect light. All subjects received an initial training series with auditory EMG feedback followed by a retest at two weeks without EMG feedback. Speed of initial learning was substantially improved by direct EMG feedback. The nature and amount of learning, including the ability to use proprioceptive cues in controlling an SMU, were not affected, nor was retention of learning.

motor unit activity operant conditioning learned control auditory feedback

G 10   Lloyd, Andree J., and Leibrecht, Bruce C.: Conditioning of a single motor unit. *J Exp Psychol, 88:*391, 1971.

Seventeen human Ss were injected with bipolar fine-wire electrodes into the tibialis anterior muscle. A start light indicated the onset of a trial. If Ss activated a single motor unit, a correct light appeared. With no additional feedback, individuals learned to isolate and control a single motor unit within 500 trials and demonstrated significant improvement during a relearning series.

motor units
feedback
conditioning

G 11   Petajan, Jack H., and Philip, Betty Anne: Frequency control of motor unit action potentials. *Electroencephalogr Clin Neurophysiol, 27:*66, 1969.

The onset interval of the single motor unit action potential (MUAP), defined as the longest regular interval of firing at minimal effort, was determined for various skeletal muscles. Intervals found were 132 ±32 msec, mean for all limb and girdle muscles, and 86 ±29 msec, mean for all facial muscles studied. Distal muscles in the upper extremities had significantly longer onset intervals than did proximal shoulder girdle and lower extremity muscles. In studying single units, awareness of the level of effort seemed more critical to the control of firing rate than did movement. The recruitment interval was less variable than onset interval, with a mean of 90 ±19 msec for limb and girdle muscles and 40 ±16 msec for facial muscles. The range of control, expressed as the difference in frequency of a MUAP between onset and recruitment relative to the recruitment frequency, decreased with cephalocaudal location of the muscle from 0.55 for the frontalis muscle to 0.29 for the biceps femoris muscle.

motor units
learned
control
visual
feedback

G 12   Petajan, J.H.: Motor unit frequency control in facial neuropathy. *Electroencephalogr Clin Neurophysiol, 27:*718, 1969.

Using audiovisual feedback of motor unit action potentials, the ability of eleven patients with facial neuropathy to control firing rate was examined. The following mean interspike intervals were determined when firing rate was (1) at its lowest most stable level, onset interval and (2) increased to a level at which recruitment of a second motor unit occurred, a recruitment interval. Mean onset interval was decreased while mean recruitment interval was unchanged. In

motor unit
activity
applications
facial neuro-
pathy
audio/visual
feedback

20 percent of orbicularis oris and 12 percent of frontalis motor units studied, a second motor unit was not recruited despite high firing rates while in normal subjects recruitment always occurs. The findings can be explained by a loss of large motor units as would be produced by ischemia or pressure block. Regardless of the number of motor units lost in any territory, if recruitment can occur, then it occurs when the primary unit reaches a critical firing rate, the normal recruitment interval.

G 13   Scully, Hugh E., and Basmajian, John V.: Motor-unit training and influence of manual skill. *Psychophysiology, 5:*625, 1969.

Employing the recently devised technique of training conscious control over individual motor units of skeletal muscles, the influence of prior manual skills was tested in twenty-nine young adults. Twenty-five subjects succeeded with a median training-time of twenty minutes. The manually skilled took longer to train single motor units than the less skilled (at the .05 level of significance). The initial period of time to isolate a single motor unit is shorter than to train it to react on command. The technique offers a novel and useful method of testing the acquisition of a fundamental motor skill and factors which influence it. Further exploration is justified because trained motor units are now being harnessed to drive myoelectrical man-machine cybernetic devices.

conscious control motor skills

G 14   Simard, Therese G., and Basmajian, John V.: Methods in training the conscious control of motor units. *Arch Phys Med, 48:*12, 1967.

Electromyography can be used to demonstrate that the finest level of control of the motor system can be obtained by adequate training. This paper deals with the development and testing of a dynamic method of training motor units in skeletal muscle. Techniques are based upon methods of control over the frequency of motor units and the inhibition of undesired activity. The training procedures include production of sets of motor unit potentials during a preliminary

training techniques audio/visual feedback learned control

period of training assisted by specific command-signals. Subjects are provided with auditory and visual cues of the motor unit activity through electromyography combined with innate proprioceptive impulses. They are trained to maintain single motor units consciously. Certain conditions are shown to be necessary for optimal results: a calm atmosphere, clear-cut commands, mandatory rest periods, a step-wise training schedule, and finally, highly competent direction of the training procedure.

G 15 Simard, T.G., and Ladd, H.W.: Pre-orthotic training. *Am J Phys Med, 48:*301, 1969. (Copyright 1969 by the Williams & Wilkins Co., Baltimore.)

Neuromuscular training can be improved by electromyographic methods. This is particularly important in view of the development of specialized myoelectric orthotic appliances. The present study deals with the functional evaluation of the three segments of the same muscle, namely the trapezius, and the training of control over isolated motor units in each of these segments. A limited number of training sessions was sufficient to obtain individual, simultaneous and consecutive control of motor units in the individual muscle segments. The successive application of some combinations of segmental control during assisted movements of the ipsilateral extremity was observed. This suggests the possibility of multiple function based on one or more functioning muscles.

pre-orthotic
EMG
training
segmental
control
multiple
function

G 16 Simard, Therese: Fine sensorimotor control in healthy children. An electromyographic study. *Pediatrics, 43:*1035, 1969.

To establish methods of training the voluntary control of the activity of a single motor unit on children (previously reported on adults), a series of electromyographic experiences was undertaken. Healthy children from three to twelve years of age were trained to gradually and consciously suppress the neuromuscular activity and to isolate and maintain in a repetitive activity a single motor unit chosen into the rhomboid muscle. The degree of motor control was verified qualitatively and quantitatively with no body move-

training
techniques
children
learned
control
rehabilita-
tion

ments and during the activity of drinking. Inhibition and maintenance of a single motor unit in the activity during drinking were successful. This was most evident among the seven- to nine-year old children. The children demonstrated the same motor ability as adults, and the variation between age groups consists mainly in the duration of attention span. The observation of doublets with young normals is at least similar in frequency as with adults.

17 Sutton, Dwight, and Kimm, Joseph: Alcohol effects on human motor unit reaction time. *Physiol Behav, 5:*889, 1970.

Studied control of single motor unit activity in five 25 to 39-year-old human Ss (59-73 kg.) by requiring a single spike discharge to a flash of light and recording the resultant (RT). Experimental sessions without alcohol were followed by ingestion of 20 cm³ 95 percent ethyl alcohol and retesting the RT performance. Median latencies were slower following intake of alcohol; however, the capacity to respond as defined simply by the ability to produce a motor unit spike was not altered. EMG RT responding also slowed following alcohol, although to a lesser degree than single motor unit RT.

alcohol
visual
*   feedback*
EMG reac-
*   tion time*

18 Sutton, D., and Kimm, J.: Reaction time of motor units in biceps and triceps. *Exp Neurol, 23:*503, 1969.

Human subjects can gain sufficient control over the firing of a single spike from motor units in biceps and triceps to perform effectively in a reaction time experiment. A comparison of reaction time latencies of the voluntarily produced single motor unit discharges in biceps and triceps reveals stable differences. Triceps units usually have shorter reaction time latencies than do biceps units. Variability of single unit reaction time is less for triceps units than for biceps units. Comparison with gross EMG performance shows consistently greater unit reaction time latency regardless of muscle of origin. Intermittent loss of control over motor unit occurs in the reaction time task.

learned
*   control*
reaction
*   time*
EMG per-
*   formance*

19 Tanji, J., and Kato, M.: Volitionally controlled single motor unit discharges and cortical motor potentials in human subjects. *Brain Res, 29:*343, 1971.

In the present experiments, attempts were made to single out motor units consciously, and also to investigate whether cortical motor potentials (MP) accompanying volitionally controlled single motor unit discharges could be recorded. When the thumb was bent gently, opponence pollicis muscle gently, after the tungsten electrode was introduced, there appeared several kinds of motor unit potential. The subject was then asked to discharge a particular single motor unit on the command of the experimenter. Summated EEG changes were studied on thirty-two units among the seventy-three singled out motor units. The analysis of cortical motor potentials accompanying a key-pressing movement with the thumb, in other words accompanying contraction of whole muscles, was performed for the sake of comparison just before or after the single-unit analysis. The cortical motor potential was recognized in all twelve subjects. It was found that the cortical motor potential related to discharge of a single motor unit is about the same size as that related to the contraction of whole muscles. Isolation of a particular motor unit—a particular alpha motoneuron—may be performed either in such supraspinal structures as the motor cortex or in the spinal cord or at both levels. The relatively large cortical motor potential accompanying a single motor unit discharge, as described above, may suggest that cerebral mechanisms play some important role in singling out a motor unit.

motor units
voluntary
control
cortical
potentials

G 20 Tanji, J., and Kato, M.: Recruitment of motor units in voluntary contraction of a finger muscle in man. *Exp Neurol, 40:*759, 1973.

The recruitment of motor units during voluntary isometric contraction was studied in the abductor digiti minimi muscle of thirteen human subjects trained to increase tension in this muscle almost linearly from zero to maximum. The subjects matched the output of a transducer, measuring the tension in this muscle, to a linear target ramp voltage. The target ramps varied in duration from two to ten seconds. When speed of contraction was kept constant there was considerable degree of constancy in the tension at which individual motor units were recruited. The recruitment order of motor

recruitment
conscious
control
muscle
tension

units, therefore, appeared to be determined at repeated contractions. However, the order was not rigidly fixed among units whose tension range of recruitment is overlapped especially among those units recruited at medium to strong contraction. When the contraction was performed more quickly the motor units were recruited at lower tension. Larger population of units were recruited at lower tension range: 45.8 percent of units were recruited before the tension attained 20 percent of maximum tension. There is a tendency for motor units with larger action potentials to be recruited at higher tension.

G 21   Thysell, Richard V.: Reaction time of single motor units. *Psychophysiology, 6:*174, 1969.

Four studies of the simple reaction time (RT) of single motor units (MU) are reported. In each study S was first trained to control the firing of a MU by observing visual and auditory feedback of MU action potentials detected by an implanted electrode. Training was followed by one or more RT testing sessions. Experiment I demonstrated that MU RT was about equal to that of a comparable Overt RT and suggested that the distribution of MU RTs was bimodal. Experiments II and III confirmed that the distribution was bimodal and eliminated the hypotheses that the bimodality was due to equipment artifacts or to S's switching between the defined visual and potentially confounding auditory reaction cues. Experiment IV tested, and rejected, the hypothesis that the bimodality was due to S's alternating between brightness and pattern information processing on RT trials. In all four experiments the bimodality was defined by a paucity of responses in the 175-199 msec interval. This fact was related to the findings that delayed auditory feedback has its maximal disruptive effect at 180 msec, and that the limit of the psychological refractory period seems to be between 175 and 200 msec. Further experiments relating these findings were suggested.

learned control audio/visual feedback reaction time

G 22   Trombly, Catherine A.: Myoelectric control of orthotic devices: For the severely paralyzed. *Am J Occup Ther, 22:*385, 1968.

Myoelectric control of upper-extremity prostheses is a clinical reality in Russia, England and Canada. The application of these principles are relevant to the control of orthotic devices by the severely paralyzed spinal cord injured patient. This relevance has been explored by the Ampersand Group for Medical Engineering in cooperation with the Engineering Design Center of Case Institute of Technology and has been found to be feasible. This paper defines and describes the principles of myoelectric control. Some clinical evaluation and training techniques involved in the application of myoelectrically controlled devices to quadriplegic patients are described.

EMG feedback prosthetic control discussion

Pre-1965 References

MUSCLE SYSTEM

Bair, J.H.: Development of voluntary control. *Psychol Rev, 8:*474, 1901.

Baitsch, V.H.: Sex and lateral differences in electrodermographic levels. *Confin Neurol, 14:*88, 1954.

Barber, T.X., and Hahn, K.W.: Hypnotic induction and relaxation: An experimental study. *Arch Gen Psychiatry, 8:*295, 1963.

Bartoshuk, A.K.: Electromyographic gradients as indicants of motivation. *Can J Psychol, 9:*215, 1955.

Basmajian, J.V.: Chacun peut apprendre a commander une par une ses cellules nerveuses motrices. *Sci Progr: La Nature, 3347:*89, 1964.

Basmajian, J.V.: Conscious control of single nerve cells. *New Scientist, 369:*662, 1963.

Basmajian, J.V.: Control and training of individual motor units. *Science, 141:*440, 1963.

Basmajian, J.V., and Stecko, G.A.: A new bipolar indwelling electrode for electromyography. *J Appl Physiol, 17:*849, 1963.

Carlsoo, S., and Edfeld, A.W.: Attempts at muscle control with visual and auditory impulses as auxiliary stimuli. *Scand J Psychol, 4:*231, 1963.

Courtis, F.A.: Relations between muscular tension and performance. *Psychol Bull, 39:*347, 1942.

Davis, F.H., and Malmo, R.B.: Electromyographic recording during interview. *Am J Psychiat, 107:*908, 1951.

Davis, R.C., Lundervold, A., and Miller, J.D.: An exploration of somatic response patterns: Stimulus and sex differences. *J Comp Physiol Psychol, 50:*44, 1957.

Dickel, H.A., Dixon, H.H., Stoner, W., and Shanklin, J.G.: Electromyographic studies on patients with chronic headaches. *Northwest Med, 57:*1458, 1958.

Goldstein, I.B., Grinker, R.R., Heath, H.A., Oken, D., and Shipman, W.G.: Study in psychophysiology of muscle tension: I. Response specificity. *Arch Gen Psychiat, 11:*322, 1964.

Harrison, V.F., and Mortensen, O.A.: Identification and voluntary control of single motor unit activity in the tibialis anterior muscle. *Anat Rec, 144:*109, 1962.

Hefferline, R.F.: The role of proprioception in the control of behavior. *Trans NY Acad Sci, 20:*739, 1958.

Hefferline, R.F., Keenan, B., and Harford, R.A.: Escape and avoidance conditioning in human subjects without their observation of the response. *Science, 136:*1338, 1959.

Hefferline, R.F., and Perera, T.B.: Proprioceptive discrimination of a covert operant without its observation by the subject. *Science, 139:*834, 1963.

Hoefer, P.F.A., and Putnam, T.J.: Action potentials of muscles in normal subjects. *Arch Neurol Psychiatry, 42:*201, 1939.

Jacobson, A., Kales, A., Lehman, D., and Hoedmaker, F.S.: Muscle tonus in human subjects during sleep and dreaming. *Exp Neurol, 10:*418, 1964.

Jacobson, E.: The effects of daily rest without training to relax on muscular tonus. *Am J Psychol, 55:*248, 1942.

Jacobson, E.: Electrical measurements concerning muscular contraction (tonus) and the cultivation of relaxation in man. *Am J Physiol, 107:*230, 1954.

Jacobson, E.: Electrical measurements of neuromuscular states during mental activities: V. Variation of specific muscles contracting during imagination. *Am J Physiol, 96:*115, 1931.

Jacobson, E.: Electrophysiology of mental activities. *Am J Psychol, 44:*677, 1932.

Jacobson, E.: Neuromuscular controls in man: methods of self-direction in health and disease. *Am J Psychol, 68:*549, 1955.

Jacobson, E.: Voluntary relaxation of the esophagus. *Am J Physiol, 72:*387, 1925.

Lindsley, D.B.: Electrical activity of human motor units during voluntary contraction. *Am J Physiol, 114:*90, 1936.

Lovaas, O.I.: The relationship of induced muscular tension, tension level, and manifest anxiety in learning. *J Exp Psychol, 59:*145, 1960.

Lundervold, A.J.S.: Electromyographic investigations of tense and relaxed subjects. *J Nerv Ment Dis, 115:*512, 1952.

Luthe, W.: Autogenic training: method, research and application in medicine. *Am J Psychother, 17:*174, 1963.

Maizelis, M.R.: Importance of a stereotype of eating, muscular activity, and sleeping in the regulation of physiological functions. *Pavlov J Higher Nerv Activity, 6:*845, 1959.

Malmo, R.B., Shagass, C., and Davis, J.F.: Electromyographic studies of muscular tension in psychiatric patients under stress. *J Clin Exp Psychopath, 12:*45, 1951.

Malmo, R.B., and Smith, A.A.: Forehead tension and motor irregularities in psychoneurotic patients under stress. *J Personality, 23:*391, 1955.

Martin, I.: Levels of muscle activity in psychiatric patients. *Acta Psychol (Amst), 12:*326, 1956.

Meyer, D.R., and Noble, C.: Summation of manifest anxiety and muscular tension. *J Exp Psychol, 55:*599, 1958.

Pascal, G.R.: The effect of relaxation upon recall. *Am J Psychol, 62:*32, 1949.

Penfield, W.: Mechanism of voluntary movement. *Brain, 77:*1, 1954.

Pierce, D.S., and Wagman, I.H.: A method of recording from single muscle fibres of motor units in human skeletal muscle. *J Appl Physiol, 19:*366, 1964.

Pishkin, V., and Wolfgang, A.: Electromyographic gradients in concept identification with numbers of irrelevant dimensions. *J Clin Psychol, 20:*61, 1964.

Sainsbury, P., and Gibson, J.G.: Symptoms of anxiety and tension and the accompanying physiological changes in the muscular system. *J Neurol Neurosurg Psychiatry, 17:*216, 1954.

Scripture, E.W., Smith, T.L., and Brown, E.M.: On the education of muscular control and power. *Stud Yale Psychol Lab, 2:*114, 1894.

Shagass, C., and Malmo, R.B.: Psychodynamic themes and localized muscular tension during psychotherapy. *Psychosom Med, 16:*295, 1954.

Shaw, W.A.: The relation of muscular action-potentials to imaginal weight lifting. *Arch Psychol, 35:5*, 1940.

Sills, F.D., and Olson, A.L.: Action potentials in unexercised arm when opposite arm is exercised. *Res Quart, 29:213*, 1958.

Smith, K.U.: Special Review: Sensory feedback analysis in medical research. II. Spatial organization of neurobehavioral systems. *Am J Phys Med, 3:49*, 1964.

Smith, O.C.: Action potentials from single motor units in voluntary contraction. *Am J Physiol, 108:629*, 1934.

Timofeev, N.N.: On the comparative physiology of exteroceptive and interoceptive conditioned reflexes. *The Central Nervous System and Human Behavior,* translated from the Russian Medical Literature. Bethesda, Russian Scientific Translation Program, 1959.

Wallerstein, H.: An electromyographic study of attentive listening. *Can J Psychol, 8:* 228, 1954.

Whatmore, G.B.: A neurophysiologic view of functional disorders. *Psychosomatics, 3:* 371, 1962.

Whatmore, G.B., and Ellis, R.M., Jr.: Further neurophysiologic aspects of depressed states: an electromyographic study. *Arch Gen Psychiatry, 6:243*, 1962.

Whatmore, G.B., and Ellis, R.M., Jr.: Some motor aspects of schizophrenia: An EMG study. *Am J Psychiat, 114:882*, 1958.

Whatmore, G.B., and Ellis, R.M., Jr.: Some neurophysiologic aspects of depressed states: An electromyographic study. *Arch Gen Psychiatry, 1:70*, 1959.

Whatmore, G.B., and Ellis, R.M., Jr.: Some neurophysiologic aspects of schizophrenia: An electromyographic study. *Am J Psychiat, 120:1166*, 1964.

Williams, J.G.L.: Use of a resonance technique to measure muscle activity in neurotic and schizophrenic patients. *Psychosom Med, 26:20*, 1964.

Wissler, C., and Richardson, W.: Diffusion of the motor impulse. *Psychol Rev, 7:29*, 1900.

Wolpert, E.A.: Studies in psychophysiology of dreams: II. An electromyographic study of dreaming. *Arch Gen Psychiatry, 2:231*, 1960.

Yates, D.H.: Relaxation in psychotherapy. *J Gen Psychol, 34:213*, 1946.

DESCRIPTOR INDEX — MUSCLE SYSTEM

PART V

EEG

INSTRUMENTS AND ANALYSIS

A 1   Boudrot, R.: An alpha detection and feedback control system. *Psychophysiology, 9:*461, 1972.

An alpha rhythm detecting and stimulus feedback display (visual and auditory) system is described. Parameters of the system can be chosen to match the psychological and behavioral processes with the EEG index in the time domain. Clocks, counters, computers, etc. are also controlled by the system which is designed for maximum flexibility.

instruments
alpha
   feedback

A 2   Goodman, David: ALFIE: Collection of EEG alpha under feedback control using time series analysis. *Psychophysiology, 10:*437, 1973.

Methods of data analysis for periods of alpha and no-alpha frequencies originating in the EEG are discussed. A package of computer programs written for a laboratory computer which performs this analysis, retaining and displaying time series information, is described.

alpha
   feedback
data
   analysis
habituation
orienting
   response

A 3   Pasquali, E.: A relay controlled by alpha rhythm. *Psychophysiology, 6:*207, 1969.

An electrical circuit energizing a relay is described, together with the response to a rectangular burst of alpha waves. This circuit is useful when a certain amount of delay in deenergizing the relay was purposely introduced so that the relay might remain continuously energized by closely spaced alpha bursts. Fundamentally the circuit action is that of a leaky integrator whose output controls a relay with different energizing and deenergizing levels.

instruments
alpha
   feedback

A 4   Pfeifer, E.A., and Usselman, L.: A versatile amplitude ana-
       lyzer for EEG signals to provide feedback stimuli to the sub-
       ject. *Med Biol Eng, 8:209,* 1970.

       The technical note describes an amplitude analyzer which   *instruments*
       provides feedback cues to subjects in studies of EEG modi-   *EEG*
       fication by feedback methods. This versatile device can be   *feedback*
       used with a variety of peripheral equipment such as band-
       pass filters, logic modules, displays, etc., and one can change
       the experiment easily without altering the electronic cir-
       cuitry. The unit can be easily assembled since it is composed
       of commercially available circuit modules.

A 5   Surwillo, Walter W.: The contingent negative variation:
       Some methodological problems in the recording of shifts in
       steady potentials. *Psychophysiology, 8:229,* 1971.

       The various methods that have been used in recording of   *CNV*
       the Contingent Negative Variation (CNV) were examined   *steady*
       with reference to developing selection criteria. Findings re-   *potentials*
       vealed that chopper amplifiers with condenser-coupled input
       circuits and DC amplifiers with zero-suppression circuits be-
       tween stages showed shifts in output level which were the
       result of changes in resistance of the input circuit. As these
       artifacts were not negligible with reference to commonly-re-
       ported CNV amplitudes, it was concluded that the two
       methods should be avoided in recording of low-level shifts
       in steady potentials like the CNV.

PSYCHOLOGIC CORRELATES
OF EEG ACTIVITY

B 1   Berlyne, D.E., and McDonnell, P.: Effects of stimulus complexity and incongruity on duration of EEG desynchronization. *Electroencephalogr Clin Neurophysiol, 18*:156, 1965.

(1) Human subjects were exposed to a sequence of visual patterns, each shown twice consecutively. Exposures lasted three seconds and were separated by intervals of fifteen seconds. The patterns belonged to eight categories, representing various complexity and incongruity variables. (2) More complex or incongruous patterns evoked, on the average, longer desynchronization than less complex or incongruous patterns (6.3 seconds as compared with 5.8 seconds). The difference was found to be statistically significant when the data for all eight categories were examined together and when the data for four of the categories (representing Irregularity of Arrangement, Amount of Material, Incongruity and Random Redistribution) were examined separately. (3) No significant difference appeared between first and second presentations of the same patterns or between subjects who were extrinsically motivated (told to attend carefully for the sake of a later recognition test) and not extrinsically motivated, and none of the interactions were significant. There was, however, a significant tendency for desynchronization to grow shorter as the session continued. (4) The findings are discussed in relation to theoretical and experimental work on motivational aspects of exploratory behavior and related phenomena.

EEG desynchronization
visual patterns
motivation
exploratory behavior

B 2   Darrow, Chester W., and Hicks, Ronald G.: Interarea electroencephalographic phase relationships following sensory and ideational stimuli. *Psychophysiology, 1*:337, 1965.

Moment-by-moment changes in the phase or relative timing of electroencephalographic (EEG) patterns in different brain areas show great lability and psychological responsiveness and are studied as possible correlates of peripheral psychophysiological reaction. Relative leading, lagging and in-phase relationships between EEGs of different brain areas are automatically recorded, and stimuli classed as simple sensory, indifferent-ideational, disturbing-ideational, and adaption routines are employed. EEG leading in anterior and central brain areas is found to characterize conditions of arousal. Rapid diphasic reversals of interarea EEG phase relationship during mental activity is possibly symptomatic of interaction between brain areas. Effects of familiarity and adaptation are evaluated.

EEG phase topography ideation mental activity adaptation

B 3   Galbraith, G.C., London, P., Leibovitz, M.P., Cooper, L.M., and Hart, J.T.: EEG and hypnotic susceptibility. *J Comp Physiol Psychol, 72*:125, 1970.

Fifty-nine subjects (twenty-four male and thirty-five female) were given the Harvard Group Susceptibility Scale (HGSS) and recorded for resting EEG. Autospectrum and cross spectrum analyses of the Oz, Cz, Fz and T3 leads of the EEG revealed a total of 20 EEG variables which were predictive of HGSS scores. The overall amplitude of the EEG was higher in the subjects with high HGSS scores with alpha showing the greatest overall difference. Due to the variability of alpha amplitude, however, it was not among the 5 variables accounting for the variance in HGSS. The 5 most important variables were: 5 Hz activity in Oz with eyes open, 5 Hz activity in the Oz-Cz pair with eyes open, 7 Hz activity in Oz with eyes closed, 6 Hz activity in Oz with eyes open, and 8 Hz activity in Oz-Cz with eyes open.

hypnotic suscepti- bility EEG patterns alpha patterns theta spectral analysis

B 4   Galin, David, and Ornstein, Robert: Lateral specialization of cognitive mode: An EEG study. *Psychophysiology, 9*:412, 1972.

We have studied EEG asymmetry in normal subjects during verbal and spatial tasks. Recordings were made from the left and right temporal and parietal areas, and the ratios of

EEG symmetry cognition

average power (1-35 Hz) in homologous leads T_4/T_3 and P_4/P_3 were computed. This ratio (right over left) was greater in the verbal tasks than in the spatial tasks. With this measure we have been able to distinguish between these two cognitive modes as they occur in normal subjects, using simple scalp recording.

lateral speciali- zation

B 5   Heinemann, L.G., and Emrich, H.: Alpha activity during inhibitory brain processes. *Psychophysiology, 7*:442, 1970.

Three studies involving quantitative changes in alpha activity are reported. Sixteen normal volunteers were shown neutral or emotionally provoking words appearing with slowly increasing intensity on a frosted glass pane in a darkened room. A differential reaction was observed, i.e. with emotional words there was a higher alpha percentage from the time before the Ss perceived the light until after they could read the word. In the second study, ten normal volunteers were stimulated with closed eyes for two-second periods of diffuse light after the hypnotic suggestion of blindness. Compared with the prestimulus interval there was an average increase in alpha amplitude, whereas the control condition showed the usual alpha decrease during stimulation. In the third study, thirty-two chronic schizophrenic patients were given a Phenothiazine derivative over three months after a two-month placebo period. Ratings of alpha activity as to occipital amplitude, group length, topographical extension, and occurrence in synchronous groups showed a progressive increase from the placebo condition to the third month.

emotion verbal stimuli alpha abundance hypnosis schizo- phrenia

B 6   Johnson, L., Lubin, A., Naitoh, P., Nute, C., and Austin, M.: Spectral analysis of the EEG of dominant and nondominant (alpha) subjects during waking and sleeping. *Electroencephalogr Clin Neurophysiol, 26*:361, 1969.

EEG spectral analysis of the left parietal lead (P3) was carried out on nine high alpha and four low alpha subjects. A 0.2 c/sec resolution interval was used on analysis periods of one minute. The most prominent feature of the spectra was a delta peak at about 1 c/sec consistently present for all

alpha dominance wakefulness sleep spectral analysis

subjects during waking as well as sleeping. The intensity of   *generators*
this delta peak increased monotonically from waking
through sleep stages 1, 2, 3 and 4 with stage REM intensity
being equal to stage 1 intensity. All subjects had a sigma
peak at about 13 c/sec during sleep stage 2, and a majority
had a similar peak in stages 3 and 4. The average spectra
show a sigma peak in all sleep stages, but none during waking. There were no consistent theta or beta peaks during
waking or any stage of sleep. The high alpha group showed
an alpha peak in waking at about 10 c/sec which decreased
to about 9 c/sec during stage 1 and stage REM. During
waking and all stages of sleep, they generally had a higher
intensity and higher variability than the low alpha subjects
for all frequencies of the spectrum. High alpha subjects had
more frequency peaks during stages 1 and REM. The two
groups have very similar spectra in sleep stages 2, 3 and 4.
The waking intensities of the delta, theta and alpha frequency bands have significant positive correlations with their
respective intensities during sleep. Waking intensity of the
alpha band never correlated with delta intensity during
waking or sleeping. These results favor the hypothesis of
constant frequency generators for delta and sigma with an
increase in energy during sleep; but they also fit the hypothesis of an alpha generator which decreases in frequency
and energy during sleep. The single, best discriminator of
waking and the sleep stages was delta. Alpha and sigma intensities add to the discrimination. However, stage 1 and
REM have very similar spectral profiles for all subjects. For
the low alpha subjects, waking, stage 1, and stage REM have
spectra that are almost indistinguishable.

B 7   Klinger, Eric, Gregoire, Kenneth C., and Barta, Steven G.:
Physiological correlates of mental activity: Eye movements,
alpha, and heart rate during imagining, suppression, concentration, search and choice. *Psychophysiology, 10:*471, 1973.

Rapid eye movements (REMs), EEG alpha, and tonic heart   *mental*
rate (HR) were measured during six types of cognitive tasks   *activity*
—imagining a liked person, suppressing thoughts of the per-   *alpha*
son, searching one's mind for alternative solutions, arith-   *abundance*
metic involving little concentration, problems involving   *eye move-*
                                                              ments

high concentration, and choosing a preferred activity. The latter three required verbalization, the former three did not. Only suppression and search did not differ significantly from each other on at least one physiological variable. Imagining, suppression, and search yielded few REMs, high alpha, and low HR. High concentration yielded many REMs, low alpha, and high HR. Choice yielded many REMs, low alpha, and intermediate HR. Low concentration yielded few REMs, low alpha, and high HR. Suppression produced somewhat less alpha than imagining but did not differ significantly in REMs.

HR

B 8   London, P., Hart, J.T., and Leibovitz, M.P.: EEG alpha rhythms and susceptibility to hypnosis. *Nature (Lond), 219:* 71, 1968.

One hundred and twenty-five subjects (sixteen to sixty-one years old) were given the Harvard Group Suggestibility Scale (HGSS), and recorded for EEG to determine the relationships between the two measures. EEG alpha incidence was determined for eyes closed recordings, while the subjects were resting and while they were producing mental images. HGSS scores were separated into four categories for analysis on the basis of percentile ranks. An analysis of variance showed a significant relationship between alpha incidence and HGSS scores in the resting and mental imagery conditions.

hypnotic suscepti- bility
alpha abundance
mental imagery

B 9   Lubin, A., Johnson, L.C., and Austin, M.T.: Discrimination among states of consciousness using EEG spectra. *Psychophysiology, 6:*122, 1969.

EEG recordings were made during waking (W) and the five sleep stages (REM, 1, 2, 3, and 4) on thirteen young adult males. For each stage, one-minute sections of the parietal EEG trace were digitized and subjected to Fourier analysis. The resulting spectral intensities were divided into five frequency bands: delta, theta, alpha, sigma and beta. Linear discriminators for all six stages were calculated using stepwise multiple regression. The overall percent agreement with visual scoring was very poor, ranging from zero for

wakefulness
sleep
computer analysis
EEG activity

stage 3 to 91 percent for stage 4. Linear discrimination between pairs of stages yielded slightly better results, but stages 1 and REM were indistinguishable. Delta is the best overall discriminator, increasing significantly through stages W, 1, 2, 3, and 4. Sigma is unique to sleep and is highest for stage 2. Theta is unimportant and beta plays no role at all. Spectral analysis of the parietal EEG lead is not sufficient to differentiate among the six states of consciousness studied here. The use of detectors for such phasic events as eye movement and K-complexes might aid sleep stage discrimination considerably.

B 10 MacNeilage, Peter F.: Changes in electroencephalogram and other physiological measures during serial mental performance. *Psychophysiology, 2:*344, 1966.

This study attempted to answer two questions: (1) Can electroencephalogram (EEG) amplitude changes be related to specific moment-to-moment changes in task performance? (2) To what extent are EEG changes related to changes in other indices of activation? Physiological responses were recorded from twenty subjects during twelve alternately fast and slow trials of a paced auditory serial addition task and three writing trials involving similar responses. Trial-by-trial results showed that EEG amplitude usually tended to covary with other physiological functions in a manner expected from activation theory. All physiological levels decreased during the session but became increasingly sensitive to differences in task difficulty. Within trials there was some concordance between alpha amplitude levels and other physiological levels, but exceptions to this trend and further analysis of palmar conductance patterns suggested that consideration of differential sensitivities of the individual measures to behavioral events might be more profitable than an activation theory approach. The only relation between EEG changes and specific behavioral events was the tendency for alpha and beta to block during motor responses.

task performance
activation
mental work
EEG
alpha amplitude
differential sensitivity
motor responses

B 11 MacNeilage, Peter F.: EEG amplitude changes during different cognitive processes involving similar stimuli and responses. *Psychophysiology, 2:*280, 1966.

In order to investigate the effects on electroencephalographic (EEG) amplitude of cognitive processes, as distinct from direct effects of sensory stimulation and motor response, subjects were given three different tasks in which the stimuli were always similar sets of spoken numbers and the responses were always written numbers. In response to sixty-one regularly occurring, randomly ordered, single-digit numbers, seven Ss wrote, on successive trials, (1) the sum of every four consecutive numbers, (2) every fourth number, and (3) every "7" and "9" heard. Since the physical stimuli were the same and the movements of response were similar for the three tasks, intertask pattern differences in EEG alpha and beta amplitude would presumably be due to differences in the cognitive processes required in the tasks. No differences due to cognitive factors were found. All short-term variations in both alpha and beta appeared related to widespread effects of response and preparation for response. Preresponse effects seemed related to motor set which was distinguished from attentional factors. The results suggest the necessity for a greater emphasis on motor effects in EEG studies.

cognitive activity
EEG amplitude
mental tasks
motor effects

B 12 McKee, G., Humphrey, B., and McAdam, D.W.: Scaled lateralization of alpha activity during linguistic and musical tasks. *Psychophysiology, 10:*441, 1973.

We have studied relative bilateral alpha activity over temporal-parietal sites in normal human Ss while they were engaged in either a musical task or one of three linguistic tasks of varying difficulty. Left/right alpha ratios were highest for the muscial tasks, and tended to decrease progressively with increasingly difficult linguistic tasks.

bilateral alpha
music task
linguistic tasks
lateral specialization

B 13 Orr, William C., and Stern, John A.: The relationship between stimulus information, reaction time, and cortical habituation. *Psychophysiology, 7:*475, 1970.

This investigation was an attempt to study systematically the effects of uncertainty, or stimulus information, on habituation rate. Subjects were randomly assigned to one of three conditions varying in uncertainty. EEG alpha desynchrony duration, electrodermal conductance change, and reaction

alpha desynchronization
orienting response

time were the dependent measures. The results showed un-   *habituation*
certainty to have no significant effect on any of the neurophysiological measures. There was a significant effect on the
reaction time measure. There was no significant correlation
between the EEG and electrodermal response measures, nor
was there any correlation between either of these measures
and reaction time. Results indicated that habituation could
occur in the presence of cortical and behavioral arousal. It
was concluded that information may be most meaningfully
measured behaviorally and that habituation parameters are
dependent upon the physiological system being measured.

B 14   Peacock, Samuel M.: Some considerations of motor and electrical activity in states of diminished awareness. *Exp Med
Surg, 27:*169, 1969.

Presents a review of the literature dealing with electrical   *EEG
activity of the brain, various phases of sleep, EEG and be-   activity*
havioral arousal, EMG findings, and effects of barbiturates.   *sleep
                                                                  arousal
                                                                  EMG
                                                                  drugs*

B 15   Stanford, R.G., and Lovin, C.: EEG alpha activity and ESP
performance. *J Am Soc Psychical Res, 64:*375, 1970.

Thirty male, college-age students were each given two   *ESP*
recognition runs using the standard ESP symbols. For several   *alpha*
minutes prior to the ESP testing, and throughout the ESP   *frequency*
testing, monopolar right occipital EEG (referenced to the
right ear lobe) was recorded. The frequency (Hz) of the
alpha rhythms recorded during the pretest (relaxation)
period correlated −.41 with the total ESP score (P < .04, 2-
tailed) . The frequency of alpha recorded during ESP testing
did not correlate significantly with ESP scoring. Change in
alpha frequency from pretest (relaxation) period to the ESP
testing correlated +.51 with the total ESP score (P < .01, 2-
tailed) . Such findings suggest that there may be an optimal
level of arousal for ESP performance in a discrete-calling
task. Thus, subjects who relax during the pretest period but
who are somewhat aroused by the actual testing seem to do
best. Additionally, correlations are reported between the per-

centage of time alpha is present in the record and ESP performance. These latter correlations are, however, regarded by the authors as inconclusive in view of difficulties which arise in using the measure of alpha percentage employed in this and certain earlier work.

B 16   Surwillo, Walter W.: Human reaction time and period of the EEG in relation to development. *Psychophysiology, 8:468,* 1971.

Simple auditory reaction time (RT) and an auditory RT task requiring a disjunctive reaction were investigated in a group of 110 boys aged forty-six to 207 months. Electroencephalograms (EEGs) were recorded during actual performance of these tasks to determine the extent to which differences in RT associated with development could be accounted for by developmental changes in the EEG. Measures of average EEG period were derived from peaks and troughs of all waves recorded in the time interval between stimulus and response of each trial. Results confirmed previous findings of a significant relationship between RT, σRT, and development. RT and σRT followed a reciprocal power-law function with age, and hence both measures decreased more rapidly in the earlier years. Choice RT showed a more rapid decline with increasing age than simple RT. Correlations were high, with log simple RT versus log Age = −.874, and log choice RT versus log Age = −.861. Developmental changes in EEG period could account for only a small fraction of these high correlations. The possible role of EEG half waves as time quanta in information processing was discussed in relation to development.

EEG development
EEG period
reaction time
children

B 17   Surwillo, Walter W.: Word-association latency in normal children during development and the relation of brain electrical activity. *Psychophysiology, 10:254,* 1973.

Electroencephalograms (EEGs) were recorded in a group of thirty-seven normal boys aged ninety-two to 206 months during performance of a word-association task. Ss were instructed to say the first word that came to mind, as quickly as possible, following presentation of each of eighteen stimulus words

word association task
children
association
reaction time

that were familiar to young children. Word-association latency, or the associative reaction time (RT), was analyzed only for trials in which a stimulus word evoked the same response word. Younger children were found to have significantly longer associative RTs than older children, with associative RT decreasing with increasing age according to a reciprocal power-law function. Comparison of this function with similar functions relating simple and disjunctive RT to age, suggested that the longer word-association latencies of children could not be attributed merely to developmental differences in nonverbal processes or processes concerned primarily with speed of responding. Sufficient EEG data for analysis were available for only five of the stimulus-response word combinations, and for these data, average EEG period from the left hemisphere was significantly different from (longer than) EEG period from the right hemisphere. Results of a partial-correlation analysis showed that left-hemisphere differences in EEG period between Ss can account, in part, for the relationship between associative RT and age, while right-hemisphere differences in EEG period cannot. Although this suggested a hypothesis which ascribes the long word-association latencies of young children to age-associated differences in EEG period of the left hemisphere, evidence was inconclusive.

hemispheric differences development

B 18 Tizard, B.: Evoked changes in EEG and electrodermal activity during the waking and sleeping states. *Electroencephalogr Clin Neurophysiol, 20:*122, 1966.

EEG and skin potential responses to repeated auditory stimuli of two different intensities were studied. Two sets of instructions, to attend to and to ignore the sounds, were given. Ratings of EEG stages of sleep and also a quantitative measure of 4 to 7 c/sec activity were used to measure drowsiness. It was found that significantly more evoked skin potential changes occurred in the "attend to sound" periods than in the "ignore sound" periods, but this variable did not affect the rate of habituation. Transient EEG responses, *viz* V waves and K complexes, did not habituate; and their number was not affected by instructions to the subject, although significantly more occurred when the stimulus was

sleep stimulus intensity instructional set habituation EEG responses GSR drowsiness

loud. Changes in ongoing EEG activity during a stimulus also did not habituate, rather there was a tendency for these to increase in number during the experimental period. The nature of the instructions to the subject was a significant variable here, but the intensity of sound was not. In the case of all three types of response there was a significant correlation, positive or negative, between the number of responses recorded and the degree of drowsiness at that time, as assessed by the amount of 4 to 7 c/sec activity. There was also a significant association between the frequency with which responses were evoked and the stage of sleep obtaining at the time. The findings are discussed in relation to Sokolov's concept of the orienting reflex.

B 19 Wolfensberger, Wolf, and O'Connor, Neil: Stimulus intensity and duration effects on EEG and GSR responses of normals and retardates. *Am J Ment Defic, 70:*21, 1965.

Normals and retardates were presented with a series of light flashes of two intensities (high and low) and three durations (.2, 3, and 15 sec.). Initial arousal, adaptation to single stimuli, and habituation to repeated stimuli were inferred from measures of alpha blocking and GSR latency, alpha blocking and GSR duration, and GSR amplitude. Retardates were less responsive on EEG, but more responsive on GSR measures. There was no systematic interaction between intelligence on the one hand, and stimulus intensity or duration on the other. Habituation rates did not differ between intelligence groups. The results are inconsistent with a number of currently prevalent theories of normal-retardate differences, and may point to a two-factor (CNS and ANS) theory of arousal. It is felt possible that an interaction between intelligence and type of learning may be consistent with the findings, in that retardates without apparent pathology may be relatively more adequate on classical learning tasks than on other, especially verbal, types of learning.

*mental
retardation
visual
stimuli
arousal
alpha
blocking
habituation*

SECTION C

CONDITIONING

C 1 Beatty, J., and Kornfeld, C.: Relative independence of conditioned EEG changes from cardiac and respiratory activity. *Physiol Behav, 9*:733, 1972.

Investigated the system specificity of learned changes in EEG spectra in man and eliminated the possibility that changes in cardiac or respiratory activity mediate the observed CNS changes. Fourteen undergraduates were trained to produce occipital alpha and beta frequency activity differentially. Standard operant methods, including a discriminative stimulus, were used. Heart and respiration rates were recorded simultaneously. Ss showed discriminant control of the EEG spectra, but no significant changes were found in either heart or respiratory systems. Data indicate that conditioned changes in the EEG spectra are not mediated by shifts in either heart or respiratory rates. Instead they suggest that the EEG generating system is relatively independent of the brain systems controlling respiration and heart function.

*operant conditioning
alpha frequency
beta frequency
learned control
somatic responses*

C 2 Beh, H.C., and Barratt, P.E.H.: Discrimination and conditioning during sleep as indicated by the electroencephalogram. *Science, 147*:1470, 1965. (Copyright 1965 by the American Association for the Advancement of Science.)

Changes in electroencephalograms indicate that subjects respond more frequently to significant or meaningful stimuli during sleep than to nonsignificant stimuli, and that conditioned reactions may be induced in sleeping subjects.

*conditioning
alpha blocking
sleep*

C 3 Birbaumer, N.: Preventive alpha-inhibition und agst. *Studia Psychologica, 12*:179, 1970.

The relationship between EEG alpha and avoidance periods was determined for subjects in a discriminated avoidance

conditioning

paradigm. During the preshock interval some subjects showed a blocking or desynchronization response. These subjects with increased alpha in the preshock interval showed more signs of anxiety than the subjects which had desynchronization of alpha.

alpha blocking
alpha enhancement
anxiety

C 4   Bry, B.M.: The operant conditioning of human EEGs. *Diss Abst,* 30 (10-B), 4805, 1970.

Following a complete review of sixty-four previous attempts to operantly condition nonskeletal and covert R's, *E* ran a series of studies to develop a procedure for operantly conditioning human EEGs without *S* awareness. Then *E* selected four *Ss* whose EEGs had from twenty to forty seconds of visible high-amplitude alpha every minute. *E* collected thirty minutes of adaptation period data from each *S* at the beginning of each of four recording days. Then *E* reinforced high amplitude alpha (HIGH) for thirty minutes in two *Ss* and reinforced all other EEG activity (differential reinforcement of other or DRO) for thirty minutes in two *Ss* during the first two days. *E* reversed the treatments between the two pairs of *Ss* for days three and four. Rest periods occurred every ten minutes to keep *Ss* alert. *Ss* indicated that they were alert during the recording by pressing a key every ten seconds. The reinforcement followed an escape avoidance paradigm. *S* heard aversive white noise until the criterion EEG amplitude appeared; then *S* heard a period of music. The interval between any criterion R, whether it occurred during music or noise, and the return of the noise was ten seconds. *E* shaped the EEG during both DRO and HIGH by gradually increasing the duration of criterion amplitude that was required before music occurred. The cumulative number of seconds per minute of high amplitude alpha increased over the baseline significantly during HIGH and fell below the baseline significantly during DRO. Postexperimental interviews revealed no *S* awareness of the reinforcement contingencies. The EEG changes were not related to eye movements nor key presses, for their incidence was significantly different during HIGH and DRO. Although *Ss* inadvertently heard more noise during HIGH than during DRO, this difference did not account for the EEG changes; the noise and music had no differential effects on the EEG during the

operant conditioning
differential EEG reinforcement
awareness

adaptation periods. *S*s showed a significantly different number of GSRs, heartbeats, and neck muscle contractions during HIGH and DRO. *E* did not interpret these differences as indicating that the EEG changes were mediated by another R, however, for the strength of association between the EEG and the reinforcement contingencies was much greater than that between the GSR, HR or EMG and the reinforcement contingencies. Also the EEG appears to be independent of the concurrent R's in their cumulative R records. That is, EEG R rate changes occur without accompanying rate changes in any of the other Rs. The significant differences in the GSR, HR and EMG data may be due to adventitious reinforcement, or the GSR, HR and EMG may have reacted unconditionally to the EEG condition. Consequently it was concluded that the EEG modifications were a direct function of the reinforcement contingencies. This conclusion is based upon the fact that the same reinforcement stimuli produced 23 percent changes in the amount of high amplitude alpha of human EEGs in both directions without obvious mediation from other Rs.

C 5   Hefferman, M.S.: The effects of self-initiated control of brain waves on digit recall. *Diss Abst, 31*:6404, 1971.

In order to test whether cortical desynchronization is necessary for the recall of digit series, thirty-three subjects were conditioned to elicit synchronized and desynchronized brain rhythms during phases in learning digit sequences. At digit presentation and digit rehearsal, recall performance during synchronized rhythms was significantly better than that during desynchronized activity; but, during the digit repeat phase of learning, no significant difference in recall between the two brain rhythms was found.

conditioning
EEG
feedback
alpha
synchrony
desynchronization
memory

C 6   Matson, L., and Urban, J.: Electrographical tests of individual differences in elementary learning processes. *Magyar Pszichologiai Szemle, 24*:33, 1967.

Correlations were found between various indices of conditioning EEG responses and GSR to optical and auditory stimuli and the introversion-extroversion scores of Ss.

conditioning
sensory
  stimuli
GSR

C 7 Milstein, V.: Contingent alpha blocking: conditioning or sensitization? *Electroencephalogr, Clin Neurophysiol, 18:* 272, 1965.

Subjects were presented with tone stimuli following a sensitization procedure and a respondent conditioning procedure to determine the nature of contingent alpha blocking. In the sensitization procedure, tones were presented to subjects following independent flashes of light. In the conditioning procedure, light-flash and tone pairs were presented to subjects in the absence of the alpha rhythm. The conditioning procedure resulted in a greater blocking effect of tone than did the sensitization procedure.

condition-ing
alpha blocking
sensitization

SECTION D

ALPHA FEEDBACK

D 1   Beatty, J., and Kornfeld, C.: Relative independence of conditioned EEG changes from cardiac and respiratory activity. *Phys Behav, 9:*733, 1972.

EEG, heart rate, and respiration were recorded from fourteen subjects who were being trained to produce occipital alpha and beta waves in order to investigate the possibility that heart rate and respiration mediate the changes in the central nervous system which are observed during learned changes in EEG activity. No significant changes in heart or respiratory activity were seen during discriminant control of the alpha and beta activity suggesting relative independence of the EEG generating system from those systems controlling the functions of heart rate and respiration.

alpha feedback
beta feedback
heart rate
respiration
generators

D 2   Beatty, J.: Similar effects of feedback signals and instructional information on EEG activity. *Phys Behav, 9:*151, 1972.

In order to evaluate the effects of prior information about psychological correlates of EEG activity and of EEG based information feedback on biofeedback of the occipital EEG, forty-five college students participated in EEG biofeedback training sessions under a variety of instructional and information conditions. Those given both ideas of how to produce alpha and beta activity and on-line feedback did no better than subjects who received only one form of information. Subjects provided with either no information or, in some cases, inappropriate feedback information showed no systematic changes. The author warns that ascribing learned changes to effects of feedback where subjects are told the nature of the task is dangerous in light of the similar results from the groups that learned in this study.

alpha feedback
beta feedback
cognition
instructions
alpha abundance

D 3   Bremner, F.J., Moritz, F., and Benignus, V.: EEG correlates
of attention in humans. *Neuropsychologia, 10*:307, 1972.

In an attempt to extend the Bremner attention model to *alpha*
humans, the expectancy subset, as well as a new one (internal *feedback*
focus) were used with twenty male college students. Ten *attention*
subjects received the Silva Mind Control course while the *expectancy*
others received a classical conditioning paradigm procedure *alpha*
which was similar to that used to obtain animal data for *frequency*
the Bremner model except that alpha activity was used in- *theory*
stead of theta. In both groups a frequency shift was seen.
When biogenic feedback was introduced, another shift or
narrowing of the spectra occurred. It is therefore concluded
that expectancy as defined by the model correlates with the
shape of the spectra and a frequency shift. The authors also
suggest that the internal focus subset is demonstrated by the
Silva group since they used no external stimuli but only
what could be called mental imagery to generate their data.
It is recognized that further study is required to validate the
subset internal focus.

D 4   Brown, B.B.: Recognition of aspects of consciousness through
association with EEG alpha activity represented by a light
signal. *Psychophysiology, 6*:442, 1970.

Forty-seven subjects (twenty-one to sixty years old; sixteen *alpha*
males and thirty-one females) were given feedback for the *feedback*
presence of the alpha rhythm in their EEGs to determine *voluntary*
whether there were particular states of consciousness associ- *control*
ated with the alpha rhythm. The recorded EEG was filtered *subjective*
for alpha activity which in turn was used to power a display *states*
light in front of the subject. The subject received real-time *alpha*
information about the incidence and amplitude of the alpha *patterns*
rhythm in his EEG. All subjects had significant increases in
alpha incidence across successive sessions and significantly
decreased alpha frequency. Subjects were asked to answer a
questionnaire about their experiences following each training session. The greatest alpha abundances were associated
with reported feelings of losing awareness of the environment, feelings of floating, concentrating on mental imagery,
and either not experiencing time or feelings that the experimental sessions were short.

D 5   Brown, B.B.: Awareness of EEG-subjective activity relation-
       ships detected within a closed feedback system. *Psychophy-
       siology, 7:*451, 1970.

The present report summaries result from feedback experiments using the three EEG frequency ranges of theta, alpha and
beta to operate lights of three different colors. The subjects
were requested to try to isolate and identify feeling (and/or
thought) activity which they felt caused successful operation
of the lights. Written descriptions of this experience from
one subject group (26 Ss) were compared to evaluations of
subjective activity obtained in a second group of subjects
(45 Ss) determined using a color Q-sort technique. Results
from the latter technique were controlled for effects of color
and for effects of the feedback experience using a control
subject group (45 Ss). Results established two sets of relationships with subjective activity: color and EEG frequency.
Each set could exist independently or in relationship to the
other. Several characteristics were postulated to account for
development of the subjective-biological relationships in this
feedback system, e.g. that generation of stimulus and response were both internal events; that both reinforcement
of the process and the behavior reinforced were selected by
subjective activity of the subject; and that positive reinforcement did not occur without effort by the subject to define it.

*alpha
  feedback
beta
  feedback
theta
  feedback
subjective
  states*

D 6   Bundzen, P.V.: Autoregulatory mechanisms of the central
       nervous system in the presence of photo-stimulation in the
       rhythm of the biopotentials. *Fiziol Zh SSSR, 54:*683, 1968.

Ten subjects were given photo-stimulation and auto-stimu-
lation from 2 to 20 cps in order to study that part of the EEG
which reflects activity of the nonspecific or diffuse mechanisms that control autoregulation of the current functional
state of the brain. Amplitude and frequency of the alpha
rhythm recorded from the occipital and central areas of the
cortex indicated a link between alpha and the activity of the
autoregulatory brain mechanisms. Autoregulation of the
tonic level of activation or excitability of higher divisions of
the central nervous system was found, in part, to be related
to "encountered" or "attendant" inhibition which in turn
is a result of the slight lability of the brain structures con-

*alpha
  feedback
photic
  flicker
alpha
  amplitude
alpha
  frequency*

trolling nonspecific mechanisms. A direct connection between the process of autoregulation of the current functional state of the brain and "optimization" of the changing strength of afferent current was also found.

D 7   Dewan, E.M.: Communication by voluntary control of the electroencephalogram. *Physical Sciences Research Papers, 284:*349, 1966.

Past suggestions that the alpha rhythm and eye position could be used to send Morse Code are followed up in this project. Working with a computer and a teletype, one can perform this function but over half a minute is required per character. Messages were also sent using muscle activity from the forehead. The possibility of practical usefulness of these techniques is suggested but not dealt with in this communication.

alpha feedback eye position voluntary control

D 8   Engstrom, D.R., London, P., and Hart, J.T.: Hypnotic susceptibility increased by EEG alpha training. *Nature (Lond), 227:*1261, 1970.

Thirty subjects (seventeen to sixty-two years old; ten males and twenty females) with low scores on the Harvard Group Susceptibility Scale (HGSS) and less than 50 percent incidence of alpha were used in the experiment. Subjects were given form A of the Stanford Hypnotic Susceptibility Scale (SHSS) before and after a training procedure of alpha brainwave feedback was given. Twenty subjects received binary alpha feedback (a light came on whenever the alpha rhythm was present in the EEG) and ten subjects received yoked feedback or were presented with the light which represented the alpha activity of another subject. Alpha incidence was found to have a significant positive correlation with scores on the SHSS. Alpha incidence increased significantly for both the feedback and the yoked control groups during the sessions with the feedback group having a significantly greater increase. The scores on the HGSS were found to have increased in the same manner as alpha; the same significant relationships were found. The subjective feelings reported to be associated with the production of the alpha rhythm were described as similar to those in a hypnotic trance.

alpha feedback hypnotic susceptability alpha abundance subjective states

D 9   Gaarder, Kenneth: Control of states of consciousness. I. Attainment through control of psychophysiological variables. *Arch Gen Psychiatry, 25:*429, 1971.

A model is made of psychological processes as a homeostatic adaptive control system describable by momentary states with transformations occurring between states. According to the model a major determinant of psychophysiological state and state of consciousness is the nature of the information transmitted between subsystems. Control of state is therefore achieved through control of the information transmitted between subsystems.

control system model
states of consciousness
information transfer
learned control

D 10   Gaarder, K.: Control of states of consciousness II. Attainment through external feedback augmenting control. *Arch Gen Psychiatry, 25:*436, 1971.

This paper reviews the theory and history of biofeedback with specific reference to its use in psychiatric treatment. Special consideration is given to biofeedback as a means of treating psychosomatic disease and states of anxiety. Possible limiting factors of feedback techniques are also discussed.

biofeedback
review
theory
history
applications

D 11   Green, E., Green, A.M., and Walters, E.D.: Self-regulation of internal states. *Proceedings of the International Congress of Cybernetics,* London, Sept. 1-6, 1969.

Techniques and tools for investigating states of internal awareness, psychological and physiological, are developed in this paper. Physiological feedback in voluntary control of normally-unconscious physiological functions of the craniospinal, autonomic and central regions is used. Successful subjects have reduced muscle tension to zero levels, increased hand temperature as much as 5°C in two minutes, to 100 percent alpha over ten-second epochs, while speaking, with eyes open. The purpose of this training is to enhance and make possible the study of those psychological states which appear as functional concomitants of a passive peripheral nervous system and an "alpha activated" central nervous system. Psychology, psychosomatic medicine, psychiatry, edu-

alpha feedback
muscle system
alpha abundance
subjective states
data analysis
applications

cation, and creativity research are all areas in which this on-going project may be valuable.

D 12   Hart, Joseph T.: Autocontrol of EEG alpha. *Psychophysiology, 5:*506, 1968, (abstr.).

Subjects were trained to increase their alpha indices by placing them in a feedback loop so that every time an alpha wave of 8 to 13 cps was produced, a tone occurred. The feedback loop included the subject, a polygraph, a bandpass filter, an oscilloscope, a trigger, a duration timer, an oscillator, and a speaker. The results replicate those from the investigations of Kamiya in showing that subjects can learn to increase alpha. Thirteen of eighteen subjects in the experimental groups significantly increased their alpha indices within ten training sessions. The subjects in Experimental Group 1, who received both in-session feedback training and postsession information about their alpha scores, demonstrated greater alpha increases than the subjects in Experimental Group 2, who received only feedback training. However, some of the control subjects also showed alpha increments. Thus it is important to include a control group (this was not done in the earlier investigations) —without a control group the influence of feedback training is likely to be overestimated.

alpha feedback conditioning alpha abundance

D 13   Honorton, C., and Carbone, M.: A preliminary study of feedback-augmented EEG alpha activity and ESP card-guessing performance. *J Am Soc Psychical Res, 65:*66, Jan 1971.

This study was performed to assess the effects of feedback-augmented EEG alpha activity on ESP card-guessing performance. It was hypothesized that increments in alpha activity following a series of operant training sessions would be associated with concomitant increments in ESP scoring level. Each of ten volunteer subjects participated in ten sessions of EEG feedback training. The subject, a digital frequency discriminator, and an audio oscillator made a closed feedback loop. Subject's alpha activity activated a 250 Hz tone. Alpha abundance was automatically registered on digital counters. Only two of the subjects showed significant

alpha feedback ESP alpha patterns

increments in alpha. A significant negative correlation (r = —0.636, P < .05) was observed between percent of alpha and ESP scores in the Non-Feedback condition. Results for the feedback condition were not significant (r = —0.042). A statistically significant decline effect was observed, post hoc, for the Non-Feedback condition (P — .006).

D 14   Honorton, C., Davidson, R., and Bindler, P.: Shifts in subjective state associated with feedback-augmented EEG alpha. *Psychophysiology, 9*:269, 1972 (abstr.).

Twenty-three subjects completed one session with auditory feedback to EEG alpha activity using a closed feedback loop. Subjects alternated two-minute trials of alpha generation, rest periods (no feedback), and suppression. Ten trials of each type were given with order counterbalanced by subject. In addition to monopolar EEG (occiput-ear lobe), EOG (supraorbital-canthus) and EMG (frontalis) were recorded. Two verbal report measures were used to assess changes in subjective activity: An on line state report scale in which subjects called numbers between 0 to 4 to indicate degree of relaxation and attention to external stimuli (elicited during alternate feedback trials) and a postexperimental interview. Successive trials of generation, suppression and resting alpha were compared: gen. M alpha = 40 percent, suppr. = 16 percent, rest = 36 percent. The three conditions differed significantly (p < .01) for the group, and each subject individually had significant gen./suppr. differences (p < .01). Alpha gen. was associated with M state report = 2.01, suppr. M = 0.63 (p < .005). Subjects with strong shifts in state reports between conditions had significantly larger alpha shifts than subjects with little shift in state reports (p < .05). High state reports were associated with significantly less REM activity and EMG activation than low state reports (p < .005). Blind-coded interview responses related significantly to state reports (p < .05). These converging measures support the hypothesis that relatively high alpha is associated with narrowing of perceptual awareness, relaxation, and with some subjects "ASCs."

alpha feedback subjective states

D 15 Hord, D., Naitoh, P., and Johnson, L.: Intensity and coherence contours during self-regulated high alpha activity. *Electroencephalogr Clin Neurophysiol, 32:*429, 1972.

Spectral intensity and coherence analysis of EEG activity during rest and during a period of self-regulated high alpha in two subjects indicate that: (1) slow frontal activity, which is due primarily to eye movements, is less intense during successful alpha regulation than during baselines. (2) There is little evidence for increased intensity in frequency ranges other than the alpha range during alpha regulation. (3) Occipital alpha tends to be more coherent with frontal than with temporal alpha during occipital alpha regulation.

alpha feedback
alpha symmetry
voluntary control
spectral analysis
coherence

D 16 Kamiya, J.: Conscious control of brain waves. *Psychology Today, 1:*56, 1968. (Reprinted from *Psychology Today* magazine, April 1968. Copyright © Communications/Research/ Machines, Inc.)

Indicates the possibility of teaching "man to perceive and control some of his brain functions." After subjects had learned to distinguish between alpha and nonalpha states, they were able to consciously produce the alpha state. Control of alpha rhythms was monitored by EEGs. Experienced Zen meditators "learned control of their alpha waves far more rapidly than did the average person. The possible value in studies of alpha wave control during the LSD experience" is indicated. The lack of connection between alpha waves and extra-sensory perception is stressed. "No evidence of electromagnetic radiation to the outside world by brain activity . . ." was found. Studies with groups other than college educated subjects are suggested.

alpha feedback
meditation
consciousness

D 17 Kaszniak, A.W.: Dichotic auditory vigilance during feedback-enhanced EEG alpha. *Psychophysiology, 10:*203, 1973, (abstr.) .

Two different groups of nonsense syllables were presented simultaneously in the right and left ears. Target syllables were specified and those given in the right ear were made

alpha feedback
vigilance

task central through instructions to pay particular attention
to them. Findings indicated decreased accuracy for target
syllable detection in the left ear during alpha enhancement
as opposed to alpha suppression trials, but no difference was
found in right ear accuracy for the two conditions. Therefore, this supports the hypothesis of decreased peripheral perceptual awareness during alpha production but does not suggest any accompanying increase in central perceptual awareness. A consideration of the results in the light of both
trained and spontaneous alpha is also offered.

*auditory
acuity
perceptual
awareness*

D 18   Keesey, U.T., and Nichols, D.J.: Changes induced in stabilized image visibility by experimental alteration of the ongoing EEG. *Electroencephalogr Clin Neurophysiol, 27:*248,
1969.

Took continuous EEG recordings while judgments of stabilized image disappearance and reappearance were made by
two adult subjects. On line use of a computer executing a
closed-loop program made it possible to detect the alpha
rhythm while it was occurring and to present a burst of white
noise shortly after each onset of alpha activity. The stimulus
could also be presented in random order. It was found that
alpha dependent presentation of the stimulus both lengthened the time the stabilized image stayed visible and changed
the temporal patterns of alpha occurrence and image disappearance and reappearance in comparison to the condition
where the stabilized image was viewed without any white
noise presentation.

*alpha
feedback
retinal
images
alpha
blocking*

D 19   Kondo, C.Y., Travis, T.A., and Knott, J.R.: Initial abundance and amplitude of alpha as determinants of performance
in an enhancement paradigm. *Electroencephalogr Clin Neurophysiol, 34:*106, 1973 (abstr.) .

While apparent enhancement of abundance has been seen in
previous work by the authors, large individual differences
in alpha amplitude and alpha abundance have also been
observed. In order to investigate this phenomenon, the records
of thirty subjects who received five alpha training sessions of
ten-minute duration with eyes open were analyzed. Initial

*alpha
feedback
alpha
abundance
alpha
amplitude*

alpha amplitude with eyes closed and initial alpha abundance with eyes open served as baselines, and data from the ten best and ten poorest performers (those with increases of alpha over trials) was compared. Large initial alpha amplitude resulted in significantly larger increases in alpha over trials than did small initial amplitude; whereas low initial alpha abundance gave way to significantly larger increases in alpha as training progressed when compared to high initial abundance.

D 20   Korein, J., Maccario, M., Carmona, A., Randt, C.T., and Miller, N.: Operant conditioning techniques in normal and abnormal EEG states. *Neurology, 21*:395, 1971 (abstr.).

A pilot study to condition EEGs involved thirteen normals, eight subjects with psychogenic and systematic disorders, and fifteen patients with seizure disorders in whom potentially induced or spontaneous spikes and bursts existed. Conditioning of the first two groups used filtered and amplified fronto-occipital 8 to 13 cps EEG activity which caused a click or photic stimulus feedback. The last group was given an auditory feedback signal when paroxysmal activity was present. Of those receiving alpha conditioning 70 percent could attain control within two weeks, and they reported alpha to be a relatively tranquil state as opposed to the nonalpha, or concentration, state. Evoked response, frequency changes, eye movements, etc. also appeared significant. Only 20 percent of the fifteen patients could control their paroxysmal spikes, and this occurred during the first trials and occasionally as one-trial learning. The authors conclude that such techniques of maintaining a steady state (alpha) may be useful in quantifying drug activity, evoked response, etc. and may also be associated with meditation. Lastly they say that therapeutic aspects of operant conditioning should be considered further.

alpha feedback psychopathology epilepsy subjective states applications

D 21   Lynch, James J., and Paskewitz, David A.: On the mechanisms of the feedback control of human brain wave activity. *J Nerv Ment Dis, 153*:205, 1971. (Copyright 1971 by the Williams & Wilkins Co., Baltimore.)

The recent attention given to the feedback control of human brain wave activity and the implications of such control prompts a careful analysis of this phenomenon. Particular emphasis is placed on the learned control of the alpha rhythm. A review of possible factors which might influence the density of alpha rhythms led to the differentiation of three general sources of influence: constitutional, physiological and cognitive-attentional factors. Each of these factors is discussed as a possible mediator of the learned control of the alpha rhythm. The view is advanced that increases in alpha density during feedback training arise from a diminution of those factors which block this rhythm, and some implications of such a view are discussed. Several of the issues raised appear generalizable to the whole question of the operant control of autonomic activity.

alpha
  feedback
learned
  control
review
theory

D 22   Machac, M., and Moravek, M.: Frekvencnizmey alfa rytmu pri psychologickych manipulacich s aktivacni urovni. *Cesk Psychologie, 11:*421, 1967.

Fourteen subjects were trained to relax with an autoregulation method. Changes in the EEG occurring through stages of increasing relaxation were observed. A 0.9 Hz increase in frequency of the alpha rhythm accompanied the relaxation produced by this method.

alpha
  feedback
relaxation
alpha
  frequency

D 23   Mulholland, T., and Evans, C.R.: Oculomotor function and the alpha activation cycle. *Nature (Lond), 211:*1278, 1966.

A biofeedback system which presented a light or tone when EEG alpha waves were present was utilized to study oculomotor functioning. Findings in five subjects showed more abundant alpha activity with eyes elevated in both eyes-open and eyes-closed conditions. Therefore, it is concluded that oculomotor function and the cortical or subcortical processes connected with the EEG alpha-activation cycle may be related. In particular, the alpha-activation cycle may in some way indicate eye movements, accommodation and position.

alpha
  feedback
visual
  system
eye position
alpha
  abundance

D 24   Mulholland, T.B.: Feedback electroencephalography. *Act Nerv Super (Praha), 10:*410, 1968.

Contents: (1) Special usefulness of feedback methods. (Nulling a closed internal loop.) Environmental clasping of a biological control system. Testing hypotheses of casualty. Testing hypotheses of difference between causes. (2) Standardization of feedback EEG. The external path. Stimulus functions. (3) The effects of feedback stimulation. Bilateral differences. Feedback as an increase or decrease of stimulation. Delayed feedback. (4) Visual control systems and occipital alpha. Control of the EEG by the subject. Accommodation, fixation and target clearness. (5) The occipital alpha-activation cycle as a controlled process. (6) The activation of the occipital EEG. (7) The alpha process. (8) Prospects for feedback methods in psychophysiology-voluntary control of physiological processes.

alpha feedback theory visual system applications

D 25 Mulholland, T.B.: Feedback method: A new look at functional EEG. *Electroencephalogr Clin Neurophysiol, 27:*688, 1969 (abstr.).

Application of feedback EEG is developed from basic research which has shown that (1) feedback from EEG to the display constrains the EEG alpha-activation cycle, reducing unpredictable or uniformative variation; (2) the constrained system can be disturbed showing an initial response followed by a recovery to near baseline conditions; (3) the disturbance and recovery of the feedback system is an index of stimulus parameters and complex variables of visual control; (4) EEG processes which are not consciously known can be brought into awareness by information feedback. Combined with training, voluntary control of these processes can be learned; (5) by means of the feedback path, information displays and appliances can be automatically regulated by the EEG processes to which they are connected. Combined with training, voluntary control of the display or appliance can be learned; (6) by controlling the parameters of the feedback path the EEG response can be controlled. If these determine a behavioral response, then it can be controlled.

alpha feedback visual system EEG activation applications

D 26 Mulholland, T.B., and Peper, E.: Occipital alpha and accommodative vergence, pursuit tracking, and fast eye movements. *Psychophysiology, 8:*556, 1971.

The parietal-occipital EEG was recorded while subjects performed various fixation, accommodation and tracking maneuvers with stationary and moving targets. For some experiments the target was continuously in view and independent of the EEG; in others, a feedback path connected the occurrence of parietal-occipital alpha with the visibility of the target. The results show that alpha attenuation or blocking is not due to visual attention but to processes of fixation, lens accommodation, and pursuit tracking. Saccadic movements were not reliably linked to alpha or alpha blocking. The utility of feedback methods for testing the hypotheses that visual control processes are linked to the parietal-occipital alpha rhythms was demonstrated.

alpha feedback
visual system
eye movements
alpha blocking

D 27   Mulholland, T.B., and Gascon, G.: A quantitative EEG index of the orienting response in children. *Electroencephalogr Clin Neurophysiol, 33:*295, 1972.

The basic assumption that all responses of the occipital EEG relevant to the orienting response are characterized by a disturbance followed by a recovery of the series of alpha intervals alternating with no-alpha intervals was made so a new method for analyzing the orienting response could be developed. This is described and illustrated under various conditions using alpha feedback. An index of orienting, developed from average disturbance and recovery series estimates, differentiated experimental conditions and ages; and, therefore, these new quantitative methods of evaluating the alpha-attenuation cycle aid in the study of EEG correlates of the human orienting response.

alpha feedback
children
orienting
EEG activation
alpha blocking
applications

D 28   Nowlis, D.P., and Kamiya, J.: The control of electroencephalographic alpha rhythms through auditory feedback and the associated mental activity. *Psychophysiology, 6:*476, 1970.

Twenty-six subjects were given baseline tests for electroencephalographic (EEG) alpha rhythm presence and then a period of fifteen minutes to gain insight into mental activity associated with alpha presence and absence while provided with an auditory feedback loop keyed to the presence of alpha. Sixteen of the subjects worked with eyes closed,

alpha feedback
subjective states

and ten, with very high initial alpha baseline scores, worked with open eyes. After the fifteen-minute practice period, permitting control of alpha through feedback, the subjects were given a trial during which they attempted to produce as much alpha as possible and a trial in which they tried to produce as little as possible. The results indicated significant appropriate change for both the generation and suppression trials. Those who were able to control alpha spontaneously reported mental states reflecting relaxation, "letting go," and pleasant affect associated with maintaining alpha.

D 29 O'Malley, J.E., and Comers, C.K.: The effect of unilateral alpha training on visual-evoked response in a Dyslexic Adolescent. *Psychophysiology, 9:*467, 1972.

This project was undertaken with a dyslexic adolescent to further elucidate the possible relationship between alpha activity and averaged visual evoked response. Baseline alpha and visual evoked responses (VER) were recorded and bilateral alpha training carried out. Analysis of variance showed that alpha training significantly increased VER amplitude (p < .001) . Baseline VER and percent alpha were not correlated, although baseline VER did fluctuate. Unilateral alpha training when 0.5 seconds alpha appeared in the left hemisphere and 0.5 seconds of beta or theta in the right hemisphere caused a significant increase over five days (four trials per day) of alpha activity on the left side and beta and theta activity on the right side. Left minus right VER amplitude difference increased and was correlated (p < .05) with percent time alpha (L) and beta and theta (R) increases.

alpha feedback
dyslexia
visual evoked response
beta
theta

D 30 Paskewitz, D.A., and Orne, M.T.: Visual effects during alpha feedback training. *Psychophysiology, 9:*269, 1972 (abstr.) .

In a study of alpha feedback training, no increases in alpha density were observed across six days (sixty trials) when auditory feedback was presented to nine subjects in total darkness. For theoretical reasons, it was predicted that the mere addition of low-level ambient light would establish lawful increases in alpha densities. A second sample of seven sub-

alpha feedback
visual system theory

jects, given ten trials a day for two days, confirmed the prediction. The original group of subjects, who failed to show
increases in total darkness, also increased densities in the
presence of light. Furthermore, with light both groups
showed significantly higher densities during feedback than
during intervening rest periods. These findings may help
reconcile some of the conflicting results in the literature.
The results support the view that increases in alpha densities
can take place only if inhibitory mechanisms are initially
present to depress density. Increases in alpha activity may
reflect an increasing ability of the subject to ignore otherwise distracting influences, and this process may account for
some of the reported subjective concomitants of alpha feedback training.

D 31   Paskewitz, D.A., and Orne, M.T.: Visual effects on alpha
       feedback training. *Science, 181:*360, 1973. (Copyright 1973
       by the American Association for the Advancement of Sci-
       ence.)

Presenting an audible indication of subjects' electroencepha-   *alpha*
lographic alpha activity under conditions of dim ambient   *feedback*
illumination led to systematic increases in alpha density,   *ambient*
while in total darkness the same procedure did not. These   *light*
results support the view that feedback training can be clear-   *voluntary*
ly demonstrated only when factors leading to a suppression   *control*
of alpha activity are present in the environment.

D 32   Peper, E.: Feedback regulation of the alpha electroencepha-
       logram activity through control of the internal and external
       parameters. *Kybernetik, 6:*107, 1970.

Experiments with feedback stimulation triggered from the   *alpha*
subject's electroencephalogram result in changing the se-   *feedback*
quential time series of intervals of occipital alpha and in-   *visual*
tervals of little or no alpha EEG activity. The rate of re-   *system*
currence of alpha and no-alpha EEG can be changed by regu-   *subjective*
lating the external feedback stimuli or by asking the sub-   *states*
ject to change his internal state. Four different paradigms
were investigated and the results interpreted in terms of the

hypothesis that oculomotor functions regulate the occurrence and nonoccurrence of alpha.

) 33 Peper, E., and Mulholland, T.: Methodological and theoretical problems in the voluntary control of electroencephalographic occipital alpha by the subject. *Kybernetik, 7:*10, 1970.

Twenty-one normal humans attempted to control the facilitation and inhibition of their EEG occipital alpha rhythm. They received auditory feedback which informed them whether or not alpha occurred. Most subjects learned to inhibit alpha, only four learned to facilitate it. Further training did not bring improved control of alpha. The results are presented to illustrate problems of method and interpretation which include the diversity of subjective attempts at control: day-to-day variability of the response, the control for alpha increase caused by habituation, and the feedback technique as an operant conditioning method.

alpha feedback voluntary control habituation

D 34 Peper, E.: Localized EEG alpha feedback training: A possible technique for mapping subjective, conscious, and behavioral experiences. *Kybernetik, 11:*166, 1972.

A subject was trained in localized control of alpha activity successfully. These preliminary results are suggestive of possible localized control to establish relationships between subjective, conscious and behavioral experiences with certain EEG patterns, thereby developing a new subjective physiological language. Particular medical and altered states of consciousness type applications are considered.

alpha feedback subjective states consciousness

D 35 Regestein, Q.R.: Prolonged continuous production of EEG alpha rhythm and desynchrony. *Psychosom Med, 34:*471, 1972.

Thirty-one subjects were trained to produce alpha waves during a four-hour session, with twenty-two being paid for success. Results included no difference between paid and unpaid groups and greater mean amounts of alpha in thirteen men versus eighteen women. Seven subjects who did

alpha feedback motivation alpha abundance

the best in this experiment participated in two additional twelve-hour paid feedback conditions study which took place on two days, two weeks apart. One of the sessions involved alpha production and the other nonalpha production with the result that the former became easier while the latter grew more difficult. Innate alpha production was attributed more to relevancy of performance than to any effects of learning.

EEG activation

D 36   Sacks, B., Fenwick, P.B.C., Marks, I., Fenton, G.W., and Hebden, A.: An investigation of the phenomenon of auto-control of the alpha rhythm and possible associated feeling states using visual feedback. *Electroencephalogr Clin Neurophysiol, 32:461, 1972.*

The aims of this study were to investigate previous reports that voluntary control of the amplitude of the alpha rhythm could be achieved by means of a visual feedback system and to confirm whether or not there were associated feeling states. Sixteen subjects were tested. Subjects were seated with their eyes open looking at the feedback lamp and were required to control the illumination of the lamp in response to instructions presented on an illuminated panel. Each subject was given only one session. Of sixteen subjects so tested, six were able to achieve voluntary control of the alpha amplitude with their eyes open. After the recording session, subjects completed two semantic differential questionnaires which referred to their feeling and mental states when the feedback lamp was on and when it was off; they were also given an unstructured interview. No correlations were found between mental or feeling states when the subject showed small or large alpha amplitudes.

alpha feedback
alpha amplitude
subjective reports

D 37   Schmeidler, G., and Lewis, L.: Mood changes after alpha feedback training. *Percept Mot Skills, 32:709, 1971.*

Thirteen young adults completed a mood checklist and Breskin Rigidity Test (measuring preference for perceptual closure) before alpha training. After two training sessions, significant increases in production of alpha EEG activity, scores for moods associated with alpha by prior research, and preference for closure were observed from retest results.

alpha feedback
subjective states
perceptual tasks

D 38 Schwartz, G.E., Shaw, G., and Shapiro, D.: Specificity of alpha and heart rate control through feedback. *Psychophysiology, 9:*269, 1972 (abstr.).

To explore the effects of repeated alpha wave training on cardiovascular functioning, twelve subjects were pre- and posttested in the laboratory on their ability to control their alpha and heart rate after four daily one-hour sessions of feedback training to increase and decrease alpha. The pretest data indicated that subjects were initially unable to differentially increase or decrease alpha, but they were able to produce 5 bpm differences in heart rate which were unaccompanied by alpha changes. However, after the four sessions of alpha training, subjects evidenced significant alpha control unaccompanied by heart changes, while their ability to control their heart rate was unaffected (identical to the pretest). Analysis of the subjective report data supports the notion that the mechanisms of alpha and heart rate control are different. Implications for the direct feedback control of patterns of alpha and heart rate are discussed.

alpha feedback
alpha abundance
heart rate

D 39 Spilker, B., Kamiya, J., Callaway, E. and Yeager, C.L.: Visual evoked responses in subjects trained to control alpha rhythms. *Psychophysiology, 5:*683, 1969.

Averaged visual evoked responses (AER) to sine wave light and to light flashes were recorded in seven subjects trained to control alpha rhythms. All seven subjects demonstrated a greater AER amplitude to sine wave light when there was high or abundant alpha in the EEG than when the alpha was low or almost entirely absent. Two of the early waves of the flash AER were usually greater in amplitude during periods of high alpha. A cycloplegic agent was shown to have no effect upon this finding, nor did varying the frequency of sine wave light stimulation. Period analysis of the EEG showed more activity at both low and high frequency bands during periods of low alpha. Auditory evoked response amplitudes were not significantly different between the high and low background alpha conditions. These results were discussed in relation to current views correlating AERs with attentive states.

alpha feedback
visual evoked response

D 40   Travis, T.A., Kondo, C.Y., and Knott, J.R.: A controlled
        study of alpha enhancement. *Psychophysiology, 9*:268, 1972,
        (abstr.).

The effects of no-noncontiguous and contiguous reinforce- *alpha*
ment on alpha enhancement were investigated. Three groups   *feedback*
were employed: (1) experimental, n = 8 (contiguous rein-   *alpha en-*
forcement); (2) Yoked Control, n = 8 (noncontiguous rein-   *hancement*
forcement); (3) Naive Control, n = 8 (no reinforcement). All
subjects experienced six 10-minute sessions on each of two
days. The feedback stimulus was a blue light and dependent
variable was percent alpha, on time. Experimental subjects
produced significantly more alpha on day 1 than subjects in
either of the control groups. On day 2, both experimental
and Yoked Control groups (who had been switched to relevant feedback) produced significantly more alpha than the
Naive Control Group. Significant increases over trials was
noted for experimental subjects on day 1 and for both Experimental and Yoked Control subjects on day 2. Naive Controls evidenced no changes on either day. Increases in alpha
output in our situation appeared to be related to a crucial
contiguity between alpha production and the delivery of
the feedback stimulus.

D 41   Travis, T.A., Kondo, C.Y., and Knott, J.R.: A comparison
        of instructed and noninstructed nonreinforcement sessions
        following alpha enhancement training. *Electroencephalogr
        Clin Neurophysiol, 34*:105, 1973.

This experiment questions whether true operant control re- *alpha*
sulted from past alpha abundance enhancement experiments.   *feedback*
The effects of removal of reinforcement following training   *condition-*
were studied under two conditions: (1) no warning and (2)   *ing*
instructions to subjects that this was a "test session" and that
they should do whatever proved most successful during feedback sessions. Eight of sixteen subjects who received five to
ten-minute enhancement training sessions with eyes open
also received a nonreinforcement trial under one of the conditions mentioned. Results tended to support the assumption
that operant control is not a consequence of such learned
control of alpha. Subjects under condition 2 (instructions

given) showed increased production of alpha during the nonreinforcement trial while the others showed no significant changes. No signs of classical extinction were seen in the nonreinforcement period.

D 42 Woodruff, D.S., and Birren, J.E.: Alpha training for the elderly. *American Psychology Association Meeting,* Hawaii, 1972.

Fifteen subjects between eighteen and twenty-nine years and fifteen subjects between sixty and eighty-one years were trained successfully in alpha production. It was concluded that these results show that alpha rhythm slowing is not an indication of irreversible deterioration in the nervous system of the aged. Hope for control of behavioral alterations associated with aging through brainwave frequency manipulation is offered.

alpha feedback
voluntary control
aging
alpha frequency

MISCELLANEOUS EEG FEEDBACK

E 1   Begleiter, Henri, Gross, Milton M., Porjesz, Bernice, and Kissin, Benjamin: The effects of awareness on cortical evoked potentials to conditioned affective stimuli. *Psychophysiology, 5:517,* 1969.

A previous paper of ours (Begleiter, Gross, and Kissin, 1967) demonstrated that it was possible to condition affective meaning to meaningless figures (CS), and significantly alter visual evoked potential (VEP) amplitudes and latencies to them, without the S's awareness of the CS-UCS relationship (Experiment I, totally unaware). In the present study some Ss were deliberately informed that a CS-UCS connection existed; however, the exact nature of their relationship was not divulged (Experiment II, slightly aware). Other Ss were explicitly informed of the correct CS-UCS contingency, and entire conditioning paradigm (Experiment III, fully aware). One physiological (VEP) and two behavioral (interflash interval and semantic differential) indices of conditioning were obtained during an extinction procedure and demonstrated significant differences between CRs in Experiment II, but none in Experiment III. VEP amplitudes to positive and negative CSs were enhanced in Experiment II and suppressed in Experiment I, in comparison to the neutral CS. This effect was most marked in responses to the negative CS. It is suggested that level of awareness of the CS-UCS contingency might be reflected in our physiological index of conditioning—VEP amplitude.

visual evoked responses classical conditioning awareness affect

E 2   Begleiter, H., and Platz, A.: Evoked potentials: Modifications by classical conditioning. *Science, 166:*769, 1969. (Copyright 1969 by the American Association for the Advancement of Science.)

446

Explored the relation between classical conditioning and the late components of the visual evoked potentials in humans. Data were derived from monopolar scalp recordings of sixteen college students. Visual evoked potentials to a positive discriminative stimulus change systematically during sensory conditioning and extinction. Changes due to conditioning are manifested in the increased amplitude of the late component of the evoked response. This effect is attenuated during extinction and reappears after reconditioning.

visual evoked responses stimulus discrimination extinction

E 3   Bundzen, P.V.: Autoregulation of functional state of the brain: An investigation using photostimulation with feedback. *Fed Proc Trans Suppl, 25:*551, 1966.

Ten healthy subjects and ten psychasthenic patients were recorded for EEG from bipolar parieto-occipital and parieto-temporal electrodes in both hemispheres. The apparatus included the usual feedback components (amplifier, filter and integrator), but in this case suppression of alpha by a flash caused stimulus (flash) cutoff. An inertia filter was used which allowed alteration of the autostimulation according to mean level of electrical activity. Automatic EEG analysis gave filtered and integrated material for four ranges (3 to 1, 8 to 14, 16 to 32, and 35 to 50 cps) which was used to make spectrochronograms showing changes in integrated values of these frequencies over time. It was concluded that (1) cyclical recurring changes in cortical neuron electrical activity was an important factor in stabilization of the functional state of the brain under autostimulation conditions; (2) functional state of the cortex autostabilization is done through the direct agency of nonspecific effects from subcortical structures and is separately connected with control of the afferent flow; and (3) disturbance of cerebral autoregulation (for example, by pathologic states) is due to weakened corticofugal control of the activity of activating structures in the brainstem.

biofeedback visual stimuli EEG activation alpha blocking theory

E 4   Bundzen, P.V., et al.: Method of automatic photostimulation in the rhythm of cerebral biopotentials with a selectively controlled feedback system. *Fiziol Zh SSSR, 54:*1239, 1968.

Technical details, drawings, etc. of equipment for auto- *biofeedback*
matic photostimulation with a direct connection between the *photic*
stimulus and amplitude, frequency, form, etc. of the cerebral *flicker*
biopotentials which has been proven in the analysis of auto- *theory*
regulatory processes of the brain are given. A direct expression of the principle of "optimal interaction" between the
nervous centers in the regulation of the "general tonic functional state of the brain" has been demonstrated using this
apparatus.

E 5   Hillyard, S.A., and Galambos, R.: Effects of stimulus and
response contingencies on a surface negative slow potential
shift in man. *Electroencephalogr Clin Neurophysiol, 22:*
297, 1967.

A slow wave potential (CNV) was recorded extracranially *CNV*
from eleven subjects during the interval between a warning *condition-*
stimulus (flash of light) and a burst of clicks which they *ing*
terminated by pressing a lever. When subjects were not re- *feedback*
quired to respond to the clicks, no CNV appeared. When
they were told to turn off the clicks, the CNV increased in
amplitude at a rate that depended on individual prior experience with the paired flash-clicks contingency. Omission
of clicks with no warning to the subjects resulted in gradual
diminution of the CNV; subsequent reinstatement of clicks
caused the CNV to increase in amplitude again. A significant
negative correlation between size of CNV and reaction time
was found over a large group of trials. The relation of the
CNV to subjective expectancy and intention to respond was
discussed.

E 6   Kuprianovich, L.: The process of instruction during sleep
can be regulated. *Technika-Molodezhi (Moscow), 11:26,*
1965.

Kuprianovich reported a method for controlling the level *EEG*
of sleep, as defined by the EEG, using a visual feedback *feedback*
stimulus. When the sleep EEG was within a particular con- *sleep*
trolled range, an auditory signal was automatically presented
to test the hypothesis that learning could occur during sleep.

E 7   McAdam, D.W., et al.: Conative control of the contingent negative variation. *Electroencephalogr Clin Neurophysiol,* *21*:194, 1966.

Experiments are described in which experimenter-subjects were able to control the amplitude of the contingent negative variation "at will." It is urged that any investigations of the psychological correlates of the CNV which make use of "trained observers" should be interpreted with this possible source of bias in mind and replicated, where feasible, using unbiased, naive subjects.

CNV feedback

E 8   Meszaros, I., and Adam, G.: Conditioned cortical evoked potentials in man. *Acta Physiol Acad Sci Hung, 37*:137, 1968.

Brief clicks were presented as conditioned auditory stimuli together with stroboscopic flashes with a delay of 200 msec. After a sufficient number of reinforcements, a conditioned response appearing 200 msec after presentation of the auditory stimulus could be recorded by occipital bipolar scale electrodes. The present observations have confirmed that conditioned cortical evoked response can be elicited also in the human.

auditory evoked responses conditioning

E 9   Peters, Jon F., Knott, John R., Miller, Lyle H., Van Veen, William J., and Cohen, Sanford I.: Response variables and magnitude of the contingent negative variation. *Electroencephalogr Clin Neurophysiol, 29*:608, 1970.

When subjects in a fixed foreperiod reaction time task are presented with a repetitive stimulus that is terminated by the manual response made to it, the contingent negative variations following the warning stimulus will be of greater magnitude than when a single stimulus, over which the subject has no control, is used. It is suggested that different levels of motivation are involved in these two conditions.

CNV reaction time task repetitive stimulus information feedback motivation

E 10   Picton, Terence W., and Low, Morton D.: The CNV and semantic content of stimuli in the experimental paradigm: Effects of feedback. *Electroencephalogr Clin Neurophysiol, 31*:451, 1971.

The usual contingent negative variation (CNV) paradigm S_1-S_2-R was modified by requiring a discrimination at S_2 and by adding a feedback stimulus: S_1-$S_{d\triangle}$-R .. FB. It was demonstrated that as the discrimination task became more difficult and therefore the feedback (FB) more important informationally, the CNV became prolonged until the FB signal and the amplitude of the evoked response to this stimulus increased in size. It is suggested that the discharge of a CNV occurs at the time of significant informational feedback. In the normal CNV paradigm this is usually intrinsic in S_2 and R, but in a discrimination task it may be delayed to an explicit feedback stimulus. The FB evoked response changes reinforce the concept that the amplitude of at least some components of an evoked response reflect the psychological significance of the stimulus. Psychiatric patients, including five schizophrenics, showed changes similar to those observed in normals, but the patient data were unusable because of significant contamination by EOG and galvanic skin response artifact.

CNV
verbal
stimuli
emotion
feedback

E 11   Rebert, Charles S.: The effect of reaction time feedback on reaction time and contingent negative variation. *Psychophysiology, 9:*334, 1972.

The contingent negative variation (CNV) and simple reaction time (RT) of human Ss were recorded when the imperative stimulus (IS) was either single flash, repetitive flash, numeric feedback of RT, or numeric no-feedback of RT. Reaction times were not significantly shorter, but CNVs were larger when IS was flicker rather than single flash. RT was slightly faster, but CNV was no larger in one study when explicit numeric feedback was provided than when it was not. Slightly larger CNVs were obtained in the no-feedback condition in a third experiment. Conclusions were (1) that the effectiveness of flicker versus flash in producing a CNV difference was due to S's attempts to obtain feedback in the flicker condition and not to feedback per se, and (2) that the general hedonic quality of the experiment produced by the degree of positive or negative reinforcement is a potent feedback variable, whereas RT feedback per se is not.

CNV
reaction
time
reaction
time
feedback
reinforce-
ment
hedonic
quality

E 12   Rosenfeld, J.P., Rudell, A.P., and Fox, S.S.: Operant control of neural events in humans. *Science, 165*:821, 1969. (Copyright 1969 by the American Association for the Advancement of Science.)

Human subjects were trained by traditional methods of instrumental conditioning to change the amplitude of a late component of the auditory evoked potential with and without oscilloscopic feedback of their performance.

auditory evoked responses operant conditioning feedback

E 13   Silverman, S.: Operant conditioning of the amplitude component of the EEG. *Psychophysiology, 9*:269, 1972 (abstr.) .

Feedback contingent on the amplitude component of the EEG irrespective of frequency changes was presented to subjects over four 1-hour sessions. The feedback signal (soft tone and dim light) was presented each time the subject's EEG equalled or exceeded a baseline amplitude obtained with eyes closed during the rest period of each session. There was no difference between EEG control in the fourth training session and the no-feedback session. There was a significant amplitude difference between "on" and "off" trials for sessions 4 and 5 combined. In all cases, high amplitude was associated with alpha frequencies, low amplitude with higher frequencies. It was concluded that learned control of EEG amplitude can transfer to a no-feedback condition.

biofeedback EEG amplitude

E 14   Smith, K.U., and Ansell, S.D.: Closed-loop digital computer system for study of sensory feedback effects of brain rhythms. *Am J Phys Med, 44*:125, 1965. (Copyright 1965 by the Williams & Wilkins Co., Baltimore.)

A computer system with appropriate transducers for physiologic and response mechanisms was designed to record and control sensory and excitatory feedback based on delay, space-displacement, kinetic modulation, etc. Experiments involving (1) the effects of brain wave generated stimulus feedback patterns on perception and EEG frequency patterns, (2) delay of these feedback stimuli relative to their source and the effects on perceptual or brain wave pattern,

feedback patterns data collection theory applications

and (3) judgment of magnitude of the delay of cyclic auditory stimuli produced by the EEG showed no significant relationships. Computer-delayed auditory-feedback effects of speech slowed, slurred, and produced repetitive defects in reading. It is suggested that these experiments make clear problems of dynamic correlation between perception and brain wave pattern in addition to proving the value of computer controlled feedback systems. It is also pointed out that these methods may help in developing new techniques of real time dynamic simulation of physiologic and behavioral disorders.

E 15   Sterman, M.B., and Friar, L.: Suppression of seizures in an epileptic following sensorimotor EEG feedback training. *Electroencephalogr Clin Neurophysiol, 33*:89, 1972.

Studies of 12 to 14 cps activity in the sensorimotor cortex of cats showed it to be related to thalamo-cortical inhibitory discharge, suppression of phasic motor behavior, and drug-induced convulsions. Similar activity of the rolandic cortex in a twenty-three-year old female with epilepsy was fed back to the subject using biofeedback techniques. Results included enhancement of abundance of the sensorimotor rhythm, differentiation of the sensorimotor rhythm from alpha activity, changes in sleep patterns, and personality and seizure suppression.

EEG
* feedback*
psychopath-
* ology*
epilepsy
alpha
* frequency*
applications

E 16   Vazquez, Alfredo J., and Toman, James E.P.: Demonstration of averaged operant potentials in the human EEG. *Electroencephalogr Clin Neurophysiol, 21*:381, 1966.

A retrospective summation method is described for study of EEG event preceding and operant patient hand-signal, together with notes on the intrinsic difficulties of such analysis. A significant cluster of small amplitude waves is found commonly present in bipolar recordings from the contralateral perietal area, in the period from 330 to 140 msec pre-trigger, in particular a 300 msec positive peak.

EEG events
operant
* motor act*

E 17   Zappoli, R.: The possibility of conditioning in man. Some types of discharges and epileptic attacks of reflex nature. *Riv Neurol, 39*:31, 1969.

This is a short review.

Pre-1965 References

EEG

Adrian, E.D., and Matthews, B.H.C.: The Berger rhythm: Potential changes from the occipital lobes in man. *Brain, 57:*355, 1934.

Albino, R., and Burnand, G.: Conditioning of alpha rhythm in man. *J Exp Psychol, 67:* 539, 1964.

Bartoshuk, A.K.: Electromyographic reactions to strong auditory stimulation as a function of alpha amplitude. *J Comp Physiol Psychol, 52:*540, 1959.

Callaway, E., and Layne, R.S.: Interaction between the visual evoked response and two spontaneous biological rhythms: The EEG alpha cycle and the cardiac arousal cycle. *Ann NY Acad Sci, 112:*421, 1964.

Chapman, R.M., and Bragdon, H.R.: Evoked responses to numerical and non-numerical visual stimuli while problem solving. *Nature (Lond), 203:*1155, 1964.

Darrow, C.W.: Electrical and circulatory responses to brief sensory and ideational stimuli. *J Exp Psychol, 12:*267, 1929.

Darrow, C.W., Lorens, S.A., Vieth, R.N., and Brues, C.: EEG and GSR latent time. *Electroencephalogr Clin Neurophysiol, 13:*146, 1961.

Darrow, C.W., Vieth, R.N., and Wilson, J.: Electroencephalographic "blocking" and "adaptation." *Science, 126:*74, 1957.

Davis, H.: Enhancement of evoked cortical potentials in humans related to a task requiring a decision. *Science, 145:*182, 1964.

Dixon, N.F.: Feedback and the visual threshold. *J Commun, 12:*97, 1962.

Eason, R.G., Aiken, L.R., White, C.T., and Lichtenstein, M.: Activation and behavior: II. Visually evoked cortical potentials in man as indicants of activation level. *Percept Mot Skills, 19:*875, 1964.

Geissman, P., and Noel, C.: Electroencephalographic study with frequency analysis and polygraphy of autogenic training. *Third World Congress Psychiatry (Montreal), 3:* 468, 1961.

Gershuni, G.V.: Conditioned cutaneous galvanic reactions and reactions of depression of alpha rhythm following subthreshold and suprathreshold sound stimulation in man. In *The Central Nervous System and Human Behavior.* (Translations from the Russian Medical Literature.) Bethesda, Russian Scientific Translation Program, 1959, p. 587.

Henry, C.E.: Electroencephalograms of normal children. *Soc Res Child Develop (Monogr), 9:*1, 1944.

Hofer, M.A., and Hinkle, L.E.: Conditioned alpha blocking and arousal: The effects of adrenaline administration. *Electroencephalogr Clin Neurophysiol, 17:*653, 1964.

Jasper, H., and Shagass, C.: Conditioning the occipital alpha rhythm in man. *J Exp Psychol, 28:*373, 1941.

Jasper, H., and Shagass, C.: Conscious time judgments related to conditioned time intervals and voluntary control of the alpha rhythms. *J Exp Psychol, 28:*503, 1941.

Johnson, L.C., and Davidoff, R.A.: Autonomic changes during paroxysmal EEG activity. *Electroencephalogr Clin Neurophysiol, 17:*25, 1964.

Kamiya, J.: Conditioned discrimination of the EEG alpha rhythm in humans. Paper presented at Western Psychological Association Meeting, San Francisco, Calif., 1962.

Kooi, K.A., and Bagchi, B.K.: Visual evoked responses in man: Normative data. *Ann NY Acad Sci, 112:*254, 1964.

Krauklis, A.A.: Autoregulation of higher nervous activity. *Riga, Latvia: Latvian Acad Sci,* 292, 1964.

Liu, Shih-yih, and Wu, Qin-e. Electroencephalographic and galvanic skin investigation of the orienting reflex in man. *Acta Psychol Sinica, 1:*1, 1963. Also in Barlow, J.S. (Ed.): *Contemporary Brain Research in China.* New York, Plenum Pub, 1971.

Mulholland, T.: The electroencephalogram as an experimental tool in the study of internal attention gradients. *Trans NY Acad Sci, 24:*664, 1962.

Mulholland, T.: Variation in the response-duration curve of successive cortical activation by a feedback stimulus. *Electroencephalogr Clin Neurophysiol, 16:*394, 1964.

Mulholland, T., and Runnals, S.: The effect of voluntarily directed attention on successive cortical activation responses. *J Psychol, 55:*427, 1963.

Mulholland, T., and Runnals, S.: Evaluation of attention and alertness with a stimulus-brain feedback loop. *Electroencephalogr Clin Neurophysiol, 14:*847, 1962.

Mulholland, T., and Runnals, S.: A stimulus-brain feedback system for evaluation of alertness. *J Psychol, 54:*69, 1962.

Mushkina, N.A.: Dynamics of formation of conditioned reflexes present and after reflexes present and after reflexes of depression of alpha rhythm and their differentiation. In *The Central Nervous System and Human Behavior.* (Translations from the Russian Medical Literature.) Bethesda, Russian Scientific Translation Program, 1959, p. 569.

Pampiglione, G., and Ackner, B.: The effects of repeated stimuli upon EEG and vasomotor activity during sleep in man. *Brain, 81:*64, 1958.

Peper, E.: Developing a biofeedback model: Alpha EEG feedback as a means for pain control. Presented in part at Biofeedback Research Society Meeting, St. Louis, 1971.

Peper, E.: Localized EEG alpha feedback training: A possible technique for mapping subjective, conscious, and behavioral experiences. Presented in part at Biofeedback Research Meeting, St. Louis, 1971.

Runnals, S., and Mulholland, T.: A method for the study of bilateral asymmetry of cortical activation. *Am J EEG Technology, 4:*15, 1964.

Shagass, C.: Conditioning the human occipital alpha rhythm to a voluntary stimulus. A quantitative study. *J Exp Psychol, 31:*367, 1942.

Shagass, C., and Johnson, E.P.: The course of acquisition of a conditioned response of the occipital alpha rhythm. *J Exp Psychol, 33:*201, 1943.

Sharpless, S., and Jasper, H.: Habituation of the arousal reaction. *Brain, 79:*655, 1956.

Slatter, K.H.: Alpha rhythms and mental imagery. *Electroencephalogr Clin Neurophysiol, 12:*851, 1960.

Stern, J.A., Das, K.C., Anderson, J.M., Biddy, R.L., and Surphlis, W.: "Conditioned" alpha desynchronization. *Science, 134:*388, 1961.

Sternbach, R.A.: Two independent indices of activation. *Electroencephalogr Clin Neurophysiol, 12:*609, 1960.

Stevens, J.R.: Endogenous conditioning to abnormal cerebral electrical transients in man. *Science, 137:*974, 1962.

Stoyva, J., and Kamiya, J.: Electrophysiological studies of dreaming as the prototype of a new strategy in the study of consciousness. *Psychol Rev, 75:*192, 1968.

Travis, L.E., and Egan, J.P.: Conditioning of the electrical response of the cortex. *J Exp Psychol, 22:*524, 1938.

Walter, R.D., and Yeager, C.L.: Visual imagery and electroencephalographic changes. *Electroencephalogr Clin Neurophysiol, 8:*193, 1956.

Walter, W.G.: The convergence and interaction of visual, auditory and tactile responses in human non-specific cortex. *Arch Psychiatr Nervenkr, 206:*309, 1964.

Walter, W.G., Cooper, R., Aldridge, V.J., McCallum, W.C., and Winter, A.L.: Contingent negative variation: An electric sign of sensorimotor association and expectancy in the human brain. *Nature (Lond), 203:*380, 1964.

White, E.H.: Subjectively equated stimulus intensities and autonomic reactivity. *J Exp Psychol, 68:*297, 1964.

DESCRIPTOR INDEX — EEG

PART VI

MISCELLANEOUS

RENAL

A 1   Dosa, S., Bojtos, A., and Houston, I.B.: The Pee-Peeper. A micturition-alert device. *Lancet, 2:*530, 1971.

A device has been developed which, by giving audible and visual signals at the moment of micturition, relieves a nurse of responsibility for the continual observation needed to note the precise time of micturition. The circuit for this instrument, when assembled, occupies a small metal box (9 × 11.5 × 5.5 cm.) with a switch for either an audible plus visual or only a visual alarm. Although usually used with an audible warning, turning off the sound while leaving a yellow flashing light is useful when disturbance must be avoided; yellow was chosen to avoid confusion with red lights used on such equipment as incubators. The "Pee-Peeper" operates from a 9 v dry battery which requires only infrequent replacement and is electrically safe.

*instrumen-
tation
operant con-
ditioning*

A 2   Gantt, W.H., Livingston, A. Jr., and Brown, E.: Renal and cardiac conditional reflex: Fractional conditioning. *Fed Proc, 28:*387, 1969.

In the study of behavior by the conditional reflex (CR) method we have previously noted that some physiological systems are adaptive; i.e. form the CR to the given agent while conditioning of other physiological systems to this agent is completely absent, viz, "fractional conditioning" (Fleck and Gantt, 1949). Fractional conditioning is valid only for the particular agent which is being used. The same physiological organ may form CRs to one type of unconditional stimulus (US) and not form CRs to another type of US. Schizokinesis refers to the difference in rate and stability of the CR in different physiological systems while fractional conditioning is an absolute difference. In renal studies we used as US: (1) milk and water, (2) pitressin, (3) phlorid-

*condition-
ing
animal*

zin. Components measured: diuresis, osmolality, electrolytes (Na, K, Cl), creatinine, pH. There was complete absence of renal conditioning to the above agents with the possible exception of Na. However, there was a cardiac CR (increase HR) to drinking and to person (exps. Frances Watt) and inhibition of HR to pitressin. These experiments indicate an absolute cleavage using the above agents between the conditionability of the cardiac function and the renal function (fractional conditioning).

A 3   Miller, Neal E., and DiCara, Leo V.: Instrumental learning of urine formation by rats; changes in renal blood flow. *Am J Physiol, 215*:677, 1968.

Rats paralyzed by curare and maintained on artificial respiration were rewarded by electrical stimulation of the medial forebrain bundle for changes in the rate of urine formation. Each of the seven rats rewarded for increases learned increases, and each of the seven rewarded for decreases learned decreases. The changes in the opposite directions were each highly reliable (p. < .001). The two groups differed in rate of glomerular filtration and renal blood flow, but not in blood pressure, heart rate, core temperature, or vasomotor activity.

conditioning
animal
blood flow

A 4   Miller, Neal E., DiCara, Leo V., and Wolf, George: Homeostasis and reward: T-maze learning induced by manipulating antidiuretic hormone. *Am J Physiol, 215*:684, 1968.

Albino rats were injected with antidiuretic hormone (ADH) if they chose one arm of a T-maze and with isotonic saline vehicle if they chose the other one. Normal rats preloaded with H_2O learned to choose the vehicle side where their kidneys could excrete the excess water more promptly, but rats with diabetes insipidus preloaded with hypertonic NaCl learned to choose the opposite side where ADH helped them to excrete excess NaCl. Normal controls that were not preloaded showed no learning. Thus, an excess of H_2O or NaCl can function as a drive, and the return to normal levels produced by an internal glandular response (instead of an external consumatory one) can function as a reward. We advance the hypothesis that drives and rewards induced in this

animal
conditioning
antidiuretic hormone

way can produce visceral learning that may serve to maintain homeostasis.

A 5   Shmavonian, B.M., DeMaria, W.J.A., Cohen, S.I., Krueger, R.P., and Hawkins, D.: Further studies in renal conditioning. *J Psychosom Res, 12*:223, 1968.

Discusses three additional experiments using renogram records, GSR, and plethysmograph records providing both blood volume measures, as well as heart rate to gain additional information on renal artery conditioning.

classical conditioning
renal artery
HR
GSR
pulse pressure

TEMPERATURE

B 1   Grabowska, M.J.: Changes of skin temperature during
hypnotic suggestions. *Pol Tyg Lek, 25:*328, 1970.

In a group of fifty-eight subjects the behavior of the tempera-   *hypnosis*
ture of the skin on the extremities was studied in various   *skin temper-*
stages of hypnosis and during hypnotic suggestion of warmth   *ature*
and cold. A statistically significant increase in the skin   *autogenic*
temperature was observed in the second stage of hypnosis and   *training*
a similarly significant rise in skin temperature during suggestion of warmth. The suggestions of warmth felt on one
hand increased the temperature of both hands. Systematic
courses of hypnosis with suggestions of warmth in association
with an own modification of the method of autogenous training based on exercises of muscle relaxation and autosugges-
tion of warmth felt in the limbs caused a statistically significant rise in the increase of skin temperature in final examinations in relation to initial examinations. These changes
were observed in healthy subjects as well as in individual
groups of patients without any significant differences between these groups. The results obtained suggest the usefulness of suggestion in hypnosis associated with the elements of
autogenous training as an additional method in comprehensive treatment of patients with circulatory disturbances in
the limbs.

B 2   Jacobson, Alan M., Hackett, Thomas P., Surman, Owen S.,
and Silverberg, Elizabeth L.: Raynaud Phenomenon. Treatment with hypnotic and operant technique. *JAMA, 225:*739,
1973.

One patient with Raynaud phenomenon was trained to in-   *hand tem-*
crease the temperature in his hands bilaterally, using com-   *perature*
bined hypnotic and operant techniques. An increase in   *Raynaud*
temperature of as much as 4.3 C was observed in both hands,   *phenome-*
    non

464

along with marked symptomatic improvement that was still in effect seven-and-one-half months after the last treatment session.

hypnosis
operant conditioning

B 3   Maslach, Christina, Marshall, Gary, and Zimbardo, Philip G.: Hypnotic control of peripheral skin temperature: A case report. *Psychophysiology, 9:*600, 1972.

In an exploratory study on the specificity of autonomic control, subjects attempted to simultaneously change the skin temperature of their two hands in opposite directions. Subjects who were trained in hypnosis were successful in achieving this bilateral difference, while waking control subjects were not. These findings demonstrate the powerful influence that cognitive processes can exert on the autonomic nervous system and also suggest the possibility of more effective therapeutic control of psychosomatic problems.

voluntary
control
bilateral
differences
hypnosis
implications

B 4   Russell, H.L.: Fingertip temperature changes during relaxation and psychotherapy. 11th Annual Meeting SPR, 1971. *Psychophysiology, 9:*279, 1972 (Abstr.) .

During therapy interviews preceded by thirty-minute relaxation procedures, Ss were given visual feedback of their fingertip temperatures. Fluctuation of ± 2 to 3°F from baseline were observed during relaxation procedures. During discussion of conflictual material in therapy there were decreases of 7 to 23°F. Concomitant with these changes, all Ss reported impressions of increased freedom from feelings of "psychic tension" with descriptions of mood state ranging from "enjoyable" to "euphoric." Those Ss most able to relate fall of temperature to fall of tension were the Ss who most increased verbalization of conflict. Preliminary results were consistent in the 8 Ss observed so far.

feedback
relaxation
therapy
interview
subjective
reports

B 5   Sargent, Joseph D., Green, Elmer E., and Walters, E. Dale: The use of autogenic feedback training in a pilot study of migraine and tension headaches. *Headache, 12:*120, 1972.

Subjects in the pilot study were either self-referred or referred by physicians in the community. The patient received instructions in the use of a "temperature trainer," which indicated the differential temperature between the mid-forehead and the right index finger, and a typewritten sheet containing autogenic phrases. Most subjects reported that a positive response with the trainer was associated chiefly with the feeling of change in the hands rather than change in the forehead. Each participant practiced daily with the temperature trainer at home and kept a record of the practice sessions on a special data sheet. Of the sixty-two patients with adequate data for clinical rating, 74 percent of the migraine sufferers were improved. There were not enough patients with tension headache to reach an adequate appraisal.

biofeedback
autogenic
training
migraine
tension
headaches

SALIVATION

C 1   Brown, Clinton C., and Katz, Ruth A.: Psychophysiologic aspects of parotid salivation in man: II. Effects of varying interstimulus intervals on delayed salivary conditioning. *Psychophysiology, 4:99*, 1967.

The aim of this study was to determine the effect of varying the interval between the onsets of CS and US on human salivary conditioning. Three interstimulus intervals (ISI's) were employed—five seconds, three seconds, and 0.25 second with an auditory CS of five-second duration and 1 ml (bilaterally) of flavored acid as US. Eighteen subjects were equally divided into the three ISI groups. Both positive (600 cps) and negative (200 cps) tones were given, and a 50 percent reinforcement schedule was followed in the last quarter of the test. The duration of the salivary unconditional response was significantly increased for the shortest (0.25 sec) ISI group for the total test period. In the last quarter of the test, the shortest ISI group showed significantly increased frequency of response to unreinforced CS presentations. The authors suggest that the change in shape of the UR was a function of the conditioning process and the increased responding to unreinforced CS's by the briefest ISI group demonstrated the importance of the temporal spacing within the conditioning paradigm.

classical conditioning
reinforcement
schedule
delayed conditioning

C 2   Brown, C.C., and Katz, R.A.: Operant salivary conditioning in man. *Psychophysiology, 4:156*, 1967.

Operant conditioning of the human parotid salivary response was attempted in order to bypass some of the difficulties encountered in classical conditioning procedures. Spontaneous, unstimulated parotid activity was collected from two groups of human subjects under two reward conditions. One group was rewarded for salivary peaks, defined as an increase in on-

salivation
operant conditioning
salivary rate

467

going salivary rate to a criteria of three drops/5 sec; the other was rewarded only at times of nonpeaking or minimal salivation. A significant increase in the number of peaks was found in the "peak reward" group, but there was no change in salivary rate in the "nonpeak reward" group. The data demonstrate salivary conditioning in human subjects by means of operant reward technique.

C 3 Brown, C.C.: The parotid puzzle: A review of the literature on human salivation and its application to psychophysiology. *Psychophysiology, 7:*66, 1970.

A survey of the literature on human salivation is presented with emphasis upon the influence of normal and psychopathologic emotional states as they affect alterations in factors relating to flow rate. Discussion includes neurological and physiological features of the gland, individuality of response, results of classical and operant conditioning, and suggested areas for future research.

salivation review emotional states neurophysiology conditioning

C 4 Delse, Frederick C., and Feather, Ben W.: The effect of augmented sensory feedback on the control of salivation. *Psychophysiology, 5:*15, 1968.

This study assessed the effect of enabling a subject to hear himself salivate while trying to increase or decrease his salivary rate. Two groups of ten subjects were instructed to try to increase their salivary rate when a light to the left was lighted and decrease when a light to the right was lighted. Acetic acid was administered periodically to the right lateral margin of the tongue, and saliva was collected by a parotid capsule and measured by a liquid displacement sialometer. Ten subjects in the feedback group (F) received a 0.2 sec, 1000-cps tone for each drop collected during a trial. Subjects in the no-feedback group (NF) received no indication of their salivary rate. Three out of ten F subjects were able to produce a significantly different (p < .05) number of drops between increase and decrease periods, and the group as a whole achieved a significant difference between increase and decrease periods. No NF subject, nor the NF group as a whole, produced a significant difference.

feedback learned control

C 5   Eysenck, Sybil B.G., and Eysenck, H.J.: Salivary response to
       lemon juice as a measure of introversion. *Percept Mot Skills,*
       *24:*1047, 1967.

Fifty men and fifty women were administered the EPI and   *salivary*
tested with respect to the increment in salivation produced   *responses*
by putting four drops of pure lemon juice on the tongue for *personality*
20 sec. It was found that in both groups introversion correlated approximately 0.7 with increase in salivation; there
was no correlation with neuroticism. When a commercial
product was substituted for pure lemon juice, all correlations
became insignificant, possibly due to the weaker concentration of the product. The results are explained (and were
predicted) in terms of a hypothesis relating introversion to
cortical arousal.

C 6   Feather, B.W., Delse, F.C., and Bryson, M.R.: Human sali-
       vary conditioning: Effect of unconditional stimulus intensity.
       *J Exp Psychol, 74:*389, 1967.

Four groups of fourteen high school students each were ad-   *classical con-*
ministered eight classical salivary conditioning trials. Each   *ditioning*
group received one of four concentrations of acetic acid em- *stimulus*
ployed as the UCS: .03 percent, .3 percent, .5 percent and   *strength*
1.5 percent. Two groups for which the CS- and UCS were   *pseudocon-*
unpaired received .3 percent and 1.5 percent acetic acid.   *ditioning*
Amount of salivation during the ten-second CS-UCS interval
was compared to amount of salivation during comparable
dummy periods. Significant levels of conditioning were
demonstrated at all four CS-UCS concentrations. There was
a significant ($p = .04$) linear relationship between UCS intensity and magnitude of CR. UCS intensity, however, did
not affect significantly the probability of response. Pseudoconditioning was not demonstrated by the unpaired groups.

C 7   Feather, B.W., and Wells, D.T.: Effects of concurrent motor
       activity on the unconditioned salivary reflex. *Psychophysiol-*
       *ogy, 2:*338, 1966.

This study tested the hypothesis that the relative amount of *salivary*
swallowing and mouth movement affects the amplitude,   *reflex*

latency, and temporal course of the salivary unconditioned reflex (UR). Twenty-four subjects were given three identical stimuli which consisted of 3 cc of 0.5 percent citric acid, delivered to the left lateral margin of the posterior half of the tongue. The stimuli were administered under three different conditions for each subject: (1) swallowing and mouth movements permitted for the first thirty seconds following stimulation, (2) swallowing and mouth movements prohibited for the first thirty seconds and permitted for the second thirty seconds following stimulation, and (3) swallowing and mouth movements permitted for sixty seconds following stimulation. Saliva was collected by a parotid capsule and measured by a sensitive liquid displacement sialometer. Motor activity was monitored by electromyogram. There was a significantly greater (p < 0.01) amount of saliva secreted during periods of motor activity, regardless of time since stimulation. Voluntary inhibition of swallowing immediately after acid stimulation resulted in significantly longer and more variable UR latencies. Implications of these findings for studies on salivary conditioning are discussed.

stimulus schedule
EMG
motor activity

C 8　　Frezza, Daniel A., and Holland, James G.: Operant conditioning of the human salivary response. *Psychophysiology, 8:* 581, 1971.

To demonstrate operant conditioning of the human salivary response, stimulus control was attempted. Unstimulated parotid saliva was collected from four Ss under two reinforcement schedules. Continuous reinforcement (CRF) alternated at regular intervals with differential reinforcement for zero responding (DRO) reinforcement for nonresponding during a specified time period. Cumulative records revealed an increase in responding under CRF and a decrease in responding under DRO for three of the four Ss. Swallowing was recorded. The conditioned salivary response appeared not to be mediated by muscle response.

operant conditioning
stimulus discrimination
learned control
EMG

C 9　　Miller, Neal E., and Carmona, Alfredo: Modification of a visceral response: Salivation in thirsty dogs by instrumental training with water reward. *J Comp Physiol Psychol, 63:*1, 1967.

Thirsty dogs rewarded by water for bursts of spontaneous salivation showed progressive increases in salivation, while other dogs, rewarded for brief periods without salivation, showed progressive decreases. No obvious motor responses were involved, but dogs rewarded for decreasing salivation appeared more drowsy than those rewarded for increasing it. Implications for learning theory and psychosomatic medicine are mentioned.

animal
operant dog
condition-
ing
stimulus dis-
crimina-
tion
implications

C 10 Wells, D.T., and Feather, B.W.: Effects of changing the CS-UCS interval in human salivary responses. *Psychophysiology,* 4:278, 1968.

An experiment was performed to test the effect of changing the CS-UCS interval on the pattern of conditioned salivation. Each of six subjects received sixty reinforced trials on each of three CS-UCS intervals: ten, twenty and forty seconds. For each CS-UCS interval ten test trials were given to determine the change in pattern to responses with change in the CS-UCS interval. An additional session included two test trials in which an extraneous stimulus was given simultaneously with the CS. The results showed little evidence of inhibition of delay in the longer intervals or of disinhibition when the extraneous stimulus was applied. The most significant result was a response which followed CS offset in the twenty- and forty-second intervals. The question of the nature of this response remains to be answered by use of different experimental design. Significance of the level of conditioning remained high (p < .00001) over the manipulation of CS-UCS interval.

salivation
classical con-
ditioning
stimulus
schedule

C 11 Wells, David T., Feather, Ben W., and Headrick, Mary W.: The effects of immediate feedback upon voluntary control of salivary rate. *Psychophysiology, 10:*501, 1973.

Thirteen human subjects (Ss) were given immediate auditory feedback concerning their salivary rates and were asked both to increase and to decrease their rates during a series of thirty-second trials. Significant decreases, but not increases, in salivary rate were obtained relative to baseline. During the second half of the experiment, when feedback was omitted until the end of each trial, Ss maintained significant dif-

feedback
voluntary
control
salivary rate
differential
responses
operant con-
ditioning

ferential response rates between increase and decrease trials,   *HR*
but the reliability of decreases from expected baseline was   *respiration*
reduced. Thirteen control Ss, who received feedback only at
the end of each trial during both halves of the experiment,
were unable to alter their rates during either half. Salivation
on increase and decrease trials was not systematically correlated with changes in either heart rate or breathing rate in
the immediate feedback group.

SECTION D

VASOMOTOR

D 1   Bloch, S., and Davies, B.: Forearm blood flow in anxious and non-anxious patients. *Aust NZ J Psychiatry, 3*:86, 1969.

A mercury in rubber strain gauge was used to assess the value of forearm blood flow estimations as a measure of anxiety. Measurements of forearm blood flow were estimated on two groups of patients, ten with features of anxiety and ten free of anxiety. In both groups of patients an increase in forearm blood flow occurred under conditions of stress, but there were no statistically significant differences in forearm blood flow between the two conditions.

measure-ment techniques
forearm
stress

D 2   DiCara, Leo V., and Miller, Neal E.: Instrumental learning of vasomotor responses by rats: Learning to respond differentially in the two ears. *Science, 159*:1485, 1968. (Copyright 1968 by the American Association for the Advancement of Science.)

Curarized and artificially respirated rats were rewarded by electrical stimulation of the brain for changes in the balance of vasomotor activity between the two ears. They learned vasomotor responses in one ear that were independent of those in the other ear, in either forepaw or in the tail, or of changes in heart rate or temperature. In addition to implications for learning theory and psychosomatic medicine, these results indicate a greater specificity of action in the sympathetic nervous system than is usually attributed to it.

animal
curare
operant conditioning
learned control
vasomotor responses
implications

D 3   DiCara, Leo V., and Miller, Neal E.: Instrumental learning of peripheral vasomotor responses by the curarized rat. *Comm Behav Biol, 1*:209, 1968.

Artificially respirated rats completely paralyzed by curare were rewarded by electrical stimulation of the medial forebrain bundle for either vasoconstriction or vasodilatation as measured by a photoelectric transducer placed at the base of the tail. Each of the four subjects rewarded for increasing vasodilatation learned reliable dilatation (P = .01), while each of the four subjects rewarded for increasing vasoconstriction learned reliable constriction (P = .01). Results also indicate that such learning is not accompanied by overall changes in heart rate, but it is associated with significant changes in core temperature; paradoxically, vasoconstriction is accompanied by decreases and vasodilatation by increases in rectal temperature.

animal operant conditioning vasomotor responses stimulis discrimination HR temperature

D 4   Gale, E.N., and Stern, J.A.: Classical conditioning of the peripheral motor orienting response. *Psychophysiology, 4:* 342, 1968.

The present study demonstrates that the peripheral vasomotor response is conditionable. The paradigm used involved a delayed, differential conditioning procedure and utilized both a conditioning and sensitization control group. The results demonstrate that the vasomotor orienting response can be differentially conditioned.

orienting responses delayed conditioning

D 5   Gelder, M.G., and Mathews, A.M.: Forearm blood flow and phobic anxiety. *Br J Psychiatry, 114:*1371, 1968.

Forearm blood flow measurements have been shown to be one of the indices sensitive enough to reflect transient increases in arousal such as those assumed to occur during desensitization treatment. Further work is needed to determine to what extent blood flow measures are preferable to the more commonly used indices of palmar skin conductance and electromyographic activity. The results are taken to indicate that, in general, reliance on forearm blood flow as a single measure of anxiety in desensitization would be ill-advised, although certain individuals may be identified by their specific responsiveness and in these the measurement of blood flow would seem an appropriate and useful clinical tool. The changes demonstrated when phobic patients

forearm phobic anxiety stress mental tasks

imagine feared objects or situations gives some objective confirmation of the supposed mechanism underlying the desensitization procedure.

D 6   Kato, L., Gozsy, B., Ban, T.A., and Sterlin, C.: Effects of psychoactive agents on the conditioning of the microcirculation in the rat. *Cond Reflex, 6*:67, 1971.

Normal vascular tonus and permeability of the microcirculatory network is mediated by catecholamines, histamine and serotonin. Following electroconvulsive treatment (ECT), histamine did not provoke local vasodilation. The inhibition was further potentiated by drugs which prevent the enzymatic or physical inactivation of free catecholamines and by locally administered norepinephrine. This system became conditioned to a visual stimulus when rats were presented in six consecutive occasions with the visual stimulus precedingly coincided with the administration of ECT. In the conditioned rats, light alone inhibited the histamine-induced vasodilatation, and this inhibition was potentiated by subeffective doses of injected norepinephrine and by drugs which prevent the enzymatic or physical inactivation of catecholamines. Sedatives, antidepressants, MAO inhibitors and the chlorpromazine-type agents as well as the psychotomimetic drugs characteristically influence either the acquisition or the extinction of the conditioned reflex. Results suggest that the obtained conditioning of the microcirculatory functions are mediated by the centrally released catecholamines.

animal microcirculation classical conditioning drugs catecholamines

D 7   Kelly, D.H.W., and Walter, C.J.S.: The relationship between clinical diagnosis and anxiety, assessed by forearm blood flow and other measurements. *Br J Psychiatry, 114*:611, 1968.

(1) "Basal" forearm blood flow has been found to be a valid and reliable index of anxiety and has been used in this investigation to measure the amount of anxiety in different diagnostic groups. Two hundred and three patients and sixty normal controls were examined. Measurements of forearm blood flow, heart rate, and anxiety self-rating were made under "basal" (resting) conditions and under "stress" pro-

anxiety forearm blood flow HR

duced by harassing mental arithmetic. The Taylor Scale of
Manifest Anxiety, Neuroticism, and Extraversion were also
measured. (2) Highly significant differences were found between forty-one patients with chronic anxiety states and
sixty normal controls. The mean "basal" forearm blood flow
of the anxious patients was more than twice as great as that
of the controls. Each investigator working separately obtained very similar results. (3) "Basal" forearm blood flow
placed nine diagnostic categories and normal controls in the
following rank order of decreasing anxiety: chronic anxiety
state, agitated depressive, chronic schizophrenic, obsessional
neurosis, phobic state, normal control, hysteria, nonagitated
depression, personality disorder, and depersonalization. The
rank order was consistent with other physiological work and
with clinical experience. The difference between the group
means of the different diagnostic categories was significant in
over 50 percent. This was the highest degree of differentiation for the parameters used. (4) There was a highly significant positive correlation between "basal" forearm blood
flow and other measures of anxiety, i.e. the Taylor Scale of
Manifest Anxiety, "basal" anxiety self-rating, and "basal"
heart rate. This is further evidence of the validity of forearm blood flow as a good objective index of anxiety.

D 8   Kelly, D.H.W., and Walter, C.J.S.: A clinical and physio-
       logical relationship between anxiety and depression. *Br J
       Psychiatry, 115:*401, 1969.

The relationship between anxiety and depression has been   *forearm*
the subject of much controversy. A simple clinical classifica-   *blood flow*
tion of anxiety and depressive states has been used and   *anxiety*
physiological and psychological measurements made to see   *depression*
if experimental data differed among the various groups.   *HR*
Anxiety states were classified as acute, phobic and chronic.   *psychiatric*
Depression was categorized as agitated and nonagitated, de-   *diagnosis*
pending on the degree of concomitant anxiety. There were
significant differences between the agitated and nonagitated
patients in mean anxiety self-ratings, basal forearm blood
flow, and heart rate. The patients with chronic anxiety states
had a mean basal forearm blood flow which was highly significantly greater than that of the patients with agitated depression. The physiological evidence presented here lends

tentative support to the classification used. The psychological measurements showed very good patient-control differences but fewer intergroup patient differences.

D 9   Kelly, Desmond, Brown, Clinton C., and Shaffer, John W.: A comparison of physiological and psychological measurements on anxious patients and normal controls. *Psychophysiology, 6:*429, 1970.

Clinical, psychophysiological and psychometric measurements were made on twenty normal controls and thirty anxious patients during rest and experimental stress. Resting forearm blood flow, a relatively new physiological index of anxiety, was found to correlate significantly with clinical and subjective ratings of anxiety and with heart rate, number of spontaneous fluctuations of skin resistance, and amplitude of forearm EMG. It did not correlate significantly with any of the measures of depression. Resting forearm blood flow and heart rate were found to be better measures of arousal in this study than skin resistance, EMG, or cutaneous vasomotor status, since the latter did not show significant differences between anxious patients and normal controls. The psychological traits of the two groups were also assessed by the Maudsley Personality Inventory, Taylor Manifest Anxiety Scale, and Zung Depression Scale; and their emotional state evaluated by the Clyde Mood Scale and Semantic Differential Scale. Twenty-one variables showed significant differences between the two groups. Some of these measures have subsequently been used, with advantage, to monitor emotional changes brought about by psychiatric treatment.

anxiety
experimental stress
forearm blood flow
HR
GSR
EMG
personality

D 10 Ledberg, Lars, Schalling, Daisy, and Levander, Sten E.: Some characteristics of digital vasomotor activity. *Psychophysiology, 9:*402, 1972.

Size and latency of responses to a series of tones, spontaneous fluctuations, and habituation in finger volume and pulse volume were studied in nineteen healthy young soldiers by means of pneumoplethysmography. The results indicate that relationships among vasomotor measures differ from those reported for skin conductance measures. Thus, in contrast to what has been shown for skin conductance, no correlation was found between habituation and number of spontaneous

vasomotor responses
finger pulse volume
skin conductance
habituation
spontaneous activity

fluctuations, and the variability of the first response to the tones did not differ from the variability of the following responses. Auditory stimulation did not increase the number of spontaneous fluctuations. There were highly significant correlations between spontaneous fluctuations during rest and stimulation periods. No significant correlations were obtained between pulse volume responses to an arithmetic task and responses to tone stimuli. Some differences in pattern of relationships were obtained between finger and pulse volume measures. Initial responses in finger volume were related to other response size measures, whereas this was not the case for pulse volume. Response latency increased during the auditory stimulation for pulse volume, but not for finger volume.

D 11   Machac, M.: Vasomotor response to intentional autoregulative operations of the relaxation activation method. *Activ Nerv Sup* (Praha), *11*:42, 1969.

A total of 111 plethysmographic measurements on finger and forearm were performed in twelve subjects. A simultaneous finger vasoconstriction and forearm vasodilation were the most frequent features (52%) during the activation phase. Vasodilation in both regions studied was found in 19 percent. Forearm vessels dilated in 77 percent of all activation phases. The observed cardiovascular changes are related to intentional manipulations with the mental state.

finger
forearm
relaxation
intention
mental state

D 12   Mathews, A.M., and Lader, M.H.: An evaluation of forearm blood flow as a psychophysiological measurement. *Psychophysiology, 8*:509, 1971.

The usefulness of forearm blood flow (FBF) as a psychophysiological measure was investigated by comparing changes occurring during mental tasks in cardiovascular, sudomotor and electromyographic measures. The measures were divided into those clearly physiologically independent and those physiologically related. ANOVA results showed that FBF, heart rate (HR), and skin conductance fluctuations (SCF) were equally reactive, and correlational analysis suggested that a close relationship existed between BFB, HR

mental tasks
forearm
  blood flow
HR
SC
EMG
correlational analyses

and SCF, although correlations fell to near zero levels when intra-individual correlations were calculated with between-task variance extracted. For some experimental purposes HR responses may be considered equivalent to FBF responses. The relationship between EMG and FBF was more variable and tends not to support the idea that FBF is an indirect measure of muscle activity. The reliability of FBF in normal subjects at rest was poor, although it improved when measured during a simple task, and is probably stable enough for most experimental purposes.

D 13   Noble, P.J., and Lader, M.H.: Depressive illness, pulse rate, and forearm blood flow. *Br J Psychiatry, 118:*261, 1971.

Recorded the forearm blood flow and pulse rate of thirty-four depressed psychiatric patients before and after a course of ECT. Ss were assessed on the Hamilton Rating Scale for Depression. In the depressed state low blood flow correlated with "retardation" and "decline in work and interests." Clinical improvement subsequent to ECT was accompanied by a significant increase in blood flow. It is suggested that depressive illness is associated with an inhibitory affect on muscle blood flow which may be mediated via hypothalamic control.

forearm blood flow psychiatric depression ECT

D 14   Rosenberg, C.M.: Forearm blood flow in response to stress. *J Abnorm Psychol, 76:*180, 1970.

The relationship between stress, forearm blood flow, and subjective anxiety was examined. In normal subjects, electric shocks applied to the opposite forearm led to a rapid rise in anxiety and forearm blood flow. With repeated regular shocks, habituation of the vasomotor response occurred and anxiety became less intense. These changes appeared to be related to the subject's ability to predict accurately the intensity and frequency of the stimulus. Mental arithmetic under harassment produced a more gradual but greater rise in blood flow without an equal rise in anxiety. Alcoholic subjects who were judged to have limited motivation and ego strength showed a significantly lower vasomotor response during mental arithmetic. It is concluded that changes in

forearm blood flow stress anxiety habituation subjective judgments mental tasks alcoholics

forearm blood flow observed during stress cannot be related
only to an increase in anxiety. This response seems to depend
also on the significance of the stimulus to the subject, his
psychiatric status, and his level of motivation.

D 15   Royer, F.L.: Cutaneous vasomotor components of the orienting reflex. *Behav Res Ther, 3* :161, 1965.

Eight normal male Ss were tested for vasomotor responses of
four skin areas to the presentation of novel auditory stimuli.
Reciprocal vasomotor responses of the finger (vasoconstriction) and head (vasodilatation) reported by Vinogradova
and Sokolov were confirmed, consistent with the known
dominant vasomotor tone of these areas. Measurement of
activity of the ear with the dominant constrictive tone and
of the skin of the neck with a dominant dilatative tone indicate that the vasomotor component of the orienting reflex
is an enhancement of normal vasomotor control.

*orienting
response
reciprocal
vasomotor
responses
response
compon-
ents*

D 16   Royer, F.L.: The "respiratory vasomotor reflex" in the forehead and the finger. *Psychophysiology, 2* :241, 1966.

The so-called respiratory vasomotor reflex, long observed
in plethysmography of the extremities, was examined in
seven normal Ss ranging in age from seventeen to thirty-eight
years. With a photometric method the vascular responses of
the skin of the forehead and the finger were found to differ
following a deep breath like a sigh. These responses were
quite similar to the vascular components of the orienting
reflex, i.e. vasodilatation in the forehead and vasoconstriction in the hand. A polyphasic response in the forehead of
some Ss followed the deliberate deep inspirations. This polyphasic response has also been observed during the orienting
reflex but without changes in respiration. This type of response appears to be associated with bradycardia and may be
related to similar vascular responses observed following
cardiac arrhythmias.

*forehead
finger
orienting
response
response
compon-
ents
respiration
cardiac
responses*

D 17   Shean, G.D.: Vasomotor conditioning and awareness. *Psychophysiology, 5* :22, 1968.

The relationship between conditioning, generalization and extinction of digital vasoconstriction and subject awareness of CS-US sequence was investigated. Subjects were randomly assigned to four groups and within-group awareness was controlled through the manipulation of instructional parameters. Results indicated that vasomotor conditioning occurred only in those subjects that were judged to be aware of relevant conditioning stimulus relationships. Conditioned responses were found to extinguish almost immediately when subjects were informed of shock cessation. These findings were interpreted as being consistent with an approach which distinguishes between conditioning and relational learning.

classical conditioning
instructions
contingency
awareness
relational learning

D 18   Shean, G.D., and Stange, P.W.: The effects of varied respiratory rate and volume upon finger pulse volume. *Psychophysiology, 8:*401, 1971.

The effects of varied conditions of respiratory rate and volume upon finger pulse volume were investigated. Results indicated that any change in ongoing respiratory activity resulted in maximal digital vasoconstriction with four to eight seconds, and that these effects were greatest during deep breathing. The relevance of these findings for investigations of vasomotor conditioning are discussed.

finger pulse volume
respiratory activity
conditioning

D 19   Silverman, Albert J., and McGough, W. Edward: Personality, stress, and venous flow rates. *J Psychosom Res, 15:*315, 1971.

Previously noted vascular differences between Field Dependent (FD) and Field Independent (FI) Ss led to an interest in Venous Flow Rates (VFR) in these two groups. Blood flow rate in a large arm vein was determined by threading a hydrogen sensitive (platinum-oxide tipped) electrode into an upper arm vein and introducing Sodium Ascorbate (as a source of H^+) into a tributory on the back of the hand. VFR was measured by dividing the time for H^+ to reach the electrode into the distance traveled. With this technique, four resting VFR in forty-one Ss were found to average 2 to 3 cm/sec. Epinephrine caused a significant increase in rate of flow,

venous flow rates
psychologic stress
epinephrine
ego strength
anxiety

while the instructions to anticipate an oral arithmetic problem, and the problem itself, caused a significant decrease. FI resting VFR in forty-one Ss were found to average 2 to 3 cm/sec. revealed more persistent elevation in VFR than FD Ss in response to epinephrine. High ego strength Ss (Barron Scale of MMPI) had faster rates at rest and after epinephrine, than low ego strength Ss. High Anxiety Ss (Taylor Scale of MMPI) revealed faster rates during epinephrine and less recovery from arithmetic than of Low Anxiety Ss.

D 20   Smith, O.A., Jr., and Stebbins, W.C.: Conditioned blood flow and heart rate in monkeys. *J Comp Physiol Psychol, 59:* 432, 1965.

Molded plastic flow sections were implanted on the terminal aorta of six monkeys, and the connecting wires brought through the back to an ultrasonic flowmeter. The Ss were then trained in a classical delayed conditioned response paradigm. Two stimulus lights of different colors were randomly presented to the animal for a fifty-six-second period; one light was followed by nothing, the other by a brief electrical shock. Conditioned increases in heart rate and blood flow were demonstrated. Discrimination was shown in five of the Ss. Records of body movements and respiration indicated that these factors have a negligible influence on the CR.

aortic blood flow
HR
respiration

D 21   Snyder, Charles, and Noble, Merrill: Operant conditioning of vasoconstriction. *J Exp Psychol, 77:*263, 1968.

A study of operant conditioning of vasoconstriction is reported. Finger volume was recorded during a five-minute baseline period, during a twenty-five-minute acquisition period, and during a twenty-minute extinction period. During the acquisition period, each of two experimental groups (n = 12) were reinforced at the peak amplitude of each criterion vasoconstriction. Two matched control groups (n = 12) received an equal number of reinforcements, but reinforcement was contingent upon vasomotor stability. A baseline control group (n = 6) received no reinforcement. During extinction, one experimental group was reinforced for

operant conditioning
vasoconstriction
finger volume
EMG
HR
respiration

vasomotor stability, while reinforcement was omitted for all other conditions. Experimental Ss showed a significant increase in number of vasoconstrictions during acquisition; control Ss did not. Conditioned vasoconstriction was independent of gross body movement, muscle tension in the forearm and finger, heart rate, and respiratory irregularities. The results were interpreted as evidence against theories which state that visceral responses can only be classically conditioned.

D 22   Spreng, Lawrence F., Johnson, Laverne C., and Lubin, Ardie: Autonomic correlates of eye movement bursts during stage REM sleep. *Psychophysiology, 4:*311, 1968.

During stage REM sleep, eye movements were found to be distributed in discrete bursts of rapid eye movement (REM-bursts). REM-burst time averaged approximately 10 percent of stage REM sleep and the rate within a subject was consistent from epoch-to-epoch and night-to-night. Consistent subject biases in eye movement direction were also found. Subject correlations were obtained between REM-burst time and autonomic activity. Significant positive correlations were found for respiration rate and number of finger pulse responses. There were positive but insignificant correlations with electrodermal activity, heart rate and decreases in respiration amplitude. Autonomic variability was not significantly associated with REM-burst time.

sleep
finger pulse
* volume*
respiration
HR
GSR

D 23   Teichner, Warren H., and Levine, Jerrold M.: Digital vasomotor conditioning and body heat regulation. *Psychophysiology, 5:*67, 1968.

Human subjects were conditioned to a tone-shock sequence during heat or cold exposure and then given ten trials of experimental extinction in the heat. In the heat, while exhibiting a general peripheral, as well as a digital, vasodilatation, vasoconstriction developed as a conditioned response; the response did not extinguish. In the cold, with general peripheral and digital vasoconstriction, vasodilatation developed as the conditioned response. Since the cold-conditioned Ss did not recover completely from their cold ex-

classical con-
* ditioning*
temperature
* stimuli*
finger
* volume*
thermoregu-
* lation*

posure during the following heat equilibrium period, the extinction data of this group could not be accepted. A comparison was also made of the differences in thermoregulation and in conditioned responses of preselected Ss varying in latency of cold-induced digital vasodilatation. Although these Ss did differ in their thermophysiological reactions, they did not differ in regard to the nature of the conditioned response developed.

D 24   Teichner, Warren H., Beals, Jacquelyn, and Giambalvo, Vincent: Conditioned vasomotor response: Thermoregulatory effects. *Psychophysiology, 10:*238, 1973.

Whether a conditioned vasomotor response will be a vasoconstriction or a vasodilatation appears to depend upon the thermal state at the time that the response is elicited and to be independent of what the response might have been during previous thermal states. For rabbits equilibrated to 18 to 20°C, the conditioned stress response tends to be a vasoconstriction. For equilibration to air temperature either higher or lower than that approximate thermal nonregulatory range, the response tends to be a vasodilatation.

vasomotor responses
animal
classical conditioning
temperature stimuli
thermoregulation

D 25   Tursky, B., and Greenblatt, D.J.: Local vascular and thermal changes that accompany electric shock. *Psychophysiology, 3:* 371, 1967.

A series of experiments was conducted to determine whether any physiological changes accompany the previously observed drop in impedance of the electrode skin circuit during the administration of electric shock. Two concentric shock electrodes were modified by the addition of devices to measure the local temperature, blood volume, and blood pulse volume changes occurring directly under the electrode. Subjects were given a series of shocks through one of these electrodes, but not the other, while the physiological measures were recorded at both sites. No significant differences in temperature and blood volume measures occurred between shocked and unshocked electrodes. However, directly correlated with the drastic drop in impedance of the shocked circuit was a marked increase in blood pulse volume, in-

mechanisms
electric shock
impedance
local temperature
blood volume

ferred to be a manifestation of the anon reflex. The two related effects were shown to be highly localized at or near the shocked electrode, and also to be characteristic only of the passage of current through electrode-skin junctions.

D 26   Volow, M.R., and Hein, P.L.: Bidirectional operant conditioning of peripheral vasomotor responses with augmented feedback and prolonged training. *Psychophysiology, 9:*271, 1972.

operant conditioning
feedback
finger pulse volume
stimulus discrimination

A program of training in voluntary control of finger pulse volume (FPV), using a discrete trials design, required dilatation and constriction from each of eight, male, undergraduate Ss. Each trial consisted of a ten-second passive baseline period; followed by a twenty-second active baseline period (S maintained some intermediate FPV level); followed by a seventy-second trial period, for which S_D was either a green slide (dilatation) or a red slide (constriction). S received continuous visual, analog feedback; and also intermittent binary feedback (tone) whenever FPV exceeded its mean active baseline level in the appropriate direction. Monetary rewards were based on Ss' performance. Approximately seventy trials were given in each direction; in alternating groups of seven each at first, and in randomized order during later test sessions. There were eleven 1-hr sessions. MANOVAs of individual difference scores (covariance-adjusted for passive baseline variability) showed: two Ss could both dilate and constrict reliably; four Ss could only constrict reliably; one S could only dilate reliably; one S learned neither task. All Ss showed a nonspecific constrictive effect, superimposed upon the first fifteen seconds of both dilatation and constriction trials.

SECTION E

RESPIRATION

E 1   Adamowicz, J.K., Gibson, D., and Kaufman, D.: Respiratory change and mental task gradient. *Psychon Sci, 9:*183, 1967.

Examined the proposed connection between mental task difficulty levels and heart rate changes using a respiration measure and pretested intensities of mental task demand and white noise for twenty-seven Ss. Similarity of direction and magnitude of results between studies based on cardiovascular measures and the present respiration findings indicate that conclusions can be generalized physiologically.

cognitive task
task diffi-culty
respiratory response
HR

E 2   Alexander, A.B.: Systematic relaxation and flow rates in asthmatic children: Relationship to emotional precipitants and anxiety. *J Psychosom Res, 16:*405, 1972.

The present experiment was an attempt to replicate with better control, and to extend, previously reported work by the author and his colleagues. In that work, relaxation train-ing, as compared to just sitting quietly, was found to result in an increase in PEFR over sessions in asthmatic children. In the present study, the relationship between the presence of emotional asthma precipitants and the amount of PEFR response, and the possibility that anxiety was mediating the effect were investigated. The previous findings were repli-cated in all important aspects, while the results suggested that anxiety changes were probably not mediating the effect and that the effect of relaxation on PEFR was generally greater for those subjects in whom emotional factors were prominent.

asthma
children
relaxation training
flow rates
emotional precipi-tants
anxiety

E 3   Bakers, J.H.C.M., and Tenney, S.M.: The perception of some sensations associated with breathing. *Resp Physiol, 10:* 85, 1970.

The ability to estimate several sensations associated with breathing was studied in man by comparing physical stimulus intensity with the subject's judgment of magnitude. The data were expressed by the psychophysical power law, $\psi = K\phi^n$, in which ψ is apparent, or psychological, magnitude, and ϕ is physical, or real, stimulus intensity. K and N are constants. The group mean value of n for pressure stimuli was about 1.5; for volume, about 1.3; and for ventilation, about 1.9. Refinements in experimental design to separate "active" (i.e. subject generated stimulus by his own motor function) as compared with "passive" (observer generated stimulus) did not reveal significant differences in manner of assessment of pressure or volume (criterion was value of n), nor were pressure assessments of either kind affected by lung volume. The origin of the sensations probably resides in the chest wall.

sensations
awareness
mechanisms

E 4   Block, James D., Lagerson, Joanne, Zohman, Lenore R., and Kelly, George: A feedback device for teaching diaphragmatic breathing. *Am Rev Resp Dis, 100*:577, 1969.

A ventilatory feedback device has been developed and seems to be effective in training patients to breathe diaphragmatically rather than thoracically. Sensory feedback of physiologic information to patients is potentially useful as an adjunct to medical therapy in chest diseases.

feedback
instruments

E 5   Heim, Edgar, Knapp, Peter H., Vachon, Louis, Globus, Gordon G., and Nemetz, S. Joseph: Emotion, breathing and speech. *J Psychosom Res, 12*:261, 1968.

Four perennial asthmatics were observed in different emotional states which arose during psychotherapeutic interviews. Respiration was monitored with a strain-gauge pneumograph during a total of thirty-nine sessions. The respiratory record allowed us to select various one-minute samples of the interview and measure the following variables: (1) respiratory rate, (2) mean amplitude, (3) variance of amplitude, (4) minute volume, (5) sighs, (6) periods of breath holding. The typescript of the tape-recorded interviews was independently studied by two psychiatric judges who selected

asthma
emotion
respiration
  parameters
speech-
  breathing
  patterns

"emotional peaks" as well as a reference "neutral" period in each interview. These were all segments during which patients were speaking. The "emotions" were operationally defined in advance and condensed in four clusters chosen to reflect different psychophysiologic states: (1) "distress" (encompassing anxiety, guilt, shame), (2) "giving-up" (encompassing sorrow, helplessness, hopelessness), (3) "drive arousal" (anger or sexual excitement), and (4) "neutral emotion" referring to the moments when the subject was judged to be in his least intense emotional phase for that hour. Predictions were made about the relative level of each physiological variable under the differing emotional conditions. Predicted outcomes were observed at a significant level for four of the six variables. Individual consistence of breathing patterns in the interviews suggested that there were individual "styles" of speech-breathing. Observation of speech-breathing patterns gives important information about inter-individual personality features and intra-individual change with changing emotional states.

E 6   Henry, John P., Junas, Richard, and Smith, Karl U.: Experimental cybernetic analysis of delayed feedback of breath-pressure control. *Am J Phys Med, 46*:1317, 1967. (Copyright 1967 by the Williams & Wilkins Co., Baltimore.)

A new method extending delayed visual feedback to the study of the voluntary control of the muscles of respiration has been devised and executed. The conclusions derived from this preliminary study are similar to those found in other studies of the control of somatic responses. (1) Increasing delays caused deterioration of performance. (2) Delays adversely affected learning. (3) By the duration of delays producing maximum effects, the muscles of respiration are classed with other skeletal muscles involving movements of a gross nature. (4) The factors of cybernetic control and design may be involved in rehabilitative training and correction of deficiencies of external respiratory control.

delayed feedback breath-pressure voluntary control

E 7   Luparello, Thomas, Lyons, Harold A., Bleecker, Eugene R., and McFadden, E.R. Jr.: Influences of suggestion on airway reactivity in asthmatic subjects. *Psychosom Med., 30*:819, 1968.

The effect of suggestion on bronchomotor tone was evaluated in a setting in which accurate, rapid and reproducible measurements of airway resistance (Ra) could be made. Subjects with asthma, emphysema, and restrictive lung disease, as well as normal subjects, were studied. All subjects were led to believe that they were inhaling irritants or allergens which cause bronchoconstriction. The actual substance used in all instances was nebulized physiologic saline solution. Nineteen of forty asthmatics reacted to the experimental situation with a significant increase in Ra. Twelve of the asthmatic subjects developed full-blown attacks of bronchospasm which was reversed with a saline solution placebo. The forty control nonasthmatic subjects did not react.

asthma
suggestion
broncho-spasm

E 8   Maher-Loughnan, G.P.: Hypnosis and autohypnosis for the treatment of asthma. *Int J Clin Exp Hypn, 18:*1, 1970.

Two controlled studies were conducted into the use of hypnosis in asthma patients. Several different control procedures were used. The methods and results of both studies were summarized, and the same conclusion was reached: hypnosis supplemented by autohypnosis was significantly more effective than control procedures. An outline is given of details of treatment methods. A current analysis of patients treated at one center, involving up to six years of follow-up, is presented to provide a working guide to the regime in regular practice. To be fully effective hypnosis should be employed before steroids are started. Steroid-dependent asthma is rarely totally relieved by hypnotherapy.

asthma
hypnosis
treatment

E 9   Maher-Loughnan, G.P.: Emotional aspects of chest disease. *Geriatrics, 26:*120, 1971.

Emotional reactions accompany and influence the course of human disease from the start to the end. The variety, quality and degree of emotional arousal and the individual reaction to the arousal differ so profoundly that each sufferer must be considered unique in this context. The sophistication of age on the one hand and the hopeless apathy on the other act as superficial masks which can lead the nurses and physicians

psychopath-ology
review

to the comfortable belief that the patient's mind is at ease or perhaps is occupied only with minor trivialities that trigger bursts of pent-up emotion, when in truth the patient may be suffering more from the emotional content of the complaint than from the physical manifestations of the disease. Diseases of the chest carry the greatest burden of disturbing emotions: fear, agitation, anxiety, worry and depression are all aroused when life itself is threatened. The contents of the thorax convey to most minds the concept of life, and failure of the heart and lungs carry higher emotional charges than failure of the liver, kidneys, or most other organs of the body. At the start of an illness, the depth of emotion, apart from being individual to the sufferer, can be influenced by many factors. These include the type of symptom and the rate of onset; the delay in seeking medical advice; the personal ideas and those engendered by friends and relations before the doctor is seen; the time that is needed for a conclusive diagnosis to be reached; any suspicion, justified or not, that the diagnosis has been delayed or that the findings have not been divulged; and the way the patient and family are informed. All of these play an important part, and the emotions aroused can play a major role in the entire course and management of the illness. It has been possible in this paper to touch on only some aspects of the emotional content of chest diseases in the aging patient. The subject is very large, but in terms of recognition and applied therapeutics, it can prove most rewarding, both in helping the living to be more contented, which can modify the course of the disease, and in easing the burden of dying.

E 10 McCollum, Mary, Burch, Neil R., and Roessler, Robert: Personality and respiratory responses to sound and light. *Psychophysiology, 6:*291, 1969.

Respiratory amplitude (RA) and respiratory rate (RR) parameters were examined in student subjects (Ss) following stimulation with five intensities of sound and five intensities of light. All Ss completed the MMPI and were then divided into high and low ego strength (Es) groups on the basis of their scores on the Barron scale. These groups were balanced for alertness-drowsiness by EEG criteria. High Es Ss responded with a greater increase in RA than low Es Ss

response character- istics

ego strength

personality

audio stimuli

visual stimuli

and there was a strong trend for high Es Ss to respond less than low Es Ss in RR. Both RA and RR increased following stimulation with the greatest changes following greater intensities of stimulation in both modalities. Light induced a greater increase in RA and RR than sound.

E 11   Moore, N.: Behavior therapy in bronchial asthma: A controlled study. *J Psychosom Res, 9*:257, 1965.

An experiment was designed to isolate the crucial factor in the behavior therapy of asthma by giving twelve asthmatic patients either relaxation with reciprocal inhibition, relaxation with suggestion, or relaxation alone in a balanced incomplete block design using patients as their own controls. Reciprocal inhibition was found to be the crucial factor, having significantly greater effect on respiratory function tests than the other treatments. All three treatments produced subjective improvement.

asthma
behavior therapy
relaxation
reciprocal inhibition
suggestion

E 12   Orwin, A.: Respiratory relief: A new and rapid method for the treatment of phobia states. *Br J Psychiatry, 119*:635, 1971.

Since anxiety caused by maximum voluntary respiratory arrest (M.V.R.A.) is abolished on breathing, it was decided to determine whether voluntary manipulation of respiratory function could lead to the use of this respiratory relief (R.R.) as an antagonist to the anxiety induced by specific phobias. It was hypothesized that the temporal pairing of R.R. with the anxiety induced by presentation of the feared object, the timing of which could be accurate to within less than a second, should result in the extinction of the anxiety response. The methods described are simple, but more complex variants have been used (Orwin, 1971). All the ingredients of desensitization (Marks and Gelder, 1968) are provided by R.R., but the speed of response is surprising. Apparently similar to exposure treatments (for example, Watson, et al., 1971) in approach, it was far more rapid in effect, and in simple phobias symptom removal occurred usually in one to two hours' treatment and with a total exposure time of minutes. Probably of more significance was the positive response in compulsive activity as compared with other tech-

voluntary control
desensitization

niques. Obviously, the importance of the various components of R.R. need investigation, and controlled trials will be necessary to establish its true efficacy in a comparison with other treatments, in particular exposure treatments.

E 13   Reckless, John B.: A behavioral treatment of bronchial asthma in modified group therapy. *Psychosomatics, 12:*168, 1971.

A number of asthmatic patients underwent a series of extinction trials (in the conditioning and deconditioning sense) in an outpatient program of modified group therapy. At intervals during the group sessions, various patients with histories of asthma would experience paroxysmal respiratory difficulty and would reach for medications in attempt to abort such attacks. A state of anxiety would become obvious. The group leader focused attention on the asthmatic patient whenever he noticed early changes suggestive of an attack. The patient was then asked to state the manifest and latent contents of therapeutic activity of the last few minutes. If the patient could not identify such contents, they were identified for him in such a way that he could incorporate them intellectually and emotionally. Another therapeutic maneuver was to discourage the patient from reaching for medications and to encourage him to tolerate the high level of anxiety so engendered. The patient was asked to select a member of the group whom he trusted and to make body contact with that person in a manner which would lead to a decrease in the level of anxiety and physical distress. After several attacks of asthma had been aborted by this method, attacks occurred less frequently and eventually ceased, even in response to themes which had originally triggered the attacks. At a three-year follow-up, patients reported a reduction in the number of attacks occurring outside the group. The author considers the most critical factor in this method of group treatment to be that of making the patient aware of the physiological changes which initiate an asthmatic attack and of the specific emotions associated with the attack. It is also important that the patient consciously link the emotion with the themes being discussed. The treatment is a deconditioning procedure utilizing the theory of reciprocal in-

asthma
group
  therapy
awareness

hibition (anxiety and a state of physical relaxation cannot coexist; Wolpe, 1958).

E 14 Weiss, J.H., Martin, C., and Riley, J.: Effects of suggestion on respiration in asthmatic children. *Psychosom Med, 32:* 409, 1970.

It has been reported that when adult asthmatics inhaled *asthma* what was suggested to them to be extracts of substances that *children* would precipitate asthma, significant changes in airway resist- *suggestion* ance developed in approximately 50 percent, accompanied in some patients by clinical symptoms. To investigate the effect of suggestion on respiration in asthmatic children, sixteen chronic, severe asthmatics, aged twelve to fourteen years, were led to believe that they were inhaling extracts of substances known to have brought on their asthma. Nine of the sixteen were on steroids at the time of the study. In fact, all of the subjects inhaled physiologic saline. Of the sixteen subjects, one showed a decrease in expiratory flow rates accompanied by audible wheezing and subjective distress, not reversible by placebo isoproterenol; and in a subsequent control session in which saline with no suggestion was administered, he showed the same reaction in this session, indicating that saline rather than suggestion was the likely potent factor. No other subjects showed any consistent reaction to suggestion on any of the objective measures, although subjective expressions of anxiety and such symptoms as tightness were not infrequent.

Pre-1965 References

MISCELLANEOUS

Abramson, D.I., Schloven, N., and Katzenstein, K.H.: Peripheral blood flow in schizophrenia and other abnormal mental states. *Arch Neurol Psychiatry, 45:*973, 1941.

Acker, L.E., and Edwards, A.E.: Transfer of vasoconstriction over a biopolar meaning of dimension. *J Exp Psychol, 67:*1, 1964.

Ackner, B.: Emotions and the peripheral vasomotor system. *J Psychosom Res, 1:*3, 1956.

Ackner, B.: The relationship between anxiety and the level of peripheral vasomotor activity. *J Psychosom Res, 1:*21, 1956.

Ackner, B., and Pampiglione, G.: Some relationships between peripheral vasomotor and EEG changes. *J Neurol Neurosurg Psychiat, 20:*58, 1957.

Adam, G.: A method for the elaboration of an interoceptive conditioned renal reflex. *Physiologia, 321,* 1957.

Altschule, M.D.: Salivary changes in emotional states. *Med Sci, 15:*60, 1964.

Barber, T.X., Chauncey, H.H., and Winer, R.A.: Effects of hypnotic and nonhypnotic suggestions on parotid gland response to gustatory stimuli. *Psychosom Med, 26:*374, 1964.

Blair, D.A., Glover, W.E., Greenfield, A.D.M., and Roddie, I.C.: Excitation of cholinergic vasodilator nerves to human skeletal muscles during emotional stress. *J Physiol, 148:*633, 1959.

Bondurant, S., Cohen, S.I., and Silverman, A.J.: Measurement of the effect of psychic stimulation in peripheral venous tone. *J Clin Invest, 37:*879, 1958.

Brothers, J.D., and Warden, D.J.: An analysis of the enzyme activity of the conditioned salivary response in human subjects. *Science, 112:*751, 1950.

Busfield, B.L., and Wechsler, H.: Studies of salivation in depression. I. A comparison of salivation rates in depressed, schizoaffective depressed, nondepressed hospitalized patients, and in normal controls. *Arch Gen Psychiatry, 4:*10, 1961.

Chauncey, H.H., Winer, R.A., and Barber, T.X.: Influence of verbal suggestion on the parotid gland response to gustatory stimuli. *Proc Soc Exp Biol Med, 116:*898, 1964.

Cohen, S.I., and Silverman, A.J.: Psychophysiological investigations of vascular response variability. *J Psychosom Res, 3:*185, 1959.

Crisler, G.: Salivation is unnecessary for the establishment of the salivary conditioned reflex induced by morphine. *Am J Physiol, 94:*553, 1930.

DeMaria, W.J.A., Shmavonian, B.M., Cohen, S.I., et al.: Renal conditioning. *Psychosom Med, 25:*538, 1963.

Fencl, V., Hejl, Z., Madlajowsek, J., and Brod, J.: Changes of blood flow in forearm muscle and skin during an acute emotional stress (mental arithmetic). *Clin Sci, 18:* 491, 1959.

Finesinger, J.E., Sutherland, G.G., and McGuire, F.F.: The postive conditional salivary reflex in psycho-neurotic patients. *Am J Psychiatry, 99:*61, 1942.

Goldie, L., and Green, J.M.: Changes in mode of respiration as an indication of level of awareness. *Nature (Lond), 189:*581, 1961.

Gottschalk, L.A.: A study of conditioned vasomotor responses in ten human subjects. *Psychosom Med, 8:*16, 1946.

Greenfield, A.D.M., Whitney, R.J., and Mowbray, J.F.: Methods for the investigation of peripheral blood flow. *Br Med Bull, 19:*101, 1963.

Hertzman, A.B.: Vasomotor regulation of cutaneous circulation. *Physiol Rev, 39:*280, 1959.

Hertzman, A.B., and Roth, L.W.: The absence of vasoconstrictor reflexes in the forehead circulation: Effects of cold. *Am J Physiol, 136:*692, 1942.

Kennard, M.A.: Vasomotor representation in the cerebral cortex. *Science, 79:*348, 1934.

Kleitman, N., and Ramsaroop, A.: Periodicity in body temperature and heart rate. *Endocrinology, 43:*1, 1948.

Kramar, J.: Endocrine regulation of the capillary resistance. *Science, 119:*790, 1954.

Menzies, R.: Conditioned vasomotor responses in human subjects. *J Psychol, 75,* 1937.

Menzies, R.: Further studies of conditioned vasomotor responses in human subjects. *J Exp Psychol, 29:*457, 1941.

Murray, H.A.: Studies of stressful interpersonal disputations. *Am Psychol, 18:*28, 1963.

Plutchik, R.: The psychophysiology of skin temperature: A critical review. *J Genet Psychol, 55:*249, 1956.

Razran, G.H.: Sentential and propositional generalizations of salivary conditioning to verbal stimuli. *Science, 109:*447, 1949.

Roessler, R.L., and Brogden, W.J.: Conditioned differentiation of vasoconstriction to subvocal stimuli. *Am J Psychol, 56:*78, 1943.

Rosenzweig, M.R.: Salivary conditioning before Pavlov. *Am J Psychol, 72:*628, 1959.

Shmavonian, B.M.: Methodological study of vasomotor conditioning in human subjects. *J Comp Physiol Psychol, 52:*315, 1959.

Stephenson, S.E., Young, W., Montgomery, L.H., and Batson, R.: Physiologic auto-control of mechanical respirators. *Dis Chest, 39:*363, 1961.

Sutherland, G.F., and Katz, R.A.: Apparatus for the study of the salivary conditional reflex in man. *J Appl Physiol, 16:*740, 1961.

Takagi, K., and Nagasaka, T.: Rhythmic circulatory changes in the peripheral vasculature. *Ann NY Acad Sci, 98:*1069, 1962.

Unger, S.M.: Habituation of the vasoconstrictive orienting reaction. *J Exp Psychol, 67:* 11, 1964.

Vanderhoof, E., and Clancy, J.: Peripheral blood flow as an indicator of emotional reaction. *J Appl Physiol, 17:*67, 1962.

Winsor, A.L.: The effect of mental effort on parotid secretion. *Am J Psychol, 43:*434, 1931.